Schi

The Battle that Forged Freemasonry

Ahiman Rezon, frontispiece (1778).

Schism

The Battle that Forged Freemasonry

RIC BERMAN

sussex
ACADEMIC
PRESS
Brighton • Portland • Toronto

2 4 6 8 10 9 7 5 3 1

First published 2013 in Great Britain by
SUSSEX ACADEMIC PRESS
PO Box 139, Eastbourne BN24 9BP

Distributed in North America by
SUSSEX ACADEMIC PRESS
ISBS Publisher Services
920 NE 58th Ave #300, Portland, OR 97213, USA

Cover design by Andy McColm.

British Library Cataloguing in Publication Data
A CIP catalogue record for this book is available from the British Library.

Library of Congress Cataloging-in-Publication Data
Berman, Ric.
Schism : the battle that forged freemasonary / Ric Berman.
pages   cm
Includes bibliographical references and index.
ISBN 978-1-84519-606-6 (h/b : alk. paper) —
ISBN 978-1-84519-607-3 (p/b : alk. paper)
   1. Freemasonry—Great Britain—History—18th century. I. Title.
HS595.A5B47 2013
366′.1094109033—dc23

2013006825

MIX
Paper from
responsible sources
FSC® C013056

Typeset & designed by Sussex Academic Press, Brighton & Eastbourne.
Printed by TJ International, Padstow, Cornwall.
Printed on acid-free paper.

Contents

List of Tables

List of Illustrations

Cover illustrations & frontispiece: FRONT – Antients' Multi Degree Masonic Apron (Painton Cowen) (date unknown); BACK – Antients *Grand Register*, Black List, extract; John Murray, 4th duke of Atholl (1755–1830), oil painting by Thomas R. Beaufort Hinkes (1901); FRONTISPIECE – *Ahiman Rezon,* frontispiece (1778).

Plate section (after page 150)
1ˢᵗ *Degree Tracing Board* (date unknown).
Antients *General Register*, Attendance List, extract.
Antients *General Register*, Membership List, extract.
'Ceremony of making a Free-Mason'; engraving from *Hiram, or The Grand Master Key* (1764).
Early Moderns' Masonic Apron (date unknown).
John Senex, *Map of London* (1720).
William Stewart, 1ˢᵗ earl of Blessington (1709–1769); oil painting by Stephen Slaughter (1744).
John Murray, 3ʳᵈ duke of Atholl (1729–1774); engraving by unknown artist (undated).
Thomas Alexander Erskine, 6ᵗʰ earl of Kelly (1731–1781); engraving by Lizars after portrait by Robert Home (*c.* 1780).
Sir Cecil Wray (1734–1805); engraving (unknown artist) published by J. Walker of Paternoster Row (1784).
Robert Freke Gould (1836–1915); engraving by Chardon-Whitman, Paris (c. 1899).
Henry Sadler (1840–1911); cabinet print of a photograph by Burt Sharp, Brighton (1879).
'Sword of State of the Moderns Grand Lodge'; engraving, printed and sold by Bro. Scott of Paternoster Road (undated).
'Reception des Compagnons'; engraving from L. Travenol, *Nouvea Catechisme des Franc-Maçon* (1749).

Acknowledgements

Many people have been generous with their time and comments during the final phases of this book and I would like to express particular thanks to Professors Toby Barnard of Oxford University and Roger Burt of Exeter University who both read and commented on a late draft, and to Doctors John Bergin, Petri Mirala and David O'Shaughnessy for their input into individual chapters and appendices. I would also like to thank the two unidentified academic readers who reviewed a pre-publication article based on this work for their encouragement and insight.

The research undertaken over the past two years required access to a considerable volume of data and I would like to acknowledge the assistance received from Rebecca Hayes, archivist and librarian, at the Library of the Grand Lodge of Ireland in Dublin, and Diane Clements, director, Martin Cherry, librarian, and Susan Snell, archivist, at the Library and Museum of the United Grand Lodge of England at Great Queen Street in London. Thank you for your patience and support.

Access to primary source material is a crucial component of any academic work and I am grateful to those Masonic lodges who allowed me access to their earliest records and, in particular, the Lodge of Antiquity, No. 2; St George's and Corner Stone lodge, No. 5; Enoch lodge, No. 11; and the Old King's Arms lodge, No. 28.

Finally, may I express my gratitude to the Modern European History Research Centre and the History Faculty of the University of Oxford through which I was provided with access to the records and data held at the Bodleian Libraries.

DR RICHARD BERMAN
February 2013

For Sue, Charlotte and Theo

Introduction

The first Grand Lodge of Freemasons was established in London in 1717. Ostensibly the product of four founding lodges seeking a structure for their mutual governance, the idea was more probably the creation of a small number of motivated members of the Horn tavern lodge led by Rev. Jean Theophilus Desaguliers, a Huguenot émigré and Oxford-educated Newtonian scientist, at the time a recently made Fellow of the Royal Society and its curator and demonstrator.[1] Although the new organisation initially sought to exercise influence over no more than those lodges established in the cities of London and Westminster, its remit expanded rapidly and within a few years, the Grand Lodge of England was positioned as a self-professed national governing authority for freemasonry and the principal force behind the movement's development in England and elsewhere.

Several factors differentiated English freemasonry from the numerous other clubs and societies then being established in eighteenth century associational Britain. Desaguliers' inner circle included Martin Folkes, later President of the Royal Society; William Cowper, the Clerk to the Parliaments, the administrative head of the Houses of Parliament; Charles Delafaye, the government's chief spymaster and a prominent undersecretary of state; and Charles, 2nd duke of Richmond and Lennox. All were members of the Horn tavern lodge, of which Richmond was Master, and each was eminent in his own right. Crucially, both they and other members of the lodge were exceptionally well connected and within a few years, leading members of the Whig aristocracy and government had been persuaded to join freemasonry, assume its leadership and provide the organisation with political protection and social imprimatur. At the same time, under the joint auspices of Desaguliers and George Payne, another member of the Horn, a new *Constitutions* was prepared that included a fresh set of Masonic charges and regulations that replaced the mediaeval 'Old Charges' that had previously governed how freemasonry and the lodge was to operate.

Published in 1723, the *Constitutions* espoused a lengthy faux history of freemasonry that detailed and lauded the Craft's ancient antecedents, introduced latitudinarianism – religious tolerance – as an operative philosophy in Masonic ritual, and adopted an almost democratic approach to freemasonry's internal governance that was at the time in a broader social context virtually unique.[2] The new regulations superimposed an implicit if not explicit Hanoverian agenda onto freemasonry and, among other aspects, revised radically the Masonic oaths to ensure that each freemason was obliged to swear to conform to and respect the law and the magistracy, be a peaceable subject of the Crown and not to become involved in any Jacobite plots or anti-government conspiracies.

In addition to the patronage of celebrity members of the aristocracy, freemasonry – and English Grand Lodge in particular – quickly became identified with numerous luminaries, including a wide range of senior members of the Royal Society and principal figures from other leading professional organisations, including the Royal College of Physicians and the Society of Apothecaries. There was, additionally, a crossover in membership with a number of socially prominent Enlightenment clubs, including the Society of Antiquarians and the Gentleman's Society of Spalding. Even the Crown was involved, with Frederick, Prince of Wales, being initiated in 1737 by Desaguliers at a specially convened lodge at Kew. Notably, many of his Gentlemen of the Bedchamber and other senior courtiers were already members of 'the Craft'. And befitting what was a profoundly pro-establishment organisation that shared and proselytised the Whig philosophy of freedom of religion and respect for property and public order, freemasonry became integrated into the establishment, developing strong ties to the military, the civil service and the magistracy, where senior members included successive chairmen of the Westminster and Middlesex benches and other judicial figures.[3]

By the late 1720s, in its now reinvented form, English freemasonry had become one of – if not the – most attractive yet accessible destinations for the aspirational gentry and middling classes. Grand Lodge and freemasonry's more eminent constituent lodges were led by a parade of noble Grand Masters from John, 2nd duke of Montagu, one of the wealthiest men in England and in 1721 the first nobleman to accept the position of Grand Master, to Thomas Howard, 8th duke of Norfolk, Grand Marshall of England, and Lord Lovell, Sir Robert Walpole's wealthy Norfolk neighbour and a key political ally, the latter two figures becoming Grand Masters in 1730 and 1731, respectively. Freemasonry had been positioned intentionally at the pinnacle of Hanoverian society. And Desaguliers and his colleagues deployed its celebrated and sometimes iconic social connections, Masonic patronage and a well-managed decade long publicity campaign to achieve a preeminent position and cement an enduring alliance with the British establishment.

Under its new Grand Lodge, freemasonry was directed by a leadership motivated by a powerful desire to safeguard the Hanoverian succession. The constitutional crisis that accompanied William and Mary's Glorious Revolution had led directly to George I succeeding Queen Anne. But the Hanoverian grasp on the British throne was neither absolute nor fully secure, and the latent threat from the Jacobite Pretender, father then son, and their allies in France, Spain and elsewhere, remained a concern and was at the forefront of eighteenth-century politics, at least until the second Jacobite rebellion was crushed in 1745.

The same if not a greater sense of insecurity and drive for self preservation was present in London's Huguenot community. Over fifty thousand Huguenot refugees had found sanctuary in England having been forced from France by Louis XIV's dragonnades and his revocation of the edict of Nantes, events that followed more than a century of persecution and sometimes genocide by the French state and Catholic church. The majority settled in London and it was not coincidental that they were represented disproportionately within London freemasonry and its leadership, including Desaguliers, Francis Sorrel, Martin Clare and Josias Villeneau. For both the Huguenots and the Whigs, Hanoverian Britain was a bulwark against the naked absolutism of France, Spain and much of continental Europe. And under Desaguliers' influence, the Grand Lodge of England and English freemasonry was in the vanguard of its defence.

But although political concerns may have shaped eighteenth-century freemasonry and altered Masonic ritual accordingly, its popularity was embedded in a relevance to its membership among the gentry and middling that went beyond Whig politics. In the 1720s and 1730s, the Masonic lodge functioned not only as a relatively exclusive secular fraternal club for the more affluent but, at the same time, many lodges became virtually an extension of Newton's scientific Enlightenment. In addition to offering the well-publicised prospect of convivial and bibulous civil association, lodge meetings would sometimes include talks and lectures and provide a potential opportunity to network with eminent professional men. Scientific lectures were at the time, in Simon Schaffer's characterisation, the 'theatre of the upper classes'.[4] But they also had a utilitarian aspect in an age when the application of science to solve practical commercial problems was integral to the processes of wealth preservation and creation. Natural philosophers, including Desaguliers, described by Larry Stewart as 'arguably the most successful scientific lecturer of the century' and, at the time, by the duke of Chandos, as 'the best mechanic in Europe', were invited to apply their knowledge and were believed to – indeed, probably could – offer their clients and audiences a valuable and direct route to personal prosperity.[5] Many were or became celebrities and their presence by association or in person offered kudos in an Enlightenment age where the pursuit of knowledge was a goal in its own right.

With Desaguliers and his colleagues from the Royal Society at its helm, freemasonry could be regarded as combining education with entertainment, politics with philosophy, and antiquarian (if sometimes faux) Masonic ritual with dining and drinking. And Britain's emergent associational culture provided a receptive growth medium. Within less than two decades, freemasonry had become the largest, best known and most influential of the nation's numerous fraternal clubs and societies. It was a unique organisation and it developed and expanded into what became virtually a mass movement among the aristocracy and middling, with perhaps a fifth becoming members and, in London, possibly more.

The Grand Lodge of England and variations on English freemasonry were emulated rapidly and widely. In an attempt to copy its cachet, Ireland, Scotland and the Low Countries each established their own Masonic grand lodges. Leading noblemen and politicians were initiated in France, Austria, Sweden, Prussia and Russia; and freemasonry was planted elsewhere, including Spain and Portugal. Outside Europe, the Craft was seeded throughout Britain's growing empire by traders, colonists and the military, with lodges warranted in India, America, Canada and the Caribbean. As a measure of its achievement, the number of lodges within the jurisdiction of the Grand Lodge of England alone increased from the founding four in 1717 to over sixty in 1725, more than one hundred in 1730 and around two hundred in 1740. Although some lodges failed to survive, by the mid-1730s, freemasonry was present on the eastern seaboard of the Americas, in Boston, New York, Charles Town and Savannah, and in India in Bengal.

But as its original founders and proselytisers aged and retired or died, circumstances changed and two decades of growth in mainstream English freemasonry came to a halt in the 1740s. Within twenty years of Desaguliers and Folkes having persuaded the 2nd duke of Montagu to accept the position of its first noble Grand Master, bureaucratic incompetency was taking over English Grand Lodge. The organisation became arrogant and self-obsessed. And disaffection grew, becoming so considerable by the end of the decade that around a quarter of London's lodges were expelled or erased from the register, while others seceded or chose to remain independent.

Partly in response, a rival 'Antients' Grand Lodge was formed in London in 1751 at the head of a small group of five predominantly London Irish Masonic lodges. While the original Grand Lodge of England stagnated, the number and membership of Antients lodges in London and provincial England climbed. Expansion was linked in part to the particular circum-stances of the Irish immigrant community in London and elsewhere and represented a response both to their social and Masonic alienation and to that of the lower middling and working class more broadly. From the handful of lodges that had been involved in the constitution of the new grand lodge, the number electing to join its orbit rose to thirteen within a year. By 1753, just two years after its launch, there were thirty lodges; and in 1754, a year later, the Antients had close to forty. Within three decades, the figure had risen to over two hundred, with around seventy-five lodges in London, over eighty in the provinces and nearly fifty overseas.

Virtually from its inception, Antients freemasonry's public persona, organisation and administration were shaped principally by one man: Laurence Dermott, an expatriate Irishman who led the organisation as its Grand Secretary and then Deputy Grand Master for over twenty-five years. Dermott dominated the Antients in a similar way to that in which Desaguliers some three decades earlier had influenced the original Grand Lodge of England. The difference was that Dermott's influence was un-rivalled and pervasive, and lasted more than a decade longer.

Many of the factors that motivated Dermott and lay behind the success of Antients freemasonry and its new grand lodge were unrelated to those that had set the foundations of the first English Grand Lodge. Unlike the pro-Hanoverian political insecurities and Newtonian science that inspired Desaguliers and the petty gentry and middling others who made up the bulk of the first Grand Lodge and its member lodges, Antients freemasonry was driven initially by the particular circumstances of London's Irish émigrés and later mirrored the urbanisation and changing work patterns associated with the emerging industrialisation of Britain. However, it also reflected the aspirations of the lower middling and working class more broadly, in particular their desire to access 'polite society' and attain economic betterment and in this there was a commonality with the aspirational threads that ran through the membership of the original Grand Lodge of England.

But despite such similarities, Antients freemasonry differed fundamentally from its predecessor lodge in two material respects: first, in terms of its social and economic function; and second, with regard to the composition of its membership. Alongside Masonic ritual, the principal purpose of Antients freemasonry was to provide and promote mutually funded welfare and an accessible social infrastructure for its predominantly lower middling and working-class membership. And as a younger organisation and one that from the late 1750s effectively competed for members, it was important that it should be positively differentiated.

Dermott positioned Antients freemasonry to offer disaffected Irish and English masons in London and elsewhere a seemingly superior and more traditional and historically legitimate alternative to that of the original grand lodge, which he pejoratively dismissed as the 'Moderns', a name which stuck to the organisation. He adopted an aggressively satirical approach towards the Moderns, about whom he was scathing, and amused, enticed and flattered rather than sought to dictate to or patronise prospective lodge members. Dermott's technique was effective and combined astute leadership with efficient press management and organisational self-promotion. However, the Antients also championed a strongly utilitarian aspect to lodge membership, a feature borne out by the aspirational nature of many of the lower and middling urban and industrial workers attracted to the organisation. In addition to its purportedly greater historical legitimacy and traditions, Antients freemasonry's superior utility was epitomised in the grant of membership certificates which provided a proto passport that facilitated access to lodges elsewhere in Britain and overseas, and thereby introduced members to a potentially beneficial network that combined social support and work and trading opportunities. In short, Antients freemasonry's success was based on a combination of Dermott's effective and aggressive leadership, and its function as a friendly society and a flexible social and commercial space open to many of those otherwise excluded.

Dermott and the Antients were at odds with their more reactive counterparts in the Moderns. Where in the first half of the eighteenth century, English freemasonry had been allied closely to the political and social establishment and their respective elites, in the second half, Antients freemasonry almost served as a repository for those more commonly rejected. Indeed, on occasions, the Antients may have appeared to be almost an anti (English) establishment force. Perhaps supportive of this interpretation, it became especially popular in many of Britain's overseas colonies where resistance to imperial economic imposition and political diktat developed along similar lines to opposition in Ireland, and across America, lodges switched allegiance from the Moderns to ally themselves with the Antients. But despite such a profile, Antients freemasonry also benefited from strong aristocratic connections and its consequential political protection. The earl of Blessington's decision in 1756 to offer his patronage and become its first noble Grand Master reinforced the Antients' standing, as did the later patronage of the 3rd and 4th dukes of Atholl and other well-placed aristocrats. The Antients gained further kudos in 1758, when the Grand Lodge of Ireland switched Masonic allegiance and ceased its fraternal relations with the Moderns to recognise the rival Antients formally as the only legitimate grand lodge in England.

Irish influence and sponsorship, direct and indirect, was a key component in the Antients' long-term success. British mercantilism had alienated and politicised the formerly loyal elite at Irish Grand Lodge and it was a powerful sense of Anglo-Irish patriotism that had motivated Blessington to become the Antients' first noble Grand Master. It is arguable that without his support, and, later, that of the Grand Lodges of Ireland and Scotland, Antients freemasonry would not have prospered to the extent that it challenged the Moderns for Masonic supremacy in England and elsewhere.

Such competition would later spur the Moderns to retaliate and reverse their decline. And after Dermott's death, the two rival grand lodges gradually ceased hostilities and would eventually amalgamate, but only in 1813 and only after the intervention of the British Crown in the form of the duke of Sussex and his brother, the duke of Kent, the younger sons of George III, and after some six decades of internecine acrimony.

However, despite being published in the two hundredth anniversary year of the union between the Antients and Moderns, *Schism* is not concerned with the later reconciliation. It seeks instead to explain and track for the first time the roots of the creation of Antients freemasonry and the Antients Grand Lodge and to examine the Antients membership as a prism through which to explore mid-eighteenth century London working class and lower middling society. Although an arcane dispute over what was the proper or more traditional form of Masonic ritual was (and continues to be) regarded as the key differentiator between the two rival grand lodges, it is contended that this rationale is overly superficial. As was later the case, there was little that could not have been resolved through flexibility and compromise. The real differences between the two organisations lay in the nature of their respective leaders, their members and the reasons they joined.

Schism has not been written to stand solely as an academic work but to introduce and make accessible the subject matter to a wider Masonic and non-Masonic audience and, most particularly, to supplement (I won't say 'replace') the now dated standard works on the subject. It is also an attempt to contribute to the history of London and the London Irish in the long eighteenth century and to confront and examine the trade and social networks that were characteristic of the lower middling and working urban class, a subject that remains substantially unexplored.

Detailed biographical and other background information on a spectrum of influential Irish and English freemasons, including many of the principal Grand Officers in the mid-eighteenth century, is incorporated into the text and appendices in the knowledge that this will be of interest to Masonic researchers and historians. I also hope that it will provide an accessible point of reference that takes note of new and now-accessible primary sources.

Schism's early chapters describe aspects of the interaction between freemasonry and contemporary eighteenth-century society and outline the axiomatic role of the London Irish and the Irish more widely in shaping both Antients freemasonry and the broader Masonic movement, an influence that has not been recognised fully, if at all. Throughout the period under review, freemasonry was in large measure a social, economic and cultural phenomenon, and to seek to divorce or examine the subject in isolation from such a framework would be to fail properly to comprehend it. *Schism* begins with an examination of the rejection of Irish freemasons by the original Grand Lodge of England. Where the final chapter suggests how the economic policies imposed by London provided a context for public alienation in Ireland and the politicisation of the elite at the helm of Irish Grand Lodge and other supporters of Antients freemasonry, CHAPTER ONE looks at a more proximate driver behind the creation of the Antients Grand Lodge: the social and economic alienation of the Irish within Britain itself.

This estrangement was epitomised in many ways by the rejection of the London Irish by English Grand Lodge and its constituent lodges. The first chapter reflects on the growth of Antients freemasonry and on the impact of the leadership and life of Laurence Dermott, the Antients' pivotal Grand Secretary and the author of *Ahiman Rezon*, their influential and bestselling 'constitution'. An attempt is made to assess Dermott's administration of Antients freemasonry and to reflect on the man himself. To the limited biographical material currently in the public domain is added new information on Dermott's personal life, including his two marriages. The chapter argues that Dermott successfully positioned the Antients as an effective and preferred alternative to the Moderns and substantially created and sustained the long-standing Masonic rivalry between the two grand lodges.

As the Antients' principal controlling mind, Dermott oversaw a period of three decades of mutual denigration that persisted from the 1750s into the 1780s. Indeed, it was only after his death that the Antients begin to row back on their criticism of the Moderns. The move paved the way for an eventual reconciliation. But criticism was not a one-way channel. The Antients and Dermott were themselves condemned by the Moderns, both at the time and subsequently, and the first chapter explores both the impact and the retaliation it provoked. One response was to seek aristocratic patronage and the section concludes with a brief exploration of the Antients' early Grand Masters.

As with the Moderns, the social and political position of Antients freemasonry was underscored by aristocratic patronage, and senior and affluent members of the Irish and Scottish aristocracy and gentry successively consented to act as its figurehead. The organisation's standing vis-à-vis the Moderns was buttressed and enhanced accordingly. William Stewart, 1st earl of Blessington, Grand Master from 1756 until 1760, was followed by leading members of the Scottish aristocracy, most especially the 3rd and 4th dukes of Atholl, who sat simultaneously as Grand Masters of the Antients and as Grand Masters of Scottish Grand Lodge. They were instrumental in o btaining the fraternal recognition of the Grand Lodge of Scotland and, in an act that sidelined and virtually isolated the Moderns, in 1773, the three grand lodges of the Antients, Ireland and Scotland established a mutual pact of Masonic recognition.

In CHAPTERS TWO, THREE and FOUR, we turn to a granular examination of the Antients' lower middling and working-class members, and to a discussion of the London Irish diaspora, the principal constituency from which Antients freemasonry was initially populated. CHAPTER TWO argues that an endemic failure to look beyond the caricature of the London Irish obscured the view of the ambitious Irish economic migrants beneath and ignored their desire to be assimilated into what might be termed polite or professional society. CHAPTERS THREE and FOUR set out a detailed breakdown of the Antients' primary membership data and examines briefly the London slums within which many lived. The records date from the early 1750s and display the social and occupational characteristics of London's grass roots members of Antients freemasonry.

Unlike many other eighteenth-century clubs and societies, Antients freemasonry was not an 'elitist' organisation. However, there is nonetheless evidence of stratification in its membership, which included the more middling and aspirational, and in acts of Masonic charity and other expenditures we can see a desire of at least some members to be marked out from their peers. Regardless, the data also reveals a high level of social integration on a local basis within London's discrete geographic districts, and a strong commitment to fraternalism and mutuality.

CHAPTER THREE also considers the evolution of the lodge as a friendly society. Contemporary records demonstrate the provision of substantial and probably effective mutual support within the Masonic and wider community, including financial assistance to the ill, unemployed and families of the deceased. Most importantly, the evidence largely dismisses the traditional image of the feckless Irishman and instead speaks to a more complex view that touches on social ambition, self-help and economic aspiration. An examination of the Antients minute books and membership records that have survived substantiates the argument. The analysis concludes that

Antients freemasonry should be regarded more as a mutual benefit club than a 'secret society' or 'society with secrets'.

CHAPTER FOUR touches on the key connection between the London magistracy and the London Irish (and other working-class defendants) that came before the bench. It argues that the then archetypical representation of the Irish working class as violent, drunken and feckless, coloured the way in which the London Irish as a whole was treated by the British establishment. This included many of those at the helm of early eighteenth-century English freemasonry – an organisation whose upper branches were dominated by members of the magistracy. The antipathy that the Irish working class encountered in England was fed by a sensationalist press and reinforced by the magistrates' bench, whose remit was to punish disorder and control those portrayed and perceived as dangerous Jacobites and disaffected papists. The chapter references a number of contemporary court reports from the Middlesex and Westminster Justices' Sessions and transcripts of trials at the Old Bailey. In addition, a first and brief attempt is made to consider the prosecution and sentencing of Irish defendants who were arraigned to appear at the Old Bailey. A selection of trial data from 1740–90 is studied, as are statistics relating to prosecution and sentencing in the mid-nineteenth century, the first occasion on which such data was broken down by nationality.

Having examined certain of the social and economic factors behind the rise of the Antients, the following three chapters look in more detail at those that drove the Irish away from English freemasonry. CHAPTER FIVE details the mid-century decline and decay of the original Grand Lodge of England from its pinnacle of influence in the late 1730s to the relative depths of the late 1740s. It explores the decline through an examination of the Moderns' Grand Officers and their actions in expelling some forty lodges, a quarter of the total, and considers the effect of what was described as a period of 'Masonic misrule' that characterised the 1740s. The issue was recognised at the time and continued to resonate in the observations of prominent Victorian commentators more than a century later.

CHAPTER SIX sets out the little that is known of Fotherley Baker, John Revis and John Jesse, the three key individuals who ran the Grand Lodge of England in the latter part of the 1740s. And CHAPTER SEVEN extends the analysis and turns to the role and position of one of the most prominent and influential of London's lodges, that at the King's Arms in the Strand: known commonly as the 'Old King's Arms' or 'OKA'. We explore its transition from an influential outpost of Enlightenment thought in the 1730s to an elitist dining club in the 1740s, and examine its uniquely close relationship with English Grand Lodge. The OKA was at the heart of the inexpedient changes taking place within the Moderns in the mid-eighteenth century and it reflected and symbolised the influence and transformational effect on London freemasonry of those then at its helm.

Finally, CHAPTER EIGHT returns to the early part of the eighteenth century to trace the political and economic milieu into which regular Irish freemasonry was born and from which Irish support for Antients free-masonry later emerged. Beginning with the Treaty of Limerick that ended the Williamite-Jacobite Wars in Ireland and emasculated Ireland's Catholic Jacobite opposition, the chapter touches on Ireland's unsteady transition from a loyal 'colony' to become one of Britain's more awkward and frac-tious neighbours. From the 1690s and early 1700s, Ireland had been governed by a minority Anglo-Irish Protestant elite who viewed their inter-ests and those of England largely as one. Such political dependability would not last. Increasingly onerous legislation forced on Ireland by London prevented the country from trading freely and restricted economic growth. Irritation and discontent was heightened by political discrimination, a mindset encapsulated by the imposition of the Irish Declaratory Act. The legislation removed the ultimate legal authority of the Irish judiciary and replaced it with that of Britain's House of Lords. The conflict between Ireland's military and economic dependency on Britain politicised many in Ireland's Anglo-Irish elite. It was present in the money bills disputes of the 1750s and Grattan's later patriotic opposition. And it was at hand in the earl of Blessington's willingness to support the Antients and become their first noble Grand Master, and in Ireland's switch away from the original Grand Lodge of England to support and recognise the Antients. Although not a subject for this book, the roots of Ireland's later quest for economic and polit-ical autonomy were as much a function of the patriotic nationalism of the Protestant Anglo-Irish in the mid- and late eighteenth century as the burgeoning Catholic opposition that followed the Acts of Union in the nine-teenth. Masonic estrangement from those previously regarded as their peers became a metaphor for the friction created by mercantilism. The chapter concludes with a brief overview of the social development of Irish freema-sonry in the latter part of the century and its parallels with Antients freemasonry in Britain.

The CONCLUSION reflects on the different dimensions that prompted the schism in English freemasonry. Masonic historians have traditionally approached 1751 and the antipathy and rancour that followed as a matter best ignored or considered as a now-resolved argument concerning minor or major differences in Masonic ritual. Perhaps worse, most mainstream histo-rians are unaware of the event, its repercussions and the metaphors and insights that it offers. *Schism* is a first attempt to analyse the subject matter in context and discuss the issues raised.

The appendices follow. The first three provide for reference purposes details of the Grand Lodge Officers from each of the Antients, Irish and English constitutions who presided at their respective grand lodges during the period under review. The fourth contains a comprehensive list of mili-tary lodges warranted by the Irish and Antients Grand Lodges.

The following two appendices are of greater length. Appendix V contains a brief history of Irish Grand Lodge and biographical information on the early Irish Grand Offices. It provides an overview of the eighteenth-century origins of Irish freemasonry and the aristocrats and gentry who stood behind the formation of the Grand Lodge of Ireland in 1725. Although the creation of an Irish Grand Lodge can be regarded as having been motivated originally to emulate the social success of its sister organisation in England, few of Ireland's early Masonic records remain extant. Instead, the development of Irish freemasonry is traced principally through press reports. They indicate that the early Irish Grand Masters were, as in England, a litany of the country's Whiggist great and good, leavened with upper middling professionals and Huguenot and Quaker merchants. Family, social and political connections bound together many of Ireland's early Grand Masters and Grand Officers, virtually all of whom, like their English counterparts, were loyal pro-Hanoverians.

Appendix VI moves back across the Irish Sea to examine the members of the lodge at the Ship behind the Royal Exchange in London. The tavern was the location of England's most prominent and possibly first principally Irish Masonic lodge and the membership represented a repository of merchants, lobbyists and expatriate Irish gentry who provide multiple examples of Ireland's social, commercial and political links with Britain. The lodge and its members offer evidence that the main centre of Irish political, legal and financial power lay in London, not Dublin. The Irish – Protestant and Catholic alike – were obliged to maintain a network of lobbyists and agents in Britain, not least to ensure that their views received attention in parliament. And since it was obligatory for many goods to be shipped via British ports, where they were taxed before being transhipped elsewhere, there were significant advantages to the Irish conducting business and trading in London. An analysis of the Ship provides a conduit through which the composite of family, business and social relationships can be explored; however, it also offers evidence of freemasonry being one of many connections shared by merchants and traders on both sides of the Irish Sea, and of the relative ease with which the affluent middling Irish were then accepted into London society.

Although Antients freemasonry can be interpreted as formalising existing Masonic divisions and buttressing what became a bitter and lengthy rivalry with the Moderns, it was principally a product of other less visible but arguably more significant factors. Put simply, the creation of the Antients Grand Lodge had two key drivers: first, England's increasingly calamitous relationship with Ireland and the Irish living on both sides of the Irish Sea; and second, the changing composition of British society and, in particular, the development of a more aspirational lower middling and urban working class.

Steered by its Grand Secretary and Grand Lodge, Antients freemasonry reflected and led changes in progress elsewhere in Britain. It extended membership and formal sociability beyond the gentry and professional classes and, in doing so, helped to create one of the first modern friendly societies. Indeed, by offering its lower middling lodge members the prospect of a broadly based, mutually financed safety net, it may even be correct to argue that Antients freemasonry helped to create and support a more confident, ambitious and less easily controlled urban working class. It is argued that Antients freemasonry not only performed an economic and social welfare function but that this, perhaps more than the ritual aspect of freemasonry, provided its main function.

Schism offers a social and economic prism through which Britain's changing relationship with Ireland and Britain's own emerging aspirational lower middling and working class can be examined. The book seeks to throw light on a hitherto neglected Irish dimension to the great English drama of the existence, pre-1813, of two rival grand lodges, each of which claimed to represent authentic English Freemasonry, and to contribute to the history of London and its eighteenth-century trade and social networks.

CHAPTER ONE

Laurence Dermott and the Antients Grand Lodge

If one were to search for a single point of origin at which London's émigré Irish began to veer away from the original Grand Lodge of England, it might be 11 December 1735. On that day, the minutes of English Grand Lodge record a meeting at the Devil Tavern in Temple Bar, central London. Three Grand Officers were absent. The Grand Master, Lord Weymouth, had 'received an express this morning from Paris concerning the death of his lordship's grandmother, the Lady Jersey so that he could not with decency attend the society this evening'; and Mr Ward, Deputy Grand Master, and Sir Edward Mansell, Senior Grand Warden, 'also happened to be out of town'.[1] In their place, George Payne was 'desired to take the Chair as Grand Master' and 'Bro. Lambell and Dr Anderson . . . took their seats as Grand Wardens pro tempore'. Martin Clare, the Junior Grand Warden, was elevated temporarily to Deputy Grand Master.

After opening the lodge and reading the minutes of the last Quarterly Communication and Charity Committee, the minutes record

> Notice being given to the Grand Lodge that the Master and Wardens of a lodge from Ireland attended without desiring to be admitted by virtue of a Deputation from the Lord Kingston, present Grand Master of Ireland. But it appearing there was no particular recommendation from his Lordship in this affair, their Request could not be complied with, unless they would accept of a new Constitution here.[2]

James King, the 4th lord Kingston (1693–1761), had served as Grand Master of English Grand Lodge in 1729, and in 1735, was sitting for the second time as Grand Master of the Grand Lodge of Ireland, having been elected in June. Given his Masonic standing and relative eminence as an Irish aristocrat, it may have been reasonable to expect that a deputation in his name would be welcomed with appropriate fraternal respect. However, with the excuse that 'there was no particular recommendation from his Lordship', the Irish were snubbed and their wish to be admitted 'could not be complied with'. The event stands out and, at least superficially, appeared to run against the fraternal philosophy that freemasonry professed to follow.

In his *Introduction* to the QCA transcript of Grand Lodge's minutes,

William Songhurst explained the rebuff by noting 'the absence of fraternal intercourse' between the Antients and Moderns.[3] And in an editorial footnote, he commented further that the decision to reject the Irish delegation 'seems to point to alterations having been made which prevented intervisitation':

> We know that the premier Grand Lodge was not recognised either in Ireland or Scotland, though both maintained fraternal correspondence with the Antients. Recognition by the Grand Lodges in the sister kingdoms, and a union with the Grand Lodge of the Antients only became possible after the resolution passed by the Moderns in 1809 "that it is not necessary any longer to continue in force those measures which were resorted to in or about the year 1739 respecting irregular masons, and do therefore enjoin the several lodges to revert to the ancient land marks of the Society".[4]

Despite these arguments having been widely accepted for many years, Songhurst's analysis is both inadequate and incorrect. First and most obviously, the Antients Grand Lodge did not come into existence until 1751, some sixteen years after the event under discussion; it was only after this point that the issue of a want of 'fraternal intercourse' between the two rival organisations developed. Second, a formal breakdown in the relationship between the Grand Lodge of Ireland and England did not develop until 1758, over two decades later. It was only in that year that Ireland recognised the Grand Lodge of the Antients formally as the sole legitimate grand lodge in England and broke off fraternal correspondence with the Moderns. Dublin's decision was linked to that of William Stewart, the 1st earl of Blessington, Grand Master of Ireland in 1738 and 1739 and a leading Irish aristocrat, who had agreed to become the Antients' first noble Grand Master two years earlier in 1756. Third, the Grand Lodge of Scotland did not recognise the Antients as the sole governing body of English freemasonry until even later, in 1773, when the 3rd duke of Atholl had become Grand Master of the Antients and was also appointed Grand Master elect of the Grand Lodge of Scotland. It was only at this point that Scotland entered into a formal Masonic pact with Ireland under which both grand lodges recognised the Antients Grand Lodge to the exclusion of the original Grand Lodge of England. The pact was a central thread in cementing the Masonic marginalisation of the Moderns in the late eighteenth century. It also reinforced a Masonic split between the Moderns and Scotland that had threatened for almost a decade. Where in 1762, the Grand Master of English Grand Lodge, Sholto Douglas, Lord Aberdour, had been the immediate past Grand Master of Scottish Grand Lodge, continuing a strong link between the two organisations, the following year the position had altered. From 1763 until 1765, Thomas Erskine, the 6th earl of Kellie, was both Grand Master of the Antients, where he presided from 1760 until 1766, and Grand Master of Scotland. Moreover, the 3rd and 4th dukes of Atholl maintained the same strong association between the Antients and Scottish Grand Lodge, serving as Grand Masters of the Antients (1771–4, 1775–81, 1791–1813) while simultaneously sitting as Grand Masters of Scotland (1773–4, 1778–80, respectively).

But notwithstanding the historical inaccuracies, perhaps the most important issue for Songhurst and other historians seeking to explain the rejection of the Irish deputation is the argument that 'alterations [had] been made [to Masonic ritual] which prevented inter-visitation'. Although not often specified, there were two sets of changes. In the early 1720s, Desaguliers, George Payne and other leading figures at English Grand Lodge had modernised Masonic ritual, adopting a more Enlightenment style that promoted religious tolerance and brought education and entertainment into lodge meetings. However, this had not prevented inter-visitation and made freemasonry less popular. It had had the opposite effect. Between the early 1720s and the mid- and late 1730s, freemasonry grew almost geometrically, both in terms of its grass roots membership and the number of lodges accepting the authority of the new Grand Lodge of England.[5] Although it is possible that Songhurst was referring to these alterations, it is more probable that he had in mind a second set of changes that took place in the late 1730s, some three or four years or so after the date on which the Irish deputation had been barred from admission to Grand Lodge. Regardless of the discrepancy between the dates, the second set of amendments to Masonic ritual were placed by Songhurst and others at the centre of the later dispute between the Antients and Moderns grand lodges. And given their role as the principal *casus belli* that instigated and sustained six decades of acrimony between the two organisations, it is appropriate to examine the issue in some detail.[6]

The adoption by the Moderns of what the Antients criticised as 'innovative ritual' was termed 'the discard . . . of the old unwritten traditions of the Order'. Two questions arise: first, did such changes occur; and second, how extensive and comprehensive were they. The answer to the first question is 'yes'. Why else would the Moderns have resolved in 1809 that it was no longer necessary for them to continue 'those measures which were resorted to in or about the year 1739'. However, the answer to the second point is harder to establish with clarity. Although the ritual used by Irish and Antients freemasons was at variance from that used by 'regular' English freemasons, the nature and extent of any divergence need to be understood in context. In addition, it is necessary to understand that the changes made in the late 1730s were demonstrably less radical and considerably less far-reaching than often supposed.

In the eighteenth century, Masonic ritual took slightly different forms in each of England, Ireland and Scotland. It is known and accepted that lodge practice also varied on a regional basis within each country and that it often differed materially from lodge to lodge. This was partly a function of an oral tradition that thwarted homogeneity, something that was achieved only later when ritual was written down. However, it was also the case that many individual lodges determined for themselves the precise nature of the ritual that they followed. Indeed, at least in the mid-eighteenth century, there was also a financial incentive to promoting and occasionally inventing additional Masonic ceremonies: extra fees could be levied by a lodge as members progressed from lower to higher degrees. It is not unreasonable to believe that this may have been a relatively important motive behind the initial spread of the Royal Arch in England and Ireland, where it only appeared on the Masonic scene in the 1730s and 1740s. And it is significant that, despite its relatively recent introduction into the Masonic ceremonial, the Royal Arch was later championed by the Antients as a principal differentiator between it and the Moderns and held out as providing evidence of the former's greater historical legitimacy and adherence to 'ancient' tradition. Tangentially, it is somewhat ironic that it was probably the popularity among freemasons of the many eighteenth-century exposés published in Britain, France and elsewhere that prompted greater uniformity in the forms of ritual used within the lodge. But standardisation in freemasonry only developed more substantially in the nineteenth century once an agreed form had been documented and disseminated by the then merged United Grand Lodge of England. And differences persisted even then. An obvious example is Bristol and the West Country, where the Masonic ritual employed had a strong commonality with that practiced in Ireland. The relationship was based on longstanding commercial ties which were mirrored in freemasonry, with merchants and traders forming and reinforcing Masonic bonds through inter-visitation and common lodge membership. Similar attachments extended to the London Irish: the first two Antients lodges to be warranted outside of London, Nos 24 and 25, were established in Bristol in October 1753. Further examples of the genre can be found in Appendix VI, which details the members of the lodge at the Ship behind the Royal Exchange and their relationships with Ireland.

Turning to the specifics of the accusations levied at the Moderns, the most common Antients complaint was that 'in or about 1739', the traditional passwords and handshakes that comprised the accepted form of Masonic recognition in the first and second degree ceremonies were transposed. The switch had purportedly been made at the suggestion of English Grand Lodge to exclude those masons whose knowledge had been gleaned from the press rather than from participating in the ceremonial. However, such a ruse would have become known rapidly. An alternative and more probable explanation is that such changes were introduced instead as an excuse to bar those thought to be of insufficient social standing. This is discussed in more detail below.

Other – lesser – Irish and Antients' criticism was directed at what was viewed as the over-secularisation of freemasonry and the omission of Christian symbolism; changes to the way in which initiates were prepared; the failure to recite the Old Charges in full (a lengthy process); and failing to use a sword in the initiation ceremony. Two further objections were directed at the use of 'stewards' to undertake roles performed in Ireland by 'deacons'; and, perhaps more tellingly, that the Moderns did not allow additional degrees to be worked in the lodge. Most of these complaints were relatively minor or even specious, and virtually all might be regarded as being undermined by the reality of eighteenth-century Masonic practice. As noted, given that Masonic ritual varied nationally, regionally and from lodge to lodge, such differences, whether minor or major, were sometimes the rule rather than an aberration. Examining the matter objectively, one can conclude with respect to ritual that in most areas of substance, the Moderns and Antients and their respective bodies of freemasons were largely aligned. Support for this interpretation is provided in *Hiram*, published in 1766, which set out to compare the two forms of ritual. The book confirms the extent to which the two overlapped and makes clear the absence of any material contradictions.[7] This should not be a surprise. There is only modest evidence that points to Masonic ritual being the primary motive for the creation of Antients freemasonry and the principal cause of the later schism. In short, the issue has been misunderstood. But if ritual was not the central factor, what was?

The work of two Victorian historians, Robert Gould and Henry Sadler, underpins the received explanation of the dispute between the Antients and Moderns and how the Antients Grand Lodge came to be established.[8] Gould's synopsis was based substantially on the minutes of what he dismissively called 'that schismatic body, commonly, but erroneously, termed the *Antient Masons*' and was limited to an analysis of freemasonry itself. Anecdotally, despite his partiality against the 'schismatics', Gould was surprisingly appreciative of the effectiveness of Laurence Dermott, the Antients' Grand Secretary, whom he termed 'the most remarkable mason of that time'. And he was correspondingly critical of the original Grand Lodge of England, Lord Byron, the then Grand Master, and its wider leadership, noting that their actions and inactions allowed the Antients to gain traction in London and elsewhere.

Sadler's assessment of the Antients focused more directly – and correctly – on the influence of the predominant majority 'Irish faction' in the new rival Antients Grand Lodge and its constituent lodges. However, unlike Gould, Sadler argued pedantically that since the London Irish had not been members of English lodges, it would be wrong to term the rivalry between the two organisations and their respective members a schism. Sadler's argument was based on the seeming tautology that, by definition, one cannot leave or fracture an organisation of which one has not been a member. He therefore contended that no schism had occurred and that the presence of two competing grand lodges was an aberration. This was a nonsense. But it was accepted without serious question in the late nineteenth century and into the twentieth. Even a century later, Dashwood, writing in support of Sadler, made the quasi-legalistic observation that the position could not have been otherwise since no 'exclusive territorial jurisdiction [for freemasonry] had [then] been formulated'.[9]

Sadler's approach, and that of many subsequent commentators, ignored the evidence. Moderns freemasons did join the Antients, and sometimes *vice versa*. Why else would the Moderns and Antients Grand Lodges sanction members who joined their respective rival? The Moderns insisted that their members meet only under their jurisdiction. Those who did otherwise risked expulsion.[10] And the Antients took a parallel view:

> if any lodge under the ancient constitution of England . . . shall have in their possessions any authority from the Grand Lodge of Moderns or in any manner assemble or meet under such authority, [they] shall be deemed unworthy of associating with the members of the Ancient Community and the warrant they hold under this Right Worshipful Grand Lodge shall be immediately cancelled.[11]

Sadler also disregarded the London Irish who were prevented or dissuaded from joining English lodges. This had been the case since the late 1730s, and probably earlier if the reaction to Lord Kingston's deputation to Grand Lodge is a guide. And he may have purposefully overlooked those freemasons who were ejected from regular English freemasonry and later found their way to the Antients. With almost a quarter of lodges expelled by the original Grand Lodge of England during the decade to 1750, the exodus is likely to have contributed substantially to the speed with which Antients freemasonry developed.

Regardless, returning to George Payne's rejection of the Irish deputation in 1735, there is another issue to be considered: the significance of the offer of 'a new constitution here', that is, the grant of an alternative English Masonic warrant. Payne would have been aware of the discrepancies that existed between Irish and English Masonic lodge warrants or constitutions. The key difference was with regard to the degree of autonomy deemed devolved to an individual lodge through the issue of a warrant by grand lodge.

Although Irish lodges placed themselves nominally under the jurisdiction of the Grand Lodge of Ireland, in practice, they retained considerable independence, with many lodges outside Dublin giving few thoughts to the edicts of Irish Grand Lodge and fewer dues. The first warrants issued in Ireland conferred extensive powers on the recipient lodges and included a license to draw up their own regulations and a grant in perpetuity to the master and wardens of the right to constitute the lodge. In such circumstances, the warrant had considerable significance and lodges were not deemed to be tied to a particular geographic location but to the location of the document itself. This gave rise to the convention and practice that a lodge could meet anywhere, whether in Ireland or overseas. It may also be one reason why peripatetic regimental lodges were first granted in Ireland.

The custom would have been anathema to English Grand Lodge in general, and to George Payne in particular. Alongside Desaguliers and Martin Folkes, Payne had been instrumental in the construction of new *Regulations* that provided the centralised federal framework that was intended to govern English freemasonry and, with other Grand Officers, he had spent more than a decade in their promotion and enforcement. In Payne's eyes, if the Irish were to meet as regular masons in London, they should do so only if they accepted an English constitution and observe English Masonic norms, most especially fealty to English Grand Lodge and acceptance of a more restrictive warrant. Consequently, given the absence of any written letter of introduction from Lord Kingston, and perhaps even if one had been forthcoming, recognition of any lodge or deputation based on an Irish warrant would have posed an unacceptable threat both to Payne and to English Masonic convention.

However, in interpreting Payne's actions, one can go further. Given his position within society, it is likely that Payne would have been subject to the same social mores as his peers. In this respect, with the exception of the Anglo-Irish gentry and aristocracy (and sometimes not even then), few Englishmen drew distinctions between different classes of Irishmen. Whether Catholic or Protestant, conformist or dissenters, rural or urban, the Irish were often lumped together as one feckless whole. Payne's negative approach to Ireland and the Irish would have mirrored the attitude of many others within English Grand Lodge. And perhaps matters were made worse by the absence of two of Grand Lodge's more aristocratic Grand Officers. Where it might have been feasible for the wealthy and socially secure Lord Weymouth and Sir Edward Mansell to have adopted a less condescending and relatively laissez faire attitude to the Irish deputation, it would certainly have been less easy for Payne, a tax official and magistrate, Jacob Lambell, a carpenter, and the Rev. James Anderson, a lowly Presbyterian minister. Although each had been associated intimately with Grand Lodge from its early years, all would have been conscious that their external social standing was at odds with their Masonic status, and this would have been guarded jealously.

Why was the anti-Irish bigotry that was so common in the eighteenth (and nineteenth) century ignored by Songhurst, Gould and Sadler as a possible cause of the rejection of Kingston's deputation. A possibility is that it would have been difficult for any of them to advance such an explanation given the subsequent union between the Antients and Moderns and the relatively more socially inclusive freemasonry that followed. Moreover, Gould and Sadler were writing in the 1880s when issues of Masonic unity (and their absence) were once again in the foreground. An argument over the precise nature of the oath to be taken in the lodge had divided international freemasonry, splitting much of the English speaking Masonic world, including the United Grand Lodge of England, the Grand Lodges of Ireland and Scotland, and the principal lodges of the United States and the British Empire, from the Grand Orient of France and European and South American freemasonry. And Songhurst, writing in 1913, would have been sensitive to the then delicate state of contemporary Hiberno-English relations given the controversy surrounding the question of Irish Home Rule.

Having had their overture summarily rejected, the reaction of the Irish delegation to Grand Lodge is unknown: bemused, annoyed or irate. Regardless, the growth of Irish freemasonry in London is likely to have been untrammelled; after all, English Grand Lodge had no sanction other than exclusion. And exclusion probably worked in favour of an émigré version of Irish freemasonry, creating a separate environment in which it thrived. In such circumstances, it would have been understandable psychology for the mainly lower middling and working-class London Irish freemasons to have accentuated the greater deemed antiquity, integrity and superiority of their own 'Antient' Masonic ritual, including the newly introduced Royal Arch ceremony. And for them to have developed and emphasised those aspects of freemasonry that had specific social and economic relevance, in particular, what evolved into the practice of mutual communal social and financial support. Given such a framework, there was perhaps an element of inevitability to the eventual aggregation of London's excluded Irish lodges. Their later agreement to create a Grand Committee and submit to an alternative central authority provided a counterpoint to the original Grand Lodge of England and offered a substitute source of prestige and patronage.

Antients freemasonry may have been established initially by the émigré London Irish but its later membership had a wider composition that included the lower middling and working class more broadly. Social and economic alienation was not limited exclusively to those from Ireland and a desire for an accessible form of polite association, an inclination for mutual protection, the dysfunction of English Grand Lodge and the later politicisation of the Anglo-Irish elite, created a confluence of different drivers and dynamics. The professed desire to protect and project a more pure form of Masonic ritual was deployed as a means of promoting the Antients Grand Lodge by casti-gating its rival and superimposed onto a construct that had other foundations. The tactic proved to be effective, but it was not the primary rationale for the existence of Antients freemasonry.

Antients Grand Lodge quickly became a focal point for London's Irish freemasons and attracted others unhappy with the original English Grand Lodge and those seeking a new form of civil association. However, with regard to propelling forward the organisation's development, perhaps the most vital feature of the new Antients Grand Lodge was that it gave a plat-form to Laurence Dermott (1720–1791), Grand Secretary from 1752 until 1770 and Deputy Grand Master from 1771 until 1777 and, again, from 1783 until 1787.

Virtually from its inception, Dermott was careful to position the Antients and Antients freemasonry as part of a long and well-established tradition: 'keeping the ancient landmarks in view'.[12] It was in this context that he iden-tified the Antients Grand Lodge with York freemasonry and took to describing the rival Grand Lodge of England as 'Moderns'. The description was, and was intended to be, heavily pejorative. In a period when the age and history of an institution had powerful implications for its legitimacy and public standing, it was a clever move. Indeed, virtually the same tactic had been employed by the first Grand Lodge of England itself some three decades earlier.

The major part of James Anderson's *1723 Constitutions* was a history of freemasonry that dated its origins to time immemorial.[13] In this, Anderson had adopted and extended a methodology used by the mediaeval Masonic guilds where the centrepiece of their 'charges', the manuscripts that constituted the guild or lodge and contained its rules, encompassed a faux history dating back to St Athelstan or St Alban, or even more remotely to Euclid or biblical times. By positioning freemasonry as an institution that could be traced back across the centuries to 'Adam, our first parent [who] had the liberal sciences, particularly geometry, written on his heart', Anderson's narrative provided the new English Grand Lodge with an aura of authenticity and an antiquarian status that an organisation recognised as more recent would have found impossible to attain.

It is unlikely that many would have considered Anderson's history to be wholly accurate or literal, rather than an account written in the context of a tradition of legend and literary hyperbole. But it is nonetheless clear that Dermott's dismissive categorisation of the original Grand Lodge as 'Moderns' and the adoption of the emotive title of 'Antients' by its younger rival was designed to reinforce the argument that the latter had the greater claim to chronological legitimacy.

Laurence Dermott recognised the value of history and tradition explicitly, most especially its potential emotional impact on prospective recruits. However, it was a mark of his confidence and intelligence that he was also willing to satirise at length the very concept of Masonic historiography. In *Ahiman Rezon*, Dermott wrote in an editor's note to his readers that he had determined to publish a history of freemasonry and had 'purchased all or most of the histories, constitutions, pocket companions and other pieces (on that subject) now extant in the English tongue'. However, having supposedly furnished himself with pens, ink and paper, and surrounded himself with the relevant compositions and started work accordingly, Dermott 'fell to dreaming', only to be woken some time later:

> A young puppy that got into the room while I slept, and seizing my papers, ate a great part of them, and was then (between my legs) shaking and tearing the last sheet . . . Like one distracted (as in truth I was) I ran to the owner of the dog and demanded immediate satisfaction. He told me he would hang the cur, but at the same time he imagined I should be under more obligation to him for so doing than he was to me for what happened. In short, I looked upon it as a bad Omen and my late dread had made so great an impression on my mind that superstition got the better of me and called me to deviate from the general custom of my worthy predecessors otherwise I would have published a History of Masonry; and as this is rather an accident than a designed fault, I hope that the reader will look over it with a favourable eye.[14]

Dermott's funny, ironic and satirical tone was pointedly and deliberately at odds with the more precious style adopted by the Moderns and their chroniclers: 'Doctor Anderson and Mr Spratt . . . Doctor D'Assigny and Doctor Desaguliers'. And Dermott's conversational introduction and relaxed literary style arguably epitomised the more open attitude adopted by the Antients and marked the organisation's greater accessibility and attraction to the lower middling and working class.

Laurence Dermot makes a first appearance in the Antients' *General Register* on 1 February 1752.[15] He was one of two men proposed for the position of Grand Secretary, replacing John Morgan who had been 'lately appointed to an office on board one of His Majesty's ships'. Selected, Dermott immediately became the driving force behind the organisation, and his administrative and marketing skills set the foundations on which its later success was built.

Dermott's early life is subject to some conjecture. Past biographies have suggested that he was born on 24 June 1720 in Co. Roscommon and thereafter moved to Dublin. However, if Dermott's date of birth is recorded correctly, the date of his initiation into lodge No. 26 in Dublin on 14 January 1741 implies that he would have been under 21. Although aristocrats and affluent gentry occasionally became freemasons before reaching the legal age of maturity, it was otherwise uncommon.

Dermott was elected Master of lodge No. 26 in June 1746. He emigrated to England the following year, arriving in London in 1747 or 1748 where he appears to have worked as a journeyman painter. In the Antients Grand Lodge minutes of 13 July 1753, Dermott noted the difficulties he had in delivering grand lodge summonses since 'he was obliged to work twelve hours in the day for the Master Painter who employed him'. Circumstantial evidence suggests that his employer was James Hagarty, variously spelt Hagerty or Hagarthy, a past master of lodge No. 4. Hagarty was also chairman of the Grand Committee that on 5 February 1752 approved Dermott as the Antients' new Grand Secretary.[16] Although Hagarty was described by Dermott as a painter who 'lives now in Leather Lane', he was more probably by then a businessman who employed others, rather than merely another jobbing employee.[17]

Séan Murphy has written that Dermott was 'almost certainly of the Jacobite-connected MacDermott family of Strokestown, Co. Roscommon'.[18] However, although the MacDermott family writ large can be linked to the Catholic Jacobite opposition, not least through the records of soldiers of that name who served with the Irish brigades in France and Spain, there is no evidence to show that Laurence Dermott was either a Catholic or a Jacobite.[19] Indeed, the opposite is more probable. Dermott's two marriages, his son's baptism and his place of burial all indicate that he was a Protestant, most probably a member of the Church of Ireland and then of the Church of England. His marriages were to Protestants, his son was baptised into the Church of England, and Dermott himself was buried at St Olave's, Southwark, in a Church of England graveyard. Other members of his family living in Dublin were also buried as Protestants, many in the Church of Ireland graveyard of St Nicholas Without in Dublin.[20] They included Thomas Dermott of New Row, Dublin (possibly his great uncle, whose date of burial was 29 September 1716); Mary Dermott and Patrick Dermott of New Street (18 October 1720 and 4 September 1717, respectively); and John Dermott of Frances Street (12 October 1729).[21] The Dermott's supposed Jacobite leanings are also questionable: Anthony Dermott, Laurence's half uncle, and other prominent members of the family were among the principal signatories to loyal addresses published in the Irish and British press. Nonetheless, Murphy was correct in linking the Dermott family to Co. Roscommon. Thomas Dermott, Laurence's father, reportedly had a country house at Strokestown. Moreover, fourteen of the nineteen members of lodge No. 340 in Strokestown, including a Michael McDermott, subscribed to the Irish edition of *Ahiman Rezon*, published in Dublin in 1760. This would have been an exceptionally high number for a small provincial lodge.[22] Tangentially, the warrant for Strokestown had been issued by the Grand Lodge of Ireland only the prior year.

Despite the connection to Co. Roscommon, the Dermott family appears to have lived principally in Dublin. Newspaper articles and classified advertisements confirm Lepper and Crossle's view that the Dermotts were middling Dublin-based merchants who traded principally with the Baltic and continental Europe.[23] Laurence Dermott's familiarity with Latin and Hebrew, a knowledge he exhibited in compiling the minutes of Antients Grand Lodge, also suggests an education that went beyond the basics and perhaps formed part of a middling upbringing. Moreover, in common with other merchant dynasties, relatives were also based overseas, including France and Spain, where they oversaw aspects of the family's foreign trading and transhipment activities and acted as agents for the importation of wine and other goods into Ireland.[24]

Dermott's grandfather and the head of the family in the early eighteenth century was Christopher Dermott (16__?–1721), who traded from Usher's Quay on the south bank of the river Liffey in central Dublin. Christopher had one child, Thomas, by his first marriage, and five children, three boys and two girls, by his second wife. It is unknown whether his first wife died in childbirth, but this was a common cause of death at the time. Christopher Dermott's will bequeathing the whole of his estate to his 'dearly beloved wife Mary Dermott [formerly Mary O'Connor, *d.*1762] and to my five children by her viz., Anthony, Michael, Stephen, Ann and Mary Dermott according to their respective merits' may indicate a falling out with his eldest son, and Thomas appears not to have received a share of the inheritance. Indeed, the principal trading business was taken over by Anthony Dermott (1700–1784), Christopher Dermott's second son but the first from his second marriage.[25]

Anthony, Laurence's half uncle, specialised in importing paper and traded mainly with the Baltic. He operated from the family's warehouses at Usher's Quay, trading from there until a fire next door forced his relocation to North

King Street.[26] Anthony and other Dermott family members appear regularly in the mid- and later eighteenth-century Dublin press alongside other well known Dublin merchants, often as prominent signatories to letters published in support of Irish bankers' credit or promoting free trade.[27] Anthony was an eminent city merchant and on several occasions represented the influential Committee of Merchants, in one instance in connection with a much publicised donation of £400 to the Inn's Quay Infirmary, which Anthony presented to the hospital on behalf of the Committee.[28] He and other members of the family were represented on the Committee for around thirty years, from the 1750s through to the 1780s.[29] Other articles and advertisements in the Dublin press confirm the family's prominence. And they suggest that the Dermotts were opportunistic and willing to conduct business across both religious and family divides. An example is their cooperative joint venture with Messrs Cosgrave, Reynolds and Plunkett in the Caribbean rum trade in the 1760s.[30]

Thomas Dermott (1699–17.?), Laurence's father, also traded with the Baltic, but mainly in timber, which had a lower added value. His premises were in New Row, the northern extension of Francis Street, a hundred yards or so to the south of Ushers Quay. However, a relative absence of press coverage suggests that he may have been less successful commercially than Anthony, his half brother. Nonetheless, with such family connections, Dermott's move to London may indicate less a journey triggered by poverty, a circumstance that motivated many, perhaps most other émigrés, than a falling out with his family or, perhaps more probably, a desire for greater independence.

London was the largest city in Europe and the centre of Britain's empire. As such, the capital attracted both economic migrants and others seeking to establish a reputation. Entrepreneurial roots have also been advanced as an explanation for Dermott's ability to upgrade both his occupation and social status from that of jobbing painter to the more middling and financially secure position of vintner. However, in this respect, his marriage in 1766 to Elizabeth Merryman, the widow of 'Mr Merryman, who kept the Wine Vaults in King Street, near Tower Hill', was probably the more significant and immediate influence.[31] Elizabeth Merryman had been widowed in 1760 and her wedding to Dermott received appropriate press coverage:

> on Saturday last was married Mr Dermott, master of the Five Bells Tavern in the Strand, to Mrs Merryman, relict of the late Mr Merryman, an eminent wine merchant in Prince's Street, Tower Hill.[32]

The marriage was the second for them both. A note in the *Public Ledger* a year earlier in November 1765 recorded Dermott's first marriage at St Clements Danes church to 'Mrs Mary Dwindle, Mistress of the Five Bells Tavern behind the New Church in the Strand'.[33] She had been widowed relatively recently. William, her late husband, the previous innkeeper at the Five Bells, had died just under two years earlier in December 1763.[34] Mary

Dwindle's second marriage to Dermott was brief and several press reports less than five months after the wedding detailed her unexpected demise:

> yesterday died Mrs Dermott, mistress of the Five Bells tavern near the New Church in the Strand.[35]

That the press coverage of Mary Dwindle's death was moderately wide suggests that both she and the tavern were well known. The implication is probably accurate. The Five Bells occupied a prominent location and was a substantial business with premises sufficiently large to accommodate musical concerts and guild and public meetings. The tavern had a good reputation and was positioned at the upper end of its market.[36] This was expressed in the Five Bells hosting 'elegant entertainments' and formal dinners, including a fund raising anniversary dinner for the governors of the Queen's Hospital, attended by its president and vice presidents, in addition to the drinking, dining and lodging more usually associated with such an establishment.[37]

Dermott would have been familiar with both the tavern and its management. The Antients' Grand Committee met at the Five Bells on a regular basis from December 1752, barely a year after its formation, until 1771, when they transferred to the Half Moon tavern in Cheapside to celebrate the installation of the 3rd duke of Atholl as Grand Master. Dermott was also known to the tavern, with Masonic correspondence addressed to him there: 'Mr Dermott, Secretary to the Grand Lodge of Free and Accepted Masons at the Five Bells in the Strand'.

Many press articles and advertisements over two decades reported on the Antients' regular, installation and ad hoc meetings at the Five Bells:

> On Saturday last a great number of the most Ancient and Honourable Fraternity of Free and Accepted Masons, met at the Five Bells Tavern in the Strand and unanimously chose the Hon Thomas Mathews, Esq., their Grand Master to succeed the earl of Kelly.[38]

And in advance of a benefit evening in March 1754 to raise funds for 'decayed Antient Masons',

> the Brothers are desired to meet on the day of the performance at the Five Bells Tavern in the Strand, at Four in the Afternoon.[39]

Despite his marriage to its mistress, Dermott did not inherit the Five Bells on Mary Dwindle's death.[40] The freehold was owned by the Worshipful Company of Haberdashers and the business was let.[41] However, operating the Five Bells in the short period he acted as its landlord was nonetheless likely to have been profitable and Dermott's departure was probably triggered by his marriage to Elizabeth Merryman and the prospect of greater remuneration and prestige as a wine merchant, an occupation shared by family members back in Ireland. Certainly, a new landlord was in residence at the Five Bells within two years; an obituary in 1769 recorded the death of a Mrs Anderson, described at that time as 'wife of Mr Anderson, master of the Five Bells Tavern, near the New Church in the Strand.'[42]

With regard to his Masonic curriculum vitae, Dermott had been initiated into lodge No. 26 in Dublin in 1740, where he rose through the ranks to become its Master in 1746. Although the records of the Grand Lodge of Ireland contain nothing that substantiates Dermott's initiation or progress through the lodge, when his *bona fides* were queried in 1757, Dermott's account of his time in Dublin was apparently verified:

> Then arose Brother Thomas Allen, Past Master of No. 2 and proved that Brother Dermott had faithfully served all Offices in a very reputable Lodge held in his house in the City of Dublin . . . [and] Brother Charles Byrne (Sr.), Master of No. 2 proved that Bro. Lau. Dermott having faithfully served the Offices of Sr. and Jr. Deacon, Jr. and Sr. Wardens and Secretary was by him Regularly Installed Master of the good lodge No. 26 in the Kingdom of Ireland upon the 24th day of June 1746 . . . Brother Dermott produced a Certificate (signed Edwd. Spratt, GS) under the seal of the Grand Lodge of Ireland of his good behaviour and Servitude . . . which gave entire satisfaction.[43]

The warrant under which lodge No. 26 had been constituted was originally issued in Co. Sligo in December 1735. The lodge moved subsequently to Dublin where it met at the house of Thomas Allen, the then Master. From there it seems to have transferred to London, the warrant possibly being taken overseas by either Allen or Dermott.[44] Smith's 1735 *Pocket Companion* supports this interpretation and, if accurate, the lodge would provide an early example of a travelling Irish warrant.[45] A Thomas Allen, possibly the same person, appears as No. 863 in the *Grand Register*. Although no more than anecdotal evidence, an advertisement in the *Dublin Journal* on 12 June 1733 suggests that Allen was a dentist who practiced in Golden Lane off Bride Street, Dublin. Tangentially, although the lodge was erased in 1801, the warrant number was later reissued to the 26th Foot, the Cameronians.

Accurate biographical information on Dermott is sparse. Many past biographies have been anecdotal and most may be wrong. Limiting analysis to what can be verified, the Antients' *General Register* details his London address in 1752 as Butler's Alley in Moorfields.[46] The location was close to Grub Street, a district that ran from Fore Street to Chiswell Street on the northern border of the City of London. Published in the 1730s, *The Grub Street Journal* was a satire on the gutter journalism with which the area became synonymous. Alexander Pope referred to the area both in his *Epistle to Arbuthnot* and in the *Dunciad*, where it was described as a 'powerful image of shabbiness of way of life [and] morals'.[47] He characterised Grub Street as 'skulking', an appropriate description for what was one of the city's more impoverished areas: overcrowded and packed with low rent housing, brothels and inns.

After his second marriage, Dermott moved east from the Five Bells tavern to King Street in St Botolph Aldgate, on the eastern borders of the City of London, where he took over his wife's vintners business. They later purchased a property in Stepney at Mile End, then a hamlet in what was the eastern extremity of semi-rural Middlesex. The latter address is given in Elizabeth's Dermott's will, the former in newspaper advertisements and in Laurence Dermott's own will, proved at probate on 15 July 1791.[48] Located on the western edge of the parish of St Botolph Aldgate, King Street bordered the Tower of London and the old Royal Mint buildings. It was another densely populated district but with a minority of more affluent residents, including Dermott, whose rates would have helped to sustain the parish's comparatively high level of poor relief.[49]

Dermott's address in King Street appeared in press advertisements in February and March 1773, when he acted an executor to the estate of Frances Allen, a fellow freemason.[50] This is one of many examples of the social and business relationships that were built or reinforced through freemasonry. And it was probably not a coincidence that Dermott's co-executor, Joseph Langser, a tallow chandler based in White Street, off Goodman's Fields, was another Antients freemason.

> All persons indebted to Mr Francis Allen, late of Woodstock Street, near New Bond Street, deceased are desired to pay the same to Mr Joseph Langser of Leman Street, Goodman's Fields, tallow chandler; or Mr Laurence Dermott of King Street, near Tower Hill, wine merchant, executors of the said Mr Allen. And all person having any demands on the said Mr Francis Allen are desired to bring in their bills in order to be paid.[51]

Like Dermott, Frances Allen had also managed to improve his social and economic status. He is recorded in the *Register* as the 290th member, having joined Antients freemasonry in 1753. He was then a victualler living at the King and Queen tavern in Capel Street, near Rosemary Lane in the East End of London. He later moved to Chandois Street, to the south of Covent Garden, and from there to the more affluent Woodstock Street, near New Bond Street and close to the Great West Road.

Laurence and Elizabeth Dermott had a son within a year of their marriage on 30 December 1767. Named for his father, he was christened into the Church of England at St Botolph Without, Aldgate, close to the Dermotts' King Street premises. Elizabeth also had a child, a daughter, from her previous marriage, Sarah, who later inherited the principal part of her estate. Laurence and Elizabeth were both buried in the Church of England grave-yard of the newly rebuilt St Olave's in Southwark.[52] Given that other members of the Dermott family had graves at the Church of Ireland St Nicholas Without in Dublin, it would be hard to argue that Dermott was not a Protestant. Nevertheless, other members of the Dermott family were Catholic.

Christopher Dermott, Laurence's grandfather, had married twice. This may explain why Anthony, Laurence's half uncle was Catholic, as were his siblings and children: they probably took their mother's faith. This was not uncommon. Indeed, according to a biographer, the Dermott family had both Protestant and Catholic branches.[53] In 1782, Anthony Dermott was one of three who signed an open letter 'on behalf of the Roman Catholics of Ireland' addressed to Luke Gardiner, 1st viscount Mountjoy.[54] This may have been either Laurence Dermott's uncle or his cousin, who had also been named for his father. The letter was published in both the British and Irish press in May 1782 and followed the partial repeal of Ireland's penal laws and the passage of legislation promoting greater religious toleration.[55] Anthony was also a signatory to another heavily published open letter dated 12 September the same year and addressed to the duke of Portland, then Lord Lieutenant of Ireland. The letter was signed similarly on behalf of 'His Majesty's dutiful and loyal subjects, the Roman Catholics of Ireland'.[56]

Anthony and his sons were prominent members of the Catholic Committee in Dublin. And they were not the first members of the family who were Catholics. The Dermott family had been Roman Catholics in earlier generations. However, in common with other merchant families with an estate to protect, it is likely that some family members, including Christopher Dermott, converted for political and financial reasons rather than out of religious conviction. Regardless, it is likely that religion was a secondary issue for Dermott. Although a Protestant, he associated with a variety of religious faiths in his role as Grand Secretary and, in this, the Antients exhibited a religious tolerance similar to that pioneered by the Moderns whose lodge members included nonconformists, Catholics, Quakers and Jews.

Dermott probably began his move towards relative affluence before his second marriage. An indication is the extent to which he was able to donate to Masonic charities and make large scale financial contributions to the Antients Grand Lodge. In 1766, before his wedding in November of that year but after his first marriage to Mary Dwindle, Dermott subscribed five guineas to help to pay the debts of a brother freemason held in Newgate and an additional ten pounds to the Antients Grand Charity. The following year and now married for the second time, Dermott commanded additional financial resources that allowed him to donate a Grand Master's throne 'which cost in the whole £34'. However, aside from the wealth he may have derived through his two marriages and briefly operating The Five Bells, another source of income and capital would have been the royalties from his publication of *Ahiman Rezon*, the Antients' popular book of constitutions.

Ahiman Rezon, or Help to a Brother was published privately by Dermott in 1756, as were at least five subsequent editions.[57] The book was dedicated to the earl of Blessington, described by Dermott as 'a father to the fraternity'. The rationale for the title is unclear and a variety of different explanations have been proposed, none of which are definitive. Mackey suggested that it was derived from three Hebrew words: *ahim*, meaning brothers; *manah*, meaning to select or choose; and *ratzon*, meaning the will or law. Taken together, Mackey offered the suggestion that the title could be construed as 'the will of selected brethren' or 'the law of a society of men who are selected as brethren'.[58] Other translations and interpretations of the title have included 'brother of the right hand secret', an allusion to the pass grip of a master mason; 'the secrets of a prepared brother'; 'royal builder'; and 'worthy brother secretary'.

Dermott himself chose not to clarify the meaning of the title other than in its by-line, 'Help to a Brother'. Notwithstanding that the central component of the text was based on Laurence Spratt's *Irish Constitutions*, which was published in Dublin in 1751 and drew heavily on Anderson's rewritten and extended 1738 *Constitutions*, *Ahiman Rezon* ran to at least six editions in England during Dermott's lifetime and at least another six in the two decades to 1813, when the Antients entered into a union and merged with the Moderns.[59] *Ahiman Rezon* was also published and sold elsewhere, including Ireland, where over twenty editions were printed, and in the American and Canadian colonies, where it was adopted as the basis for the constitutions of the grand lodges of seven American states. In addition, special editions of *Ahiman Rezon* were published by the Grand Lodge of Pennsylvania in 1783 and the Grand Lodge of Nova Scotia in 1786. Virginia and Maryland produced their own versions in 1791 and 1797, respectively, as did South Carolina and Georgia in the nineteenth century.

Ahiman Rezon codified and more importantly publicised Antients freemasonry, arguing in favour of its greater antiquity and superior ritual as compared to the (not dissimilar) form practiced by the Moderns. Dermott also used later editions of the book to highlight the pact between the Antients and the Grand Lodges of Ireland and Scotland and to emphasise the Antients' claim to Masonic pre-eminence over the Moderns. The book's impact was extensive and grew as subsequent editions gained greater traction. The value of the publisher's royalties would also have been considerable and, in September 1785, in an act that set a seal on Dermott's standing within the Antients Grand Lodge and testified to his then affluence, Dermott gifted his future royalties to the Antients' Grand Charity.

Notwithstanding his achievements and perhaps because of them, in the mid-nineteenth century, some four decades after the union and six decades after his death, it became commonplace to vilify Dermott. Laurie in his *History of Freemasonry* wrote that

> much injury has been done to the cause of the Antients . . . by Laurence Dermott . . . the unfairness with which he has stated the proceedings of the Moderns, the bitterness with which he treats them and the quackery and vainglory with which he displays his superior knowledge, deserve to be reprobated by every class of Masons who are anxious for the purity of their Order and the preservation of the clarity and mildness which ought to characterise all their proceedings.[60]

Mackey wrote of Dermott in a similar vein: 'as a polemic, he was sarcastic bitter, uncompromising and not altogether sincere or veracious'.[61] Mackey nonetheless acknowledged that Dermott was 'in intellectual attainments . . . inferior to none . . . and in a philosophical appreciation of the character of the Masonic institution he was in advance of the spirit of his age'.[62] Gould's view of Dermott was of an 'unscrupulous writer [but] a matchless administrator'.[63] Hughan called his works 'absurd and ridiculous.[64] And Sadler commented variously on Dermott's writings as 'comical', 'ridiculous' and 'scarcely worth a moment's thought'.[65] Antipathy towards Dermott dated back a century and Gould's observation that 'in Masonic circles, Dermott was probably the best abused man of his time' was almost certainly accurate. Rolling with the punches, Dermott used subsequent editions of *Ahiman Rezon* to retaliate to his vilification with biting satire. He was effective. He joked that the rival Moderns had:

> [considered it] expedient to abolish the old custom of studying geometry in the lodge and some of the young brethren made it appear that a good knife and fork in the hands of a dextrous brother (over the right materials) would give greater satisfaction and add more to the rotundity of the lodge . . . from this improvement proceeded the laudable custom of charging to a public health to every third sentence that is spoke in the lodge.[66]

And Dermott continued:

> There was another old custom that gave umbrage to the young architects, i.e. the wearing of aprons, which made the gentlemen look like so many mechanics, therefore it was proposed, that no brother (for the future) should wear an apron. This proposal was rejected by the oldest members, who declared that the aprons were all the signs of masonry then remaining amongst them and for that reason they would keep and wear them. It was then proposed, that (as they were resolved to wear aprons) they should be turned upside down, in order to avoid appearing mechanical. This proposal took place and answered the design, for that which was formerly the lower part, was now fastened round the abdomen, and the bib and strings hung downwards, dangling in such manner as might convince the spectators that there was not a working mason amongst them. Agreeable as this alteration might seem to the gentlemen, nevertheless it was attended with an ugly circumstance: for, in traversing the lodge, the brethren were subject to tread upon the strings, which often caused them to fall with great violence, so that it was thought necessary to invent several methods of walking, in order to avoid treading upon the strings.[67]

The Moderns published their retaliation in *A Defence of Freemasonry . . . as practiced in the regular lodges*, published in 1765. Advertisements for the book noted that it contained 'a refutation of Mr Dermott's ridiculous account of that ancient society, in his book entitled *Ahiman Rezon*'.[68] But in the event, the Moderns' *Defence* achieved only limited success. Worse, the decision of the earl of Blessington to accept the position of Grand Master and thus validate Antients Grand Lodge with his imprimatur, and the later decision of Irish Grand Lodge to cease fraternal communication with the Moderns, was regarded with incredulity by the Moderns. Even a century later their apologists considered the decision inexplicable. Gould wrote that it was

> a little singular that Dermott secured the services as titular Grand Master [of a] nobleman under whose presidency the Grand Lodge of Ireland conformed to the laws and regulations enacted by the Regular or Original Grand Lodge of England.[69]

Gould's analysis, like that of many other Masonic commentators, was incomplete. He and others ignored the political and economic dynamics that underlay Blessington's decision and the Antients' success. In any event, even within the terms of his own analysis, Ireland had adapted rather than adopted the laws and regulations of the Grand Lodge of England. And perhaps equally importantly, Ireland's evolving socially inclusive approach to freemasonry and less proscriptive governance was an approach readily emulated by the Antients.

With Dermott's guidance, Antients freemasonry traded successfully on the combination of inclusivity and notionally superior antiquity. Underlining this, in his second edition of *Ahiman Rezon*, Dermott's 'Philacteria for such gentleman as may be inclined to become Free-Masons' accentuated the pre-eminence of Antients freemasonry through a catechism. Probably more than any other element of *Ahiman Rezon*, it created, captured and cemented the perception of the Antients as superior Masonic beings. It was to be instrumental in attracting and retaining new members:

First Question: Whether freemasonry, as practiced in antients lodges, is universal?
Answer: Yes

Second: Whether what is called modern masonry is universal?
Answer: No

Third: Whether there is any material difference between antient and modern?
Answer: A great deal, because an antient mason can not only make himself known to his brother but in cases of necessity can discover his very thoughts to him, in the presence of a modern, without being able to distinguish that either of them are free masons.

Fourth: Whether a modern mason may with safety communicate all his secrets to an antient mason?
Answer: Yes

Fifth: Whether an antient mason may with the like safety commu-
                nicate all his secrets to a modern mason without further
                ceremony?

Answer: No. For as a Science comprehends an Art (though an artist
                cannot comprehend a science) even so antient masonry
                contains everything valuable amongst the modern, as well as
                many other things that cannot be revealed without addi-
                tional ceremonies. . . .

Ninth: Whether the present members of modern lodges are blame-
                able for deviating from the old landmarks?

Answer: No. Because the innovation was made in the reign of George
                I and the new form was delivered as orthodox to the present
                members.

Tenth: Therefore as it is natural for each party to maintain the
                orthodoxy of their Masonical preceptor, how shall we
                distinguish the original and most useful system?

Answer: The number of antient masons compared with the moderns
                being as ninety-nine to one proves the universality of the old
                order . . .

Of course, what Dermott held out to be facts were either falsehoods or
opinions. However, together they comprised a powerful polemic and encouragement to join Antients freemasonry whether *ab initio* or by way of a
conversion from the Moderns. (In later years, many freemasons became
members of both organisations.) The force and persuasive power of
Dermott's arguments were directed to prospective masons both at home and
overseas, especially at British and Irish colonists in the Americas, whose
'right worshipful and very worthy gentlemen' were singled out for particular
flattery in the second edition of *Ahiman Rezon*.

As the Antients expanded their membership in London, across provincial
England and in Britain's colonies and elsewhere, Dermott posed a challenge
to the authority of the original Grand Lodge of England and that of the
(English) establishment. He championed the potentially seditious nature of
Antients freemasonry and embedded it in its workings and literature. For
example, Dermott's frontispiece to the revised third edition of *Ahiman
Rezon*, published in 1778, featured a design that reflected the exclusion and
marginalisation of the Moderns in favour of the Irish, Scottish and Antients
branches of freemasonry, the last an offshoot of Ireland:

The three figures upon the dome represent the great masters of the tabernacle . . . The two crowned figures with that on their right hand represent
the three great masters of the holy temple at Jerusalem. The three figures
on the left hand represent the three great masters of the second temple at
Jerusalem.

The three columns bearing Masons aprons with the arms of England, Ireland and Scotland and supporting the whole fabric, represents the three Grand Masters . . . who wisely and nobly have formed a triple union to support the honour and dignity of the Ancient Craft, for which their Lordship's names will be honoured and revered while Freemasonry exists in these kingdoms.[70]

Dermott's text reminded the reader that it was Antients freemasonry that offered the more widespread support to the indigent, quoting an unfortunately phrased letter from the Moderns to a 'a certified petitioner from Ireland' that stated 'your being an Antient Mason, you are not entitled to any of our charity'. The Moderns' letter continued, digging a deeper hole, with the author, the then Grand Secretary, stating that the 'Society is neither Arch, Royal Arch or Ancient, so that you have no right to partake of our charity'.[71] The minutes of the Moderns Grand Lodge confirm the position. Although there are few direct references to the rival Antients, a resolution passed on 29 November 1754 is significant. Under the Marquis of Carnarvon, then Grand Master, English Grand Lodge resolved:

> that if any mason shall attend, tyle or assist as tyler at any meetings or pretended lodges of persons calling themselves masons not being a regular constituted lodge acknowledging the authority of our Rt. Worshipful Grand Master and conforming to the Laws of the Grand Lodge, he shall be forever incapable of being a tyler or attendant on a lodge or partaking of the General Charity.[72]

In short, the primary response of the Moderns to the challenge posed by the Antients was to rule that no Masonic charity would be available to any Antients freemason, that they would not be allowed to act as an attendant or tyler, a role often performed by indigent freemasons, and that they would be excluded from any and all 'regular' Masonic lodge meetings.

Within six months the rule was put to the test. The Master and Wardens of the lodge at the Ben Johnson's Head tavern were summoned to Grand Lodge to answer an accusation that they had been meeting as Antients. The lodge responded by arguing that, as private persons, they had the right to meet in any manner they deemed fit. In order to seek a resolution, Thomas Manningham, the acting Grand Master, asked the Master and Wardens on behalf of the lodge to put forward a proposal to determine the issue.[73] The minutes continue, noting that 'after some debate about the question to be proposed', a suggestion was tabled that 'the Members of the Lodge at the Ben Johnson's Head be permitted to meet independent of their Constitution from this Society under the Denomination of a Lodge of Ancient Masons'. The resolution was voted down almost unanimously. The representatives of only two lodges voted in favour: those from the Ben Johnson's Head itself and a delegation from the Fish and Bell tavern in Soho. Subsequently, the members of the Ben Johnson's Head having been invited to 'refrain from their said irregular Meetings [and] reconcile themselves to Grand Lodge', the minutes note that the request was 'without effect'. Accordingly,

> a question was then put, that the lodge No. 94, held at the Ben Johnson's Head in Pelham Street, Spitalfields, be erased from the Book of Lodges and that such of the Brethren thereof who shall continue those irregular Meetings be not admitted as Visitors in any Lodge.[74]

The resolution was carried 'almost unanimously, with the same Brethren as above only dissenting'.[75]

Two aspects to the affair can be noted. First, the Fish and Bell in Soho, the only lodge voting to support the Ben Johnson's Head, was one of four lodges who together had founded the first Grand Lodge of England. The lodge had met previously at the Apple Tree Tavern and was then known by that name.[76] The Fish and Bell was one of a number of lodges who had not modified their ritual to the new form approved by Grand Lodge but instead retained their own older form of working. The lodge's resistance to the central diktat of English Grand Lodge was shared by several other lodges that pre-dated Grand Lodge. And its stance had a counterpart in the decision of the Horn tavern, the senior founding lodge, not to attend Grand Lodge's Quarterly Communications for much of the 1740s. As a result, the Horn ceased to be recognised as a 'regular' lodge and stood erased until 1751, when George Payne interceded on its behalf and persuaded both sides to agree to a reinstatement. The issue is discussed further in CHAPTER SIX. However, the point is that the positive approbation of Grand Lodge was not a requirement for a lodge to function. Many would both survive and prosper as independent lodges. Second, Dermott used the fallout from the incident as yet another means to heap derision and opprobrium on the Moderns. The episode was described at length in the third edition of *Ahiman Rezon* published some two decades later. As usual, Dermott's comments were pointed, designed to show his rivals in a less than favourable light and to emphasise the consequential superiority of the Antients. Dermott spun a summary of what had occurred, writing that the Ben Johnson's Head:

> [was] composed mainly of Antient Masons, though under the Modern Constitution. Some of them had been abroad and received extraordinary benefits on account of Antient Masonry. Therefore they agreed to practice Antient Masonry on every third lodge night. Upon one of those nights some Modern Masons attempted to visit them but were refused admittance; the persons so refused laid a formal complaint before the Modern Grand Lodge . . . [who] ordered that the Ben Johnson's Head should admit all sorts of Masons without distinction. And upon non compliance to that order, they were censured.[77]

Dermott continued. Quoting from a protest pamphlet that he assured his readers had been issued by the maligned lodge, he observed that the 'injustice' to the Ben Johnson's Head was due to the Moderns' crass ignorance of freemasonry. In a memorable analogy, Dermott compared the futility of the Moderns' position to that of 'a blind man . . . in the art of mixing colour'. And as a final thrust and with intentional irony, albeit that it was in conflict with his earlier remarks, Dermott stated that the relevant members of the Ben Johnson's Head had not even been Antients freemasons, although '(from [his] personal knowledge and public report) they were persons of the most amiable character as men and masons'.[78]

Dermott's actions on this and other occasions encapsulate three key aspects to his success in positioning the Antients as an attractive organisation, maligning the Moderns, and thereby recruiting and retaining new members. First, he emphasised that the Antients provided a conduit for Masonic benevolence, even when members were overseas; after all, members of the Ben Johnson's Head 'had been abroad and received extraordinary benefits on account of Antient Masonry'. Second, he drew attention to the Antients' greater exclusivity and possession of superior ritual, arguing that the lodge at the Ben Johnson's Head was, in this sense, correct to refuse admittance to the lesser qualified Moderns. And third, he suggested that the behaviour of the Moderns Grand Lodge was at the same time both dictatorial and ignorant. In particular, their decision to order the admittance of 'all sorts of Masons without distinction' indicated an absence of knowledge of the 'true' nature of freemasonry. They were, in short, 'as a blind man is in the art of mixing colour'.

The disparagement of the Moderns was a constant thread throughout Dermott's terms of office. Twenty years after having first been appointed, in April 1772, Dermott chaired a meeting of a lodge at the Half Moon tavern on Cheapside at which a letter from the 3rd duke of Atholl was read and later reported in the press. In the letter, quoted verbatim,

> the duke thanked them for the great honour they had conferred upon him by continuing him Grand Master for the year ending and he likewise acquainted them that he was of opinion (and it is the opinion of the Society in general) *the Modern Masons are acting entirely inconsistently with the antient customs and principles of the craft.*[79] [Author's italics.]

The letter was almost certainly genuine. Another addressed to the Grand Secretary of the Moderns dated 15 October 1776 and signed on behalf of the 4th duke by Captain George Smith of the Royal Military Academy posed four questions and expressed similar sentiments.[80] The questions are as set out in the original document held at the UGLE Library:

> 1. His Grace the duke of Athol would wish to know by what authority the GLE pretends to supremacy over the GLS, instituted by Royal Charter granted by King James the sixth to the family of Roslin in the year 1589 and there acknowledged to be the head and first lodge in Europe.

2. Why the GLE has thought proper to alter the mode of initiation; also the Word, password, and grip of the different degrees in Masonry.
3. Whether Dermot constitutes lodges in his own name or in the name and authority of the duke of Athol, and whether anything can be said to his charge inconsistent with the character of an honest man and a Mason.
4. Whether any mode of Union could be thought of and in such manner that might appear probable to both parties.

The third question is of particular interest. It indicates, if not confirms, the duke's lack of knowledge of Antients workings, asking 'whether Dermot constitutes lodges in his own name or in the name and authority of the duke of Athol'. It also raises the issue of why the duke, the Antients' Grand Master, would question the Grand Secretary of the Moderns with regard to Dermott's probity. However, the duke was barely 21 and had been initiated, passed and raised during a single ceremony barely a year earlier. It is probable that, at the time, he had no more than a limited knowledge of freemasonry and was a simple figurehead. Tangentially, the fourth question is also worth underlining in that it may represent one of the first occasions on which the question of a union between the Antients and Moderns was posited. The theme was revisited and taken further by the duke in the early nineteenth century when he retired as Grand Master specifically to facilitate the later union.

Dermott continued to remain vigilant in press management throughout his Masonic career, even into the 1780s. Like Desaguliers with respect to the Moderns some fifty years earlier, he was adamant that the London press should report the Antients in a favourable light.

The December 1786 installation of the earl of Antrim as Grand Master (and Dermott as his deputy) was accompanied by the installation of officers of several hundred Antients lodges and Dermott ensured that it received widespread and positive publicity. A line in one press article stating that 'the day was spent in the utmost harmony and much to the honour of the *true system of ancient and legitimate masons*' points strongly to Dermott's influence and suggests that even after thirty-four years, he was unwilling to forego the opportunity to sideswipe the rival Moderns and place the Antients in the better light.[81]

A change to a less confrontational approach occurred only after Dermott's death when the tone and content of those editions of *Ahiman Rezon* published after 1791 were substantially moderated. The more judicious methodology was an important factor in allowing the later union to be negotiated and to proceed. A second was the more collegiate approach adopted by the Grand Masters who preceded and presided over the negotiations leading to union in 1813.

The search for a noble Grand Master to take the nominal leadership position at Antients Grand Lodge had commenced almost immediately after its formation. The minutes of 1 April 1752 record three members – Morgan, Hagan and Dermott – being asked to explain their success in petitioning Lord

Sackville (1716–85), the duke of Dorset's youngest son, to accept the position of Grand Master. They reported that:

> they had waited on Lord George Sackville at Somerset House in the Strand, that having read the petition His Lordship told them politely that he had the highest veneration for the Ancient Craft, and [wished] to promote it; but he was engaged to attend his father the Lord Lieutenant of Ireland, and was informed that the Grand Lodge of Ireland had lately chosen him Grand Master; and that upon his return to England he would accept the Chair, or recommend them to another Noble Man.

While a reasonable response, it posed a problem for the Antients: should they wait for his return to London or seek an interim or permanent alternative.

A Grand Committee had been established a year earlier to manage the Antients lodges in London and Westminster until 'an opportunity offers for the choice of a noble personage to govern our antient fraternity'. Looking to the Moderns and to Ireland and Scotland, the point was made that:

> the Craft has flourished most and best when governed by a Noble Grand Master [and] although Grand Committees have power to form new laws for the fraternity . . . a Grand Master is absolutely necessary.[82]

However, Dermott cautioned against moving in haste. He argued that Sackville would soon return and believed it would be 'most prudent to wait . . . as he had formerly given a very friendly and obliging answer'.[83] There was also the question as to whether the Antients were correctly positioned to receive a noble Grand Master. A number of members of the Grand Committee considered the Temple Eating House, their then home, an inappropriate location, unsuitable for the installation of a noble Grand Master. It was Dermott who proposed that they relocate to the Five Bells tavern – a location both 'suitable and reputable'. The vote was carried by 16 to 11.

Given the apparently strong possibility that he might accept the position of the Antients' first noble Grand Master, Dermott's suggestion that the Grand Committee wait for Sackville's response is understandable. Sackville was potentially an excellent choice. Most particularly, he was familiar with and sympathetic to Ireland and its interests. Sackville had graduated from Trinity College Dublin in 1733 during his father's first term as Lord Lieutenant, been elected a member of the Irish bar and served as a past clerk to the Irish privy council, appointed in 1737, the same year he was made a captain in Lord Cathcart's horse, the 6th dragoon guards, then on the Irish establishment. Sackville later became lieutenant colonel of Bragg's 28th Foot (appointed in 1740), and in 1748, having soldiered on the continent and in Scotland, he was awarded the colonelcy of the 12th and, subsequently, the 3rd dragoon guards.

Sackville had also been connected to freemasonry for some time. Captain John Arabin, the Grand Treasurer of Irish Grand Lodge in 1736–7, had served alongside Sackville as a captain-lieutenant in the 6th dragoon guards in 1737 and in 1740 joined Bragg's 28th Foot as lieutenant colonel. Arabin was appointed lieutenant colonel of the 8th dragoons in 1745 and, a decade later, received the colonelcy of the 57th Foot. Sackville would also have known Philip Chevenix, a brother officer in the 6th dragoon guards and another freemason. And Captain John Corneille, Junior Grand Warden in 1735 and Senior Grand Warden the following year was director of the Irish Ordnance, which Sackville later commanded as lieutenant general.

It is not known when Sackville first became a freemason but in common with his brother, Charles, the earl of Middlesex, later the 2nd duke of Dorset (1711–1769), it is likely to have been in his youth.[84] Moreover, given the extent to which he was resident in Ireland, it is likely that he would have been initiated into an Irish lodge. Support for the argument can be found in his personal application to Irish Grand Lodge in 1748, while colonel of the 20th Foot, for a warrant to be re-issued to the regiment. The warrant was granted to Sackville, signed by Sir Marmaduke Wyvill as Grand Master, John Putland, his deputy, and his two Grand Wardens, Boyle Lennox and Hans Bailie. Sackville also knew other senior members of Irish freemasonry, including many of the principal politicians and aristocrats at its head. However, in the event, although he acted as Grand Master of the Grand Lodge of Ireland from 1750 until 1753, he did not sit as Grand Master of the Antients. Consequently, in December 1753, no nobleman having been secured for the role and with unease dominating the mood of the Grand Committee, Dermott, as Grand Secretary, proposed:

> that as the fraternity had not made choice of any of the noble personages formerly mentioned . . . and it being doubtful whether the Antient Craft could be honoured with a noble GM at this time, he humbly begged that the brethren would make choice of some worthy and skilful Master to fill the Chair for the space of six month successively.[85]

Robert Turner, the Master of lodge No. 15, was accordingly nominated to the role and served for twelve months. And the Hon Edward Vaughan, the Senior Warden of lodge No. 4, succeeded him and served for the following two years. During this period, four names were raised as possible alternatives to Sackville, those of Blessington, Chesterfield, Inchiquin and Ponsonby. Philip Dormer Stanhope, 4th earl of Chesterfield had been a successful and popular Lord Lieutenant of Ireland between 1744 and 1746, and thereafter was briefly Secretary of State. He was a member of the duke of Richmond's Horn tavern lodge and had been an active freemason both in Britain and in continental Europe where, as ambassador to the Low Countries, he was instrumental in the initiation of the duke of Lorraine, later Holy Roman Emperor.

Inchiquin was William O'Brien, the 4th earl, a past Grand Master of English Grand Lodge, Whig MP for Aylesbury between 1747 and 1754 and Governor of Co. Clare from 1741 until 1777. And Ponsonby was William

Ponsonby, Junior Grand Warden of Irish Grand Lodge in 1731, the elder son of Brabazon Ponsonby, earl of Bessborough, and chief secretary to the duke of Devonshire when he had first been appointed to Ireland's lord lieutenancy. Ponsonby subsequently married Devonshire's elder daughter and became active in British politics in the Devonshire interest.

However, it was William Stewart, 1st earl of Blessington, who acceded. It is unclear what means were used to approach Blessington and whether Sackville intermediated with him as had originally been suggested. Regardless, on 1 December 1756, having given the committee prior notification of his consent, Blessington was accepted unanimously as the Antients' prospective Grand Master and first noble figurehead. Confirming the appointment, Dermott read out a letter that he had written to the noble lord:

To the Right Honourable William, earl of Blesinton, in Margaret Street

My Lord,

I have the Honour of conveying the unanimous thanks of the Grand Lodge of the most antient and honourable Fraternity of Free and Accepted Masons, for the great honour your Lordship has done the Fraternity in condescending to fill Solomon's Chair, I am also ordered to assure your Lordship that the several members which compose this Grand Lodge are firmly resolved to pursue such measures as will convince your Lordship that this great favour is not ill bestowed.

I have the honour to be my Lord &c. &c.

LAURENCE DERMOTT, Grand Secretary

Ironically, the letter had not been delivered at the first attempt; however, when eventually received by Blessington, he had replied in kind.

To Mr Dermott, Secretary to the Grand Lodge of Free and Accepted Masons at the Five Bells Tavern in the Strand

December 16, 1756

Sir,

I am much concerned that I happened not to see you when you called on me the other day but my being denied was owing to a mistake having given my orders not with regard to you but another person who has been very troublesome. As I shall be out of town St John's day, I must beg leave to act by Deputy. I am very sensible of the honour done me by the fraternity in choosing me Grand Master, and if you shall hereafter have any business to transact with me, you have but to let me know beforehand when you will call, and I shall give proper orders to receive you.

I am Sir, your Humble Servant
BLESINTON

Dermott had ostensibly delayed publishing *Ahiman Rezon* until it could be dedicated to a noble Grand Master and Blessington's consent allowed printing to proceed. Gould's comment that Blessington did not attend any meetings of the Antients Grand Lodge misses the point. The Antients had sought aristocratic imprimatur; they did not expect Blessington to make any contribution to the day-to-day management of the lodges, nor would Blessington have intended or expected to do so. His appeal to the Irish émigrés in London was the seal of approval that an affluent and well-known Irish aristocrat provided. And it went further. Blessington commanded a flattering reputation for his charitable benevolence and, as Lord Mountjoy, while Grand Master of Ireland in 1738–40, had led fund raising and food distribution efforts to support the poor in Dublin and relieve the famine. His actions were part of working-class Irish folklore and remembered as much as three decades later. A letter to the *Gazetteer and New Daily Advertiser* in 1766 complaining of the then current lack of action in dealing with Irish poverty reminded its readers that 'the present earl of Blessington, then Lord Mountjoy, went in his coach . . . and collected money . . . with great success.'[86]

Blessington was installed as Grand Master of the Antients privately in the library of his London townhouse in Margaret Street. His acceptance was as significant as that of John, 2nd duke of Montagu, had been with respect to the original Grand Lodge of England in 1720 and would have spurred recruitment and sanctioned the position of the Antients as a legitimate outpost of Irish freemasonry and as a grand lodge in its own right. Moreover, as with the Grand Lodges of England, Ireland and Scotland, Blessington's decision and presence as Grand Master cut a path for others to follow, most notably the 3rd and 4th dukes of Atholl, both of whom also sat as Grand Master of Scotland.[87]

Blessington had inherited as viscount in 1728 and was created earl in 1745.[88] First mentioned as a freemason in 1731 when a member of Viscount Montagu's exclusive Bear and Harrow lodge in Butcher Row near Temple Bar in London, a few yards from the Five Bells in the Strand, Blessington had been a popular Grand Master of Ireland.[89] However, it was his position as the Antients' first noble Grand Master from 1756 to 1760, and the aristocratic imprimatur he bestowed upon the organisation, that was arguably more significant.

Blessington's family had settled in Ulster from Scotland in the sixteenth century and been loyal undertakers in the Irish parliament for six generations. His grandfather, a second-generation baronet, had fought against the Irish rebellion as commander of a foot regiment and, in 1682, was rewarded with a viscountcy. A Protestant, he was suspected of disloyalty by Richard Talbot, earl of Tyrconnell, the Anglo-Catholic commander of James II's army in Ireland, and sent on a false diplomatic mission to Paris where, as intended, he was arrested and imprisoned in the Bastille. Joining William's army on his release in 1692, he was killed at Steenkerque later the same year. Blessington's father, 2nd viscount Mountjoy, was also a talented soldier. Given command of a foot regiment, he was promoted to successively higher military offices, becoming a lieutenant general. In 1714, he was advanced to Master General of the Ordnance, given the colonelcy of a regiment of dragoons and made Keeper of the Great Seal.[90]

At his father's death, Blessington inherited estates in Co. Tyrone and Co. Wicklow and held property in England at Silchester in Hampshire and town houses successively in Grosvenor Square and Hill Street, Mayfair.[91] He was one of many absentee property owners criticised by Thomas Prior in his *List of absentees of Ireland*, who accused him of annual expenditure abroad of £2,500.[92] The criticism was largely misplaced. Blessington was an active contributor to charities in Ireland, and in Britain, where he was a prominent supporter of the Middlesex Hospital, among other institutions.[93] In 1748, consolidating his position as a person of quality and one of the great and good, Blessington was appointed Governor of Co. Tyrone and sworn a member of the Irish privy council.[94] He received the governorship of Carlisle Castle in 1763.[95]

Although Blessington's loyalty to the Hanoverian dynasty may have been absolute, this did not translate into blind support for its government and their policies. His concern for Irish agriculture and manufacture and for the right to trade freely was notable and noted, not least by the London agents and representatives of the West Indies merchant community who sought his backing to promote the cause of free trade both in parliament and more widely.[96] And his wider interest in Ireland's wellbeing was expressed in membership of organisations ranging from the Incorporated Society for the Promotion of Protestant Working Schools in Ireland to the Dublin Society, where he was a member across two decades from 1741 until 1762.

British condescension towards Irish accomplishments, Ireland and its aristocracy would have grated with Blessington, as it did with others. Toby Barnard's comment that Sir John Perceval, 1st earl of Egmont, alongside other Irish peers, was 'shouldered aside' in the procession marking the wedding of the Prince of Orange to George II's eldest daughter, and that Irish peers were unable to obtain proper recognition of the precedence due to their rank, encapsulates the position.[97] Stung, the alienation of Ireland's elite was reflected in a changed relationship with English freemasonry. What began as a supportive and fraternal affiliation with common cross membership of English and Irish lodges became more antipathetic. It was expressed in the decision of the Grand Lodge of Ireland to recognise the Antients Grand Lodge and to cease fraternal communications with the original Grand Lodge of England. And it had underpinned Blessington's decision to accept the role of Grand Master some two years earlier.

Blessington declined to be reappointed in 1760 and was succeeded as the Antients' Grand Master by Thomas Erskine, 6th earl of Kellie [or Kelly] (1732–1781), who was in turn succeeded six years later by the Hon Thomas Mathew, the Provincial Grand Master of Munster, then one of the wealthiest and most influential commoners in Ireland.[98] Mathew's estates purportedly generated an annual income exceeding £30,000. He was widely believed to have been promised a peerage but in the event this was not forth-coming:

> we hear that Thomas Mathew Esq. of Thomastown in the county of Tipperary, Ireland, will be created a peer of that kingdom by the style and title of earl of Clonwilliam, Viscount Anfield and Baron Mathew.[99]

The family was obliged to wait until the next generation to obtain the peerage, Mathew's son, MP for and later Governor of Co. Tipperary, then being created earl of Llandaff.

The Antients Grand Lodge's minutes record openly the dissension and disputes among the lodges and the membership that became a central characteristic of its development. And despite Blessington and Kellie, there were periodic difficulties in obtaining and retaining an aristocrat as the organisation's nominal head. The 4th duke of Atholl declined to be reappointed as Grand Master in 1782 and the duke of Leinster, when asked, refused the position. Indeed, in the temporary absence of a willing member of the aristocracy to take the chair, the Deputy Grand Master, William Dickey, presided over the Antients' Grand Committee for fifteen months until Randal MacDonnell, 6th earl of Antrim, eventually acceded to act as Grand Master.[100] Antrim held office from 1783 until his death in 1791. And at that time, despite his earlier reluctance, the 4th duke of Atholl agreed to succeed. He would serve for over two decades until 1812, when he stepped down in favour of the duke of Kent, whose brief year as Grand Master preceded a union with the Moderns in 1813.

At the time of the union, and subsequently, the issue of the Royal Arch ceremony came to the fore. The degree was significant in that it had evolved to become one of the more fundamental differences in the ritual schematic as practiced by the Antients and Moderns, and it was a key to their later reconciliation. Dermott had been exalted into the Royal Arch degree in Dublin in 1746. The precise nature of the ceremony at that time is not known, nor are its origins, whether invented, corrupted or replicated from Scotland or elsewhere. The degree may have been instituted in Ireland in the 1740s or earlier partly for financial reasons. *Faulkner's Dublin Journal* mentions the Royal Arch in January 1744 in connection with a Masonic procession in Youghal, Co. Cork, as does D'Assigny, among other sources.[101] It is also recorded in Scotland in the 1730s and early 1740s. However, whether this was the same degree and ceremony cannot be assumed with any certainty. Nevertheless, regardless of its origins, the Royal Arch proved popular and developed a following among freemasons, especially Irish masons. Indeed, Royal Arch appears to have been introduced to England by the London Irish.

It first appears in the early minutes of Antients Grand Lodge in connection with the censure of two of its members, Thomas Plealon and John Macky:

Grand Committee at the Griffin Tavern Holborn
March 4, 1752
Brother John Gaunt, Master of No. 5, in the Chair

The following Brethren viz., Thomas Figg of No. 5, Laurence Folliot of the same Lodge, Samuel Quay of No. 2, Richard Price of No. 3 & Henry Lewis of No. 4, made formal complaints against Thomas Phealon and John Macky, better known by the name of the leg of mutton Masons.

In course of the examination it appeared that Phealon and Mackey had initiated many persons for the mean consideration of a leg of mutton for dinner or supper to the disgrace of the Ancient Craft [and] that it was difficult to discover who assisted them, if any, as they seldom met twice in the same Alehouse. That Macky was an Empiric in physic; and both impostors in Masonry. That upon examining some brothers whom they pretended to have made Royal Archmen, the parties had not the least idea of that secret. That Doctor Macky (for so he was called) pretended to teach a Masonical Art by which any man could (in a moment) render himself invisible. That the Grand Secretary had examined Macky, at the house of Mr James Duffy, tobacconist, in East Smithfield who was not a Mason and that Macky appear'd incapable of making an Apprentice with any degree of propriety. Nor had Mackey the least idea or knowledge of Royal Arch masonry. But instead thereof he had told the people whom he deceived a long story about 12 white Marble stones etc. etc. and that the rainbow was the Royal Arch, with many other absurdities equally foreign and ridiculous.

The Grand Committee Unanimously Agreed and Ordered that neither Thomas Phealon nor John Mackey be admitted into any Ancient Lodge during their natural lives.

On 2 September the same year, the Antients' minutes noted that:

The Lodge was opened in Ancient Form of Grand Lodge and every part of Real freemasonry was traced and explained, except the Royal Arch.

And on 2 March 1757, they recorded an Order that:

the Masters of the Royal Arch shall also be Summoned to meet in order to regulate things relative to that most valuable branch of the Craft.

Dermott referred to Royal Arch in *Ahiman Rezon* as 'the root, heart and marrow of masonry'.[102] There may have been two reasons. The Royal Arch had become quite rapidly a highly popular aspect of the Antients' Masonic ritual and had garnered a strong following. Indeed, many Moderns were also attracted to the Royal Arch and the ceremony was practiced by the Moderns, albeit unofficially, from at least the 1760s. But perhaps most importantly, the ritual had not been adopted formally by the Moderns. In fact, it had been rejected. Samuel Spencer, the Moderns' Grand Secretary, argued that the degree 'seduced the brethren' and that it did not form part of the core traditional ritual. In his words, 'our Society is neither Arch, Royal Arch or Antient'. [103] Spencer's sentiments allowed Dermott to increase the distance between the Antients and the Moderns still further and to use the issue as yet another means to malign his rivals. This was a principal reason why the issue of incorporating the Royal Arch degree into post-union freemasonry later assumed such symbolic importance.

CHAPTER TWO

Antients Freemasonry
and the London Irish

Detailed in Appendix VI, the members of the lodge at the Ship behind the Royal Exchange demonstrate the presence, function and integration of wealthy upper middling Irish in London in the 1720s. However, as this and later chapters make clear, the professionals, politicians and merchants who made up the lodge and are often the subject of study by both academic and Masonic historians were a minority and unrepresentative of London's larger émigré Irish population. Unsurprisingly, they also had limited commonality with the members of Antients freemasonry.

Research into the London Irish working class in the eighteenth century and its strong connections with Antients freemasonry has generally been bypassed. One reason has been the false consensus view that there is an absence of relevant primary data. In fact, the early records of the Antients Grand Lodge and its constituent lodges contain details of over a thousand individual lodge members. A few of those listed, around eighty, appear more than once: a function of members moving from lodge to lodge. In addition to their names, approximately half the entries provide the addresses and occupations of the relevant members. In many instances, the date on which such members joined or rejoined their respective lodges is also recorded. And from the disaggregated data, multiple social relationships can be identified and a range of associations explored. Taken as a whole, the Antients' lodge minutes and membership registers provide a unique and to date almost uncultivated resource that complements parish records and exposes the individual and communal characteristics of an important segment of London's social sub strata, many of whom would have been first or second generation émigré Irish.

Estimates of the size of London's Irish population in the mid-eighteenth century vary from the mid-thousands to the low tens of thousands. However, given the relatively large number that appear as members of Antients freemasonry, it is not unreasonable to assume that the latter figure is the more probable and perhaps an underestimate. Accurate census data began only in 1801. At that date, the Irish-born population in London was calculated to be around 40,000. The number is thought to have reached a peak of around 110,000 in 1851 after the mass migration that accompanied and followed Ireland's great famine of the 1840s.[1] However, later census data only captures Irish-born respondents and excludes second, third and later generation Irish who were born in the capital. And it is clear that from the second and third decades of the 1700s, the number of Irish migrants settling in London became a rising proportion of the city's population.

Irish migration to England had generally been seasonal, with workers travelling across the Irish Sea each year to work on the harvest. In contrast, the majority of Irish émigrés in the mid- and later eighteenth century were a combination of skilled workers seeking improved employment opportunities and unskilled labourers driven by poverty. Seasonal working continued and such migrants remained a large presence but, over time, they were outweighed by those who settled permanently. There were several reasons. The interconnection between Dublin and London's respective linen and silk industries drew weavers from Ireland to Spitalfields and elsewhere, where they worked alongside the Huguenot community. Yet more economic migrants found employment as unskilled or semi-skilled labourers, building the emerging infrastructure, from canals, bridges and mines to London's docks, as Britain industrialised. Many were engaged in a variety of other relatively low-end occupations, including domestic workers, chairmen and porters, or pedlars, hawkers and street sellers, employments where the absence of start-up capital was no bar to working and where the increasing wealth of the capital and other growing urban areas provided a regular demand for such services. Irishmen also served in the British army and navy. Up to a third of the lower ranks were thought to be Irish and from there they were often discharged jobless onto the capital's streets. It is not known how many among London's Irish émigré community drifted into vagrancy and criminality but anecdotal evidence and contemporary crime reports suggest that the figure may have been disproportionately large.

Although London's Irish were disbursed widely across the metropolis, many congregated in the slums or rookeries of St Giles and St Martin's, and the crowded courts and lanes east of the City of London around Rosemary Lane, the Ratcliffe Highway, Wapping and the docks, where poverty was often the common denominator. Even by contemporary standards, conditions were deprived, and often dire, and both new and old arrivals tended to subsist in crammed lodging houses and tenements similar to if not worse than those described by Dickens nearly a century later:

> wretched houses with broken windows patched with rags and paper: every room let out to a different family, and in many instances to two or even three. Fruit and sweet-stuff manufacturers in the cellars, barbers and red-herring vendors in the front parlours, cobblers in the back; a bird-fancier in the first floor, three families on the second, starvation in the attics, Irishmen in the passage, a 'musician' in the front kitchen and a charwoman and five hungry children in the back one. Filth everywhere, a gutter before the houses and a drain behind, clothes drying and slops emptying, from the windows . . . men and women, in every variety of scanty and dirty apparel, lounging, scolding, drinking, smoking, squabbling, fighting and swearing.[2]

For the majority with limited or no education and few skills, London had limited potential financial rewards. Those in the jobbing building trades such as painters, plasterers, carpenters and bricklayers, or providing basic services such as tailoring, wig making or cobbling, were likely to obtain only irregular and poorly paid casual work. And even as regular waged labour became more common, workers were frequently subjected to low pay and sweated conditions, with security of employment threatened by seasonal layoffs, their employer's vicissitudes and the economic cycle of boom and bust. It is estimated that up to two-thirds of low paid workers would have been forced periodically to draw on parish funds or charity to supplement their earnings. And more – if not almost all – would have needed to do so if unemployed, sick or following the death of the main earner in the family. Living conditions in this layer of London society were miserable and characterised by overcrowding, inadequate sanitation and squalor. And life was often short, a function of poor diet, alcoholism and rampant disease.

But despite the many barriers to economic and social achievement, a small but growing minority of the lower middling and working-class Irish community attained relative success, climbing some rungs higher on the financial ladder and gaining the refuge of improved occupations or the security of more remunerative employment or self-employment. Some, indeed many, provided services to their compatriots and, over time, there developed a network of Irish-owned and Irish-run lodging houses, chop and alehouses, gin distilleries and brothels. Others used their determination and expertise to become traders or more skilled artisans, or became teachers, apothecaries or even lawyers, doctors or barber surgeons, some providing services within their own communities and others serving the burgeoning stratum of wealthier Londoners. In this sense, the rookeries and slums were not simply a sink but also a font of entrepreneurialism. Those resolved to escape poverty had few options other than to look after their own interests and rely on their own resources or that of their family or close community. Those with the necessary drive and determination would strike out, embracing commerce, building capital and sometimes achieving success. Those that prospered (if only in relative terms) and broke free from the constraints of absolute poverty and escaped the worst aspects of the rookeries grew in status and were able to exercise greater influence upon and within their communities, if only by example. Although only around 20 or 25 per cent of those considered below might fall into such upwardly mobile categories, they are of especial interest in determining the changing nature of Antients freemasonry and its membership as it developed over the course of the second half of the eighteenth century. Indeed, it was from this group that many of the more aspirational lower middling and middling London Irish came into Antients freemasonry, perhaps attracted by the prospect of its ritual, faux history and, perhaps most crucially, a social space that was considered comparatively exclusive and could provide both fraternal association and sustainable mutual financial support.

Although a gross simplification, many in eighteenth-century England held the Irish (and not only their working class) to be uniformly feckless and there was little popular distinction between the indigent and the aspirational. Perhaps unsurprisingly given its lack of dimension, the common perception was a misrepresentation. The membership registers and minutes of London's Antients Masonic lodges provide strong evidence that many within the Irish and larger working-class community in London were motivated, entrepreneurial and driven by a desire for social and financial self-improvement. The Antients' *General Register* lists a heterogeneous group of men in a range of occupations from the lower rungs of society to an unexpectedly high number of more middling and lower middling occupations. It suggests that the Antients created an effective interdenominational mutual support structure for both the Irish community in London (and elsewhere) and for the urban working class and lower middling more broadly.

Established in London in 1751, the Antients Grand Lodge and the freemasonry it represented was shaped and supported by London's Irish diaspora. The new organisation provided an accessible social space as well as a focal point for Irish Masonic lodges in London and a home to members of previously independent or 'St John's' lodges, as well as those expelled by or estranged from the original and now rival Grand Lodge of England. In doing so, the Antients opened freemasonry intentionally to a more diverse membership and offered potential mutual financial assistance and a support structure that was available not only to the expatriate Irish community but also more broadly to the lower middling and working class. From a relatively small base – just five lodges were in the founding nucleus and only nine lodges were listed in the first minutes written in 1752 – the Antients grew rapidly such that by 1756, there were over a thousand members across more than forty lodges.[3] The organisation gained traction and, in 1758, a union was established between the Antients and the Grand Lodge of Ireland to the exclusion of the original Grand Lodge of England. The pact was made tri-partite in 1773 when Scotland joined. In that year, the 3rd duke of Atholl was both Grand Master of the Antients and Grand Master-elect of the Grand Lodge of Scotland, a pattern repeated in subsequent years. By 1770, Antients' membership had grown to more than five thousand within London and the provinces and the rival Moderns were at risk of being sidelined permanently. A decade later, the Antients had over 200 affiliated lodges; 75 were based in London; more than 80 in the provinces; and 45 had been warranted overseas.[4] And by the early 1800s, the number had nearly doubled again to a total of more than 350 Antients' lodges nationally and internationally, with a total of perhaps 20,000 or so members.

Data on individual members was held centrally between 1751 and 1755, and also locally, where it was recorded by individual lodges, usually as part of the lodge minute books or treasurer's records. Although trying to determine either nationality or religious affiliation from an analysis of members' surnames is notoriously difficult (and probably impractical in the absence of corroborative data such as the corresponding records of births, marriages and deaths), it is nonetheless likely that the Antients' membership included a mixture of Irish and English Protestants (conformist and non-conformist) as well as Catholics. Scottish (possibly Ulster) and Jewish émigré surnames are also present, as is evidence that Quakers also joined freemasonry.[5] The *General Register* records members' occupations in approximately 500 cases and a place of residence or contact address in around 450, albeit that there is data repetition where a member appears in the register more than once.[6] In a minority of instances, additional data is recorded, including the name of any proposer, current lodge, rank and/or prior lodge.

ANTIENTS FREEMASONRY:
THE LONDON MEMBERSHIP, 1751–5

With respect to the 500 or so members whose addresses were listed in the *General Register*, approximately half (around 250) were located in Middlesex and Westminster to the west of the City of London. Over eighty lived in the central London slum district stretching from St Giles and Seven Dials through to Covent Garden; nearly fifty were to the east of Covent Garden in an area from Drury Lane to Gray's Inn and north to Holborn; and about the same number were to the south of Covent Garden in the Strand and Temple Bar. A further forty or so members lived to the west and south-west of the Strand in the contiguous district of St Martin's Lane, with smaller groups in Soho, Golden Square, Leicester Fields and Piccadilly.

The majority of the remainder lived and worked around the eastern and northern borders of the still partly walled City of London. Twenty-five members were resident in east London, around the Ratcliffe Highway, Goodman's Fields, Rosemary Lane and Wapping; with a similar number in Bethnal Green, Whitechapel and Shoreditch, of whom seven gave their address as Holywell Lane. Close to seventy came from the arc around the north east of the City from Spitalfields to Clerkenwell, of whom nine alone gave an address in Quaker Street. Seven members lived or worked in Farringdon; fifteen in Bishopsgate, mostly without the City walls; and eleven in Moorgate and Moorfields. Over forty lived elsewhere in the City, from Aldersgate, Smithfield, Little Britain and Cheapside to Wallbrook and Lower Thames Street. And across London Bridge and south of the Thames, some thirty members gave a Southwark address, with a lesser number in Bermondsey, Borough and a handful in Lambeth and elsewhere.

Location is generally a useful sociological tag, however, it is important to recognise that in eighteenth-century London, the segregation of social class by neighbourhood was relatively undeveloped and the middling classes and gentry often lived in close proximity to the poor. This was the case not only in those neighbourhoods that were downshifting from affluence to relative poverty, such as Covent Garden, but a pattern that could be followed across

London as a whole, including some of the most impoverished areas such as St Martin's, and relatively prosperous districts such as Grosvenor Square and St James's, both of which housed servants, shopkeepers and other tradesmen. However, although residence in Seven Dials, for example, could not be advanced as proof of penury, or in Mayfair, of affluence, it could be viewed as raising the probability. Regardless, despite the difficulties of using location as a simple proxy for social status and relative wealth or poverty, the social and financial standing of many Antients' lodge members is given greater clarity by the specifics of their addresses – the courts, alleys and lodging houses in which they lived – and attains still higher probability through a granular examination of their occupations.

Assessing the data at such a level reveals a frequent reoccurrence of specific locations and members with the same or proximate addresses living in the same streets and sometimes sharing a common tavern or boarding house. In addition, many had similar or related occupations. Both demonstrate local clusters of Masonic sociability and suggest strongly that social and business networking was not limited to middling and upper class eighteenth-century society but stretched across the social divide. Perhaps the clearest confirmation of such associations and sociability among the London Irish and other members is the number of neighbours and near neighbours who joined at the same time, together with the large number of members with common and linked occupations. Taking only a small number from many possible examples, we can point to Barnaby Fox, Thomas O'Harah and John Morris, three weavers, who joined the Antients at virtually the same time, each giving the same address 'opposite The Two Brewers' in Spitalfields. Similarly, the Ship & Anchor in Quaker Street, Spitalfields, was home to four weavers: Thomas Kaan, John Disrael, Edward Butcher and William Pendlebury, as well as Isaac Daking, a cooper, and Moses Willoughby, a victualler. Tangentially, Laurence Dermott gave the same address on 24 February 1752.

Members who joined the Antients as a group included John Woodward, Mathew Doyle, James Moran, John Eustace and Thomas McGuire, five linen printers who lived in Broadwall in Southwark, and three of their neighbours, William Bryant, a pipe maker, Thomas Sneath, a victualler, and John Sheridan, a hatter. The same commonalities linked George Rochford and Anthony Morley, both weavers and neighbours in Old Coach Lane in Spitalfields; and James Say, a glazier, and Robert Blount, a wine merchant, both of whom lived at Upper Ground, Church Street, Southwark. Other examples of colleagues, friends or neighbours joining in tandem include twelve shoemakers, seven of whom lived in the streets immediately surrounding Red Lion Square in Holborn and three others close by in Drury Lane; and two silversmiths, John McCormick and Samuel Galbraith, both of whom lived in Horse Shoe Alley in Moorfields, both members of lodge No. 20. Two painters, Richard Storer and Benjamin Hobbs, who lived in Tower Street in Seven Dials, moved lodges together, transferring their membership to lodge No. 5 from lodge No. 9. And Daniel Neil, Daniel

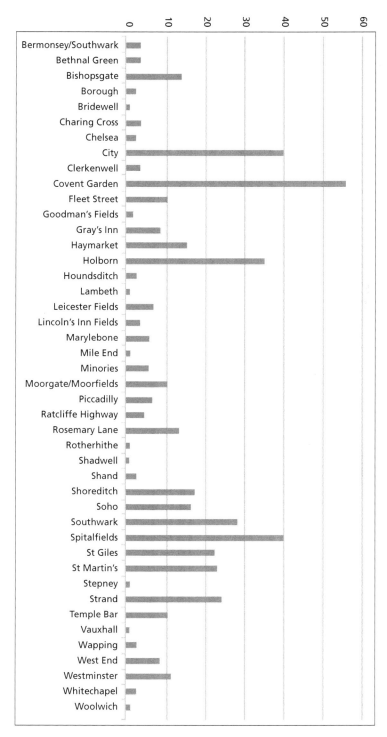

Figure 1 Antients' Members, 1751–5: Analysis by Location

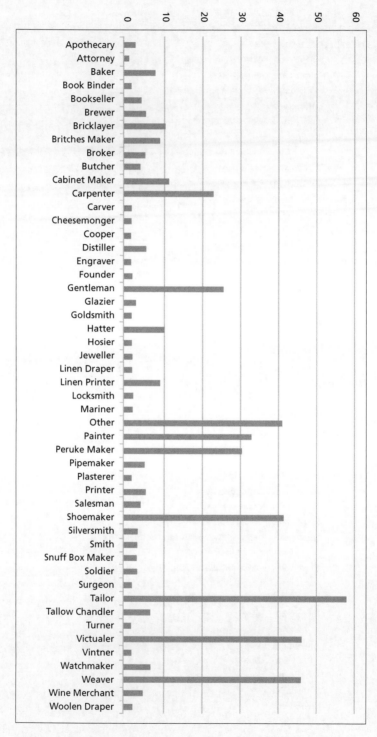

Figure 2 Antients' Members, 1751–5: Analysis by Occupation

Dawson and Peter Dunhaven, three carpenters living at Mr Steed's in King Street near Bloomsbury Square, are recorded simultaneously joining the same lodge.

Family connections are apparent with brothers, or possibly fathers and sons, becoming members of the same lodges. Examples include John and William McDowell, carpenters, both of whom initially lived at the Crown tavern in Green Street Leicester Fields before relocating to Chandois Street in Covent Garden, and Coventry Court, Haymarket, respectively. The McDowells joined lodge No. 7, introduced by James Hagan. And Evan and Alexander McKenzie, both introduced by John Bradshawe, each became a member of lodge No. 8. Numerous other examples reinforce a sense of communal sociability that is marked by members from the same streets or courts joining successively or simultaneously. The evidence suggests that Antients freemasonry was from its earliest years an association of friends, neighbours and co-workers, the large majority of whom lived and laboured in a relatively small number of compact adjacent areas within London. It was a medium in which a mutual benefit society might be expected to take root; and it did.

Although there is only a limited number of examples extant, the minutes of eighteenth-century Antients' lodge meetings that have survived underline that freemasonry offered London's émigré Irish and others from the lower middling and working class not only a social medium but also access to potential mutual financial support through mutually financed Masonic benevolence. Among the many hundreds of instances recorded, we can quote the following three representative examples:

paid to Bro. Jackson, SW No. 5, for Bro Evans, he being ill, 2s 7½d;[7]

debated on the funeral charges of Brother Mitchell late of No. 2 [and] unanimously and cheerfully agreed that the said funeral charges shall be paid for by a voluntary contribution of two shillings [from] each lodge;[8] and

heard a petition from Thomas Warren Master of No. 20 (sick) – ordered that the petitioner shall receive forty shillings at the rate of five shillings per week. Ditto from Michael Wade of No. 8 (sick) – ordered that the petitioner shall receive one pound five shillings at five shilling per week, both these donations to be paid by the hands of our worthy SGW, John Jackson.[9]

And there was more. Antients freemasonry provided a *de facto* passport to those visiting London from Ireland and leaving London for elsewhere. Moreover, the utility offered by Masonic membership was not confined to those permanently resident in the city. The lodge's milieu was also exploited by London's transient population with members periodically returning to the mother country – 'gone to Ireland' – and others recorded as travelling elsewhere – 'gone to Liverpool'. Indeed, the evidence includes New York

(Nicholas Horton, a mariner, No. 773 in the list of members) and Jamaica (Roderick Rose, No. 192).

The cachet of membership should also be considered. Given its faux antiquarian history, well-publicised aristocratic leadership in each of Ireland, English and Scotland, and in all three countries, but especially in England, a past association with Enlightenment luminaries, freemasonry would have been perceived as having a prestige and exclusivity otherwise unavailable to the socially marginalised. Perhaps as a consequence, lodge membership came with what were considered and treated as serious moral and financial obligations. First and probably most importantly, in addition to funding the cost of regular weekly or (more commonly) bi-weekly dining and drinking, members were obliged to pay lodge fees and charity dues. This was the natural *sine qua non* of any mutual support framework and the Antients' *General Register* hints at the probability that at least some members were obliged to leave or left because such dues, which in general were not low, proved too onerous. In certain instances, members who were recorded as barred for non-payment appear later to have rejoined the same or a different lodge, presumably at a time when their financial circumstances had improved. The collection of lodge arrears by the Antients Grand Lodge was also a problem and in September 1754, five lodges were excluded for this reason. Second, regular if not strict attendance was expected and the Antients' lodge registers catalogue both habitual attendees and a minority of members subsequently excluded by virtue of their inability or unwillingness to be present. One such member, presumably unable rather than unwilling, was Samuel Watson, the housekeeper at Harwood's Bell Brewhouse in Shoreditch. Watson had originally been introduced to lodge No. 10 by Lawrence Dermot, the Antients' proselytising Grand Secretary.

The range of livelihoods recorded in the *General Register* and other lodge membership data comprises a surprisingly broad spectrum of occupations, employments, income and status. A comparatively large number, twenty-five or over 5 per cent of those whose work status was recorded, were categorised as 'gentlemen'. However, whether the description was ironic, genuine or the product of social inflation is unclear and several members have addresses that may appear to be in conflict with their assumed status. Examples include Isaac Simon living in White Lion Street in Seven Dials; Colin Bruce of Lancaster Court at Shand in Southwark; William Hindlestone of the Star in Salisbury Court off Fleet Street; Benjamin Dove at Mr Gardener's in Hedge Lane, Southwark; Thomas Heathcott of Borough, who was later excluded for non-payment; and Thomas Porteus of 18 Gillum's Court in Rotherhithe. Each address was in an area of some poverty although, as noted, that does not preclude the presence of better-off residents.

Certain members appear genuinely to have been gentlemen, for example, James Rowe, who lived at Alderman Hoare's house in Fleet Street; Robert Turner at the Eagle & Child in Petty France; John McCormick, whose address was at the popular Spring Gardens in Vauxhall; and James Hartley

Table 1 'Gentlemen' Members of Antients Freemasonry, 1751–5

Membership Number	Name	Address
91	James Hartley	Golden Fan, Bucklersbury, Cheapside
170	James Lauder	
240	Thomas Porteous	No 18 Gilham's Court, Rotherhithe Wall
242	Richard Partridge	Chandois Street
284	Austin Allen	
285	Isaac Simon	White Lion Street
300	Robert Turner	Eagle & Child, Petty France, Westminster
344	James Rowe	Alderman Hoare's, Fleet Street
352	Nathaniel Franks	Mr Frank's, Skinner Street
354	Benjamin Dove	Mr Gardener's, Hedge Lane
368	Collin Bruce	Lancaster Court, Strand
385	Thornhill Heathcoat	Borough
393	Alexander Drumond	
411	Alexander Fraizer	
435	John Rob	
456	John Holloway	
476	Richard Partridge	Chandois Street
502	Robert Gray	
510	Peter Reily	Long Acre, Covent Garden
518	Jerome Robinson	Mr Chambers' near Opera House
521	Francis Vignolas	
534	John McCormick	Spring Gardens, Vauxhall
550	William Davis	Malpas Arms
586	Henry Jellybrain	Chapel Street, Westminster
756	William [Hindle]stone	Star, Salisbury Court, Fleet Street

of the Golden Fan at Bucklersbury, a few yards to the south of the Royal Exchange at the centre of the City.

Other addresses are more ambivalent social indicators. For example, that of Richard Partridge of Chandois Street, and William Davis, whose address was given as the Malpas Arms in Charles Street. There were several 'Charles Streets' in London. One was close to the affluent Grosvenor Square; a second located less salubriously on the edge of the rookeries. To quote from Frank McLynn:

> the species of London criminal feared most was the footpad, the armed robber operating on foot, usually in gangs. They infested London on the

outskirts. [Their] operating haunts . . . were around Knightsbridge and Tottenham Court Road, then surrounded by ditches and open fields. After the robbery, the favourite retreat would be one at Holborn, Gray's Inn Lane, Great Queen Street, Long Acre, St Martin's Lane, Bedford Street and Charles Street.[11]

Although many of the factors that drove the growth in Antients member-ship had their counterparts in the Moderns, including patronage by wealthy members of the aristocracy and gentry, a loose connection to the Enlightenment, an impressive if faux history and relative social exclusivity, other aspects were more specifically Irish. The inter-denominational nature of the Craft was probably a significant attraction for prospective Catholic members and the relatively ornate Masonic ritual may have proved a draw where access to liturgy was difficult to access. Indeed, depending on county, towards the last quarter of the eighteenth century, between 20–40 per cent of Irish freemasons are thought to have comprised Catholics.[12] In England, notwithstanding greater religious toleration, the Tests and Corporations Act remained in force, and Sarah Knott's analysis, although not directed at Antients freemasonry, is relevant:

> as a politically defeated and confessionally excluded community, [Catholics] articulated civil society as a realm superior to politics which might incarnate virtue, especially that of religious charity.[13]

Linked to this, perhaps the leading factors behind the growth in membership for all denominations was Antients freemasonry's function as a social forum for the otherwise marginalised and provision of a mutually financed support structure.

Aside from those described as gentlemen, only nine of the *c.*470 or so Antients' members whose occupations were disclosed might be categorised as 'professional' men. There were two surgeons, albeit that they were possibly barber surgeons; three apothecaries; two attorneys; and two merchants. Neither of the two surgeons, Thomas Brothwick and Edward Vaughan, were members of the Royal College of Physicians. In any event, the categories of physician and surgeon were socially and professionally distinct at this period, with surgeon being the lesser of the two. However, there is press evidence that John Gillum, whose occupation was stated as merchant, was exactly that, and that James Shee and David Jennings, were both attorneys.[14] Shee's address at Fetter Lane and Jennings' at 4 Brick Court in the Temple, were also both close to the Law Courts. John Wright, the apothecary living in Great Wild Street, may have been the same John Wright who in 1736 was admitted to the Society of Apothecaries.

But although there were only a few 'professional' men, at least 7 per cent of Antients members can be categorised as having relatively upwardly mobile 'semi-middling' occupations. The number included five wine merchants, two vintners and others with comparatively well-paid occupations including

Table 2 The 'Professional' Members of Antients Freemasonry, 1751–5

Membership Number	Name	Occupation	Address
35	William Boullough	Apothecary	
105	William Garven	Apothecary	at Mr Hooper, St Martin's Lane
612	John Wright	Apothecary	Great Wild Street [Drury Lane]
40	James Shee	Attorney	Fetter Lane
184	David Jennings	Attorney	No. 4 Brick Court, Temple
192	Roderick Rose	Merchant	Jamaica
214	John Gillum	Merchant	Hog Lane, Norton Folgate
163	Edward Vaughan	Churgeon (surgeon)	Blue Ball, Fleet Street
314	Thomas Brothwick	Surgeon	Preston Court, Great Minories

Table 3 Middling & Lower Middling Occupations among Antients Freemasons, 1751–5

Occupation	No.	Occupation	No.
Apothecary	3	Book Binder	2
Attorney	2	Bookseller	3
Goldsmith	2	Butcher	4
Jeweller	2	Cabinet Maker	10
Merchant	2	Clerk	1
Silversmith	4	Clock/Watchmaker	11
Surgeon	2	Coachmaker	1
Vintner	2	Engraver/Painter	3
Watchmaker	9	Grocer	1
Wine Merchant	5	Gunsmith	1
		Linen Draper	2
Total	**33**	Printer	6
		Schoolmaster	1
		Shipwright	1
		Snuff Box Maker	3
		Tallow Chandler	5
		Tobacconist	1
		Undertaker	1
		Wool Draper	2
		Total	**59**

goldsmiths, silversmiths and jewellers, some of whom would have doubled as bankers. Yet more appear to have been talented and possibly better paid artisans: clock and watchmakers; bookbinders; printers; a gunsmith and so on. Such men were likely to be capable of avoiding cyclical poverty and amassing capital, if only on a small scale. As noted, they may also have been disproportionately influential within the community and in Antients freemasonry, not least because of their status and the financial contribution they made to the lodge. In aggregate, the proportion of such middling, semi-middling and skilled artisans amounted to approximately 20 per cent of the members whose occupations are disclosed.

After allowing for the duplication of entries in the *Register*, the number of gentlemen, middling, semi-middling and skilled artisans totals just over a quarter of those Antients members whose occupations were disclosed. However, the actual percentage is likely to have been higher. Although the majority of those described, for example, as 'tailors', 'weavers' or 'painters', were probably employed or self-employed and low-skilled, a minority, perhaps a large minority, would have been the small or medium scale entrepreneurs and businessmen that employed them. An obvious example would be James Hagarty, the Past Master of lodge No. 4, the master painter who at one time probably employed Laurence Dermott.

However, not surprisingly, by far the largest element of Antients' members is likely to have comprised less skilled and unskilled workers. These included bakers, brewers, bricklayers, britches makers, coopers, distillers, hatters and linen printers. The most common occupations were those of carpenter (with around twenty members); cobbler or shoemaker (thirty-five); painter and decorator (twenty-eight); peruke [wig] maker (twenty-six); weaver (thirty-nine); and tailor, the most widespread occupation at fifty-seven members, or around 13 per cent of the total. The relatively high proportion of peruke makers is of interest; although fashionable in the early 1700s, wearing wigs was rapidly going out of style by the mid-eighteenth century and such men may have been among the more impoverished. Even further down the social ladder were shop workers and street salesmen, with around fifty members, the majority victuallers and drapers (in total, forty-three). Although some, perhaps many or even most of their number may have been the more affluent shop owners rather than shop workers, others were probably hawkers or peddlers, for example, those living near Rag Fair in Rosemary Lane. But although few or none would have been regarded as well-paid or steady occupations, not all such men and their families would have lived close to subsistence, although most would have been in need of charity during periods of unemployed and illness, if not more regularly.

Data in the *General Register* suggests that in the same way that English and Irish lodges such as the Horn at Westminster, Rummer at Charing Cross, Ship behind the Royal Exchange and the Yellow Lion in Dublin, tended to encompass men with a similar social standing and a common business and/or political outlook, Antients freemasonry developed along similar lines. This is not unexpected given that lodge membership was generally a function of

Table 4 The Membership of lodge No. 20 at the Hampshire Hog, Goswell Street, London

Joined	Name	Occupation	Contact Address
First Year			
09.07.1753	John McCormick (WM)	Silversmith	Horse Shoe Alley, Moorfields
	Samuel Galbraith (SW)	Watchmaker	Great Arthur Street[9]
	James Bedford (JW)	Victualler	Crown, St Paul's Churchyard
	Thomas Warren	Britches Maker	Catherine Wheel Alley, Whitechapel
	John Houghton	Silversmith	Mrs Bows, Fleet Lane
	Noblet O'Keefe (Sec)	Watchmaker	Great Arthur Street
	John Hosier	Back Maker	Brick Lane, Old Street
20.08.1753	John Finch	Silversmith	Horse Shoe Alley, Moorfields
	Thomas Stones	Silversmith	Barley Bow, Mile End Green
01.10.1753	John Scovill	Clockmaker	Horse Shoe Alley, Moorfields
	John Cleminson	Silversmith	Green Gun, Mile End Green
15.10.1753	Fenwick Weddrinton	Watchmaker	Shorter Street, Wel[close] Square[10]
	James Newham	Shoemaker	Daggers Court, Moorfields
	Samuel Welbeck	Gold Chain Maker	Ham[p]shire Court, Whitechapel
14.01.1754	William Healy	Peruke Maker	St John's Square[11]
18.02.1754	John Summers	Jeweller	Blue Anchor Alley, B[unhill] Row[12]
28.03.1754	John Hogan	Tailor	Blackfriars[13]
01.04.1754	William Beckerton	Watchmaker	Mr Maud, St Martin's Lane
	Thomas Weir	Hatter	Mitchel Street, St Luke's Church[14]
20.05.1754	William Fox	Mariner	Horse Shoe Alley, Moorfields
Second Year			
29.07.1754	Paul Blunt	Mariner	Gone to sea
	William Green	Victualler	White Lion, White Lion Street[15]
	Samuel Hutchins		
16.09.1754	Robert Barnett	Victualler	Red Cross, Minories
05.05.1755	William Corp	Shoemaker	Great Arthur Street
25.05.1755	Thomas Dowsett	Shagreen Case Maker	Warwick Lane
02.06.1755	John Forsaith	Brewer	Bell Lane, Spitalfields
Third Year			
19.01.1756	George Lankston	Glover	Great Arthur Street

invitations to friends, colleagues or neighbours and, in common with most societies, only a minority might have been active in issuing such invitations. Further evidence for this interpretation can be seen in the membership registers and minute books of individual Antients lodges.

Although only a small number of such mid-eighteenth century lodge records have survived, one that has is that of lodge No. 20, which met at the Hampshire Hog in Goswell Street near Aldersgate. The composition of its membership supports the argument that commonalities of occupation and address, and an association with a few key figures, drove the lodge and created and cemented social and business relationships.

Seven members formed the lodge on 9 July 1753 and a further thirteen joined in the first twelve months. Of these, just over half appear to have been relatively high status artisans including five silversmiths, four watchmakers, a jeweller, a clockmaker and a gold chain maker. John McCormick, the Master of the lodge, a silversmith living at Horse Shoe Alley in Moorfields on the outskirts of the City, appears to have been responsible for inviting John Finch and John Scovill to join. The minutes for 20 August record that 'John Scholefield [was] reported by the Master and Senior Warden to be made a mason on our regular Lodge night next ensuing'. They were neighbours: Finch, another silversmith, and Scovill, a clockmaker, also lived in Horse Shoe Alley. Other early joiners connected through silversmithing were John Houghton, Thomas Jones and John Cleminson. Once again, the minutes for 3 September note that 'John Cleminson [was] reported by the Master, Bro Stone[s] and Bro Lewis M[aster] No. 4 to be made a mason on our regular Lodge night next ensuing'. Similarly, Samuel Galbraith, a watchmaker living in Great Arthur Street on the northern rim of the City of London at the Barbican, can be linked to Noblet O'Keefe, another watchmaker at the same address, and to others. The minutes of 23 December 1753, record that 'Bro Galbraith reported Mr William Healy [a peruke maker of St John's Square, Spitalfields] to be a member of this most honourable and antient lodge of free and accepted mason[s]'. And on 6 May 1754, a 'Bro Weir [was] reported to become a member of our Lodge by Bro Galbraith'.

Six new members joined in the lodge's second year when membership reached a plateau, with exclusions that year, most for non-payment, equalling the number of new entrants. Two new members, William Green and Robert Barnett, both victuallers, lived east of the City, around the Minories and Goodman's Fields; it is unclear at whose invitation they were invited to join. However, at this time, freemasonry was entirely open and those wishing to join a lodge would simply have to ask a known member.

The principal fulcrums on which the lodge turned appear to be John McCormick, the first Master, and Samuel Galbraith, the Senior Warden, who in 1755 was appointed the Antients' Junior Grand Warden. Evidence of Galbraith's influence is apparent in the volume of visitors from lodge No. 3, of which he had been Master, and the number of proposals Galbraith made with respect to new members.[22] Galbraith also financed the lodge's initial establishment. If his influence was central to maintaining the lodge's vitality, his subsequent absence would provide a reasonable explanation for the lodge's demise in the latter part of 1756, which followed Galbraith's return to Ireland in March of that year.

Taken as a whole, lodge No. 20 epitomises the characteristics found elsewhere in Antients freemasonry: a close concentration of addresses, in this instance around the northern perimeter of the City; related occupations, here principally within the jewellery trade; and a sense of friends and colleagues coming together. Although lodge numbers were relatively small, the membership register records that most members attended the twice monthly meetings with only limited absences: McCormick was away on five occasions in 1754; Galbraith was absent once ('sick'); and the majority of other members are shown as failing to attend on only a handful of occasions. There were a few exceptions. John Finch moved to Lisbon in January 1754 and was not present again. That he paid his lodge fees may indicate that freemasonry was of some use to him in Portugal. John Scovill and John Cleminson ceased to attend after May 1754. Like Finch, Cleminson paid his lodge fees, despite having 'gone to the country'; however, Scovill was later excluded for non payment.[23] Six others were similarly excluded: Frances Weddrinton, John Summers and Samuel Hutchins in September 1754; and Samuel Welbeck, Thomas Weir and William Fox in May 1755. Welbeck had been recorded 'sick' for virtually the whole year and had been able to attend only once.

In a paper transcribing the minutes and describing the lodge, Songhurst noted that the minute book had been prepared in the first instance by Laurence Dermott, who received 8s for its supply and for writing out the by-laws and preparing the minutes of the first two meetings.[24] An implication is that the lodge would have been relatively affluent in order to pay for such a service. The supposition is supported further by the employment of Richard Gough, the Antients' Grand Tyler, as the lodge tyler, that is, the external guard and lodge servant, who may have charged a premium for his services.

The lodge by-laws, an extract from which is replicated, set out the fees and system of fines levied in relation to various events and infringements. Based on a retail price index deflator, the fee per meeting of 1s 2d would be equivalent to c. £12 today, which would have excluded any charitable contribution; and a dining fee of half a crown, 2s 6d, would be c. £25.[25] The adjustment of such data for inflation is not an exact science and the figures would be considerably higher (by a factor of 7–10), based on the increase in average earnings between 1750 and 2010. Nevertheless, even at the lower level, the inference is that a member's earnings would necessarily have had to be relatively high and that joining such a lodge was a status improving act. There may also have been an implicit assumption by members that the benefits of joining, both social and financial, were perceived as having tangible value. Conversely, it would also be correct to assume that the high level of lodge fees would have provided the rationale for those members forced to leave or subsequently excluded for non-payment.

V

AND if any Member refuse to Serve any of the afores⁴. Offices shall be Fin'd as follows Viz. the Mast'. 5 Shill⁸. each Ward⁸. and Secretary two Shill⁸. each Deacon One Shilling, and to be Fined the Same if they don't Serve their full time Except for the Reasons mention'd in the 2⁴. Rule.   That the Master and Brethren meet on every S'. JOHN day to dine together between the Hours of 12 and two o'Clock and that each Mem'. pay 2 Shill⁸. the Lodge night before each S'. JOHNS day towards defraying the Charges of the Festival that the Wardens be appointed as Stewards to Transact all matters Relateing to the Feast that the new Officers be in Stall'd immadiately after Dinner, and all Visiters who dine, In this Lodge on said days Shall pay 2⁸.6 for Dinner.

VI

THAT on each Lodge Night every Mem'. pay one Shilling and put 2 pence in the Box that the Jun'. Ward. keep an Exact Account of the Reckoning and Acquaint the Body when all are in. and upon his neglegence or Omifsion he Shall be Answerable for the Difficiency.

VIII

ANY Person desireous of being made a Mason Shall be reported a Lodge night before his making by a Member of the Lodge and if not well known Shall be farther reported to the Grand Secretary with his Name, Occupation, and place of Abode with the intended time of his makeing, that the Secretary may make a Strict Enquiry into his Character, (and if approv'd off) Shall pay £1.5, one pound five shillings one moiety to be spent as a Wellcome to the New Bro'. and the Other part to be put in yᵉ Chest of this Lodge and at his making Shall Cloath the Lodge if Requir'd and when Enter'd Shall be Register'd in the Grand Lodge Book.

IX

WHEN any Mason is desireous of becoming a Member of this Lodge he Shall be Reported a Lodge Night before, as above and Balloted for and when Admitted, Shall pay 2⁸./6ᵈ into the box and One Shilling to the Grand Secretary for Registering him to the Number of this Lodge.

Unlike English lodges where meetings tended not to occur during the summer when the aristocracy and gentry were out of town, lodge No. 20 met bi-weekly throughout the year. Fees were payable by members on each occasion, jointly with dining charges and charitable contributions. The overall cost, per meeting and annually, would accordingly have been high. Nevertheless, although relatively affluent, the lodge was not rich. Indeed, much to its embarrassment, McCormick, as Master, supposedly complained at a meeting of Antients Grand Lodge that he had 'no jewels to open the Lodge'.[26] However, his grumbling is not borne out by the lodge's accounts, the first item of which notes a donation of 10s 6d from Bro. Hosier to purchase such jewels.

Belying the London Irish reputation for insobriety, by-law eleven dealt with the penalties payable for drunkenness. It implies that the members of the lodge considered their activities to have significance beyond the purely social and that lodge meetings should and could command a more appropriate level of respect. Where levied, fines were payable 'the third lodge night after they are due, otherwise the transgressor shall have no vote in the lodge and if not cleared on St John's day, shall be excluded'. Indeed, the sanction for a third offence was potentially considerable:

XI

IF any Member of this Lodge come disguis'd in Licquor he Shall be Admonish'd by the Mast^r. for the First Offence, for the 2^d Offence he Shall be Fin'd One Shill^s. for the 3^d he Shall be Excluded without Certifycate or Benefit from the Lodge and reported to the Grand.

The minutes of lodge No. 20 indicate that Masonic ritual assumed a central role in the lodge's proceedings. The lectures given by the officers of the lodge, members and visitors were not the scientific or self-improving addresses that had been and may have remained a part of at least some English lodge evenings, but rather recitals and explanations of Masonic ceremony. Lectures 'in the Craft', 'in the first branch' (the initiation ceremony) or 'in the second part' (passing to the degree of a fellowcraft), were given at virtually every meeting and not limited to those where members were actually initiated, passed or raised. An obvious question is whether the Antients' focus on and championing of a more ornate form of traditional Masonic ritual was a factor in the popularity of Irish freemasonry in England, Ireland and elsewhere. Indeed, for some members it may have become a substitute for Catholic liturgy or a proxy for the High Church Anglicanism of at least some Church of Ireland services. Moreover, despite the absence of tangible evidence, there are understandable reasons to suppose that many Irishmen, in the main poorly educated and at some distance from home, would have welcomed that form of freemasonry.

But apart from any quasi religious or spiritual benefits, it is also reasonable to conclude that two of the main advantages of lodge membership were economic and social. Individual lodges and Antients Grand Lodge acted as proto friendly societies, provided a forum for social interaction and a testament to a member's reliability and financial status: a 'good man and true' whose lodge fees were up to date. In this context, membership may well have been viewed as evidence of financial rectitude and improved a member's opportunities for trade and employment. This was certainly the position in the latter part of the eighteenth century and in the nineteenth. One example is that of certain harbour pilots both in the Americas and in Britain's colonies who used a Masonic pennant as an identifier when competing for trade from incoming vessels.

Unlike current practice, Masonic membership certificates were not provided to members automatically when they were made a mason but on request and only where that member was in good standing. Certificates acted as a passport to allow the bearer to be recognised and accepted by lodges elsewhere. As such, they provided access to a ready-made support structure and would have been a valuable possession. They may also have assisted labour mobility. The minutes of 2 September 1754 record that following a lecture by Laurence Dermott, Bro. Blunt requested a membership certificate from the lodge 'as he is going to Jamaica'. After discussion, the certificate was granted, 'received honourably, as he has paid all his dues in our lodge'. The following year, on 25 May 1755, Thomas Dowsett joined the lodge, introduced by Galbraith. Proof of Dowsett's Masonic position, his 'being worthy of being a member', was attested by 'his certificate from No. 218, Ireland'. Dowsett may have been a former soldier who had previously been stationed in Ireland. The warrant constituting lodge No. 218 had been issued to the 48th Regiment of Foot by Irish Grand Lodge on 27 December 1750.

Of course, a certificate was not always required as proof of Masonic membership. Men seeking to join or visit another lodge within the same district or town might normally expect to be known to a current member who could vouch for his *bona fides*. But in a large city this was not always easy to achieve and there are instances of complaints raised by those whose admission had been rejected:

> Bros Mercado and Hood [complained] against the lodge held at the Anchor & Baptist Head in Chancery Lane for refusing to admit them as visitors as they were not known to any member.[27]

However, Antients freemasons travelling overseas or to other parts of the country where they were unknown would require a membership certificate as proof of their identity and of their good standing. With such a certificate, they would be freely admitted to the local lodge and to the support and infrastructure it offered.

The speed with which provincial and overseas lodges were created by the Antients is an excellent indication of their social and commercial utility.[28] Two lodges were warranted in Bristol in 1753, and by 1755, others had been established elsewhere, in Coventry, Liverpool, Manchester and Warrington. Over the next two decades, the Antients built a significant presence across England that stretched from Kent in the south east to Cumberland in the north west, and from Devon in the south west to Durham in the north east. Most Antients lodges were established in the newly industrialising communities where Irish and other workers were drawn to work in the new factories or laboured on construction projects. And overseas, Antients lodges were active in each of America's thirteen colonies, and in the Caribbean and Canada; they were also present across continental Europe and in Scandinavia. Adding to the total, by 1790, fifty Antients regimental warrants had been granted within the British army, the majority of which were issued to regiments posted to North America.

Lodge No. 37, constituted on 19 April 1754, represents a second Antients lodge whose membership register and late eighteenth century minutes have survived, albeit only in part.[29] Although the earliest lodge minute books have

Table 5 The Membership of lodge No. 37 at the Red Cow,
Holywell Street, Strand, 1754–5

Registration	Name	Rank
19 August 1754	William Cowen[26]	WM
	William Osborne	SW
	John Nelson	JW
	Charles Buss[27]	
	Leonard Holiday	JD
	William Child	Sec.
	William Dickey	
	William Grayson	DGM
	Thomas Field	
	Richard Houlditch	
	Nathaniel Morgan	
	William Moore	
6 November 1754	Giles Powell	
	John Turner	
4 December 1754	Alexander McDowell	
2 April 1755	Charles Smith	
	John Masters	
	Thomas Stodard	
	James Logan	
	Thomas Morgan	
	Omitted Tottershell	
	James Hagan	

been lost, the records of Antients Grand Lodge indicate that in 1754, the lodge applied to exchange its warrant for a now vacant earlier (and thus lower and thereby more prestigious) number: that of No. 6, granted on 17 July 1751. The minutes record that on 2 October 1754,

> Brother William Cowen, Master of the Lodge No. 37, proposed paying one guinea into the Grand Fund for No. 6 (now vacant).[30]

Grand Lodge agreed the application and for the consideration of a guinea, paid by instalments and completed on 18 June 1755, lodge No. 37 was elevated thirty-one places.[31] The first members of the lodge are listed in the *General Register*, albeit that the address and occupation of each member was not recorded.

The lodge returns to Antients Grand Lodge show three new members in 1754; seven in 1755; and 29 in 1756, of whom six ceased to attend after the December meeting. Four joined in 1757 and one in 1758, being Laurence Dermott, the Grand Secretary. John Lane's *Masonic Records* note that the lodge moved to the King's Arms tavern in Holywell Street in 1755. It

Table 6 The Membership of lodge No. 6 at the Admiral Vernon,
Bishopsgate Without, 1771

Name	Rank	Occupation	Contact Address
William Bayley	WM	Buckle maker	Duck Lane, West Smithfield
Luke Conniff	SW	Tailor	Wardour Street, Soho Square
William Dagnin	JW	Gentleman	31 Cateaton Street
Thomas Blair	PM	Tailor	3 Fishmonger's Alley, Fenchurch Street
John Bexwell	SD	Attorney	near the London Infirmary, Whitechapel
John McCormick	JD	Goldsmith	Messrs. Fox & Lovos, Worship Street, Moorfield[29]
Charles Bearblock	Sec.	Victualler	'Admiral Vernon', 114 Bishopsgate St Without
James Douglas			at Bro. Blair's [3 Fishmonger's Alley]
Patrick Murphy[30]		Locksmith	at Mr Brown's, Winsley Street, Oxford Market
William Ford		Victualler	at 'Two Blue Posts', Cockpit Alley, Drury Lane
John Tirrell		Breeches maker	'Sun and Dove', opp. Red Lion St, Holborn
William Finch		Baker	Bunhill Row, Artillery Fields
Robert Erwin		Brandy merchant	Fashion Street, Artillery Lane, Spitalfields
John Burford		Tailor	11 Great Wild Street, Lincolns-Inn-Fields
Thomas Withers			
James Barnard		Weaver	Wheeler Street, Spitalfields.
Timothy Doyle[31]			[Holywell Lane, Shoreditch][32]
John H. Ayckbourn		Glass maker	9 Back Lane, Princes Square
Moses Meyers			Gone to Holland
Abraham Abrahams		Glass seller	[Mitre Court, Leadenhall Street][33]
Antony Strawback		Glass engraver	9 Back Lane, Princes Square
Andrew Robertson		Peruke maker	Wormwood Street, Bishopsgate Within
William Griffiths		Attorney	opposite the New Road, Whitechapel
Moses Chopin		Victualler	at 'London Apprentice', Adam and Eve Court, Whitechapel

remained there until 1770, when the lodge transferred its meeting place to the Admiral Vernon tavern at 114 Bishopsgate Street Without. The surviving minutes commence on 17 December 1770 at the Admiral Vernon and contain the list of members set out below.[34] In 1819, lodge No. 6 took the name 'Enoch Lodge'.

Lodge No. 6 shares similar characteristics to No. 20, with a concentration of members around the north of the City of London and a combination of middling and lower ranking occupations that range from the relative affluence of two attorneys, a gentleman and a goldsmith, to a weaver, victuallers and tailors. Interestingly, the lodge's membership also included two Jews: Moses Myers and Abraham Abrahams. At the 17 December 1770 meeting, Thomas Blair sat as Master of the lodge and Robert Irwin, a brandy merchant, was proposed, initiated and passed to a fellowcraft. Irwin was already a freemason, albeit a Modern, and consequently paid a fee of 10s 6d rather than the standard joining fee of 2 guineas. The same arrangement applied in March, when Moses Meyers, another Modern, joined the lodge, on this occasion proposed by Charles Bearblock.[40] The discounted fee suggests that the Antients were happy to encourage Moderns to defect to their ranks and indicates the continuing competition between the two rival grand lodges. That Meyers and Abrahams had to undergo an initiation for a second time under Antients' ritual speaks to the lack of regard in which the Moderns were held by the Antients (and vice versa). Both organisations imposed the same obligation on those joining from their respective rival, albeit that each set of candidates was 're-made' using a similar ceremonial. The scale of fee – even at 10s 6d – speaks to the expense of lodge membership.

The first page of the earliest surviving Treasurer's Book for lodge No. 4, dated June 1769 and covering the period 1769–91, lists twenty-two lodge members. However, the first named fifteen, probably those who had constituted the lodge, are recorded in name only, and it is only the subsequent six members whose occupation and address were also noted.

The membership register of lodge No. 3, dated 1773, contains a more detailed list.[43] The lodge was originally numbered 55; it acquired the vacant

Table 7 The Membership of lodge No. 4, 1769

Joining Date (in 1769)	Name	Occupation	Address
3 August	Samuel Stead	Haberdasher	Ludgate Street
3 August	Thomas Thorp	Vintner	Fleet Street
7 September	William Wynch		Shoe Lane, Fleet Street
5 October	John Alewood	Bookbinder[35]	Addle Hill
2 November	Joseph Browning	Tailor[36]	Christopher Court, St Martin's Le Grand
30 November	Thomas Wood	Haberdasher	Cheapside

Table 8 The Membership of lodge No. 3, 1773

Name	Occupation
Thomas Carter	Cook
John Moody	Undertaker
Robert Jones	in Sir W.W. Wynn's Service
Samuel Sidebottom	ditto
John Yeomans	Hair [unclear, possibly 'merchant']
Edward Meredith	Musician
William Dennison	Shoemaker
Omitted Kelly	Servant to Lord Thomand
Edward Marsh	Baker
Omitted Storer	Plumber
Omitted Llandale	Taylor
Omitted Cook	Silversmith
John Pilkington	Coal Merchant
Omitted Stade	Tailor
Omitted Chamless	Baker
Omitted Cullom	Tailor
Omitted Parker	Joiner
John Neal	Hatter
Omitted Parmistone	Breeches Maker
John Wild	Framework Knitter
Omitted Wood	Victualler
Charles Sidebotham	in Sir W.W. Wynn's Service
William Pixley	ditto
Griff Williams	ditto
Omitted White	Victualler
Omitted Rogers	
Omitted Ross	of the Treasury
Omitted Morris	Victualler
Omitted Collins	Builder
Spencer Draper	Cheesemonger
Omitted Lightwood	Victualler
Omitted Charme	Carver
Omitted Lindenburgh	Tailor
Omitted Looseley	Smith
John Sergeant	

warrant for No. 3 on 6 June 1759 for a donation of £4 14*s* 6*d*.[44] The lodge later took the name 'St George's Lodge'.

The lodge register illustrates a principally artisanal and working-class membership. That five members were in the employ of Sir Watkins Williams Wynn, 4th Bt., (1748–1789), is of interest. Given the probability – if not certainty – that Wynn's permission would have been required for his servants to attend lodge meetings, their presence and his patronage, albeit indirect, suggest a possible (if loose) tie to opposition politics. Wynn's father, the third baronet, had been an active and influential Jacobite sympathiser, a leading Tory and at the forefront of opposition to Walpole. Although Wynn did not pursue a political career with the same vigour and his parliamentary attendance was more limited, as MP for Shropshire (1772–4) and Denbighshire (1774–89), he nonetheless carried influence and was noted for voting with the opposition.

Despite his Tory politics, Wynn's wealth nonetheless made him a mainstay of the north Wales gentry and in April 1775, he applied for the lord lieutenancy of Merionethshire. Reluctantly acceding to a request to grant the honour, the king replied to Lord North that he would 'consent to Sir Watkins Williams being lieutenant of Merioneth, if he means to be grateful, otherwise favours granted to persons in opposition is not very political'.[45] Wynn supported the government accordingly for the next four years but, following a threat to his commercial interests in Wales, reverted to the opposition and thereafter voted against North and the administration until his death. One other factor might be mentioned. Wynn was in 1770, Junior Grand Warden of the Moderns and, in 1771, their Senior Grand Warden. His decision substantiates the social divide between Antients and Moderns freemasonry and also speaks to the different attraction that freemasonry had to Tories in Wales, an issue explored in *Foundations*. Whether it also indicates Wynn's temporary conversion to pro-establishment politics is more open to debate.

Wynn's multitude of servants represented a pattern of domestic service that was becoming overshadowed albeit not replaced by a changing commercial and industrial dynamic.[46] Despite onerous employment legislation and harsh penalties, the concept of the worker as a servant subject to the Master and Servants Acts who could and should be compelled to work was being substituted by the notion of the employer and employee. A growing minority of the urban working class was beginning to benefit financially from real wage growth and, psychologically, from a new ability to choose their employer as much as be chosen. As such pockets of urban prosperity expanded, the freedom to allocate time between labour and leisure became its corollary. Urban interaction within the lower middling and working class also created a space for greater social confidence allied to improved access to information. Both helped to create a more secure and certain labour force where the prospect of climbing out of poverty and creating personal wealth, if only on a small scale, was for many an extension of the same social and moral imperatives as those that motivated others higher up the financial and social ladder.

Greater and growing income disparity was a consequence of British economic development. However, it existed not just in the chasm between those at society's pinnacles and the bulk of the remainder, but also within the labour force itself. Urban workers' earnings accelerated away from those of their rural counterparts and, within towns and cities, the skilled artisans who provided the differentiated services and goods demanded by an increasingly affluent urban social elite could command a wage premium. Both developments can be identified in the composition of the Antients lodges and in the sometimes generous contributions of their members towards local mutual support and fraternal benevolence. They are also present in the fees, costs and expenses associated with lodge membership, and nuanced in the reputation of the different taverns that hosted lodge meetings and in the dining arrangements that distinguished one lodge from another. Similar clues to status and association are marked in the relationships that linked members of similar – and different – social and financial standing.

Over time, Antients freemasonry reflected and added to the rollback of social deference and to greater self-reliance and more open debate.[47] Where the Moderns sidelined controversy and considered such matters in private meetings or within the loyal and discreet Charity Committee of Grand Lodge, the Antients debated issues more freely. An extract from the minutes of the meeting of the Antients Grand Lodge on 2 April 1755 provides an example of the confidence exhibited and the mutual support in which that confidence was rooted:

> Thomas Eastman the Master of No. 18 stood up and declared that his business to the Grand Lodge on this night was to make a formal declaration that neither he nor any of the members of his lodge, No. 18, would contribute to the Grand Fund nor attend this Grand Lodge for the future, upon which the GM [Edward Vaughan] told Mr Eastman that he was welcome to stay away and, further, that if he knew anybody of like principles in this Assembly he was also at liberty to take him or them.

> Heard the petition of Thomas Byrne, Past Master of No. 32, in distress (through sickness). Ordered that the petitioner shall receive one pound fifteen shillings at the rate of seven shillings per week by the hands of George Birney, Master of No. 32 aforesaid, providing that in case the said petitioner, Thomas Byrne, should die within five weeks, the said George Birney shall return the remainder of the money to the Grand Lodge.

> Heard a petition from James Towbin, a Sojourner in distress. A private collection was immediately made for and delivered to him.

> GW Galbraith begged leave to resign his office on account of the ill usage which he received from Laurence Rooke, the Master of No. 17. The Grand Warden was reconciled to his Office and Laurence Rooke declared off the Grand Charity and demanded two shillings which he had formerly contributed to the fund for relief of worthy brethren in distress. The GM told him that taking him in every sense, he did really believe him to be one of the poorest creatures in London, but wanted merit to receive a single farthing out of any charitable fund in the universe.

This is not to argue that England's workforce was uniformly or even predominantly upwardly mobile and aspirational. That was far from the case. But it is to contend that many of those who found a home within Antients freemasonry were within that category. That such a considerable proportion were Irish speaks to the determination and drive of many of those economic migrants who made their way to England. Indeed, Laurence Dermott is a pre-eminent examples of the diligence, confidence and above all success that characterised this section of London's labour force. His sharp elbowed promotion of the Antients was extraordinarily effective, as was his emulation of the gentry in his use of marriage as a path to social mobility and relative affluence. Where the Moderns had created a mid-century vacuum in English freemasonry, Dermott placed the Antients at the front and centre of lower middling community life.

CHAPTER THREE

The Antients' General Register

Within this chapter we examine briefly a number of the principal London districts where most Antients freemasons listed in the *General Register* lived and worked, and detail the names, addresses and occupations of those known to have lived in each area. In practice, certain districts merged into one another, however, for our purposes, they have been grouped loosely into five broad areas. The first comprised a swathe of central London including much of the city of Westminster; the second, an arc that stretched north and north-east of the City of London; the third, the City itself; the fourth, the area to the east of the Tower of London, including the Minories, Ratcliffe Highway and Goodman's Fields; and the fifth, Southwark and south of the Thames. And, of course, within each district were sub-districts.

COVENT GARDEN & DRURY LANE

The earls of Bedford had been granted land in Covent Garden after its sequestration by Henry VIII. They employed Inigo Jones to design and layout a central square and planned to create a residential district that would attract the gentry and aristocracy as a means of increasing the value of the land. A small fruit and vegetable market serving the area later developed to the south. However, as with St Giles-in-the-Fields and Seven Dials, what had been intended in the seventeenth century as an affluent and fashionable quarter gradually fell into decline. As the gentry relocated further west, taverns, coffee houses and brothels filled the vacuum and proliferated. By the early eighteenth century, the district had become a notable location for popular entertainment and attracted a demimonde of pleasure seekers, becoming synonymous with drink and prostitution. Drury Lane, an area to the immediate east, was equally notorious and insalubrious:

> the Hundred of Drury [with its] one hundred and seven pleasure houses within and about the settlement, the Ladies whereof ply the passengers at noon.[1]

Contemporary guidebooks listed those streets and districts where prostitution, both hetero and homosexual, might easily be found, together with the rates charged for such services. *A Trip through London* was one of many popular guidebooks to the area.[2] Another, *A second part of A view of London and Westminster: or, the Town Spy*, encouraging 'lewdness unrestrained by shame', provided a list of courtesans and their respective addresses.[3] And *Harris's List of Covent Garden Ladies*, setting out a description of each courtesan to be found in the area, was in such demand that successive editions were published almost annually from 1746 until Harris's death in 1766, and thereafter by other enterprising compilers through to the 1790s. Indeed, the book's popularity was such that it was believed to sell around 8,000 copies a year, a vast number given the cost, let alone the percentage of the population that was illiterate.

Despite a focus on central London, prostitution was omnipresent across the metropolis and far from limited to the theatre and entertainment districts of Covent Garden and Drury Lane. The adjacent St Giles, St Martin's, the Haymarket and the Strand were also renowned for their brothels and streetwalkers, as was the City, Spitalfields, the Commercial Road, the Ratcliffe Highway and Southwark. Estimates of the numbers of women (and men) involved vary widely. Randolph Trumbach in *Sex and the Gender Revolution* refers to the reforming magistrate, Saunders Welch, who concluded in 1758 that approximately three thousand women worked in prostitution; a number that was also adopted by Jonas Hanway in 1760.[4] Trumbach analysed the locations of London's disorderly or 'bawdy' houses, noting an estimated 408 in the decade 1720–9, over 70 per cent of which, 290 such establishments, were located in the West End. The greatest number was in St Giles (with 193) and St Martin's (69), with a smaller figure located in the Strand (16). The data are similar to the number of pleasure houses mentioned by the *Town Spy*. Of the balance, 15 per cent or some 60 houses were situated to the north of the City in Clerkenwell and Cripplegate; with the same number to the east of the City along the Ratcliffe Highway and in Stepney, Whitechapel and Wapping, an area that also attracted substantial custom from the port of London and its docks.[5]

As might be expected, the Antients members living in Covent Garden and Drury Lane appear generally to have been in less well paid occupations, a combination of tailors, jobbing painters and other unskilled or low skilled employments. However, a few rise clearly above the mass: Richard Partridge, a gentleman living in Chandois Street; another, Jerome Robinson, at Mr Chambers' near the Opera House; John Wright, an apothecary in Great Wild Street; Maliche Delany, a vintner in Charles Street; and Peter Reilly, another gentleman living in Long Acre.

Table 9 sets out the names and occupations of those recorded in the *General Register* living and working in Covent Garden and Drury Lane, together with their respective occupations.

John Rocque's 1746 map of London illustrates Drury Lane running south from Broad Street St Giles to Wych Street and the Strand. A few major thoroughfares branch out in perpendiculars out along its length, including Long Acre, Russell Street and Princes Street. But such principal thoroughfares are massively outnumbered by an abundance of cross-streets,

Table 9 Covent Garden & Drury Lane, 1751–5

List #	Name	Occupation	Address
1	Samuel Quay	Habit Maker	P W, Tavistock Street
5	John Smith	Tailor	Steuart's Rents, Drury Lane
23	Abraham Ardizaif		Broad Court, Bow Street, Covent Garden
41	John Gaunt	Painter	Middlesex Court, Drury Lane
42	Hugh Cheevers	Painter	Orange Court, Drury Lane
53	John Dowling	Peruke Maker	No. 3, Orange Court, Drury Lane
56	Lawrence Folliot	Tailor	Golden Seal, Castle Street, Long Acre
59	Evan Gabriel	Bricklayer	next door to The Black Dog, Drury Lane
61	Joseph Kelly	Cheesemonger	Seymour Court, Chandois Street, Covent Garden
69	James Drummond	Tailor	4, Seymour Court, Chandois Street, Covent Garden
79	John Keelly	Victualler	The Globe, Bridges Street, Covent Garden
102	Samuel Ferguson		Horseshoe, Chandois Street
152	Patrick Kenny	Tailor	Go[o]dwins Court, Bedfordbury
156	Thomas Moffat	Tailor	Chandos Street
166	William Kinnaird	Tailor	next door to The White Lion, Chandois Street
172	Joseph Kelly	Cheesemonger	Seymour Court, Chandois Street, Covent Garden
185	James Broaders	Undertaker	Drury Lane
186	Thomas Rawlinson	Victualler	King's Head, Drury Lane
211	Ambrose McCormick	Broker	Drury Lane
237	Anthony Richard	Tailor	Opposite Seymour Court, Chandois Street
242	Richard Partridge	Gentleman	Chandois Street
250	Francis Betty	Shoemaker	Nelson's Court, Drury Lane
256	Henry Hunter	Shoemaker	Old Playhouse Passage, Drury Lane
260	Roger Madden	Peruke Maker	Fox Court, Gray's Inn Lane
268	Maliche Delany	Vintner	Charles Street, Covent Garden
280	William Nowlan	Shoemaker	Bricklayer's Arms, Drury Lane
298	John Morrison	Peruke Maker	Earls Court, Bow Street
302	John Allen	Staymaker	Chandois Street
303	Thomas Haig	Cabinetmaker	Glassenbury Court, Long Acre
307	James Pindie	Cabinetmaker	Glassenbury Court, Long Acre
312	John Scott	Linen Draper	Chandois Street
319	Alexander Taite	Cabinetmaker	Conduit Court, Long Acre

323	William McGare	Carver	Near St James's Street, Long Acre
324	Andrew Leakey		Chandois Street
348	Thomas Jordan	Victualler	Red Lion, Dirty Lane, Long Acre
389	James Noland	Tailor	Pipemaker Alley, Bedfordbury
400	John McDowell	Carpenter	Chandois Street
429	John Panvisol	Hatter	Drury Lane
443	Thomas Pully	Founder	Three Bells, Castle Street, Long Acre
446	William Shaw	Tailor	Three Crowns, White Lion Street, Seven Dials
447	James Brennan	Baker	Brown Bear, Bow Street, Covent Garden
457	Christopher Wallace	Cabinetmaker	Long Acre
477	James Nolan	Tailor	Pipemaker Alley, Bedfordbury
510	Peter Reily	Gentleman	Long Acre
511	John Hiett	Broker	Castle Street, Long Acre
518	Jerome Robinson	Gentleman	Mr Chambers' near Opera House
526	John Ward	Woolen Draper	New Street, Covent Garden
529	Michael Sandipher	Peruke Maker	Dirty Lane, Long Acre
530	John Eare	Glazier	Dirty Lane, Long Acre
540	Laurence Folliot	Tailor	Middlesex Court, Drury Lane
548	Thomas Hancock	Tailor	Mrs Hart's Baker, Long Acre
549	James Kelly	Carpenter	Shorts Gardens
554	James Black	Carver	Middx Court, Drury Lane
591	Peter Callan		Chandois Street
612	John Wright	Apothecary	Great Wild Street
803	William Kinnaird	Tailor	next door to The White Lion, Chandois Street
951	James Broaders	Undertaker	Drury Lane

cul-de-sacs and courts, many accessible only via narrow alleys. It is these smaller and more penurious addresses that appear against the majority of members' names in the *General Register*: Blackmoor Street, leading to Stanhope Street; Broad Court; Maypole Alley; Middlesex Court; Old Playhouse Passage; Orange Court, made infamous by Gustav Doré in the nineteenth century; Stewart's (or Stuart's) Rents, joining Drury Lane to Great Wild Street; Tash Court and others. Many of the streets were the named locations in criminal trials at the Old Bailey and in cases brought before the Middlesex and Westminster Justices. And they and others are cited in poor relief, vagrancy and bastardy examinations at local parish hearings.[6] And they appear and reappear in later parliamentary enquiries investigating the effects of contagious fever among those in the city's most overcrowded districts:

one house in Saffron Hill supplied eight patients from its different apartments; one in Tash Court, Gray's Inn Lane, four; and from three or four houses in St Giles, upwards of twenty patients were admitted in the course of a month.[7]

A high proportion of London Irish lived in such overcrowded closed streets and passages. They were described by Thomas Beames, the Victorian commentator, as London's 'Irish colonies' which he viewed as both a physical manifestation of the community's social isolation and, importantly, as a testament to its strong intra-communal support network.[8]

But despite its association with the Irish and with Antients freemasonry, Covent Garden also contained Moderns lodges, attracted by the proliferation of taverns and coffee houses. Meetings were held at an array of locations including the Two Black Posts and Lebeck's Head in Maiden Lane; the Cross Keys in Henrietta Street; the Mitre and the Globe, both in Globe Lane; and the Bedford Arms in the main piazza. Others lodges met at the Shakespeare's Head to the north east of the piazza; at the Bedford Coffee House, where Desaguliers stayed after leaving Channel Row; and in Bury's Coffee House and the Theatre Coffee House, both in Bridges Street. One of the better known and more popular taverns was the Bedford Head in Southampton Street, a 'luxurious refractory' celebrated for its food and gaming.[9] As Pope noted: 'when sharp with hunger, scorn you to be fed, except on pea-chicks at the Bedford-head?'[10]

St Giles and St Martin's

Overcrowded, insanitary and in an even more reduced state, St Giles was adjacent to Covent Garden and to its north-west. It was regarded accurately as one of the worst slums in Britain and 'abounding in poor'.[11] The district was home to so many of those Engels later termed the 'poorest of the poor', that it came to epitomise poverty in London, especially among the Irish, and was widely known as Little Dublin.[12] To its south was the equally unfashionable St Martin's, another slum dominated by Irish émigrés, colloquially called 'porridge island' for the plethora of takeaway shops that fed those too impoverished to have access to a kitchen or who were otherwise unable or could not afford the raw materials and equipment to cook for themselves. It was then the case – as it is now – that cheap takeout shops proliferated in the poorest urban areas where the cost of labour and premises was low and translated to cheap, if not always nutritious, food.

Like Covent Garden, St Giles-in-the-Fields and St Martin's-in-the-Fields had in the past been destinations for the affluent gentry and merchant classes. However, from the late seventeenth century they had subsided into decay as the gentry gravitated west towards the newly built Berkeley, Grosvenor and St James's Squares. And as decline took hold, new landlords, mainly the gentry and professionals, but also merchants, traders and more affluent shopkeepers, leased or purchased property portfolios of multiple houses and even whole streets. Individual tenements would be under-leased to lesser landlords, who would themselves sub-lease or rent rooms to under-tenants. Individual rooms were in turn subdivided and rented on a monthly, weekly or even daily basis to families or manifold individual lodgers. In such circumstances, overcrowding and a lack of sanitation was endemic. Over the course of the eighteenth century and into the nineteenth, St Giles and St Martin's became two of the most densely populated areas of London, 'a core of increasingly crowded and shabby housing ringed by the Haymarket, Long Acre, Drury Lane, the Strand and Charing Cross'.[13] Both parishes developed into bywords for disease, vagrancy and unemployment. Prostitution of both sexes was pervasive, as was alcoholism, assisted and promoted by the proliferation of distilleries and inexpensive gin shops.

Of the two, St Giles came to embody most egregiously the evil of poverty in popular culture. In *Gin Lane* (1750) and the first scene of *Four Stages of Cruelty* (1751), Hogarth illustrated the cruelty, misery and squalor associated with the alcohol dependency and destitution for which the district was known. Consumption of gin was regarded by the establishment as a particular iniquity and viewed as a threat not just to public health and morality but, more subtly, as the means by which the middling classes and the gentry were deprived of an effective labour force and productive consumption. In the Bishop of Worcester's words, 'how many . . . are annually killed and how many commodities . . . does this pernicious gin supplant'.[14] Kent has emphasised the scale of the problem, noting the St Martin's parish officers' complaints to parliament, which argued – and demonstrated – that the excessive consumption of spirits led to crime, disorder and idleness. The constables' reports indicated that as many as one in eight houses in Westminster sold spirits. In St Giles, the number was thought to be higher, at one in four.[15] Small-scale distillers proliferated in London and, in 1735, the number was estimated at more than 1,500 across the capital. The retailing of spirits was similarly widespread. The Middlesex justices calculated in 1736 that around 7,000 premises sold gin and brandy, of which just over half sold nothing else.[16] William Maitland's survey corroborated the data. Considering the area covered by the Bills of Mortality as a whole, Maitland calculated the number of retail wine merchants to be 1,148; alehouses, 5,975; and spirit retailers, 8,659.[17] The consumption and production of alcohol grew in tandem, almost doubling between 1730 and 1736, with excise duty levied on a total of around 6.4 million gallons of British spirits in the latter year.[18] Unsurprisingly, spirit outlets had a particularly high density in the most deprived areas of London, with an especially large number to the east of the City in Whitechapel and in the rookeries of central London. The same districts were also home to other spirit vendors, including barrowmen, stall holders and chandlers shops, most of whom needed little initial capital to set up in business.

Ranged against the spread of Mother Gin was an alliance of genteel forces spearheaded by the Middlesex and Westminster magistrates benches. Clark has described their relationship in the 1730s and 1740s with fellow opponents of the spirits trade in London, including parliamentarians, the SPCK and other forces supported and encouraged by the sensationalist London press. Allegations of drunken disorder and drink-fuelled crimes spurred letter writers to deplore 'this destructive vice' and to rally 'some of the wisest and best men who have long lamented this evil'.[19] Lurid reports of intoxication, robbery and even murder proliferated and were given credence by episodes such as the fire started at Mrs Calloway's, an Irish-owned brandy shop, in Cecil Court off St Martin's Lane. The fire spread rapidly, destroying thirteen houses and requiring the mobilisation of the local military to put it down.[20] Brought before Thomas de Veil, London's leading magistrate, Elizabeth Calloway was indicted for maliciously setting fire to her own house with the intent to burn those of two of her neighbours. Amid an upsurge of anti-Irish sentiment, Calloway was committed to Newgate to await trial. But although the fire and its aftermath received extensive publicity, the trial itself was almost unreported, perhaps because Calloway was acquitted.[21]

Among the foremost promoters of the Gin Act was Sir Joseph Jekyll, the then Master of the Rolls, who used his parliamentary and judicial contacts and a close cooperation with the SPCK and the magistrates' benches to mobilise public, judicial and parliamentary support. He was assisted by Sir John Gonson, chairman of the Westminster bench, as well as Thomas de Veil, Nathaniel Blackerby and Benjamin Burrowes, all influential magistrates. Other prominent supporters included James Oglethorpe and James Vernon, a commissioner of the excise. Not coincidentally and as discussed in CHAPTER FOUR, many leading figures, including de Veil, Blackerby, Vernon and Oglethorpe were also prominent freemasons, as were other justices of the peace.

SEVEN DIALS

Seven Dials, a junction that linked St Martin's Lane with Broad St Giles to the north, had also once been intended for the aristocracy. Designed by Thomas Neale in the late 1700s as a fashionable residential development, the area had then, in John Strype's words, been 'inhabited by the nobility and the gentry'.[22] However, over a few decades it was gradually absorbed by the decay of St Giles and became 'unhappily associated . . . with the extremes of wretchedness and vice'.[23] Dickens' later description of the 'maze of streets, courts, lanes and alleys' around Seven Dials would have been recognisable in the eighteenth century.[24] And contemporary press reports reinforce a sense of social disrepair where the absence of foundations and destruction of a tenement house becomes a metaphor for the lives of its residents:

Thursday Night a House near Seven Dials in which were 25 persons, mostly lodgers, fell down; providentially no person was killed but several were much bruised and wounded.[25]

Contemporary newspaper reports also speak to a caricature of the Irish and other outcasts living there: 'Yesterday Pheneas Balthazar, a Jew Dealer in clothes, quarrelling with two Irish traders in the same branch in a public house near the Seven Dials, received so violent a blow in his right eye as totally to extinguish all future use . . . and was otherwise so much bruised, that it is thought he cannot recover.'[26] And the near fatal after-effects of excess alcohol were so common as to be a joke: 'Sunday evening a tradesman who lives near the Seven Dials, being with his wife in a public house . . . insisting on more liquor, she was obliged to leave him, and next morning he was found in the road with both legs broken, supposed to have been occasioned by his having taken asleep and a carriage going over him in the dark.'[27] Albeit expressed in the 1840s, Engels' comment would have been equally valid a century earlier:

> here live the poorest of the poor, the worst paid workers with thieves and the victims of prostitution indiscriminately huddled together, the majority Irish, or of Irish extraction, and those who have not yet sunk in the whirlpool of moral ruin which surrounds them, sinking daily deeper, losing daily more and more of their power to resist the demoralising influence of want, filth, and evil surroundings.[28]

Table 10 details those Antients members living in St Giles, Seven Dials and St Martin's. The stated occupations reflect the possibility of their predominantly low social status and suggest that many may have been employed as poorly paid or sweated labour, including the painters, tailors and casual building workers who lived and worked in the area. Only a few stand out as potentially more middling, including, Isaac Simon, a gentleman living in White Lion Street; and William Garven, an apothecary at Mr Hooper, St Martin's Lane.

Commentators have suggested that one reason for the concentration of Irish residents in St Giles was a prevailing understanding that parish charitable relief was accessible to incomers with relative ease.[31] It is unclear why this should be so. In most instances, the Poor Laws were of limited use to recent Irish émigrés. Under the terms of the 1692 Poor Relief Act, a claimant could obtain access to relief only after a minimum period of employment or residency.[32] And any potential entitlement was determined only after examination, which was often thorough:

> Christopher Dallmange aged 38 years saith he hath no lodging these five nights and that his last lodging was at one Mr Peacocks in Earls Street by the Seven Dials where he lodged a year, that he was bound apprentice by indenture for seven years to Mr Robert Waterfield, a Painter in Half Moon Street in the Parish of St Martin in the Fields where and with whom he

Table 10 Seven Dials, St Martin's & St Giles, 1751–5

List #	Name	Occupation	Address
80	John Hamilton	Painter	Monmouth Street, Seven Dials
83	John Holland	Mason	Monmouth Street, Seven Dials
87	Stephen Deveaux	Peruke Maker	Tower Street, Seven Dials
90	John Fern	Tailor	Great St Andrews Street, Seven Dials
95	William Brown	Pipemaker	Vinegar Yard, St Giles
108	William Woodman	Smith	Golden Key, Tower Street, Seven Dials
215	Richard Storer	Painter	Tower Street, Seven Dials
216	Benjamin Hobbs	Painter	Tower Street, Seven Dials
232	William Huddleston	Painter	Tower Street, Seven Dials
282	Hugh Horan	Britches maker	White Lion Street
285	Isaac Simon	Gentleman	White Lion Street
387	Laurence Rooke	Carpenter	Thistle & Crown, Monmouth Street, Seven Dials
440	Daniel Manser	Broker	Black Moor's Head, Castle Street, [Seven] Dials
442	John Hamilton	Painter	Monmouth Street, Seven Dials
515	Laurence Wheaton	Plasterer	Green Man, St Giles's
516	William Eyres	Plasterer	Green Man, St Giles's
902	Daniel Manser	Broker	Black Moor's Head, Castle Street, [Seven] Dials
899	John Conner		next door to the [illegible] St Martin's Lane
900	Charles Conner		Bull's Head in St Martin's Lane
901	Omitted Doverthy		Bull's Head in St Martin's Lane
38	George Fay	Tallow Chandler	Bull's Head, Church Court, St Martin in the Fields
47	William Waters	Painter	Coarch & Horses, St Martin's Lane
105	William Garven	Apothecary	at Mr Hooper, St Martin's Lane
187	Michael McDaniel	Tailor	at the Highlander, Bedford Bury
243	Andrew Fallon	Tailor	Corner of Hewitt's Court
274	Alexander McDougall	Tailor	Angel, St Martin's Court
310	James Russell	Tailor	Dawson's Alley, St Martin's Lane
320	Alexander Cowen	Peruke Maker	Star & Garter, St Martin's Lane
321	James McDougall	Tailor	Star & Garter Court, St Martin's Lane
328	James McBride	Tailor	St Martin's Street
334	John Bonner	Painter	Church Lane, St Martin's
420	James Dempsey		next to Chandler's shop, Little St Martin's [Lane]
552	Alexander Clark	Victualler	White Lion, Hemming's Row [St Martin's Lane]

served all his said apprenticeship which expired 16 years ago, since which he took an apartment of 14 pounds per ann. which was not separate unto itself, the house being let out in tenements, and that he never took any house rented £10 per ann. paid any parish taxes or was a yearly hired servant afterwards, that he was married to Isabella his wife (who has been absent from him these seven years) at Marylebone Church 12 years ago and hath no children. Sworn the seventh Day of January 1740 before me'.[33]

It is not known to what extent, if any, the availability of benevolent relief from the Antients may have swayed attitudes to the openness of poor relief on a larger scale, however, it is likely that the Irish sought to offer what support they could to their fellow countrymen.

HOLBORN AND THE OXFORD ROAD

Adjacent to St Giles to the north, Holborn and Bloomsbury were in part an extension of the rookeries and had similar characteristics. The area had a justifiable reputation for being unsafe, and not only at night. Press reports of attempted and successful daylight robberies in Holborn and the immediate district, including the Oxford Road, were published on a daily basis in the early 1750s:

Sunday about 7 o'clock in the evening, Mr Nevill returning from Gloucester Street to his chambers in Gray's Inn, crossing Red Lyon Square, was attacked by six fellows armed with drawn cutlasses and pistols, who robbed him of his gold watch and thirty guineas . . . the same night, about 11 o'clock, a man was robbed in Red Lyon Square, and it is presumed by the same fellows, but he making some resistance, one of the villains gave him a blow with a cutlass whereby it is feared he will lose one of his eyes.[34]

The press and public commonly blamed the Irish for what was regarded in the eighteenth century as a crime epidemic, albeit that rising urban poverty and the absence of an effective policing force were the principal causes. And crime was not simply a function of frequent drunken brawling. Correctly or otherwise, many footpads were thought to be Irish and at least some of them believed to be deserters from the continental Irish brigades.[35] The Oxford Road, one of the principal routes running west from the City of London, passed through Holborn to Tyburn and Oxford beyond, and the travellers that it attracted had their counterparts in those that preyed on them. The highway was known for its theatres and other varied entertainments. Cock fights were staged, including several well-advertised bouts such as that 'between the gentlemen of London and Westminster and the gentlemen of Suffolk'.[36] The route provided a focal point not only for gamblers but also prostitutes and their clients, becoming 'a rendezvous for loose, idle and disorderly persons'.[37] However, as elsewhere, the poor and rich lived in close

Table 11 Bloomsbury, Holborn & the Oxford Road, 1751–5

List #	Name	Occupation	Address
10	Francis Mathews	Shoemaker	Opp. W[hite] B[ear], Princes Street, Red Lion Square
89	John Kennedy	Framework Knitter	King Street, Bloomsbury
136	John Stalker	Glazier	Glass Shop, Bloomsbury
145	Andrew Francis	Tailor	next door to The Dial, Little Wild Street
161	James Evans	Painter	Queen Street, Oxford Road
246	Jeremiah Coleman	Shoemaker	6 Cans, Turnstile, Holborn
247	James England	Shoemaker	Trumpet, Shire Lane, Holborn
249	Richard Nowlan	Shoemaker	Sun in Wood Street, Turnstile, Holborn
253	Michael Lutterel	Shoemaker	Princes Street, Red Lion Square
254	Thomas Reilly	Shoemaker	Fishers Street, Red Lion Square
255	Anthony Jones	Shoemaker	Princes Street, Red Lion Square
257	Grafton Shepperd	Shoemaker	Next door, Thatched House, Red Lion Square, Holborn
259	Richard Duffy	Weaver	Star, Holborn
270	Joseph Johnson	Britches maker	East Street, Red Lion Square
271	John Gear	Locksmith	Lamb's Conduit Street
278	John Mahony	Shoemaker	Opp. Black Horse, Little Wild Street
279	John Lane	Shoemaker	Two Blue Posts, Great Turnstile, Holborn
313	James Kerr	Peruke Maker	Hatton Garden
347	Thomas Dawson	Painter	Diet St, St George's Bloomsbury
349	Richardson Sharp	Painter	Oxford Road
356	Thomas Gibbons	Senior Broker	Holborn
359	James Golden	Shoemaker	Prince's Street, Red Lion Square
361	Edward Ashley	Peruke Maker	Holborn
392	William Smith	Butcher	Little Turnstile, Holborn
428	John Taylor	Victualler	Turk's Head, East Street, Red Lion Square
430	Thomas Gear	Locksmith	Lambs Conduit Street Passage, Red Lion Square
431	Richard Storer	Shoemaker	Bedford Street, Bedford Row, Holborn
434	John Gear	Locksmith	Lamb's Conduit Street
437	James McKane	Printer	Mr James's Printer, Cursitor Street
455	Samuel Ellson	Bricklayer	Gloucester Street, Queen Square
512	Daniel Neil	Carpenter	King's Street, Bloomsbury Square

513	Daniel Dawson	Carpenter	at Mr Steeds, King's Street, Bloomsbury Square
514	Peter Dunhaven	Carpenter	at Mr Steeds, King's Street, Bloomsbury Square
539	Bernard Jackson	Painter	Queen Street, Oxford Road
543	George Kennedy	Bricklayer	at the Boot, Tibals Row [Theobalds Road]
546	John Brown	Tailor	Malpas Arms, Charles Street
550	William Davis	Gentleman	Malpas Arms
553	William Pollock		Malpas Arms
664	Jeremiah Coleman	Shoemaker	6 Cans, Turnstile, Holborn
924	Richard Smith	Victualler	Carpenters' Arms, Montague Street
965	John Pearce	Victualler	Red Lion, Oxford Road

proximity and despite its sometimes negative reputation, 'fine streets . . . from Great Russell Street down to St Giles' and 'from King Street to the Oxford Road' were constructed in the belief that they would prove attractive to those that could afford them.[38] Table 11 details those Antients members living in Holborn, Bloomsbury and along the Oxford Road where their address and/or occupation was recorded.

The majority of members listed appear to be from the working classes, the majority in poorly paid occupations, including thirteen cobblers. Other similarly paid trades include those of bricklayer, carpenter, painter and tailor. However, perhaps the most notable aspect of the data is the concentration of members living and working around Red Lion Square, many of whom joined the Antients simultaneously.

THE STRAND AND TEMPLE BAR

Once lined by grand aristocratic mansions, the Strand, the main artery linking the cities of London and Westminster, was in the late seventeenth and eighteenth centuries more noted for its entertainments, coffee houses and taverns. Mottley's description of the 'streets, lanes, alleys and courts in this parish', recorded the contrast between 'good built houses, well inhabited by gentry' situated next to 'passage[s] . . . pestered with carts . . . bringing coals and other goods from the wharfs by the water side'. His 'ill inhabited lanes', 'a small place called Piffling Alley, a very proper name', jostle against larger and older houses converted to multiple occupation or converted for business use. The description of the area between Temple Bar and St Clement's Inn is representative.

On the North side of the Butcher Row . . . are several courts, most of which are but small. The first is Ship Yard, a through fare into little Shear Lane, with a pretty broad passage; on the east side is an open place going into a

Table 12 The Strand & Temple Bar, 1751–5

List #	Name	Occupation	Address
127	Alexander Fife		Beaufort Buildings, Strand
144	David Lyon	Tailor	White Horse, Hungerford Market
147	William Weir	Painter/Stainer	Church Court, Strand
149	Alexander Ligerwood	Victualler	Thistle & Crown, Church Court, Strand
154	Alexander Shand	Peruke Maker	Savoy
158	George Gray	Peruke Maker	Church Court, Strand
188	Thomas Fowler	Hatter	Church Lane, Strand
205	George Mittens	Painter	Church Court, Strand
248	James Callan	Shoemaker	Next door, Bell, Exeter Street, Strand
288	Henry Chambers	Goldsmith	Northumberland Place [Passage]
305	Peter Kerr	Tailor	Lancaster Court, Strand
309	John Crookshanks	Tailor	Hewite's Court, Strand
327	Thomas Crocket	Peruke Maker	Catherine Street, Strand
337	John Duff	Watchmaker	Peacock, New Round Court, Strand
357	John Hill	Pastry Cook	Cr., Burford Buildings, Strand
364	George Forbes	Wine Merchant	York Buildings
368	Collin Bruce	Gentleman	Lancaster Court, Stand
370	William Hone	Victualler	Angel Inn, Wich St, Strand
468	John Doughty	Shoemaker	Church Court, Strand
472	Edward Dooley	Victualler	Crown, Mary Gold [Marigold] Court, Strand
473	Joseph Prosser	Victualler	One Tun, Strand
474	Richard Janes	Coal Merchant	Barford Buildings, Strand
485	James Slade	Cheesemonger	at Mr William's Blackmoor St, St Clem't Danes
486	Francis Richmond		Cheshire Cheese, Savoy Alley
487	William Pratt	Printer	Hudson's Court, Strand
13	Richard Price	Carpenter	Sheer Lane, Temple Bar
124	James Bradshaw	Peruke Maker	Temple
125	Thomas Blower	Tallow Chandler	Temple Bar
128	Robert Glave	Vintner	Sheer Lane, Temple Bar
130	Henry Jones		Temple & Sun, Sheer Lane, Temple Bar
132	John Smith	Britches Maker	Sheer Lane, Temple Bar
157	John Gordon	Gentleman's Tailor	Garden Court, Temple
184	David Jennings	Attorney	No. 4 Brick Court, Temple
339	James Bouillon	Tobacconist	Butcher's Row, Temple Bar

small court, called Chair Court with a fair Freestone Pavement. This yard seems to take its name from the Ship Tavern at the entrance thereof. Next to Ship Yard are . . . Swan Court, very small; Star Court, indifferent good and large with an open air; White Hart Court, long but narrow; Lock Alley, but small; Windmill Court, very small and inconsiderable. Crown Court hath an open air about the midst and leads into little Shear Lane. Bear & Harrow Court, so called from such a sign, a noted eating house at the entrance into it. This court, (or rather alley, for its length and narrowness) runs into Boswell Court. Then beyond St Clements Lane is the Angel Inn, a very large place and of a great resort, especially for the Cornish and West Country Lawyers.[40]

The area was particularly popular with Irish émigrés and transients, not least for its proximity to the Inns of Court that lined the upper reaches of the Strand, and the Five Bells tavern, where the Antients Grand Lodge met, and other grand inns that provided a range of popular entertainments and accommodations. Table 12 lists the Antients members living in the Strand and Temple Bar to its east.

SPITALFIELDS AND THE EAST

To the other side of the City of London was Spitalfields, an area bounded by Bishopsgate Without in the east, Brick Lane to the west, Shoreditch in the north and Houndsditch to the south. The area housed over thirty-five Antients freemasons with others living in the adjacent districts of Shoreditch, Bethnal Green and Bishopsgate within the City walls. Prominent among the addresses stated was Brick Lane, home to at least ten members; Holywell Lane, with seven; and Quaker Street, with nine. Just under half, nearly thirty members, gave their occupation as 'weaver'; and it is likely that other members living in the area whose jobs were not specified would also been employed on or associated with the looms. Brewing was another relatively common occupation, with at least three working in the industry. The remainder worked in an assortment of unskilled and semi-skilled occupations ranging from baking and bricklaying, carpentry and cabinet making, to a shoemaker and victualler.

Outside the City walls and nominally free of guild constraints, Spitalfields, originally pastures owned by the New Hospital of St Mary without Bishopsgate, better known as 'St Mary Spital', had been a destination and home to thousands of Huguenot refugees who had settled in the area after fleeing France in the late seventeenth century.[44] Many terraced houses had been constructed to combine accommodation, workshops and showrooms, with silk weaving on the upper floors and a sales and display area at ground level. Houses built by successful master weavers, such as those in Fournier Street, approached small urban mansions. Others were or became slums.

Irish weavers began to arrive in Spitalfields in numbers from the 1730s, as the decline in Ireland's domestic linen industry forced both linen and silk workers to seek employment elsewhere. Although the greatest migratory flows occurred in the mid-nineteenth century following the famine and agricultural depression of the 1840s, successive waves of emigration also accompanied and followed the severe famines of the 1720s and early 1740s. The irony of the Irish seeking refuge in the capital city of the country that was at least partly to blame for their poverty and circumstance may not have been lost on those concerned. The London Irish had been an influence on the city's population since before the seventeenth century. And over time, seasonal harvest workers were joined by permanent migrants as successive generations of Irish sought better economic prospects across a spectrum of skilled and semi-skilled occupations. But despite the influx of Irish migrants, a flow complemented by immigration from the surrounding rural counties and continental Europe, London's population remained virtually static until the latter part of the eighteenth century. Estimates for Middlesex suggest only a nominal rise in population between 1701 and 1751, from 582,000 to 590,000, and within London as a whole, a figure of around 630,000 in 1715 is thought to have grown by little more than 100,000 to perhaps 740,000 in 1765. If so, this would have represented an increase of just over 2,000 per year over half a century.

High mortality was a product of overcrowded housing compounded by an inadequate diet, and non-existent or poor sanitation accelerated the speed with which contagion and infection took hold within London's densely packed population and brought death early to many, and not just those in the lower middling and working classes. During the first half of the eighteenth century within the areas covered by the Bills, the number of recorded burials consistently exceeded that of baptisms. The statistics underline the importance of migration, without which London's population would have declined in absolute terms.[45] Indeed, even such population growth as occurred was often uneven and periods of expansion were commonly followed by decline or stagnation as agricultural cycles and economic depressions caused adult and infant deaths to soar. The latter was a particular issue and infant mortality was calculated to be around 20 per cent in the 1750s, that is, a rate of twenty deaths per hundred live births within the first two years of birth. Deane and Cole estimated London's rate of natural population increase between 1701–50 at a negative 10.8 per thousand, rising to negative 4.8 per thousand in 1751–80 and only becoming positive – at 2.7 per thousand – in the last two decades of the century. Only migration offset the decline; between 1701 and 1780, this was estimated to be around 11.4 per thousand, falling slightly to 9.6 per thousand in 1781–1800.[46]

Whether migrants or longer term residents, the relative poverty of many of those recorded in the *Register* is suggested by the details of their address. Examples include James Ryan, a weaver living in Half Moon Alley off Bishopsgate, a member of lodge No. 10; James Loury, a cobbler, in Long Alley off Moorfields; John Jackson of lodge No. 5, a tailor in Angel Alley,

Houndsditch; Michael Wade, a general dealer in Dunnings Alley; and John Duff, a weaver in Brick Court, Brick Lane. Others lodged at taverns and boarding houses, at least six alone at the Ship & Anchor tavern in Spitalfields. Edward Ryan, a peruke maker, roomed at the John of Gaunt tavern in Duke Street; Loghlin McIntosh of lodge No. 3, at the Crow in Patrick's Alley; and Thomas Nowlan, a shoemaker from lodge No. 14, at the Sun-in-the-Woods, Spitalfields. Perhaps another indication of limited means, Nowlan was later excluded for non-payment of lodge dues.

Spitalfields had been a centre for small-scale woollen, linen and silk manufacture, printing and dying since the seventeenth century. But it also housed carpenters, cobblers, tailors, shopkeepers and others serving the local community, and held a mixture of other industries. Brewing had developed there in the late seventeenth century. This was the Huguenot-influenced Truman's brewery, whose Black Eagle site in Brick Lane had been built in the 1680s.[47] The brewery expanded almost continuously in the eighteenth century to cover more than six acres, becoming a substantial employer and supplying nearly three hundred publicans by 1739.[48] Other breweries in east London included the Red Lion in Lower East Smithfield; Harwood's at the High Street in Shoreditch; Meux's Griffin brewery located in the aptly named Liquorpond Street, now Clerkenwell Road; and Whitbread's in Chiswell Street. Further west, central London had another assortment including the Woodyard brewery in Castle Street, Long Acre; the Horseshoe on Tottenham Court Road; and the Stag in Pimlico.[49]

But regardless of other industries, the manufacture of cloth and tailoring continued to be Spitalfields' main activity. The concentration of skills created economies of scale in weaving and its allied trades but this had both advantages and disadvantages. In better times, the prospect for those employed was buoyant; but in recession, with reduced demand, many dependent on the looms were forced out of work and unable to find alternatives. Although the distribution of poor relief provided an element of support, the consequential effect, as Thornbury noted a century later, could be the near pauperisation of the district.[50]

A number of Spitalfields lodges, including No. 10, formerly 11, at the Duke's Head in Winfield Street, had local catchment areas with members drawn almost exclusively from the immediate vicinity, including Bishopsgate, Shoreditch and Spitalfields itself. Around half the members were weavers, with the balance in other low paid employments; the only member not obviously in unskilled or semi-skilled work was Nathaniel Frank, who gave his address 'at H. Frank's in Skinner Street, Bishopsgate' and his occupation as gentleman. However, as noted, it is possible, perhaps probable, that at least some of the members listed may have been master weavers, that is, employers rather than employees. The lodge was later erased for 'disobedience of the 21st rule'.

The membership of lodge No. 5 was comparably narrow. However, as the lodge relocated successively to different meeting places across the metropolis, its members' addresses and occupations broadened accordingly. The

Table 13 Spitalfields, 1751–5

List #	Name	Occupation	Address
49	Barnaby Fox	Weaver	Opposite The Two Brewers, Spitalfields
50	Thomas O'Harah	Weaver	Opposite The Two Brewers, Spitalfields
58	John Morris	Weaver	Opposite The Two Brewers, Brick Lane, Spitalfields
117	Thomas Kaan	Weaver	Ship & Anchor, Brick Lane, Spitalfields
118	Isaac Daking	Cooper	Ship & Anchor, Quaker Street, Spitalfields
119	John Disrael	Weaver	Ship & Anchor, Quaker Street, Spitalfields
120	Moses Willoughby	Victualler	Ship & Anchor, Quaker Street, Spitalfields
131	Laurence Dermott		Ship & Anchor, Quaker Street, Spitalfields
137	Edward Butcher	Weaver	Ship & Anchor, Quaker Street, Spitalfields
142	Thomas Floyd	Turner	Browns Lane, Spitalfields
164	John Drake Hutchin	Cabinetmaker	Browns Lane, Spitalfields
168	William Pendlebury	Weaver	Ship & Anchor, Quaker Street, Spitalfields
174	Peter Lacour	Baker	Phoenix Street, Spitalfields
175	George Wilson	Hosier	Opposite [illegible], Bell Lane, Spitalfields
176	Benjamin Fournear	Weaver	Brick Lane, Spitalfields
177	John Woodward	Weaver	Brick Lane, Spitalfields
194	James Ryan	Weaver	Elder Street, Spitalfields
195	Barnaby Fox	Weaver	Opp. The Two Brewers, Spitalfields
196	George Hebden	Weaver	Elder Street, Spitalfields
201	Samuel Sturges	Pipe maker	Booth Street, Spitalfields
244	Thomas Warren	Britches maker	Red Lion Court, Spitalfields
293	Peter McLaughlin	Log Cutter	Old George Street, Spitalfields
365	John Cope	Weaver	Birch Court, Brick Lane, Spitalfields
366	James Duncon	Weaver	Quaker St, Spitalfields
371	John Kinyon	Turner	Brick Lane, Spitalfields
422	Barnaby Fox	Weaver	Opposite The Two Brewers, Spitalfields
424	George Rochford	Weaver	Old Coach Lane, Spitalfields
425	Anthony Morley	Weaver	Old Coach Lane, Spitalfields
426	John Mathews	Shoemaker	Corner Churchyard and Brick Lane, Spitalfields

439	Abraham Juers	Weaver	Brick Lane, Spitalfields
449	Thomas Garity	Weaver	near Corner, Old Coach Lane, Spitalfields
465	Thomas Warren	Britches maker	Red Lion Court, Spitalfields
469	Edward Ryan	Peruke Maker	at the John of Gaunt, Duke Street, Spitalfields
497	Abiah Waller	Weaver	Three Neat's Tongues, Pearl Street, Spitalfields
532	William Lay	Bricklayer	George Street, Spitalfields
542	Thomas Nowlan	Shoemaker	at the Sun in the Wood, Spitalfields
817	Thomas Weir	Hatter	Mitchell Street, near St Luke's Church, [Brick Lane]
854	Richard Doyle	Weaver	near the Queens Head, [illegible], Spitalfields

lodge met at three locations between 1751 and 1754, moving from the Plaisterers' Arms in Little Gray's Inn Lane to the Horse Shoe tavern on Ludgate Hill and, from there, to the Red Lion in Dirty Lane, an alley that ran across to Long Acre in Covent Garden that was home to several Antients freemasons. The last entry in the lodge records was on 21 January 1761 and the lodge lapsed later that year.

Shoreditch to Bishopsgate

London Wall, the northern border of the City of London, bisected Bishopsgate, dividing it into two more or less equal sections within and without the City's walls. Bishopsgate itself marked the beginning of the Old North Road and a number of large coaching inns and taverns had been constructed alongside the road to accommodate passengers. These relatively grand buildings were interspersed with cheap and overcrowded housing for those working in the surrounding sweat shops outside and within the City proper. Strype described the neighbourhood outside the City wall as a 'continual building of tenements' that stretched to Shoreditch – named after Sir John de Soerditch – until eventually reaching open fields. Shoreditch itself extended from Norton Folgate to Old Street and from Finsbury to Bethnal Green. As development expanded north, what had once been a village became increasingly a pauperised continuation of Bishopsgate Street.

Of the thirty or so members resident in the area, seven specified an address in Holywell Lane in Shoreditch; three in Skinner's Street; and two at the Admiral Vernon, a tavern that hosted several Masonic lodges. Other members lived within a radius of a few hundred metres. Holywell Lane was located on the western side of Shoreditch and, according to Stow, was named after a water well which, by the early eighteenth century, had become spoiled by the manure heaps of the surrounding fields and market gardens that

Table 14 Shoreditch & Bishopsgate, 1751–5

List #	Name	Occupation	Address
96	John Scarr	Weaver	Holywell Lane, Shoreditch
98	Richard Stringer	Carpenter	Holywell Lane, Shoreditch
99	John Hopkins	Weaver	Holywell Lane, Shoreditch
104	William Gordon	Weaver	Holywell Lane, Shoreditch
121	Charles Murray	Weaver	Castle Street, Shoreditch
123	Joseph Henley	Baker	Shoreditch
139	Thomas Lynch	Weaver	King John's Court, Holy[well] Lane, Shoreditch
159	Samuel Watson	Housekeeper	Harwood's [Bell] Brewhouse, Shoreditch
160	George Pinfold	Weaver	King John's Court, Holywell Lane, Shoreditch
199	Joseph Henley	Baker	Shoreditch
245	John Osborne	Brewer	Shoreditch
261	Samuel Watson	Housekeeper	Harwood's Brewhouse, Shoreditch
295	John Neugent	Velvet Weaver	Black Jack, Porter's Fields
852	John Purcell	Weaver	near the Crown, Webb Square, Shoreditch
853	William Emery	Weaver	Castle Street, near Shoreditch Church
856	Michael White	Weaver	Red Lion, Holywell Lane, Shoreditch
140	James Ryan	Weaver	Half Moon Alley, Bishopsgate Street
180	John Jackson	Victualler	Admiral Vernon, Bishopsgate Street without
198	Patrick Scurloch		Mr Walkers' Half Moon Alley, Bishopsgate
200	John Coleman	Tailor	White Hart Court, Bishopsgate
352	Nathaniel Franks	Gentleman	Mr Frank's, Skinner Street
353	Joseph Pullum	Butcher	Bishopsgate Street Without
405	Omitted Holland	Bricklayer	Skinner Street, Bishopsgate Without
412	Daniel Rush	Painter	Norton Folgate
453	John Jackson	Victualler	Admiral Vernon, Bishopsgate Street without
496	Michael Wade	Dealer	Dunnings Alley, Bishopsgate Street
544	Patrick Flanagan	Victualler	Rosemary Branch, Artillery Lane, Bishopsgate Without
601	James Clifton	Staymaker	Skinner Street, Bishopsgate Without
919	James Stephens	Brewer	Primrose Street, Bishopsgate

served London. Holywell Mount, close by, was one of several local plague burial pits that dated from the Black Death of the seventeenth century. Another was further to the west in the artillery grounds of Finsbury. The parish was the site of a notable building workers strike and riot in the late 1730s. Local labourers had refused the low wages on offer for work on the reconstruction of St Leonard's church and were replaced by cheaper Irish labourers. The move triggered an anti-Irish riot that required the militia to be called out.

THE MINORIES, RATCLIFFE HIGHWAY, ROSEMARY LANE AND GOODMAN'S FIELDS

A warren of narrow streets advanced to the east of the Minories, with slum housing extending from the naval victualling office, slaughterhouse, pickle yards and the old Mint buildings east of the Tower of London, alongside and between Rosemary Lane, East Smithfield and the Ratcliffe Highway to Wapping, its warehouses and the docks. Although a slum, the district was more cosmopolitan than St Giles and St Martin's, with a leavening of discharged sailors, soldiers and failed or returned colonists. In the 1750s and later, it was also notorious for its prostitution, criminality and for its large expatriate Irish and Jewish communities. And in *Rookeries of London*, Thomas Beames described the area, what he termed 'this Cimmerian region':

> bounded on the south by the Thames, on the west by the Minories, on the north by the Commercial Road, on the east by the basin of the Regent's Canal . . . The rookeries of this neighbourhood, then, are among the oldest in London. They are bona fide rookeries built for the habitations of the poorest classes two hundred and fifty years since. Many of the buildings . . . are of wood – for the Great Fire, that wholesale purifier of these iniquities, did not extend to the Tower; so that the long narrow streets, with their branches and intersections of courts and alleys, remain in a condition little removed from their original form. The streets are not wider, less tortuous; the alleys are as formerly cul-de-sacs [and] the only entrance [is] from the street . . . the main thoroughfares are uneven, the roads narrow, the houses crumbling with age, with fronts of every variety.[58]

As London had expanded eastwards along the Ratcliffe Highway, Goodman's Field, a once open space to the north became progressively more the site of cheap housing, in Strype's words 'small, nasty and beggarly'. The area was beyond the formal legal jurisdiction of the City of London and gradually became associated with theatres, taverns and other entertainments, particularly prostitution, whose relationship with the docks and sailors on shore leave was parasitic and lasted into the twentieth century:

Table 15 Minories, Ratcliffe Highway and East London to the docks, 1751–5

List #	Name	Occupation	Address
Minories & the Tower			
314	Thomas Brothwick	Surgeon	Preston Court, Great Minories
316	William Dawes	Paper Stainer	Great Minories
338	Joseph Dover	Paper Stainer	Goodman's Yard, Minories
594	John Merryman	Wine Merchant	King Street, Tower Hill
812	Laurence Deering	Tailor	Angel & Sugar Loaf, [Minories]
906	Samuel Hutchins	Victualler	Red Cross, Minories
Ratcliffe Highway, Rosemary Lane & Rag Fair			
495	Thomas Brien	Bricklayer	Mrs Morgan's near Bluecoat
Fields, Ratcliffe Highway			
500	John Grainger	Victualler	Black Dog, Ratcliffe Highway
587	Alexander Dixon		Bull & Butcher, Rag Fair
588	William Byrne	Tailor	Bull's Head, R[adcliffe] Highway
595	Nathaniel Clarkson	Distiller	White Street, Goodmans Fields
596	Joseph Langser	Tallow Chandler	White Street, Goodmans Fields
602	Isaac Ducker		Maudlin's Rents, East Smithfield
286	Hugh Molloy	Shoemaker	Rosemary Lane
289	Thomas Cuddy	Hosier	Capel Street
290	Frances Allen	Victualler	King & Queen, Capel Street
291	Patrick Murphy	Baker	Old Gravel Lane, Wapping
294	William Kidney	Butcher	Capel Street
296	Jonathan Crafford	Tailor	King & Queen, Caple [Capel] Street
297	Corin Donovan	Salesman	New Exchange, Rosemary Lane
498	John Sullivan	Chapman	Rosemary Lane
501	Abraham Jacob	Salesman	Rosemary Lane
589	John Sullivan	Tailor	Rosemary Lane
590	Isaac Simon		Capel Street
597	James Lacy	Salesman	Rosemary Lane
603	Alexander Dixon		Bull & Butcher, Rag Fair
Wapping			
292	Peter Callan	Tailor	Capel Street
416	John Hamilton	Distiller	Hermitage, Wapping
417	Samuel Grant	Victualler	Thistle & Crown, Hermitage

the women associate chiefly with sailors and foreign mechanics and they have habits differing from those of the more destitute prostitutes of other districts but are even more closely congregated together than the former.[59]

By the mid-eighteenth century, the locality had also become a by-word for criminality and poverty. It remained so for over a century. An 1840 report on public health described it as 'a district proverbial for fever and filth' and its residents 'miserably neglected'.[60]

Pope, in the *Dunciad*, used the Rag Fair, a vast second hand clothes market stretching along Rosemary Lane, as a metaphor for the condition of those who lived there, as well as declining moral standards more widely:

Where wave the tatter'd ensigns of Rag-Fair,
A yawning ruin hangs and nods in air;
Keen, hollow winds howl thro' the bleak recess,
Emblem of Music caus'd by Emptiness.[62]

Rag Fair was more than merely a 'place near the Tower of London where old clothes and fripperies are sold'.[63] Many of the second hand goods for sale were stolen and the market was notorious across London both for fenced goods and the cheapest prostitutes in the city: 'a rare place for a miser to lay his lechery at a small expense, for two-pence will go as far here in woman's flesh as half a crown at Madam Quarles'.[64] Like St Giles, Ratcliffe Highway and Rag Fair were allegories for the underside of mid-eighteenth century London life. Newspaper reports throughout the period provide a vivid commentary on the violence, disorder and immorality with which both locations were associated, whether 'a squabble . . . in Rag Fair between some soldiers, two of whom were killed on the spot and several others wounded';[65] or a more general observation concerning 'the inhabitants of blind alehouses . . . the various clans of pedlars and hawkers that patrol through the streets or ply in Rag Fair'.[66]

Although Jewish traders were prominent participants in Rag Fair's second hand clothing market, the majority of the lodging houses and taverns were Irish. Over twenty Antients members gave an address in this somewhat insalubrious part of London. Examples include John Sullivan, a chapman or pedlar, and James Belles, a cobbler, both living in Rosemary Lane. Thomas Brien, a bricklayer and member of lodge No. 16, and John Grainger, a victualler. Both lived close to the Ratcliffe Highway, the former at 'Mrs Morgan's near Bluecoat Fields' and the latter at the 'Black Dog'. Joseph Langser, a distiller, and Nathaniel Clarkson, a tallow chandler, each lived in White Street in Goodman's Fields. Rosemary Lane was also home to at least one Jewish Antients freemason, Abraham Jacob, who gave his occupation as salesman. Other Jews noted in the Antients' register include Abraham Ardizaif of Broad Court, Covent Garden; Abraham Juers, a weaver, in Brick Lane; Isaac Wolfe, a shoemaker, in Old Playhouse Passage, Drury Lane; and Mordechai Isaacs, whose address was not stated. However, not all members from this part of London were from the working class. One member living to the west in King Street near Tower Hill, a more upmarket address, was John Merryman, the wine merchant whose widow Laurence Dermott subsequently married. His lodge number is not given in the register but his name appears at No. 594 in the chronological list of members. Another middling figure is Thomas Brothwick, a surgeon, and the aptly named William Kidney, a butcher in Capel Street, who would have been at least among the lower middling.

FLEET STREET, THE CITY AND ITS NORTHERN/WESTERN BORDERS

The City's membership list comprised several more middling members. It included James Shee, an attorney in Fetter Lane; and James Hartley, William Hindlestone and James Rowe, gentlemen living respectively at the Golden Fan at the centre of the City at Bucklersbury, the Star tavern in Salisbury Court off Fleet Street and Alderman Hoare's house in Fleet Street, probably linked to Hoare & Co., the merchant bankers. It also included John Gillum, a merchant in Norton Folgate, and Edward Vaughan, a surgeon living at the Blue Ball in Fleet Street. Many others appear to have been relatively affluent artisans, such as Richard Allen, a snuff box maker behind the Inns of Court in Gray's Inn Lane, and include those in the jewellery trade who were members of lodge No. 20. Tradesmen were also present: victuallers, distillers, weavers and shoemakers. But many were likely to be factory or shop owners and major or minor employers rather than poorly paid employees. Thomas Ginsell, for example, described as a weaver, lived at 13 Old Bridewell off Fleet Street. Bridewell was the location of a prison and a hospital, both run by the Corporation of London. William Ginsell, possibly his father, was one of those who had been appointed a governor by the City Corporation. As Stow noted: 'the private riches of London rest chiefly in the hands of the merchants and retailers, for artificers have not much to spare and labourers had need that it were given unto them'.[71] Many may have been among the more affluent members of the Antients and some of the more influential.

SOUTHWARK AND SOUTH OF THE THAMES

According to Strype's *Survey*, 'no part of London . . . is more populous than the borough of Southwark and parts adjacent.'[72] The comment was something of an overstatement. London south of the Thames was a relative backwater and, even in 1800, Southwark's population of 60–70,000 was only around 6 or 7 per cent of London's total population which was then approaching the million mark. Nonetheless, the completion of Westminster Bridge in 1750 and that at Blackfriars in 1770 greatly improved connections between the north and south banks of the Thames and the southern

Table 16 Fleet Street, Gray's Inn and the City of London, 1751–5

List #	Name	Occupation	Address
Fleet Street			
9	Nale McColm	Tailor	Ship, Fleet Ditch
48	Owen Tuder	Painter	Bride Lane
163	Edward Vaughan	Churgeon	Blue Ball, Fleet Street
189	Bryan Eagan	Clerk	Serjeant's Inn, Fleet Street
344	James Rowe	Gentleman	Alderman Hoare's, Fleet Street
350	Reginald Trotter	Victualler	Salisbury Court, Fleet Street
351	James Swift	Tailor	Salisbury Court, Fleet Street
380	Edmund Thomas	Distiller	Fleet Ditch
382	Thomas Ginsell	Weaver	Old Bridewell (No. 13) [Fleet Street]
756	William [Hindle]stone	Gentleman	Star, Salisbury Court, Fleet Street
967	Robert Hughes	Shoemaker	Maypole Alley, Stanhope Street
Clerkenwell			
18	Thomas Humber	Watchmaker	Bishop's Court, St James's, Clerkenwell
30	James Owen	Snuff Box Painter	Coldbath Fields [Clerkenwell]
269	Richard Roodes	Bricklayer	next door, [Baffners, Hick's Hall]
377	Thomas Humber	Watchmaker	Bishop's Court, St James's, Clerkenwell
Gray's Inn			
44	George Robinson	Painter	Leicester Street, Gray's Inn Lane
45	Thomas Figg	Victualler	Plaisterers' Arms, Little Gray's Inn Lane
46	Charles McCarty	Painter	Flower de Luce Court, Gray's Inn Lane
51	Richard Allen	Snuff Box Maker	Tash Court, Gray's Inn Lane
55	James George Smith	Britches Maker	No. 2, Tash Court, Gray's Inn Lane
57	John Adams	Painter	Plaisterers' Arms, Little Gray's Inn Lane
264	James Henderson	Hair Merchant	Corner, Gray's Inn Lane
450	William Bowen	Peruke Maker	Gray's Inn Passage
1004	Edward Hurley	Shoemaker	Gray's Inn Lane
City of London			
22	John Smith	Victualler	The Cripple, Little Britain
25	James Hagerty	Painter	Leather Lane
27	Henry Lewis	Jeweller	Mr Foster's Jeweller, Wood Street, Cheapside
29	George Hebden	Cabinetmaker	Pied Bull, Whitecross Street
32	Christian Pidgeon	Shopkeeper	Aldersgate Street
34	Owen Tuder	Painter	Mr Bromidge [Bromwich], Ludgate Hill
54	John Casey	Hair Curler	near The Boot, Dowgate Hill

60	Bartholomew Scully	Paper smith	next to the White Horse, Hosier Lane
91	James Hartley	Gentleman	Gold[en] Fan, Bucklersbury
92	Thomas Brenen	Hosier	opposite The Stationers' Arms, Saffron Hill
133	John Freebold	Jeweller	St Martin's le Grand
171	Joseph Settrec	Tallow Chandler	St Martin's le Grand
162	John Wilson	Peruke Maker	Snow Hill, [Farringdon]
182	John Cartwright	Watchmaker	Red Lion Court, Church Lane
206	John Coleman	Victualler	Horse Shoe, Ludgate Hill
208	John Spence	Carpenter	Grey Hound Court
209	Joseph Gifford	Carpenter	Little Britain
214	John Gillum	Merchant	Hog Lane, Norton Folgate
231	Robert McNeal	Linen Draper	Lukes Court, St Martin's-le-Grand
241	Edward Flanagan	Tailor	Globe Court, Fish Street Hill
251	Robert Hall	Shoemaker	Next door Temple & Sun, Shoe Lane
378	John Callheath	Tyler	Little Britain
381	Noblet O'Keefe	Watchmaker	Great Arthur Street
383	John Haughton	Silversmith	Great Arthur Street
397	James Allen	Lapidary	Dean's Court, St Martin's le Grand
408	William Cranfield	Painter	Basinghall Street
458	Samuel Gabraith	Watchmaker	Great Arthur Street
459	George Stretton	Printer	Cursitor Street, Chancery Lane
461	David Jacks	Book Binder	Addle Hill, Upper Thames Street
467	John Hosier	Britches Maker	Gosswell Street or Brick Lane, Old Street
489	James McLaughlin	Victualler	Red Hart, Shoe Lane, Farringdon
506	John Hogan	Tailor	Mr Greenwood's Shoemaker, Blackfriars
522	Thomas Edes	Victualler	Hampshire Hog, Gosswell Street
528	John Bowring	Peruke Maker	Mr Rayners' Cannon Street
541	Isaac Ducker	Carpenter	Maudlin's Rents, East Smithfield
674	Henry Lewis	Jeweller	Mr Foster's Jeweller, Wood Street, Cheapside
890	Samuel Galbraith	Watchmaker	Great Arthur Street (cf. 458)
898	Omitted Hickey		next door to Queens Head in the Old Bailey
910	John Pick	Tailor	Opposite the Horse Shoe, Blackfriars
918	John Hare	Victualler	Queens Head, Leadenhall Street
1003	Thomas Mansell	Shoemaker	Fetter Lane

Table 17 Southwark & South of the Thames, 1751–5

List #	Name	Occupation	Address
103	Britton Peter	Hatter	Gravel Lane, Southwark
134	Samuel Church	Tailor	White Hart Yard [Southwark]
178	Mathew Doyle	Linen Printer	Broadwall, Southwark
179	James Moran	Linen Printer	Broadwall, Southwark
181	William Bryant	Pipemaker	Broadwall, Southwark
222	John Woodward	Linen Printer	Broadwall, Southwark
223	Mathew Doyle	Linen Printer	Broadwall, Southwark
224	James Moran	Linen Printer	Broadwall, Southwark
225	William Bryant	Pipemaker	Broadwall, Southwark
226	Thomas Sneath	Victualler	Mitre, Broadwall, Southwark
227	John Eustace	Linen Printer	Mitre, Broadwall, Southwark
229	Thomas McGuire	Linen Printer	Southwark
230	John Sheridan	Hatter	Broadwall, Southwark
234	James Say	Glazier	Upper Ground, Church Street, Southwark
235	Robert Blount	Wine Merchant	Upper Ground, Church Street, Southwark
262	James Glover	Pipemaker	Broadwall, Southwark
283	Martin Norton	Watchmaker	Next door, Ship, New Street [Illegible]
332	Richard Dawson	Grocer	Sugar Loaf, Long Lane
333	Patrick Simpson	Cabinetmaker	Glassenbury Ct, Long Lane
345	Thomas Whitney	Smith	Upper Ground, X's Church, Southwark
358	Laurence Reilly	Hatter	Mint, Southwark
433	Miles Burke	Hatter	White Hart, Gravel Lane, Southwark
545	William Sherry	Blacksmith	Upper Ground, Southwark
556	Mathew Doyle	Linen Printer	Southwark
557	James Moran	Linen Printer	Southwark
558	Thomas McGuire	Linen Printer	Southwark
813	Edward Angel	Painter	Green Walk, near the Falcon, Southwark
814	John Hall	Distiller	Gravel Lane, Southwark
922	William Atkins	Smith	Near Eight Bells Church, Southwark
354	Benjamin Dove	Gentleman	Mr Gardener's, Hedge Lane
390	William Brangan	Tailor	Black Boy, Hedge Lane
444	Abraham Stones	Founder	Black Moor's Head, Hedge Lane
478	William Brangan	Tailor	Black Boy, Hedge Lane
238	John Abercromby	Victualler	Marsh's Tap House, Borough
239	Israel Wolfe	Victualler	Marsh's Tap House, Borough

385	Thornhill Heathcoat	Gentleman	Borough
183	John Scholefield	Watchmaker	Shand
263	Thomas Stuart	Linen Printer	Round Court, Shand
281	Alexander Dixon	Tailor	Ship Alley, Well Close Square
375	Samuel Green	Victualler	Brown Bear, Shand
585	James Main	Shipwright	at the Success, Woolwich

parishes of Southwark, Bermondsey and Borough developed to house those providing good and services to Westminster and the City. The result was a small economic boom south of the Thames and an expansion in local construction.

Apart from the building trades, the majority of south-bank residents were in the riverside trades or worked in brewing, small-scale manufacture, or as shopkeepers, taverns and street hawkers. Others serviced the many prisons in the borough: the notorious Marshalsea and King's Bench debtors' prisons; the Surrey Gaol;[73] the Clink, a prison burned down in the 1780 Gordon Riots; and the Borough Compter on Southwark High Street. Southwark was also home to St Thomas's Hospital, one of London's largest, rebuilt in the early eighteenth century. Around thirty Antients freemasons lived in the district, with a handful further downstream in Bermondsey, Rotherhithe and Woolwich. Nearly half were in or near Broadwall and Upper Ground, with its timber yards and wharfs; others were located at Shand and on Gravel Lane, also close to the Thames. Almost all members appear to have had semi skilled or unskilled occupations, including seven linen printers and three hatters. The other occupations stated included tailor, victualler, blacksmith, cook and pipe maker.

Moderns' freemasonry had been active in Southwark since the 1720s. The Bull's Head tavern at Southwark was one of London's earliest lodges, No. 15 on the 1729 engraved list at Grand Lodge with a warrant that dated from 1 April 1723. It survived until 1776. Other lodges had been established at the King's Arms on St Margaret's Hill; at the Fountain Tavern; the Prince of Orange's Head; and at the Mitre in Mint Street. In the 1740s, Masonic lodges met at the Queen's Arms, the Swan, the Fox in Castle Street and the Golden Horseshoe, which later relocated to the Woolpack. In contrast, there were relatively few Antients' lodges. The first, established on 13 November 1752, met at the Mitre on Broadwall. The last entry in its minute book was in 1763 and the lodge number was declared vacant in 1787. The second, warranted on 7 December 1752, met at the Marshalsea Tap House, within the debtors' prison. It later moved to the Tiger's Head in Borough and thereafter to the Black Bull. The lodge failed in 1757 and the warrant number was reassigned the following year. That only two out of some thirty-seven Antients' lodges established between 1751 and 1754 met south of the Thames and that both failed to survive may speak to the relative paucity of members (and of the London Irish) who lived in the district.

WESTMINSTER, SOHO AND PICCADILLY

The relatively large number of Antients' freemasons living and working in and around Westminster does not imply a uniform or high level of affluence. A few, such as William Lansdowne, a goldsmith, and Robert Turner and Henry Jellybrain, gentlemen, had occupations or titles that might be regarded as middling. Others may also have employed rather than been employees. However, the detail contained in certain members' addresses is instructive. Green Street to the south east of Leicester Fields, home to Thomas Weer, William Carney and Robert Keely, was also known as Dirty Lane and linked the area to Long Acre and Covent Garden. Dirty Lane was the address given by two other Antients masons, Michael Sandipher and John Eare, who lived at the eastern end of the street. And Carnaby and St James's markets were both active street markets in the mid-eighteenth century and not the more fashionable areas they would later become. The Haymarket was also an accurate description, with carts regularly blocking the area on the three days a week the market operated – Tuesdays, Thursdays and Saturdays.[76] Mottley's *Survey* described the Haymarket as 'a spacious street of great resort, full of inns and houses of entertainment, especially on the west side', with coaching inns and yards providing stabling, food and drink.[77] Additional entertainment was offered by two theatres, one 'in which operas are performed in the Italian language, and singers for that purpose brought from Italy at excessive price'; the second 'presently taken up by a pack of French strollers'.[78] And as in Covent Garden and elsewhere, such entertainment attracted brothels, street walkers and similar aspects of the vice trade.

Other streets were equally questionable as residential locations. Suffolk Street and Little Suffolk Street at the southern end of the Haymarket were described as having 'fallen into decay and disrepute'.[79] Shug Lane was 'an old and narrow thoroughfare', 'meanly built', linking Davies Street at the north of Berkeley Square to the Oxford Road.[80] Perhaps worse, 'neither are its inhabitants much to be boasted of'.[81] And although the location of several large mansions, including Burlington House and Devonshire House, and, by the 1720s, developed four or five blocks west of its junction with St James's Street, Piccadilly was at the western border of the metropolis. It bordered the country and was considered by Mottley and others to be 'a place of no great account'.[82] Soho lay roughly between St Martin's and St Giles to the east, Leicester Fields to the south and the Oxford Road to the north. The area reflected in mosaic the different and varied characteristics of its residents and neighbours. While Dean Street may have been 'a very good street, well built and inhabited by the gentry', others were mainly occupied by Huguenot émigrés.[83] Thus, although Compton Street had well-fashioned houses, it was considered 'of no great account for its inhabitants, which are chiefly French'; Wardour Street was 'very ordinary and ill inhabited'; and Greek Street blighted by 'dead walls, which generally are dirty and ill kept'.[84]

Table 18 Westminster & the West End of London, 1751–5

List #	Name	Occupation	Address
3	William Taylor	Bookseller	Little Suffolk Street, Haymarket
82	John Willis	Upholder	Haymarket
84	William Taylor	Bookseller	Little Suffolk Street, Haymarket
301	William Rankin	Cardmaker	Knave of Clubs, Haymarket
325	John Atkinson	Shoemaker	Shug Lane
330	Edward Broadstreet	Poulterer	Shug Lane
336	William Dixon	Peruke Maker	Bell & Goat, Haymarket
343	Michael Wilcox	Tinman	Shug Lane
391	Patrick Carr	Tailor	Highlander, Suffolk Street
401	William McDowell	Carpenter	Coventry Court, Haymarket
409	Andrew Porteus	Bookseller	Shug Lane
480	Patrick Carr	Tailor	Highlander, Suffolk Street
504	Thomas Fannin	Tailor	Little Suffolk Street, Haymarket
505	George Butler	Tailor	Mr Cosgriss's, Suffolk Street, Haymarket
517	John Hartley		Norris Street, St James's Market [off Haymarket]
536	Omitted Timewell	Victualler	White Hart, Shug Lane
97	William Furlong		Crown, Green Street, Leicester Fields
100	John McDowell	Carpenter	the Crown, Green Street, Leicester Fields
101	William McDowell	Carpenter	the Crown, Green Street, Leicester Fields
315	John Montgomery	Peruke Maker	Leicester Street
340	Jeremiah Evans	Engraver	Blue Last, Bear St, Leicester Fields
765	Omitted Yateman	Tallow Chandler	Bear Street [Leicester Fields]
903	John Byrne		Next Horse & Groom, Castle St, Leicester Fields
135	Thomas Bradbury	Printer	Grafton Street [Piccadilly]
146	William Turner	Peruke Maker	Mr Fry's, Swallow Street
150	John MacFarquhar	Peruke Maker	at the corner of Clifford Street
151	Richard Kitchen	Victualler	the George, opp. the Church, Piccadilly
335	John Barnet	Shoemaker	Albemarle House
622	William Turner	Peruke Maker	Mr Fry's, Swallow Street
628	Richard Kitchen	Victualler	The George, opp. the Church, Piccadilly
16	Loghlin McIntosh	Printer	Crow, Patrick's Alley, St Patrick's Churchyard
88	Barnaby Hackett		next to the Red Lion, Portland Street, Soho

203	Evan McKenzie	Victualler	Carlisle Arms [Soho]
218	William Lansdowne	Goldsmith	Soho Square
221	Evan McKenzie	Victualler	Carlisle Arms, Soho
308	John Craig	Watchmaker	Litchfield Street, Soho
331	John Fulton	Cabinetmaker	Great Poultney Street
342	Omitted Brown	Shoemaker	White Horse, Hungerford Market
363	Collin McKenzie	Tailor	Carlisle Arms, Queen Street, Soho
438	Edward Shea	Shoemaker	The Boot, Compton Street, St Anne's, Soho
464	James Bedford	Victualler	Crown Street, St Patrick's Churchyard
484	George Hutchinson	Cabinetmaker	at Mr Doby's in Litchfield Street, Soho
509	Thomas Pyke	Glazier	Greek Street, Soho
527	John Pittot	Cabinetmaker	Rathbone Place, Soho
537	John Curtis	Peruke Maker	Dean Street, Soho
547	John McCoy	Slater	No. 4, Crown Court, Dean Street, Soho
233	John Corbet	Joiner	Carnaby Street
326	James Ward	Peruke Maker	Clifford St, Bond St
394	Thomas O'Hara	Hatter	Carnaby Market
395	Peter Ward	Hatter	Carnaby Market
524	James Newman	Feltmaker	Marshall Street, Carnaby Market
525	Charles Ward	Engraver	Heddon Street, Golden Square
535	Jeremiah Egan	Tailor	Duke Street
584	Alexander Giddes	Peruke maker	Vine Street
974	Peter Ward	Hatter	Carnaby Market
2	James Hagan	Peruke Maker	Goat & Ass, Pall Mall
4	John Doughty	Shoemaker	Prince of Wales Arms, Pall Mall
300	Robert Turner	Gentleman	Eagle & Child, Petty France, Westminster
418	Richard Pierce	Carpenter	Westminster
419	Francis White	Carpenter	Westminster
441	James Hagan	Peruke Maker	Goat & Ass, Pall Mall
448	William Hubbard		Blue Last, Petty France, Westminster
454	Archibald McDiarmid	Musician	Crown Court, Westminster
538	Benjamin Turner	Pipemaker	Great St Anne's Lane, Westminster
583	Philip Hillier	Cooper	Gardener's Lane, Westminster
586	Henry Jellybrain	Gentleman	Chapel Street, Westminster
961	Richard Hodgson	Baker	New Street, St James's, Westminster

Table 19 The First Antients' Lodges, 1751–3

Lodge	Location	Year
No. 2	Turk's Head, Greek Street, Soho[87]	1751
	Rising Sun, Suffolk Street, Haymarket	1752
	Thistle & Crown, Church Court, Strand	1752
	King's Head, Hewitt's Court, Strand	1754
No. 3	Cripple, Little Britain[88]	1751
	Crown, St Paul's Churchyard	1752
No. 4	Cannon, Water Lane, Fleet Street[89]	1751
	Temple & Sun, Shire Lane, Temple Bar	1752
	Red Hart, Shoe Lane, Covent Garden	1753
	Bedford Arms, Bedford Court, Covent Garden	1754
	Swan & Cross Keys, Long Acre	1755
No. 5	Plaisterers' Arms, Little Gray's Inn Lane[90]	1751
	Horse Shoe, Ludgate Hill	1752
	Red Lion, Dirty Lane, Long Acre	1754
No. 6	Globe, Bridges Street, Covent Garden[91]	1751
	Brown Bear, Strand	1752
	Rose & Crown, Clare Court, Drury Lane	1753
No. 7	Fountain, Monmouth Street, Seven Dials[92]	Erased 1752
No. 7	Temple & Sun, Shire Lane, Temple Bar[93]	1752
	Angel Inn, Wich [Wych] Street, Strand	1754
	Two Blue Posts, Cockpit Alley, Drury Lane	1755
No. 8	Admiral Vernon, Bishopsgate Street Without[94]	1752
No. 9	Ship & Anchor, Quaker Street, Spitalfields[95]	1752
	Thistle & Crown, Church Court, Strand	1752
No. 10	Duke's Head, Winfield Street, Spitalfields[96]	Erased 1752
No. 10	Admiral Vernon, Bishopsgate Street Without[97]	1752
No. 11	Mitre, Broadwall, Southwark[98]	1752
No. 12	Carlisle Arms, Queen Street, Soho[99]	1752
	White Hart, Shug Lane	1753
	White Swan, New Street, Covent Garden	1753
No. 13	Marshalsea Taphouse[100]	1753
	Tiger's Head, Borough	1754
	Black Bull, Borough	1754

No. 14	Plaisterers Arms, Little Gray's Inn Lane[101]	1753
	Thistle & Crown, Church Court, Strand	1753
	Turk's Head, East St, Red Lion Square	1754
	Crown, Church Court, Fleet Street	1755
No. 15	King's Head, Marylebone Street, Golden Square[102]	1753
	Thistle & Crown, Swallow Street	1755
No. 16	King & Queen, Capel Street, Rosemary Lane[103]	1753
No. 17	Scots Arms, Haymarket	1753
	White Hart, Shug Lane	
No. 18	Admiral Vernon, Bishopsgate Street Without[104]	1753
	Three Sugar Loaves, St John's Street	1754
	Bull & Butcher, Rag Fair	1754
No. 19	Fountain Inn, Monmouth Street, Seven Dials[105]	1753
	George, Broad Street, St Giles	1754
No. 20	Hampshire Hog, Goswell Street[106]	1753
No. 21	One Tun, Strand[107]	1753
	Cheshire Cheese, Savoy Alley	1754
No. 22	King's Head, Little Suffolk Street[108]	1753
	Bull's Head, St Martin's Lane	1754
No. 23	White Lion, Hemmings Row[109]	1753
	George, Piccadilly	1754
	Prince of Wales' Head, Long Acre, Covent Garden	1754
No. 24	Edinburgh Castle, Marsh Street, Bristol[110]	1753
No. 25	Unicorn, West Street, Lafford's Gate, Bristol[111]	1753
	Three Indian Kings, Small Street, Bristol	1754
No. 26	Rosemary Branch, Rosemary Lane[112]	1753
No. 27	Prince of Wales' Head, Capel Street, Rosemary Lane[113]	1753
	Prince of Wales' Head, Rag Fair	1755
No. 28	Royal Oak, Charing Cross[114]	1753
No. 29	George, Piccadilly[115]	1753

✷ ✷ ✷

In addition to providing a solid basis for analysing the character and composition of the Antients membership during the period 1751–55, the *General Register* also details where the earliest lodges were located. As might be expected, these overlap with those districts that feature most frequently in the membership lists themselves: St Giles, Covent Garden and the Strand; Temple Bar, Fleet Street, Gray's Inn, the City and the east by the docks; and south of the Thames.

Despite the efforts expended by John Lane in compiling his *Masonic Records*, accurately tracing the history of individual Antients lodges is not straightforward. The first problem is that on 27 December 1752, the lodges were renumbered:

> Bro. Thomas Blower, Master of (the then) No. 8 in the Chair, ordered that lodge Nos. 7 and 10 be 'discontinued . . . for their disobedience.

Lodge No. 8 accordingly became No. 7; No. 9 moved to No. 8; and each lodge from No. 11 to No. 16 moved up two places. Second, and complicating matters further, they were renumbered repeatedly thereafter. In addition and as noted, when older warrants became available because a lodge had failed or been expelled, the vacant number was either sold to raise money for the Antients' Grand Charity, or reutilised, by moving another lodge to the unoccupied location. The same practice applied in Ireland from where it may have been inherited. Another problem is that many lodges were peripatetic, moving the location of their meeting place often, and frequently more than once a year.

In the absence of a complete set of minute books, it is hard to track individual lodges with absolute certainty and historians, including Lane, sometimes confuse Antients and Moderns lodges before the 1813 union where the same lodge number is common to both. Notwithstanding such hurdles, Table 19 sets out the details of those Antients lodges warranted in the two years immediately following the creation of Antients Grand Lodge. The first position on the lodge register was left blank intentionally. The conceit was copied from the Grand Lodge of Ireland where the Grand Master's Lodge headed the roll of lodges, albeit unnumbered.[85] The position was filled five years later. Antients lodge No. 1, the Grand Master's lodge, was formed in 1756 following the appointment of the earl of Blessington and formally received its warrant on 13 August 1759. Tangentially, at its first minuted meeting on 5 September 1759, a petition was granted to issue a Provincial Grand Warrant for 'the Brethren at Philadelphia', the first step in the Antients' colonisation of American freemasonry.[86]

CHAPTER FOUR

London's Magistracy and the London Irish

The freemasonry associated with the Moderns, the original Grand Lodge of England, had reflected the mores of its founders. Established in 1717, it was from the start a dynamic and explicitly pro-establishment organisation with strong government connections. As such, it was linked closely to the Whig magistracy, especially in London, where the government held a particularly tight sway over appointments to the bench.[1] London freemasonry's association with the Middlesex and Westminster benches and the packed grand juries of the Quarter Sessions was based on common political, economic and philosophical interests that embraced a strongly pro-Hanoverian and Whiggist approach: 'the cause of your God, your king and your country'.[2] The freemasons who sat on the bench and the magistrates who sat in the lodge believed in, upheld and enforced the laws that protected the gentry and the middling against the mob.

> Justices would be vigilant to detect and produce to punishment all those who . . . attempt the subversion of the great basis upon which stands all that is or can be dear to England and Protestants . . . our religion, our liberty and our property.[3]

It is almost self-evident that the stereotypical perception and treatment of the eighteenth-century London Irish as drunken, criminal, papist and disaffected, would prejudice or prevent their fraternal embrace by the Grand Lodge of England and its constituent lodges. Writ large, London's lower middling and working classes – especially the Irish – were placed as social outcasts at the margins of organised society and the Middlesex and Westminster benches worked to ensure that the majority remained there.[4]

The lowly economic and social position of the London Irish was not simply a function of their status as recent émigrés. Many if not most would have been subject to anti-Irish and anti-Catholic prejudice that ran from legal discrimination to periodic mob violence. The Spitalfields riot in 1736 against competition from cheaper Irish labour is an obvious example. Perhaps more insidiously, the economic and institutional bias against the London Irish working class was such that by the 1740s and 1750s, anti-Irish bigotry was endemic. Mainly absent from the treatment of the Welsh and Scots, it pushed the Irish to the borders of the capital's economic activities and entrenched their poverty. Several of London's many slums became effectively Irish

Table 20 Frequency Analysis of Irish Surnames in Criminal Trials at the Old Bailey, 1740–90

Surname	Frequency
Boyle	29
Burke	54
Byrne	27
Callahan/Callaghan	8
Carroll/O'Carroll	39
Collins	316
Conner/Connor/O'Connor	155
Connolly	20
Daly	18
Doherty/O'Doherty	0
Donnelly	15
Doyle	100
Duff/Duffy	32
Donne/Dunn/Dunne	132
Gallagher	0
Hughes	420
Kelly	201
Kennedy	129
Lynch	60
Martin	536
McGuire	2
Moore	325
Murphy	360
Murray	188
Neal/Neil/O'Neil	23
Nolan	3
O'Brian/O'Brien	55
O'Donnel/O'Donnell	5
Quin/Quinn	70
Reilly/O'Reilly	9
Ryan	96
Sullivan/O'Sullivan	143
Thompson	715
Walsh	17
Total	**4,302**

ghettos, nicknamed 'Little Dublin', 'The Holy Land' or 'Paddy Town', the designations reflected the vast numbers of Irish congregating there.[5]

Life in the rookeries often precluded social and economic assimilation and cemented many into penury at the bottom of society's ladder. Perhaps inevitably, poverty begat crime, and although criminality was far from limited to the London Irish and seasonal Irish workers, the publicity given to prosecutions and convictions from within those quarters reinforced the popular image of the Irish as feckless and violent. In short, they were portrayed and treated as the epitome of the undeserving poor.

Although it would be incorrect to reach a firm conclusion on the basis of inadequate data, a preliminary analysis suggests that the number of Irish appearing before the various magistrates' benches in London and the Central Criminal Court at the Old Bailey was disproportionately high as a percentage of London's working classes. Criminal records for the period 1740–90 document only a modest number of instances – just over a hundred – where the defendant's nationality is stated specifically as Irish. However, an analysis using the surname of those appearing before the bench may provide greater insight.[6] A basic data search of criminal trials at the Old Bailey using thirty-four common Irish surnames (but excluding 'Smith') indicates that the number of trials that probably involved at least one Irishman or woman was around 4,300, albeit that certain cases are reported more than once and that some of those appearing may not have been Irish or descended from Irish-born parents or grandparents.[7] A second round analysis of the same data using metaphones and phonetic spellings, rather than the modern spelling of each surname, raises the number of relevant cases significantly. Moreover, given that the analysis is with respect to a numerical minority of those surnames commonly linked to Ireland, it may be reasonable to assume that the total number of criminal prosecutions involving an Irish defendant or victim (and often both) would have been considerably in excess of 4,300.

The majority of Old Bailey trials were for assault, stealing or petty theft. However, a minority were more serious and included breaking and entering, counterfeiting, and robbery and violence, including murder. Of course, Irish defendants were not always found guilty. However, where the Court ruled against them, punishment was often severe, and seemingly more so than in the case of non-Irish offenders.[8] It should be noted that the following analysis excludes all less serious offences which were brought before the magistrates' benches. Were the relevant data to be included, the number of Irish-linked cases would be far higher. To take only one example, the name 'Collins' featured on over 700 occasions in the period 1740–90 in the Middlesex Sessions alone.

It is necessary to emphasise again that the above data is designed only to point towards the probability or strong possibility of Irish nationality; it is not definitive and many of those named may have been English or Scottish. Reliable judicial statistics disaggregated by nationality were not compiled officially before the 1860s. However, an examination of the nineteenth century data indicates that the Irish were five times more likely to be prosecuted and convicted than were the English or Welsh.[9] And it can be argued that the later data provides a reasonable indication of what may have occurred fifty to a hundred years earlier. Public and private attitudes did not alter materially and were not dissimilar in the mid-eighteenth century, nor did the approach adopted by the British judiciary benefit from any fundamental change. Roger Swift, commenting on the mid-Victorian view of the Irish and criminality, might have been speaking of the 1760s when he suggested that 'the link between Irish immigration, crime and disorder . . . was widely regarded . . . as axiomatic'.[10] In Swift's characterisation:

> [English] society's widespread belief in the innate criminality of the Irish – and, more particularly, of the Irish poor – formed an integral component of the negative side of the Irish stereotype.[11]

Indeed, Georgian literature, press and court reports all offer strong confirmation that such views were not new in the 1850s and 1860s but had powerful antecedents a century earlier.

Despite the acquittal for lack of evidence of many of those accused, the general and popular view of the Irish as drunken, lazy and criminal remained disabused: the Victorian view that the London Irish 'lived off thievery' was current in the 1750s.[12] The press added to the prejudices of their readers and a pejorative description of Irish defendants commonly preceded accounts of eighteenth-century cases. Court reports were more factual, often reporting verbatim. However, the extent of anti-Irish bigotry was nonetheless detailed with clarity: 'you Irish bog-trotting dog';[13] and 'an hundred Irish dogs'.[14]

Three cases from the many thousands that featured at the Old Bailey cannot provide a representative sample of the multitude that involved Irish defendants. However, they do support the argument that discrimination was visibly present on the bench as elsewhere.

In the first case, Martin Malone and William Bruce had been arraigned for the assault on the public highway of a Post Office employee, Thomas Smith, and accused of robbing him of 'a peruke, a silk handkerchief and 8s 10d in money'.[15] Witness statements make clear that the accused were present when the crime occurred. The following lines are extracted from the trial record on the final day. The evidence of prejudice is overt: 'I would have paid for lodging but they said I was an Irishman and they would not let me have any'. The poverty and displacement of those accused is equally obvious. Having failed to find work in London, the defendants were seeking employment elsewhere in order to earn sufficient funds to return to Ireland, 'to get what would carry us home'. Martin Malone, was acquitted. William Bruce was found guilty and sentenced to death:

> Prisoner: Please your Honour I came out of Ireland to look for work, I was scarce of money and was returning home; I lay at the upper end of Barnet; I would have paid for lodging, but they said I was an Irishman and they would not let me have any. We were very cold when the daylight came; as

we were cold we said to one another, we had better be going to Coventry, to get what would carry us home.

In the second case, Michael Magennis had been indicted for the murder of Richard Shears.[16] Having heard conflicting evidence as to the facts of the charge, the court heard witness evidence attesting to the accused's character. Despite the defendant's referees, he was found guilty and sentenced to death:

Mary Callowham: I live servant with the prisoner; I never saw a hanger or cutlass or any such weapon in his house in my life; I did not hear the man was killed till about a month after he was dead and buried.

Thomas Reed: I am a milkman, I have known the prisoner between five and six years, I never saw anything amiss of him in my life, he has been a lodger of mine above a year and half.
Q. What business is he of? Reed. He is a milkman.
Q. What country man is he? Reed. He is an Irishman.

Mary Palace: I have known him six years, he deals where I deal; I never heard he was quarrelsome in all my life, or to have such arms as he is accused with.

John Jones: I have known him about four or five years; I am not greatly acquainted with his life and conversation, I have had dealings with him.

Tho. Burchell: I have known him about four years, I never saw anything of him that was like quarrelsome ; he once owed me a debt and when he was in gaol he paid me £3 of it.

Owen Jones: I have known him about a year, he used my house; I never heard anything bad of him.

Tho. Richards: I have known him about a year and half, I am little acquainted with his character; I have had dealings with him, he paid me very honestly.

In the third example, John Barry had been indicted for stealing two guineas, one moidore, and a shirt, with a value of 10s. The goods and money were the property of John Gutteridge, Barry's employer.[17] The following extract is taken from the record of the trial at the Old Bailey. The verdict was guilty and the sentence transportation:

John Gutteridge: I am a brush maker and live at the corner of Long Lane, West Smithfield; the prisoner was my journeyman. On Saturday, 14th of June, in the evening, I went out of town and left the prisoner at work in the shop; and the money and shirt mentioned were locked up. I returned on the 16th; I found my till below-stairs broke open and the things above stairs tumbled about; and upon missing the shirt and money I took up the prisner.

Mr Pool: I was with the prosecutor and prisoner at the Ram Inn and heard the prisoner confess that he secreted himself in his master's house on Saturday-night and lay there till Sunday at noon; that he robbed him of a moidore, two guineas and eighteen-pence, and a shirt; and he delivered what money he had left back again.

Prisoner: I am an Irishman, a stranger in this country. I leave it to the mercy of the court.

The benchmark public view of the London Irish was a caricature. But it provides a context for the broader attitude of the English establishment in the early and mid-eighteenth century, including many of those at the Grand Lodge of England and its more influential constituent lodges. London's freemasons had financial, political and social concerns regarding the influx of Irish freemasons, including their reliance on and proclivity for alcohol and gin, in particular. In contrast to what might be regarded as the respectable poor, it was widely if incorrectly held that the London Irish were broadly criminal and probably papist, and the antithesis of deserving. However, even where charitable support might be due, the sheer volume of migration and the rising number of those settling in London posed a threat to the system of poor relief and the financial viability of individual lodge charities and, possibly, that of the central Grand Charity itself.

Providing aid and support for indigent masons had been a tenet of Masonic benevolence for many years, but there were caveats. These were explicit, for example, that a recipient should be a member of a recognised and regular Masonic lodge for at least five years, and implicit, that those destitute should be deserving of Masonic support.[18] Resistance to émigré freemasons being recognised as genuine masons and therefore legitimate recipients of Masonic charity translated into an effective bar and it was not until 30 November 1752 that the Grand Lodge of England gave permission to its Charity Committee to dispose of up to £5 'to relieve any foreign indigent brother', and only then 'after due examination'.[19] However, although financial concerns may have had resonance, perhaps the crucial factor that determined English and London freemasonry's widespread condescension towards the London Irish was the influence of senior members of the Westminster, Middlesex and City magistracy. Magistrates were positioned on the establishment's front line; their principal function was to deter and punish offences against property and the person, prevent individual and mass disorder, uphold the tenets of parliament's 'wise administration' and castigate sedition.

In 1738, shortly after his appointment as a Deputy Lord Lieutenant for Middlesex, Nathaniel Blackerby, a former Deputy Grand Master of English

Grand Lodge and its first Grand Treasurer, was elected chairman of the Westminster bench.[20] Blackerby had served as a justice of the peace for over two decades and succeeded in the chair other Masonic colleagues including William Cowper, previously Grand Secretary and Deputy Grand Master, and Leonard Streate, both of whom were members with Blackerby of the duke of Richmond's influential Horn Tavern lodge. Blackerby's speech to the Westminster justices on his election was designed to remind his colleagues of their political and moral obligations:

> as you expect a blessing on yourselves, families and posterity . . . exert yourselves for the preservation of the laws of your country . . . consider the duty you owe as subjects to your King, under whose mild government and wise administration every man enjoys the fruits of his labour, his liberty, his property.[21]

His words echoed those of William Cowper a decade before:

> It ought always to be a matter of particular distinction . . . that justices would be vigilant to detect and produce to punishment all those who . . . attempt the subversion of the great basis upon which stands all that is or can be dear to England and Protestants . . . it is . . . for our religion, our liberty and our property.[22]

Indeed,

> the magistrate . . . is trusted to uphold the honour, the dignity and the majesty of the state; to see that order is observed; that equal right be done according to known and approved law . . . and whoever assumes . . . such powers upon any other principle is and should be treated as a subverter of peace, order and good government . . . and an enemy to human society.[23]

The parallels with Desaguliers and Payne's Masonic charges are clear. Each newly-made freemason was obliged to swear an oath to be not only 'a good man and true' but also:

> strictly to obey the moral law . . . to be a peaceable subject and cheerfully to conform to the laws of the country . . . not to be concerned in plots and conspiracies against government [and] submit to the decisions of the supreme legislature [and] . . . the civil magistrate.[24]

Aside from the function of the bench in penalising crime and punishing disorder, the barrier between the magistracy and the working classes, and not just the London Irish, was compounded and reinforced by the role of the bench in adjudicating and implementing employment law. This was governed by Master and Servant Acts which were based on the sixteenth-century Statute of Artificers, supplemented by secondary legislation and case law. Together they defined and regulated what was becoming an increasingly fractious relationship between employers and employees.[25] On one side, workers were required to labour diligently and obediently; on the other, the employer, among other matters, was obliged to pay wages when due and give appropriate notice before termination. Under the delegated authority of the High Court, the magistracy had the authority to provide summary judgment on employment matters brought before it and although the Master and Servant Acts provided for fines on employers found to be in breach, action was more usually taken against the servant or employees, including imprisonment for breach of contract, fines and the termination of employment with loss of wages.

Perhaps unsurprisingly, the nature of labour legislation and the manner in which it was enforced became increasingly one-sided in the eighteenth century as successively more onerous employment legislation was passed by parliament as a means of controlling what was seen as an increasingly unruly labour force. In the 1720s, new acts increased the maximum term of imprisonment from one month to three and added hard labour to the penalties available to the bench; and in 1747, parliament added corporal punishment.[26] Most tellingly, as Douglas Hay has noted, 'the worker in breach was often treated as a criminal; the master never was.'[27]

Among the many influential freemasons who were prominent on the bench in the 1730s and beyond were some of its most rigorous and exacting jurists. They included Sir Thomas de Veil, Henry Norris, Richard Gifford, Richard Manley and Clifford William Philips.

De Veil (1684–1746), a past Master of William Hogarth's lodge at the Apple Tree tavern, was the principal subject satirised by Hogarth in *Night*, where he was depicted hypocritically drunk and in Masonic regalia on his return home from a lodge meeting.[28] A magistrate on both the Middlesex and Westminster benches throughout the 1730s, de Veil sat at Leicester Fields and in Soho until establishing the first formal magistrate's court in 1739 at his house in Bow Street. His pro-government approach and dedication to enforcing the penal code were such 'that the government turned to de Veil whenever it needed a magistrate's services'.[29] As a reward for his services to the administration, de Veil was given a colonelcy in the Westminster militia, numerous sinecures and, in 1744, was invested a knight. At the time of his death, he was regarded by many as the leading magistrate in London; he also sat as a commissioner for the peace in Essex, Hertfordshire and Surrey.

The wealthy Russia merchant, Henry Norris, a member of the lodge at the Cheshire Cheese in Arundell Street, who had extensive properties in Hackney, as well as the City and Southwark, was the author of the 'justicing notebook' that was the subject of *Justice in eighteenth century Hackney*.[30] At the time, Hackney was still largely agricultural countryside, accessible to the City and popular with wealthy merchants such as Norris. However, a nascent small-scale industry was growing, based around the local brickfields. The area also had a mixed and growing population that combined Protestant dissenters with émigré Jews and Irish communities, a combination of nationalities that was reflected in the cases brought before Norris and the bench. In her editorial commentary, Ruth Paley noted tellingly that 'all these groups were likely to attract considerable hostility . . . [but] to be Irish (and even worse to be an Irish Catholic) at this time was to be subjected to stereotypes of irresponsibility, lawlessness and criminality'.[31] Norris was tough on those brought before him and was regarded as 'a man of somewhat harsh and authoritarian views'.[32] In common with most of his judicial colleagues, he was also fervently pro-government. The administration used his magisterial services much as it did those of de Veil: to promote its purposes. In 1731, for example, Norris was selected to participate as a member of the carefully chosen Quarter Sessions jury that convicted Richard Francklin, the publisher of the leading opposition journal, the *Craftsman*'.[33]

Among other strongly loyalist magistrates, Richard Gifford was a warden of the lodge at the Castle Tavern in St Giles; Richard Manley a member of Martin Folkes' influential Bedford Head lodge in Covent Garden; and Clifford Philips a member and later warden of the Rose & Crown in King Street, Westminster. Paley has described all three as among the most active magistrates in London, a view substantiated by the multitude of records of the cases they tried.[34] Indeed, the main burden of criminal cases in urban Middlesex appears to have been shouldered by only six justices, including Gifford, Manley and Philips, who were responsible for just under half of the two thousand or so recognizances returned to the General and Quarter Sessions in 1732.[35]

Charles Delafaye, another member of Richmond's Horn, was a prominent figure, influential both masonically and as an active magistrate. A senior civil servant who from 1717–39 was under secretary of state at the northern and southern departments, and deputy secretary of state for Scotland, Delafaye was also the government's chief spymaster and coordinator of its anti-Jacobite spy network. He was appointed to the bench in 1714 or 1715 and served as a magistrate for several decades. Like de Veil, he was considered a 'go to' member of the magistracy. A substantial number of the cases brought before him were political; all were found in favour of the Whig administration.

Unfortunately, primary sources listing the membership of lodges warranted by English Grand Lodge are available only for an estimated two-thirds of lodge members and for no more than a handful of years from 1723 to 1730. Data after that point and until the beginning of the nineteenth century is accessible only piecemeal and is more a function of the limited records of individual lodges that have survived rather than the product of a possibly more reliable central database. As a consequence, it is possible to examine the extent to which there was a significant overlap between the magistracy and London freemasonry only within a relatively narrow time from the 1720s to the early 1730s. One of the last occasions within this period on which a new intake was appointed to the bench was November 1727.[36] The list of one hundred and thirty new entrants sworn to the magistracy at that time constituted one of the largest rolls of incoming appointees.

It was headed by Charles Lennox, duke of Richmond, Grand Master of England in 1725–6, and known and probable freemasons comprised around 15 per cent of the total listed. However, the actual number may have been higher. The proportion of probable freemasons in earlier lists of newly appointed magistrates where lodge membership is more readily documented generally ranged from 20 to 25 per cent.

The new intake to the bench in 1727 included Sir William Billers (1689–1745), and Sir George Cook (16__?–1740). Both were members of the aristocratic lodge meeting at the Rummer, Charing Cross. Billers has been portrayed correctly by Nicholas Rogers as a member of the 'big bourgeoisie of Hanoverian London'.[37] He was a stalwart of the Worshipful Company of Haberdashers and became a City Sheriff in 1721, an alderman in 1722 and was elected the City's Lord Mayor in 1734.[38] The link with Fotherley Baker, elected Clerk of the Haberdashers' Company in 1741 and later Deputy Grand Master of English Grand Lodge (discussed below) should be noted. Billers commanded the Honourable Artillery Company, the oldest regiment in the British army and considered a principal safeguard against the London mob; he also had command of the Blue regiment of Trained Bands, one of six London militia regiments under the jurisdiction and command of the Lord Mayor. Later sworn to the privy council, Billers' unforgiving judicial approach is detailed in over seven hundred contemporary press reports of court cases from 1727 until his death.

Sir George Cook was another mainstay of London's affluent bourgeoisie, holding office as Chief Prothonotary or chief administrator of the Court of Common Pleas from his legal chambers in the Temple.[39] Cook owned a townhouse in Lincoln's Inn Fields and substantial estates in Uxbridge.[40] He was close politically to the Whig establishment and gained the duke of Newcastle's political recommendation for the position of knight of the shire for Middlesex, albeit that his election bid was unsuccessful.[41]

Following their appointment to the bench, justices might sit individually or more commonly jointly or in committee, especially at the Quarter Sessions. These were local courts, held quarterly, that tried those cases that could not be dealt with summarily by the justices without a jury. At most Quarter Sessions, the jury comprised members of the bench and others considered loyal to the government. A relevant example is the twelve magistrates who presided as a jury at the Middlesex Sessions on 31 March 1733. They included five prominent freemasons: William Cowper, the former Grand Secretary and Deputy Grand Master mentioned above; Alexander Chocke, another former DGM and member of Richmond's Horn tavern lodge; Samuel Saville, a member of the Cock & Bottle lodge in Little Britain; Richard Gifford, a Warden at the Castle Tavern in St Giles; and Thomas de Veil.[42]

There is no evidence to suggest and it would be wrong to argue that there was any explicit conspiracy, government or Masonic, to crowd the bench with freemasons.[43] However, it is reasonable to conclude that many within London's lodges had a social commonality and similar if not identical polit-

Table 21 The Horn Tavern, 1720–35

Horn Tavern Member	Masonic Rank	Magistracy
Duke of Montagu	GM, 1721/2	JP
Duke of Richmond	GM, 1725/6	JP
George Payne	GM, 1718 & 1720; GW, 1724; DGM, 1735	JP
William Cowper	DGM, 1726; GS 1723–7	JP (Chair)
Alexander Chocke	DGM, 1727; GW 1726	JP (Chair)
Nathaniel Blackerby	DGM, 1728–9; GW, 1727; GT 1731	JP (Chair)
Francis Sorrel	GW, 1723–24	JP
William Burdon	GW, 1726	JP
Col. George Carpenter	GW, 1729	JP
Alexander Hardine	Master	JP
Samuel Edwards	Warden	JP
Thomas Brereton	Member	JP
William Burdon	Member	JP
Theophilus Cole	Member	JP
Charles Delafaye	Member	JP
Raphael Dubois	Member	JP
Samuel Horsey	Member	JP
Charles Medlicott	Member	JP
Thomas Medlicott	Member	JP
Simon Mitchell	Member	JP
Col. Thomas Paget	Member	JP
Col. Edward Riley	Member	JP
Leonard Streate	Member	JP (Chair)

ical and moral outlook to those at the heart of the Whig administration. They were natural and vigorous defenders of the status quo and many sat on or aspired to the government benches in parliament.[44]

Charles, duke of Richmond and Lennox, was an important government supporter and a leading Whig who was close to both Newcastle and Walpole. Richmond had been Grand Master of English Grand Lodge in 1723 and both before and after sat as Master of his own lodge at the Horn tavern in Westminster, close to parliament. Of the lodge's more than seventy members, around a third or more were magistrates, albeit that some were more active than others.

Table 21 is compiled from data drawn from the *Middlesex and Westminster Sessions' Papers, Justices' Working Documents* and lists those members of the Horn who are known to have sat or been appointed during the 1720s and/or 1730s.[45]

Table 22 The Rummer Tavern, 1723

Rummer Tavern Member	Masonic Rank	Magistracy
Col. Daniel Houghton	GW, 1725	JP
Sir Henry Bateman	Member	JP
Sir William Billers	Member	JP
William Bucknall	Member	JP
James Cook	Member	JP
Sir George Cook	Member	JP
Capt. Giles Earle, MP	Member	JP
Charles Hayes	Member	JP
Francis Reynolds	Member	JP
Alexander Strahan	Member	JP
Joseph Taylor	Member	JP
Robert Viner	Member	JP
Col. George Watkins	Member	JP

As noted, it is not possible to determine with certainty the aggregate number of freemasons among the London magistracy. Partial Masonic records and the phonetic spelling of freemasons and magistrates names alike prevent the data from being sufficiently precise. However, where the data is capable of analysis, it suggests that up to a quarter were or may have been freemasons.[46] The argument is supported anecdotally by an analysis of the membership of a second Masonic lodge, the Rummer tavern at Charing Cross. Like the Horn, the Rummer's membership was drawn from among the gentry and upper middling segment of London society. Of its fifty-six members in 1723, around half were recorded by their surname alone. At least thirteen can be identified as magistrates.

The level and scale of interaction between the two organisations suggests strongly that the influence of the judiciary on freemasonry and its outlook with regard to the London Irish and the working class more generally, should be considered potentially significant. The Whiggist political characteristics of early eighteenth-century London freemasonry that were central to its success in attracting members from both the gentry and affluent profes-sionals included loyalty, probity and respect for property. They were the same factors as those prized by the government in choosing its appointees to the bench. It is unsurprising that the relatively narrow social composition of mainstream London freemasonry and English Grand Lodge in the 1720s, 1730s, 1740s and thereafter was mirrored within the magistracy. It rein-forced the social chasm between Moderns freemasonry and London's lower middling and working class and drew a barrier that prevented interaction. Indeed, the difficulty, perhaps impossibility, of men such Billers, Chocke, Cowper, de Veil and Norris associating masonically and socially with London's working class, especially the London Irish, is perhaps self-evident.

Middling merchants, landowners and professionals were accepted into English freemasonry with relative ease, the less affluent, which included most of London's Irish community, were rejected. At odds socially and economically, it should not be a revelation that many chose to strike out independently.

CHAPTER FIVE

An Age of Decline – English Grand Lodge, 1740–1751

English freemasonry's early and mid-eighteenth century rejection of the working class and lower middling, and what Robert Gould later characterised as its mid-century period of Masonic misrule, was coloured not only by anti-Irish prejudice. During the 1740s, over forty lodges, around a fifth of those on its register of lodges, were expelled by the Grand Lodge of England. Others left of their own accord or chose to operate independently. Cessation and erasure where lodge membership had declined to an unsustainably low level was a relative commonplace. But exclusion for not attending Grand Lodge's set piece Quarterly Communications or the failure to contribute to the Grand Charity (and thus demonstrating insufficient respect for Grand Lodge) was more novel. The policy marked a new and uncompromising approach and was a significant shift compared to the more emollient stance of the preceding two decades. It also provided a context for the creation of the Antients Grand Lodge and the expansion of Antients freemasonry across London and elsewhere.

The minutes of the lodge at the Shakespeare's Head in Little Marlborough Street give an insight into the deteriorating relationship between English Grand Lodge and at least some of its constituent lodges.[1] On 12 January 1740, a letter from the Grand Secretary was read to the lodge. Referring to the absence of the lodge's representatives from the most recent Quarterly Communication, the Grand Secretary informed the Master that 'unless the officers of the lodge . . . attend Quarterly Communication . . . or send in their charity, the [lodge's] constitution would be lost'. The reprimand was intended to be taken seriously and the Master advised the members that he had responded to the letter and on behalf of the lodge had sent half a guinea to the Grand Secretary with a request that it be paid to the Grand Charity 'on behalf of this society' at the next Quarterly Communication. However, at the meeting on 23 February 1740, only six weeks later, the minutes record the receipt of a second letter from the Grand Secretary. Read by the Master to the members, the letter commanded the senior officers of the lodge to attend the Grand Master at the Quarterly Communication to be held the following night. The minutes record that the lodge was reluctant to comply, the Master commenting that 'as the interests of the lodge had been secured [at] the last QC, it was not thought fit at this time to put the society to the charge of this attendance'.

Only a small number of individual lodge minute books from the early and mid-eighteenth century survive and most are anodyne, listing the names of those members present, the officers of the lodge and the fees paid or outstanding, and few provide detailed reports of individual meetings. Nonetheless, despite the absence of such corroborative evidence, it is reasonable to assume that the letter received by the Shakespeare's Head was probably not unusual and that lodges in a similar position would have received the same or analogous correspondence. It is also clear that the Shakespeare's Head's unease at being obliged to follow the bidding of Grand Lodge was not new. The minutes of 11 December 1738 and 9 April 1739 both record the lodge's disapproval of Grand Lodge's insistence on the central collection of Masonic charity and the members' discomfort over their lack of influence over its disbursement.

The Shakespeare's Head was not a naturally rebellious lodge; indeed, the opposite was probably the case. Fourteen members, around half the total, were members of the influential and aristocratic King's Arms lodge in the Strand, later the Old King's Arm's, lodge No. 28 (or 'OKA').[2] A driving force at both was Martin Clare (1688–1751). Clare was in several ways the epitome of Masonic loyalty. He had been selected as a Grand Steward in 1734, appointed Junior Grand Warden in 1735 and made Deputy Grand Master in 1741. Clare was also connected to many of freemasonry's elder statesmen. As the founder and headmaster of the well-regarded Soho Academy in Soho Square, he had been elected a Fellow of the Royal Society in 1735, proposed by a slate of influential freemasons including the pivotal Desaguliers, Sir Richard Manningham, Ephraim Chambers (the publisher of the eponymous dictionary), James Gibbs and Dr Alexander Stuart, among others.[3] Clare was, in addition, the reputed author of *A Defence of Masonry* and a prolific educational and Masonic lecturer who had been one of freemasonry's principal flag carriers in promoting educational self-improvement and the new body of knowledge that flowed from Newton's scientific Enlightenment.[4] His *Discourse* on the subject summarised both his approach and that of many within the inner orbit of English Grand Lodge:

> The chief pleasure of society – viz., good conversation and the consequent improvements – are rightly presumed . . . to be the principal motive of our first entering into then propagating the Craft . . . We are intimately related to those great and worthy spirits who have ever made it their business and aim to improve themselves and inform mankind.[5]

Clare had been elected Master of the Shakespeare's Head in 1736. Many of the entries in the minute books are in his handwriting and his lectures appear to have been a mainstay of its activities. Clare was re-elected to the chair in 1738 and again in 1740. However, despite a close association with several prominent freemasons, attendance at the lodge declined. Only five members were left in 1745 and, the following year, Clare was obliged to pay half a guinea to Grand Lodge to ensure that the lodge was not erased immediately. Without an obvious future, the remaining members agreed with Clare that they should seek to identify potential purchasers for the lodge's Masonic furniture and other assets. They were unsuccessful and in the absence of a buyer, Clare agreed to acquire the assets himself in 1747. Two years later and just over a year before his death, Clare agreed to sell the constitution, jewels, furniture and books to the lodge that then met at the George and Dragon in Grafton Street, now the Lodge of Friendship, No. 6. The Shakespeare's Head lodge was disbanded formally at the same time.[6]

If a lodge such as the Shakespeare's Head was demonstrably unhappy with the strictures of Grand Lodge, it is reasonable to believe that Masonic discontent may have been relatively common, if not widespread. Certainly, other lodges experienced the same or a similar decline in membership numbers. Another lodge with which Clare was associated, No. 185, at the British Coffee House in Cockspur Street near Charing Cross, also failed to survive and was erased in 1745; and lodge No. 63, later the Corner Stone lodge, meeting at the Masons' Arms in Maddox Street, was reduced to only seven active members in 1742 and 1743.[7]

The response of English Grand Lodge was to encourage ailing lodges to surrender their warrants and merge with those in a better condition. At the Quarterly Communication of 24 June 1742, Lord Ward (1704–1774), a Midlands landowner and minor politician who had been appointed Grand Master after inheriting a peerage, 'took notice of the great decay of many lodges'. Ward believed the problem to be caused by an excess number of lodges, in his word, a 'multiplicity', and in response to the merger of the Turk's Head lodge with that at the King's Arms, made it Grand Lodge policy to encourage other unsuccessful lodges to identify prospective partners. Ward also tried to enforce a restriction on the number of lodges to which a London freemason could belong, limiting membership to a single lodge, and to encourage prospective freemasons to join failing lodges rather than support the constitution of new lodges. Both rules had been on the books for many years but had rarely if ever been enforced. There were good reasons not to do so. As with many clubs and societies, the bulk of a lodge's activities was undertaken by a minority of its membership. Moreover, those who were devoted to freemasonry or ambitious for Masonic advancement were often members of more than one lodge and took an active part in each. Richard Rawlinson offers an excellent example of the genre: in the 1730s he was Master of the lodge meeting at the Oxford Arms in Ludgate Street, warden of a second, and a member of two more.[8] Ward's insistence on restricting the number of lodges to which a freemason could belong and the imposition of constraints on the formation of new lodges may have been designed to foster the survival of failing lodges as well as demonstrate Grand Lodge's authority over such matters, but the strictures were also a direct affront to many of the most dedicated freemasons involved in London freemasonry and fell at an early hurdle when it came to guaranteeing the success of ailing lodges.

Ward's successor Grand Masters compounded Masonic discontent, most particularly the absentee William Byron, 5th lord Byron (1722–1798). During Byron's reign as Grand Master, disaffection and unease percolated out to even the most loyal of lodges, including the Grand Stewards' lodge, which expressed its dissent in 1749 by declining to contribute to the Grand Charity collection and neither attending Grand Lodge nor contributing to charity in succeeding years. Indeed, withholding charity and declining to participate in the formal Masonic processions that accompanied meetings of Grand Lodge became a standard means by which the Grand Stewards registered their opposition.[9]

The disciplinary procedures adopted by Grand Lodge to enforce its rules were harsh and contentious. On 24 June 1742, Ward ordered that four lodges be erased from the official list for 'not attending the Grand Master in Quarterly Communication pursuant to several notices respectively sent them'. The lodges were No. 37, which at that date met at the Angel & Crown in Whitechapel; No. 60, at the Vine in Long Acre, Covent Garden; No. 161, at the Swan, Fish Street Hill; and No. 165, at the Flower Pot in Bishopsgate. The specific lodges are hard to identify from Lane's *Masonic Records*, however, lodge No. 37 may have been that which originally met at King Henry VIII's Head in Seven Dials and from there moved to Billingsgate and thereafter Whitechapel, although it is possible that the lodge at Billingsgate was a newly constituted lodge. Lodge No. 60 had met at the Golden Spikes tavern in Hampstead before moving to Long Acre. And it is likely that lodge No. 165 had only been warranted in 1739, taking the place of the lodge that had convened at Cameron's Coffee House.

At the following Quarterly Communication on 8 February 1743, the masters and wardens of thirteen lodges, including that at the Flower Pot tavern, were summoned to attend the Grand Master to explain their non-attendance for over two years. However, representatives of only four of these lodges attended the following meeting held on 9 April. Two apologised, making 'an excuse for their non attendance and promising to attend more punctually for the future'; and two were given additional time to explain. Ward commanded that the remaining seven be erased:

> Ordered that the following lodges be erased out of the Book of Lodges they not attending pursuant to the Summons' directed at the last QC nor any speaking on their behalf:

No.		
	40	Globe, Fleet Street
	45	Globe, Strand
	59	Castle, St Giles's
	80	Three Tuns, Grosvenor Street
	145	Three Tuns & Half Moon, Snowhill
	156	Red Lion, Red Lion Street
	165	Flower Pot, Bishopsgate Street

The two lodges given dispensation to explain their non-attendance were dismissed subsequently by Ward in April 1744, citing their persistent failure to attend. These were No. 7, at the King's Arms, Temple Bar, originally warranted in 1722, which had previously met at the Devil's Tavern in Temple Bar and at Daniel's Coffee House; and No. 39, at the Mitre in King Street, Westminster. The latter had been established in 1725 at the Golden Lion in Dean Street, Soho, and later met at the Swan in Grafton Street and then at the Swan in Long Acre.

Ward's inflexible approach was continued by his successor, Thomas Lyon, the earl of Strathmore and Kinghorne (1704–1753). On 26 February 1745, Lyon, as Grand Master

> Ordered that the Secretary do Summon the eight following lodges to show cause at the next QC why they have Omitted to attend the Rt Worshipful GM at the general meetings of the Society for upwards of two years past, viz.:

No.		
	3	Crown, behind the Royal Exchange
	9	King's Arms, New Bond Street
	17	Sun, Holborn
	19	Vine, Long Acre
	26	Forrest's Coffee House, Charing Cross
	146	King's Head, Old Jewry
	159	Gloucester Lodge at Canon, Charing Cross
	173	British Coffee House, Charing Cross'

The lodge at the Crown had received its warrant in 1721 and had since that time met in the City close to the Royal Exchange building. Although erased, lodge No. 9 was reinstated in 1748 and is the present day Tuscan Lodge, now lodge No. 14. Lodges 17 and 19 were warranted in 1723. The latter had been known as the French Lodge, which had met at the Dolphin in Tower Street before moving to the Swan in Long Acre and then the Vine tavern. The French lodge had enjoyed a close association with Desaguliers and the wider Huguenot community, a group whose support for freemasonry and its Whiggist stance had been unyielding over the years. Although most Huguenots had become by the 1740s more closely integrated into mainstream British society, the erasure of the French lodge can nonetheless be viewed as a serious indictment of Grand Lodge policy. The remaining three lodges had been warranted in 1737, 1738 and 1739. In a footnote to the relevant entry in the QCA reprint of Grand Lodge Minutes, Dashwood, the editor, commented that the lodges summoned had not attended the Quarterly Communication for three years or more. However, 'if the list had been extended to include those who had not attended for two years, twenty-two more summonses would have been sent'.[10] Tellingly, Dashwood also observed that less than seventy of London's remaining 120 lodges were at the time attending Grand Lodge on a regular basis. None of the lodges summoned by Lyon chose to appear before the Grand Master at the next Quarterly Communication, nor was any representation made on their behalf. Consequently, at the following meeting on 25 March 1745, all were ordered erased from the register for non-attendance.

James Cranstoun, 6th lord Cranstoun (17__?–d.1773), was appointed Grand Master in April 1745. Unlike Lyon for whom Ward deputised on each occasion other than at his installation, Cranstoun personally chaired each of the Quarterly Communications held during his period of office. Those attending his installation were invited to take breakfast at the Braund's Head in New Bond Street and from there go in procession to the Drapers' Hall.[11] The installation was popular and ten days later an advertisement informed 'the Brethren . . . of the Society' that those intending to join Cranstoun at Bro. Parry's Bowling Green House on Putney Heath should obtain their tickets 'by tomorrow at farthest, that suitable provisions may be made for their reception . . . dinner to be on the Table at Two o'clock precisely'.[12] Cranstoun also continued the practice of Masonic theatrical evenings and the Masonic pomp that often preceded and followed:

> A great number of gentlemen have appointed to meet this evening at five o'clock at the Shakespear's Head tavern in Covent Garden to wait on the Rt Hon the Grand Master and the rest of the brethren of the Antient and Honourable Society of Free and Accepted Masons and from thence to proceed in their proper cloathing to see the Old Batchelor which is to be played for their entertainment at Covent Garden Theatre.[13]

On 21 November 1745 at the first Quarterly Communication at which he presided, eight lodges were ordered to receive summonses demanding their attendance 'to answer for their not attending the Grand Master at the General Meetings of the Society for a considerable time past'. The lodges summoned were:

No.		
	2	Horn, Westminster
	4	Shakespeare's Head, Little Marlborough Street
	33	Sash and Cocoa Tree, Moorfields
	68	Bull's Head, Whitechapel
	88	Hoop & Griffin, Leadenhall Street
	133	Bell, Little Eastcheap
	140	King's Arms, Cateaton Street
	153	Fountain, Bartholomew Lane

Cranstoun also commanded that twelve lodges be erased:

> Ordered that the twelve following Lodges be Erased out of the Book of Lodges they not having attended the GM at the general meetings of the Society nor regularly met so as to be Summoned for some years past.

No.	15	Bedford Arms, Covent Garden
	16	Bear & Rummer, Gerard Street, Soho

25	Dog, St James's Market
48	Royal Oak, Earl Street, Seven Dials
54	George, St Mary Axe
79	King's Head, St Paul's Churchyard
107	Fountain, Snow Hill
112	Horn & Dolphin, Crutched Friars
142	White Horse, Piccadilly
160	Horn & Feathers, Doctors' Commons
171	Standard, Leicester Fields
155	Mansion House, Steel Yard, Thames street

The first named lodge in the list of those called before Grand Lodge was the Horn, the duke of Richmond's lodge, *de facto* the most senior of all London's Masonic lodges and, historically, one of, if not the most influential, whose members had dominated both Grand Lodge and English freemasonry for nearly two decades. The lodge was one of several that predated Grand Lodge; moreover, it had been the principal instrument in its creation. Aristocratic and by a substantial margin the largest of the founding lodges, the Horn's membership throughout the 1720s and 1730s included a mixture of influential aristocrats, ranking army officers, parliamentarians, civil servants, diplomats and scientists, many of whom, around a third, also held positions in the Middlesex and Westminster magistracy.

In the 1720s, the Horn's seventy plus members included thirteen English and European aristocrats, many with close connections to the British crown, including Richmond, whose father was the illegitimate son of Charles II. The lodge's parliamentary connections were distinguished. Many members were MPs or, like the duke of Richmond, wielded influence over who would be selected for seats within their local jurisdiction. The lodge also had influence within the military, with two generals, ten colonels and other officers below field rank within the membership. The connection with the Royal Society was equally strong. At least eleven were FRSs, including Richmond; John, duke of Montagu; Charles, duke of Queensberry; James Hamilton, Lord Paisley; and the Hon George Carpenter. In addition to Desaguliers, among the lodge's non-aristocratic FRSs were Charles du Bois, the botanist and cashier-general of the East India Company; Nathan Hickman, the physician; Sir Richard Manningham, a pre-eminent male midwife whose clients included the royal family; Charles Delafaye, undersecretary of state and the government's spymaster; and George Stanley, a merchant married to Hans Sloane's daughter. There were also two French FRSs: Jean Erdman, Baron Dieskau, a soldier and diplomat; and Charles du Fay, a member of the Royal Academy of Science. Politically, with few exceptions, the lodge was loyally Whiggist.

The Horn was probably at its most influential as a spawning ground for Masonic Grand Officers. Table 23 illustrates how many of its members took prominent roles within freemasonry, and how the Horn's members governed the influential Grand Charity Committee to which many of the more sensitive decisions of Grand Lodge were later delegated.

Table 23 The Members of the Horn Tavern lodge Holding Grand Office, 1718–35

Name	Grand Office	Grand Charity Committee
George Payne	GM 1718 & 1720, GW 1724 DGM 1735	
J.T. Desaguliers	GM 1719, DGM 1722–3 & 1725	Yes
John, duke of Montagu	GM 1721	Yes
Charles, duke of Richmond	GM 1724	
James, Lord Paisley	GM 1726	Yes
William Cowper	DGM 1726 GS 1723–7	Yes
Alexander Chocke	GW 1726 DGM 1727	
Nathaniel Blackerby	GW 1727 DGM 1728–9 GT 1731	
Thomas Batson	GW 1729 DGM 1730–4	
Francis Sorrel	GW 1723–4	
Sir Thomas Prendergast	GW 1725	Yes
William Burdon	GW 1726	
Col. George Carpenter	GW 1729	
Major Alexander Harding		Yes
Thomas Edwards		Yes

The Masonic importance of the Horn was without parallel from the 1720s through to the mid-1730s. But although its Masonic star may have been on the wane in the 1740s, the threat of sanction and erasure by Grand Lodge from the list of recognised lodges was probably nonetheless a relatively empty gesture. The Horn had sufficient stature to allow it to function without recourse to or recognition from Grand Lodge. But even where lodges had less eminence and a more middling membership, they were also able to survive independently. Many chose to function as 'St John's' lodges, a generic name given to a lodge not associated with any self-proclaimed ruling body; and, in due course, a number (or their members) chose to affiliate with the Antients. The Horn itself remained unaffiliated for six years until George Payne, then a member of the OKA, interceded on its behalf. Following Payne's compromise agreement that the Horn would pay a contribution of two guineas to the Grand Charity, the lodge was in 1751 reinstated to Grand Lodge's register of regular lodges. That this occurred close to the end of Lord

Byron's period as absentee Grand Master is unlikely to have been a coincidence.

In 1746, Lord Cranstoun was asked to remain in office for a further year. There was a general concern that the numbers attending the Grand Feast would be embarrassingly low. Some members, including many from the nobility, were fighting in Flanders, but the prevalent malaise in freemasonry was equally at fault. In testament, a further four lodges were ordered erased at the same April meeting. Indeed, no further Quarterly Communication was held until a year later when a motion discontinuing the procession to the Grand Feast was passed and Lord Byron proposed as the Grand Master elect. Underlining the Masonic depression, of the new lodge warrants granted by Cranstoun on behalf of Grand Lodge, only two survived to be 'continued in the present list of lodges'.[14] But despite its problems, the imperious attitude of Grand Lodge in the latter half of the 1740s was unrelenting. In March 1748, Ward, chairing a meeting in Byron's absence, ordered the Grand Secretary to write to a further twelve lodges requiring them to explain their failure to attend. Seven of the lodges summoned appeared before him and dutifully 'made their excuses'; the remaining five were erased. As a single offset, Ward reinstated lodge No. 9, then meeting at the King's Arms in New Bond Street, on the grounds that its prior failure to attend the Grand Master had been caused by an alleged mistake.

The decreasing regard with which Grand Lodge (and freemasonry) came to be held in the mid- and late 1740s was reflected in a change in the general public's attitude towards the annual Masonic Grand Feast. Dating from Montagu's installation in 1721, the installation of a new Grand Master had been preceded by a ceremonial and ornately choreographed public procession. The event had been generally well-publicised with a proliferation of classified advertisements in the press designed to attract attention and raise the profile of freemasonry and Grand Lodge. This had been remarkably successful, and the parade attracted a large audience from the London public and gained positive press comment. Processions comprised, in Anderson's words, 'many Brothers duly clothed [proceeding] in Coaches from the West to the East'.[15] That of the duke of Norfolk in 1730 was preceded by Lord Kingston, the outgoing Grand Master, attending the duke at his London mansion 'with ceremony', together with 'a vast number of brothers duly clothed'.[16] And from his house in St James's Square, the Grand Master elect and his retinue paraded formally to the City led by

> six of the stewards clothed proper with their badges and white rods, two in each chariot . . . noble and eminent brethren duly clothed . . . former Grand Officers clothed proper . . . former noble Grand Officers clothed proper . . . the secretary alone with his badge and bag, clothed . . . the two Grand Wardens clothed proper with their badges . . . the Deputy Grand Master alone clothed proper with his badge in a chariot . . . and in the final coach, Kingston, Grand Master clothed proper with his badge [and] Norfolk, Grand Master elect, clothed only as a Mason.[17]

The annual parade and installation dinner was the pinnacle of the Masonic year. So many sought to attend Norfolk's installation and the feast that followed that the venue needed to be relocated to the Merchant Taylor's hall from the Stationers', the latter 'being too small to entertain so numerous'.[18] Indeed, the annual cavalcade was intentionally organised for optimum impact: 'the stewards [halting] at Charing Cross until the messenger brought orders to move on slowly'.[19] In 1734, John Lindsay, earl Crawford's spectacular display included 'trumpets, hautboys, kettle drums and French-horns to lead the van and play at the gate till all arrive'. Two years later, that of John Campbell, earl of Loudoun, was even more elaborate, the Grand Master elect travelling

> in a chariot richly carved and gilt drawn by six beautiful grey horses [with three] sets of music . . . consisting of a pair of kettle drums, four trumpets and four French horns, the others of a pair of kettle drums, two trumpets and two French horns.

And the *London Evening Post* reported that Edward Bligh, earl Darnley's procession in 1737 was

> attended by kettle-drums [and] trumpets', with an array of coaches and chariots that culminated in 'the earl of Darnley in a fine, rich, gilt chariot, drawn by six long tail grey horses, with fine morocco harness and green silk reins.[20]

Reporting the same event, the *Daily Advertiser* referred to 'upwards of a hundred coaches' and an estimated cost of £200 for the pre-installation breakfast alone.[21] This was the zenith. A decade later on 3 April 1747, Grand Lodge passed a resolution discontinuing the event:

> The occasion of this prudent regulation was that some unfaithful Brethren, disappointed in their expectation of high offices and honours of the society, had joined a number of buffoons of the day, in a scheme to make a mockery of the public procession to the Grand Feast.

Anti-Masonic protests had grown over the preceding years and the activities of those such as the Scald Miserable Masons who arranged processions designed to mock freemasonry were duly recorded by the press:

> Yesterday, some mock freemasons marched through Pall Mall and the Strand as far as Temple Bar in procession; first went fellows as jackasses, with cow's horns in their hands; then a kettle drummer on a jackass, having two butter firkins for kettle drums; then followed to carts drawn by jackasses, having in them the stewards with several badges of their order; then came a mourning coach drawn by six horses, each of a different size and colour, which were the Grand Master and Wardens; the whole attended by

a vast mob. They stayed without Temple Bar until the Masons came by and paid their compliments to them, who returned the same with an agreeable humour.[22]

Other mock processions were organized but although favoured by the London mob, they were held in less regard by the authorities, with some prevented and others rerouted.[23] Nonetheless, in response to possibility of ridicule, rather than processing from his townhouse, Lord Byron instead invited those attending his installation to 'meet him at the hall at 12 o'clock at Noon'. Although the press recorded that 'an elegant entertainment was provided', the installation meeting was held in private and appears to have been more prosaic.[24] In his speech to those attending, Byron undertook that 'he would to the utmost of his power promote the benefit of the Craft'. However, his promise was broken almost immediately. Byron was present in Grand Lodge on only one occasion after his installation: on 16 March 1752, when he proposed that Lord Carysfort be installed as his successor. During the intervening five years, Grand Lodge would fall under the domain of Byron's Grand Officers with press coverage muted and public interest at bay. The five year absence of a Grand Master effectively set a seal on English freemasonry's mid-century decline.

Byron had inherited his title at the age of 14 and volunteered for the navy two years later, serving in the Mediterranean and off West Africa. He was promoted lieutenant but resigned in 1743 on reaching his majority and returned to England. Byron married in March 1747, a month before he was appointed Grand Master elect. His wife, Elizabeth Shaw, was 'a very beautiful lady with [a] £70,000 fortune' and the wedding took place at his in-laws house in Albemarle Street.[25] Their first son was born the following year but died at eleven months;[26] a second son, William, was born in October 1749 and survived.[27] Outside of family, Byron's principal diversions were gambling and horseracing. They were common to many of his set and he engaged actively in both. A newspaper noted his presence at the Burford races in Gloucestershire shortly after his return to England in 1743 and the report describes clearly the attraction of such events:

The field was honoured with the presence of the duke of Beaufort, duke Hamilton, earl of Lichfield and brothers, earl of Portmore, earl of Shrewsbury, Lord Gower, Lord Chedworth and brothers, Lord Byron, Lord Castlehaven, Lord Craven, Lord Noel Somerset, Lord Barrington, great numbers of baronets, members of parliament and the gentlemen of the best fashion in all the adjacent counties who diverted themselves with hawking or hind hunting every morning, racing at noon, dining together every day to the number of 200, and concluding their nights at the town hall, where there was a grand ball and entertainment for the ladies, whose beauty, richness of apparel and heights of spirits rendered the whole meeting most agreeable as well as the most magnificent that has been seen for many years.[28]

Within two years, Byron had moved from spectator to participant. The *London Evening Post* of 2 April 1745 advertised the forthcoming race between the duke of Kingston, Lord Byron, Sir Charles Sedley and a Mr Parson. Each entered 'a horse, mare or gelding past six years old on the round course carrying fourteen stone, the best of three heats, for fifty guineas a side, sweep stakes'. Apart from Kingston, each competitor rode their own horse. Parson won the first two races with Byron finishing third and second, respectively.[29] He was more fortunate the following year at Northampton when his horse, Quiet Ball, finished first in an eight horse race.[30] Byron's wagers and success or otherwise at or on the track were described throughout the 1740s and into the 1750s and provide the counterpart to his Masonic non-attendance. The *General Evening Post* of 13-15 April 1751 reported him among twenty-eight other peers present at the Newmarket races that week and there are numerous other instances of his exploits at the track.[31]

It would be an understatement to say that Lord Byron was not regarded as a positive role model. Some two decades later, *The Complete Freemason* assessed his time in office as 'very inactive' and commented that 'several years passed by without his coming to a Grand Assembly, nay [he] even neglected to nominate his successor'.[32] Indeed, there is evidence of only one instance when he offered his imprimatur to freemasonry or was otherwise supportive. On 11 May 1747, two weeks after his installation, an advertisement appeared promoting a performance of the *Merchant of Venice* at the Theatre Royal in Drury Lane to be attended by the Grand Master and fraternity of freemasons and accompanied by the 'usual masons' songs'.[33] The following week, the advertisement was expanded, noting that 'Mr Custos is to sing a song, who was long confined in the Inquisition in Portugal on account of his freemasonry'.[34] And attendees were invited to 'meet his Lordship clothed' at the Rose Tavern in Covent Garden, from where they intended to process to the theatre where 'three rows of the pit will be railed in for Masons only'. But Byron's interest in freemasonry never germinated. And without aristocratic patronage and under the ineffective leadership of his officers, freemasonry's attractions and popularity relentlessly diminished:

> Whereas several summons have been sent to the several members of the Society of Free and Accepted Masons, held at the Salutation Tavern lately in Newgate Street, and now in Grey Friars, and several have absented themselves; this is therefore to give Notice to such members as pretend to belong to the said Society that if they do not appear on Monday night, the 13th July instant, they will be excluded any pretensions to the Society or the furniture thereof.[35]

Although not relevant to his lack of interest in freemasonry, Byron is probably now known best for his drunken duel in 1765 with his cousin, William Chaworth, which resulted in the latter's death.[36] Byron was arrested and tried by his peers in the House of Lords where he was found guilty of manslaughter; he received a fine and was discharged under the Statute of Privilege. After his trial, his marriage disintegrated and his wife left him. His son, from whom he was estranged, and grandson, predeceased him, and his title and a heavily mortgaged Newstead Abbey, the family seat, were taken over by George Gordon Byron, the poet, who became the 6th lord.

Under Byron's absentee leadership, Grand Lodge's negative transformation continued to the point where Horace Walpole could comment ironically that freemasonry and freemasons were 'in so low repute now in England, that . . . nothing but a persecution could bring them into vogue again'.[37] Where English freemasonry had once beguiled, it now alienated. Only two decades earlier, prominent aristocrats, politicians and scientists had placed freemasonry at a social, political and intellectual hub, offering a fashionable club of some consequence that attracted a growing aspirational membership both nationally and internationally. But by the 1740s, freemasonry's defining characteristics had begun to wane. The change in the public's perception was influenced not only by those at its helm but also by a political backlash in Europe where, from the late 1730s, many continental monarchies had adopted an anti-Masonic stance. In 1736, Sweden's Frederick I prohibited freemasons from meeting on penalty of death. France proscribed Masonic assemblies the following year, and in Italy, the Inquisition closed the English lodge meeting in Rome. Pope Clement XII published his anti-Masonic papal bull in 1738 and, that year, Charles VI issued an edict prohibiting freemasonry in the Austrian Netherlands. Poland followed in 1739, when Augustus III interdicted freemasonry. This affected Saxony and the Baltic, since Augustus was Elector of the duchy of Saxony and Grand Duke of Lithuania. And in 1740, Philip V of Spain issued a decree against freemasonry which condemned freemasons to the galleys.[38] These edicts and proscriptions were not filed and forgotten. As late as 1751, a news report from Naples confirmed that 'ever since his Majesty's edict against the free and accepted Masons, it was generally conjectured that there were several persons of distinction possessed of important posts who would be obliged soon to resign'.[39] The threat that freemasonry was perceived to pose to Catholicism and Europe's absolute monarchies were at the root of European concerns. In Protestant England, as Marie Mulvey-Roberts noted with respect to the Moderns, there was simply a 'malaise' that began in the 1730s and endured until the 1760s.[40]

Fotherley Baker, DGM, presided in Byron's absence. At his first Quarterly Communication in December 1747, he was supported by several former Grand Officers and members of the OKA including Robert Lawley, Edward Hody and Benjamin Gascoyne. The next meeting on 7 March 1748 was chaired by Ward. The principal business was again largely negative and included the order that twelve lodges be summoned to Grand Lodge for 'not attending . . . for a considerable time past'. The list was headed by the lodge at the Shakespeare's Head in Little Marlborough Street. Grand Lodge failed to meet again until December, when Baker once again deputised. Seven of the twelve lodges summoned by Ward, including the Shakespeare's Head, appeared before Grand Lodge to 'make their excuses and promise to be more regular in the future'. Their apologies were accepted. The remaining lodges were erased:

> Ordered that the five following lodges be erased out of the Book of Lodges none attending for them although duly Summoned as aforesaid

No.	41	Mounts Coffee House, Grosvenor Street
	70	Salutation, Newgate Street
	83	Sun, Ludgate Street
	125	Ashley's London Punch House
	143	Swan, Southwark

Lodge No. 41 had been established in 1727 at the Mount Coffee House; No. 70, warranted in 1731, had met previously at the Crown in Prujean Court near the Old Bailey; No. 83 dated from 1732 and met at the Oxford Arms in Ludgate Street; No. 125 was constituted in 1736; and No. 143 had moved to Southwark in 1742, having originally been formed at the Westminster Hall Tavern in Bishopsgate in 1737.

The next Quarterly Communication was held in May 1749, a gap of fifteen months. In prior years, the June meeting would have been the installation meeting and occasion of the annual Grand Feast. Instead, Baker more mundanely

> informed the Lodge that himself and several Brethren intended to dine at Bro. Viponts at Hampstead on Saturday the 17th June & desired the Company of such as it suited to dine with him.

This was the second year that no Grand Feast had taken place. Grand Lodge met again thirteen months later in June 1750. The lodges were called over, paid their charity and the charity's accounts were examined and approved. The dining arrangements, once the principal attraction, were again informal with Baker advising those attending that he intended to be

> at Bro Perry's [at] the Bowling Green House at Putney on Saturday 14 July next and hoped that such brethren as it suited would attend him there.

Discontent was by now rife.

> The Fraternity, finding themselves entirely neglected, it was the opinion of many old masons to have a consultation about electing a new and more active Grand Master, and assembled for that purpose, according to an advertisement.[41]

Thomas Manningham, Sir Richard Manningham's second son, headed off the putative rebellion and Grand Lodge met twice more under Baker in September and October 1751. There was no obvious reason for the short gap between the two meetings and attendance at the latter was sparse with only thirty-three lodges represented. However, Byron's return to Grand Lodge on 16 March 1752 was marked by an upsurge, with fifty-six lodges attending represented by 166 masters and wardens. The Grand Feast was reinstated and scheduled for 20 March. But notwithstanding Lord Byron's return, the treatment of two lodge petitions suggests that attitudes at Grand Lodge remained largely unaltered. The first, an appeal from the brethren meeting at the Crown in Parkers Lane, asked that the lodge formerly held there might be restored and return to its former place in the register of lodges. However, rather than approve the restoration of the lodge with or without its former place of precedence, the request was rejected. A second petition was tabled from lodge No. 83. The lodge had met at the Sun in Ludgate Street prior to being erased in December 1748. The lodge also prayed for reinstatement. But the petition was rebuffed.[42] The autocracy which had alienated so many in earlier years appeared set to be maintained.

CHAPTER SIX

Masonic Misrule, Continued

The description of 'misrule' that was appended to Byron's term in office from 1747 to 1752 could also have applied to the preceding years, which included Lord Ward's reign as Grand Master. It was also applicable to the mismanagement of those who presided in Byron's absence: Fotherley Baker, the Deputy Grand Master, a lawyer and semi-professional bureaucrat; John Jesse, the Grand Treasurer, an official at the Post Office; and John Revis, Grand Secretary, a middling linen draper.

FOTHERLEY BAKER

One of the most important freemasons in the 1740s, Fotherley Baker (*d*.1754) held a succession of key grand offices for nearly a decade: JGW in 1744, SGW in the following two years and DGM in 1747, remaining as such until 1752.[1] A City-based lawyer and later Clerk to the Worshipful Company of Haberdashers, he was a member and later a warden of the lodge at the St Paul's Head tavern in Ludgate Street.[2] The lodge was large, with sixty-four members in the list submitted to Grand Lodge in 1730. Although not obviously aristocratic, it had a relatively wealthy and predominantly City-based membership. On 31 March 1735, for example, the lodge was one of the largest contributors to the Grand Charity with a donation of two guineas, twenty-one of the twenty-three other lodges present at that Quarterly Communication donating either half or a quarter of the amount.[3] The quantum of charity contributed by a lodge was a convenient proxy for the affluence of its membership and a deemed expression of loyalty to Grand Lodge. Another sign of the St Paul's Head's favoured status was that its Master was permitted to carry a sword belonging to the lodge before the Grand Master in formal processions.[4] However, the privilege was lost shortly after the duke of Norfolk presented Grand Lodge with a 'richly embellished' sword of state and appointed his own personal sword bearer. The event triggered a petition in favour of the St Paul's Head continuing in the role but despite the support of sixteen masters and wardens under the lead signatory of John Jesse, the Master of the Queen's Head, and Richard Rawlinson, it was rejected.[5] The Grand Master was considered to have an absolute entitlement to appoint his own officers, including a sword bearer, and no argument to the contrary would be accepted.

Aside from the abortive petition, the St Paul's Head had a further claim to notoriety. A relatively large number of its members had been connected to *Philo-Musicae et Architecture Societas-Apollini*, an irregular Masonic lodge established for the benefit of those who appreciated classical music and architecture. The episode provides an example of the interplay between the centralising tendencies of Grand Lodge and London's independent lodges in the 1720s, and contrasts how Masonic disobedience was handled in earlier years in comparison to the approach adopted two decades later.

PHILO-MUSICAE ET ARCHITECTURE SOCIETAS-APOLLINI

Established at the Queen's Head tavern in Temple Bar on 18 February 1725, *Philo-Musicae* was an independent lodge and art club with an emphasis on Italian music. Eight freemasons were present at the inauguration. Seven were also members of the regular lodge at the Queen's Head in Hollis Street, two of whom had been initiated on 24 December 1724 by the duke of Richmond, then Grand Master.[6] Subsequent members included middling lawyers and merchants, minor gentry, government officials and professional musicians. Andrew Pink commented accurately that notwithstanding its lack of affiliation to Grand Lodge and musical focus, *Philo-Musicae* was in all other ways a 'regular' Masonic lodge. Its minutes record the usual Masonic proceedings, including a petition on 5 August 1725 from a John Ellam that he be made a freemason in order to be admitted a member of the lodge, and Ellam's subsequent initiation.[7] However, perhaps because of the its Enlightenment nature and the social standing and connections of many of its members, *Philo-Musicae*'s independence and the absence of formal recognition by Grand Lodge was the source of some friction.

The mid-1720s was a period of accelerating centralisation by English Grand Lodge as it developed and then sought to impose a federal structure and uniform code of behaviour and ritual across London and later provincial English freemasonry. One component in its strategy was an edict issued unilaterally on 21 November 1724 which deemed unaffiliated lodges within ten miles of London 'irregular' and imposed a penalty for supporting or attending an initiation at any such lodge: a ban on associating with 'regular' lodges and with Grand Lodge itself:

> That if any Brethren shall met Irregularly and make Masons at any place within ten mile of London, the persons present at the making (the new brethren excepted) shall not be admitted even as Visitors into any Regular Lodge whatsoever unless they come and make such submission to the Grand Master and Grand Lodge as they shall think fit to impose upon them.[8]

Consequently, *Philo-Musicae* and its associates were to be deemed *personae non gratae* and prohibited from regular London freemasonry.

Perhaps to the chagrin of those imposing it, the edict was widely ignored and *Philo-Musicae* prospered, admitting new initiates and joining members at its popular regular meetings. For Grand Lodge, this was at best inconvenient. At its meeting on 20 May 1725, an order was issued 'that there be a letter wrote to the following brethren to desire them to attend the Grand Lodge viz. William Gulston, Coort Knevitt, William Jones, Charles Cotton, Thomas Fisher, Thomas Harbin and Francesco Xaviero Geminiani'.[9] But despite the appearance of firm authority the true position was more complex. On one hand, Grand Lodge needed to be seen to be exerting control and responding to the alarm of concerned Grand Officers, such as George Payne. On the other, members of *Philo-Musicae* were well-connected, both masonically and more broadly. The duke of Richmond as Grand Master had initiated at least three members: William Jones, the mathematician and a close friend to both Richmond and Martin Folkes;[10] Coort Knevit, a member of Richmond's own Horn Tavern lodge;[11] and Charles Cotton, a City merchant, later appointed a governor of the Bridewell Hospital.[12]

George Payne had made a point of attending a meeting of *Philo-Musicae* in order to assess the position for himself. But perhaps more significantly, he had also spent close to eight years designing and implementing the new federal structure and regulations to which *Philo-Musicae* and other independent lodges posed a threat. None of those summoned to Grand Lodge attended and, offended, Payne insisted that Richmond pursue the matter. A note from Payne to *Philo-Musicae* enclosing a cease and desist letter from Richmond was dated and delivered on 8 December 1725. *Philo-Musicae's* minutes for 16 December 1725 record its receipt and their apparent outrage that Richmond 'erroneously insists and assumes to himself a Pretended Authority to call our Right Worshipful and Highly Esteemed Society to account for making Masons irregularly'. However, it is more likely that Richmond's letter was more form than substance and *Philo-Musicae's* minuted response was ironic. In the event, *Philo-Musicae* ignored Richmond's missive and Grand Lodge also took the matter no further.

The context for the exchange is important. Historically, individual lodges had been self-governing with autonomy to make masons as each saw fit. It was only Grand Lodge's edict issued some twelve months earlier that deemed such activity apostasy in the absence of an affiliation with itself. The public censure of *Philo-Musicae* allowed Grand Lodge to be seen as making a stand on the issue, most probably with the intention of encouraging compliance among London lodges more widely. Privately, it is likely that Grand Lodge allowed matters at *Philo-Musicae* to proceed more or less unhindered. Richmond's connection to Jones, Knevit and Cotton has been mentioned. All three were members of the Queen's Head in Hollis Street: Knevit its Master and Jones its Senior Warden. By the end of 1725, ignoring Grand Lodge's strictures, eleven of the fourteen members of the Queen's Head had become 'directors' or members of *Philo-Musicae*.[13] They included William Gulston, a wine merchant, the president of *Philo-Musicae* and its principal guiding hand; Papillon Ball, another wealthy merchant and later a director of Royal

Exchange Assurance; Francesco Geminiani, an eminent Italian violinist then living in London;[14] and three gentlemen: Anthony Corville, the Junior Warden, Edward Squire and Thomas Marshall. Two other members, Edward Bedford and Thomas Harbin, completed the group.[15] Even those members of the Queen's Head who were not formally part of *Philo-Musicae* appear as visitors. Peter Reefer [also written as Reffer] was minuted as a guest on at least three occasions, the last being 30 September 1725, six months after the Grand Lodge edict; Thomas Fisher was present twice; and Thomas Gilbert at least once. Philip Hordern, described as a member of the Queen's Head in *Philo-Musicae's* minutes but not mentioned in the membership list returned to Grand Lodge, visited on 16 December 1725.[16]

However, *Philo-Musicae's* circle of influence was far wider than Hollis Street alone. Pink has identified around thirty-five members of the lodge;[17] Gould thought its membership above one hundred.[18] Whichever is correct, the lodge had a substantial loyal following and Francis Sorrel and Alexander Harding, two former Grand Wardens, and Charles Delafaye, another member of the Horn, were all minuted as visitors on 23 December 1725, barely two weeks after the despatch of Richmond's letter. Indeed, had Grand Lodge's official pronouncement been enforced, over thirty lodges would have been compromised by their members' visits to *Philo-Musicae* between 1 April 1725 and 9 March 1727 alone.[19] The number represented over a third of all regular lodges. Perhaps worse from Grand Lodge's standpoint, Geminiani had been invited to join *Philo-Musicae* and became its director of music principally in order that the first six of Corelli's violin solos could be made into an orchestral concerti grossi. Dedicated to the king, the works were immensely popular and had a large number of subscribers, including five other members of the royal family and numerous members of the aristocracy.

Nonetheless, despite its – albeit indirect – royal patronage and a steady flow of potential new members, including four who petitioned for membership in February 1727, *Philo-Musicae* wound down its activities in early 1727 and its last recorded meeting took place on 23 March. No direct pressure appears to have been exerted by Grand Lodge and it impossible to know whether the organisation had naturally run its course or, as the influence of Grand Lodge expanded, some of *Philo-Musicae's* members wished to avoid potential acrimony and secure their status in what was becoming a consequential organisation. If the latter is correct, and perhaps as compensation, within a few years, several *Philo-Musicae* alumni including Fotherley Baker, John Jesse, John Revis and Richard Rawlinson had been appointed to Grand Office.[20] And at least eleven members of *Philo-Musicae* were later members of the St Paul's Head with several joining the OKA, in the mid-1740s, London's most influential Masonic lodge.[21]

THE ST PAUL'S HEAD

Although conjecture, the substitution of the Master of the St Paul's Head as the Grand Master's sword bearer may have been a factor in the – perhaps compensatory – selection on 7 June 1733 of two of its members as Grand Stewards: Fotherley Baker and Richard Rawlinson. The appointments were made less than ten days after the rejection of the St Paul's petition to Grand Lodge. Twelve stewards were responsible each year for arranging the Grand Feast and underwriting any loss that arose. At the time, such losses were a strong possibility. However, in addition to signifying a financial commitment to freemasonry, the role was probably more significant in that it generally presaged higher Masonic rank for those appointed. From around 1730, virtually every Deputy Grand Master and Grand Warden had been chosen from the ranks of the Grand Stewards. Indeed, on 31 March 1735, reflecting what had become established practice, Grand Lodge 'resolved, that for the future all Grand Officers (except the Grand Master) should be selected out of [the Grand Stewards]'.[22]

The St Paul's Head was honoured again in June 1735, when John Jesse, the immediate past master, also became a Grand Steward, albeit as a replacement. Jesse was later to become treasurer of Grand Lodge, serving from 1739 until his death in 1753. He was friends with Fotherley Baker, who provided his security to Grand Lodge in respect of the Grand Charity's funds.[23] They were both later directors of the Amicable Society, a life assurance company, and sponsored two hospitals: the Small Pox Hospital and the London Infirmary. Their jointly rising Masonic status was marked publicly in the press in 1741:

> On Tuesday Night at the Devil Tavern Temple Bar, was held a Quarterly Communication of the most ancient and Honourable Society of Free and Accepted Masons, when a handsome contribution was made for the Relief of decay'd Brethren, and the Right Hon the earl of Morton was chose Grand Master Elect for the Year ensuing, who re-elected the former Deputy Grand Master and warden. There were nearly 300 Brethren present, and among them were the Count de Truches the Prussian Minister, the earl of Hyndford, the earl of Loudon, the Lord Ward, the Lord Raymond, George Payne Esq., Fotherby Baker Esq., John Jesse Esq. and other Persons of Distinction.[24]

Baker attended Grand Lodge frequently. He was made acting Junior Grand Warden on 24 June 1741 and appointed to the role formally on 2 May 1744 by the earl of Strathmore, the then Grand Master. The following year, Strathmore's successor, Lord Cranstoun, appointed Baker his Senior Grand Warden and, on succeeding Cranstoun in 1747, Byron appointed him Deputy Grand Master with 'full authority and right' in his absence. Described as a gentleman in the list of subscribers for Bishop Burnet's *History of His Own Time*, Baker was in 1724 an attorney with an office in Bread

Street in the City of London, a secondary road running perpendicular from Cheapside to Watling Street.[25] In 1740 he relocated to the more prestigious Queen Street, a few yards to the east.[26] The St Paul's Head tavern in Ludgate would have been a brief stroll from either location.

Baker's father, Nicholas, had also been an attorney, Solicitor to the Treasury from 1695–1700 and then Clerk to the Commission of Lieutenancy for the City of London.[27] In addition to his legal work and perhaps partly because of it, Baker was appointed Clerk to the Haberdashers' Company on 21 October 1741, one of the principal City livery companies.[28] His appointment was recorded in the *Daily Gazetteer* and *London Evening Post*, among others.[29] It may not have been coincidental that the annual Grand Feast was held at the Haberdashers' hall in 1740 and for the next five years with the exception of 1743, when a concern over numbers led to the feast being 'deferred to a more proper opportunity'.[30] The event's decreasing popularity is substantiated by a shift to the Drapers' hall in 1745, which held around 250, far less than the number accommodated at the Haberdashers'.[31] The following year, the Grand Feast was cancelled again; that in 1747 went ahead, again at the Drapers'. The next feast would not be held until 1752.

Baker's role as Clerk may not have been particularly remunerative but it carried prestige and provided both accommodation and an office.[32] The Haberdashers' Company was located centrally in the City at the junction of Maiden Lane and Staining Lane, just off Wood Street to the north of Cheapside. Baker took advantage of the location and although he had a country house at Bromley in Kent, classified advertisements and published reports in connection with his charity work gave his address at the 'house at the hall' until his death on 8 May 1754.[33]

Baker's charitable activities would have proved a large financial drain and point to the need for a relatively healthy income. Baker's legal practice and, to a lesser extent, position as Clerk to the Haberdashers' may have produced reasonable earnings. Indeed, Baker was described mid-career, correctly or otherwise, as an 'attorney of great practice'.[34] However, any wealth may have been the product of a dowry from his marriage to the only daughter of Sir Richard Brocas, a City alderman.[35] Brocas, a senior City figure, had been Master of the Grocers' Company (1724);[36] a City sheriff (1729) and, in 1730, was elected Lord Mayor.[37] He was also an exceptionally active magistrate, a role that formed part of his civic duties. The LMA contains records of over seventy hearings at the City of London's Sessions and more than fifty at the Old Bailey.[38] Indeed, Hitchcock made a salient if slightly exaggerated observation that 'for a time in the 1720s and 1730s he seems to have almost entirely monopolized the dispensation of justice in the City'.[39] In keeping with his status, Brocas was also a governor of St Thomas's Hospital and of the Bridewell; and treasurer and later president of St Bartholomew's Hospital.[40]

Participation in charitable undertakings was a corollary and obligation of wealth and like his father-in-law, Baker embraced the milieu and was heavily involved with the creation, governance and fund raising for the London Infirmary, later renamed the London Hospital.

THE LONDON INFIRMARY

The London Infirmary was one of five new general hospitals set up in London between 1720 and 1745. Financed by public subscription and voluntary contributions, it was incorporated in September 1740 with an initial capital of 100 guineas provided by seven founders.[41] At least three were freemasons: Baker, its treasurer; John Harrison, a member of the Lebeck's Head lodge in Maiden Lane and the hospital's first surgeon; and Josiah Cole, Master of the Vine Tavern lodge in Holborn and its apothecary. Baker's influence may have been instrumental in obtaining the duke of Richmond's patronage as the hospital's first president, although no correspondence has been located. Richmond accepted the position in 1741 and in *An Account of the Rise, Progress and State of the London Infirmary* published the following year, Baker is shown as Richmond's deputy and the sole vice president.[42] The third most senior figure was Thomas Boehm, a City merchant who succeeded Baker as treasurer; Boehm had been elected a Grand Steward in 1736.[43]

As the number of patients treated by the London Infirmary rose from just over 2,700 in 1742 to more than 8,000 in 1749, its annual disbursements also increased, from *c.*£1,200 to over £3,000. The workload of the hospital's management committee rose accordingly.[44] By the late 1740s, the committee met at least weekly with Baker presiding as vice president. Richmond was a figurehead; indeed, it had been agreed as early as 1742 that peers could vote by proxy.[45] His presidency was designed to encourage others. And he succeeded. The number of those providing sponsorship grew and by December 1743, numbered around ninety, including three of Baker's current colleagues at Grand Lodge: Benjamin Gascoyne, William Graeme and John Jesse, all past Grand Stewards. Other Masonic supporters were John Hawkins, then Master of the Ship at the Royal Exchange; George Thornborough, a member of the Swan at Greenwich; Major General Williamson of the Horn tavern; and Charles, Lord Baltimore, another from Richmond's inner circle. Baker, Boehm, Jesse and Williamson were all life governors of the hospital, having donated at least 30 guineas to secure the title.[46] Baker extended his commitment to the hospital in 1743 and was one of eight stewards appointed by the governors to organise its annual fund raising anniversary feast. The evening was held at the Haberdashers' hall on 25 March 1743. In addition to Richmond, Baker and Boehm, the stewards that year included John Atwood, a Grand Steward in 1731, a member of the lodge at the Star & Garter in Covent Garden and the Fleece in Fleet Street, and Thomas Jeffreys, a Grand Steward in 1736. Jeffreys was also a member of the St Paul's Head lodge and later Junior Grand Warden under Baker's Deputy Grand Mastership.[47]

The London Infirmary's profile rose rapidly and the number of contributors supporting the hospital tripled. Among the organisation's new supporters were aristocrats, politicians and the clergy, including the archbishops of Canterbury and York, the late primate of Ireland, and the bishops of Bristol, Chichester and Oxford.[48] Baker remained one of the trustees of the hospital until 1751, receiving, holding and disbursing funds on its behalf and with his name displayed in the financial statements published annually from 1744.[49] But perhaps recognising that his social position and personal wealth were insufficient to command the respect of many of the hospital's new supporters, Baker stood down as vice president in 1747. He was replaced by Sir James Lowther, 4th Bt. (1673–1755), and Peter Du Cane (1713–1804).[50] Lowther, a coal magnate and one of the wealthiest commoners in England, had estates in Whitehaven, Cumberland which generated an annual income of around £25,000 and were worth above £600,000 at his death.[51] Du Cane became a governor of the hospital in 1743 and treasurer in 1746.[52] A Huguenot City merchant, he had estates at Braxstead in Essex and a house in St James's Square. Du Cane was a governor of the Bank of England, a director of the Honourable East India Company and a member of the Court of St Thomas's Hospital.[53] He was married to Mary Norris, the daughter of Henry Norris.[54]

THE AMICABLE SOCIETY FOR A PERPETUAL INSURANCE UPON LIVES

Baker was elected a director of the Amicable Society in 1736 and served initially for a year. Unlike many of his co-directors, he had been a subscribing member of the Society since 1730, described in the members' register as a gentleman.[55] Baker was re-elected in 1739 and remained on the Court or board until 1753, taking periodic one-year statutory breaks between each three year term.[56] In 1743, Edward Hody joined the board, and in 1746, John Jesse. The three served together continuously until 1753.[57] Freemasons had a notable presence on the Court. In the 1740s and into the early 1750s, and in addition to Baker, Jesse and Hody, the Society's directors included Thomas Cuthbert, a warden at the Nag's Head lodge in Prince's Street and Ambrose Dickens, probably the 'Mr Dickens' of the Vine Tavern lodge in Holborn.[58] Five directors were merchants: Jonathan Ewer, Isaac Hunter, Elijah Impey, John Ridge and Thomas Symes; and five attorneys, Baker, Samuel Calverley, Robert Handley, Robert Michel and Robert Waddilove.[59] An average of around ten directors served annually.[60]

The Amicable was Britain's first mutual life assurance society. Incorporated by charter of Queen Anne in 1706 with a slate of prominent sponsors including William Talbot, later Bishop of Oxford, the Society was structured such that a maximum of 2,000 members would each pay initial fees of 10s and a fixed annual contribution of £6 4s.[61] Subscribers owned both their policies and a stake in the Society, with membership open to anyone aged between 12 and 45. Each year, the members' annual contributions less operating costs were divided between the representatives of those members who had died. The arrangement avoided actuarial risk, high mortality in any year resulted in a lower payout rather than in a reduction in reserves, but there were commercial risks, including fraud and losses on investments. Indeed, embezzlement occurred virtually from inception.

A history of the Society published in 1732 indicated that the value of its stock rose from £25,000 in 1710 to £34,000 in 1715, and to over £45,000 immediately prior to the collapse of the South Sea Bubble.[62] In 1731, asset value had declined to just over £27,300, mainly due to the fall in value of the South Sea stock which caused a drop of some £13,000 alone. However, fraud was at the root of other losses. An accountant, 'Mr Wall', had fled with £300; a prior treasurer, 'Higgs', had 'lost' £2,500 in 1713; and perhaps most egregiously, Mr Hodgson, another former treasurer, had absconded in 1730 after embezzling £4,400.[63] Whiston also calculated that a failure to collect full annual premiums on outstanding policies caused additional losses of £8,200. However, better management, improved investment returns and the absence of further fraud turned matters around. By 1742, finances had improved sufficiently for the Court to reduce annual subscriptions to £5, payable quarterly.[64] Geoffrey Clark has noted that a number of companies, including the Amicable, had intended that income from accumulated assets would allow them to become self-financing without the need for annual contributions. This almost occurred. The bull market in the second decade of the eighteenth century saw individual policy interests sold at a premium as the value of the portfolio rose; and even after losses on the South Sea stock, by the second half of the century, the Society set a minimum payout on death notwithstanding actual mortality rates.[65]

Both superficially and at its core, the Amicable embodied the bourgeois virtue of prudence. Clark was correct in noting that by agreeing to an association with other professional households 'the middling sort could lay claim to the political virtue and moral legitimacy that had generally been regarded as the preserve of landed families'. In Clark's words,

> to the many urban households of middling means lacking the security of landed wealth, the prospect of acquiring part-title to a growing fund of money (and of doing so while actually reducing their financial exposure) must have seemed a golden means to entrench their economic position against mortal risks while also providing an enduring vehicle for the conveyance of their fortunes down the generations.[66]

Of course, the words 'many' and 'middling' need defining. The number of households able financially to take advantage of mutual societies such as the Amicable, probably represented at most around 10 per cent, perhaps less, of London's population. Membership was inevitably tilted towards professional men, merchants and the more affluent who could afford the annual fee, a bias substantiated by the *List of the Members of the Corporation* which gives both occupation and address.[67] (The difference that existed between such middling associations and their Moderns members and the more accessible mutual support framework offered by the Antients is self-evident.) Moreover, unlike a friendly society, the Amicable also offered an opportunity for financial speculation. Because there was no restriction on the lives insured nor any requirement to substantiate an insurable interest, policies were often written as wagers. The presence of assorted dukes and other prominent public figures among the lives insured provides evidence that gambling was prevalent. The only barrier to fraud was the acceptance of the policy by the Court. As Gary Salzman noted, such arrangements remained unchanged until 1774, when parliament eventually acted to regulate the industry and require that there be an insurable interest in order for a policy to be valid.[68] The purpose was squarely to remove the temptation to gamble and reduce the risk of fraud; in its own words, the Act '[regulated] insurance upon lives . . . prohibiting all such insurance except in cases where the persons insuring shall have an interest in the life or death of the person insured'.[69]

It is impossible to know whether Baker had a financial motive to accepting a position on the Amicable's Court rather than enhancing his social status or exercising his public spirit. The board's remuneration, at least in the 1730s, was modest, with direct payments amounting to only around £100 in total and covering expenses and disbursements approved by the Court. However, the first mention of an independent audit was not until the late 1740s when five gentlemen were chosen as auditors: Thomas Rawling, John Read, Charles Cotton, James Cole and John Unwin'.[70] Several had links to Baker, Jesse and Hody. Cotton had been a member of the Queen's Head lodge in Hollis Street and a member of *Philo-Musicae*; Read a past Grand Steward, appointed in 1732; and John Unwyn (or Unwin), a member of the lodge at the Ship behind the Royal Exchange. Cole may have been the then Master of the lodge at the Vine in Holborn.

The Small Pox Hospital

Baker was also instrumental in the development of London's Small Pox Hospital. Established by subscription in 1746, sufficient seed funds had been raised by 1749 to allow inoculations to commence later that year.[71] Baker was elected a governor in 1750, chairman of the Court the following year and the hospital's treasurer in 1752.[72] The Court was responsible for collecting and supervising the disbursement of close to £6,000, the majority of which was linked to property improvements, and Baker's role would have been time intensive.[73] It may also have been profitable. Conventionally, the treasurer had control of the whole of an institution's funds.

Like the London Infirmary, the Small Pox Hospital held anniversary feasts as annual fund raising events and as with the Masonic Grand Feast, stewards were appointed to underwrite the dinner and encourage ticket sales by example or persuasion. That in 1752 was held on 5 March after a sermon preached at St Andrew's church in Holborn before the duke of Marlborough and the Court. The sermon, by the Bishop of Worcester, was reported in the press and 'answered the objection to inoculations . . . showed the salutariness of that method . . . and took notice of how great use this Hospital was to the poor'. The *London Daily Advertiser* wrote that the church service was 'accompanied by a full band of vocal and instrumental music' and *The London Magazine* praised 'a very fine performance of music vocal and instrumental by above 70 performers'.[74] At its end, a parade of carriages processed from Holborn to the Drapers' hall, carrying the governors, the stewards and their supporters.[75] In addition to its value as a spectacle, the event was a financial success:

> there was collected at the church £225 16s and the collection at the hall after dinner, and the several benefactions then given to that charity, with what was received at the church, amounted to £820 and upwards.[76]

Such events were designed to appeal to both the gentry and the aspirational middling classes. The *London Daily Advertiser* noted the presence of 'a very numerous company of the Nobility, Gentlemen and Merchants' at the dinner.[77] And the *London Magazine* recorded the attendance of some '3,000 ladies' at the church service, for which event tickets were available specifically.[78] The stewards ranged across a narrow spectrum from the aristocracy to affluent City figures and included the 4th earl of Cardigan, George Brudenell, the son-in-law of the duke of Montagu, the first noble Grand Master;[79] and George Parker, 2nd earl of Macclesfield, the Teller of the Exchequer and another prominent freemason.[80] Among the other grandees who lent their names and pocket books were Sir William Beauchamp, a lawyer and Whig MP for Middlesex;[81] William Calvert, Master of the Brewers' Company and Lord Mayor in 1748;[82] John Hopkins who had inherited a £300,000 estate from his cousin of the same name;[83] and Moses Mendes, a successful stockjobber.[84]

The fund raising the following year was even more substantial and married dinner at the Merchant Taylors' hall with a performance of Handel's *Alexander's Feast* at the King's Theatre in the Haymarket.[85] The evening was bisected by a carriage procession from the theatre to the Merchant Taylors' in Threadneedle Street. It was promoted heavily with daily press advertisements and in addition to the monies raised from ticket sales, the collection at dinner brought a further £600 to the hospital with a second taken the following day.[86] Money-raising advertisements nonetheless continued:

> Yesterday the Committee of the Small Pox Hospital met at the Hospital in Cold Bath Fields (where they met every first Thursday in the Month in the Morning) and upon viewing the Patients, twelve Men and Boys, and twelve Women and Girls, by Inoculation, with twelve Men and Boys, and twelve Women and Girls, in the natural Way, appeared perfectly cured, and will be discharged in two or three days. The Public may observe by this, the great Benefit of this most useful Charity. Benefactions and Subscriptions are received by Sir Joseph and Sir Thomas Hankey & Co., Bankers in Fenchurch Street; Messrs Ironside, Belchier and How, in Lombard Street;

Mr George Campbell, Banker, in the Strand; Andrew Drummond Esq., & Co. at Charing Cross; Fotherley Baker, treasurer to the Hospital, at Haberdashers' hall.[87]

The likely impact on Baker of his portfolio of activities and interests can be imagined. As a practicing City solicitor, Clerk to the Haberdashers', a director of the Amicable Society and an active governor, treasurer or trustee of two expanding hospitals, each of which was busy fund raising and developing their respective properties, Baker would have had only limited time for administrative duties as Deputy Grand Master. But this would have been a matter of choice. It can be assumed that the kudos and responsibilities attached to his extra-Masonic activities were more attractive and gave greater opportunities for networking. He was also following an established trend for many men to express their benevolence less through freemasonry and more directly by serving as governors and subscribers to specific socially attractive causes. Moreover, London freemasonry was in decline. With Baker focused elsewhere, Byron's non-attendance at Grand Lodge between 1747 and 1752 was marked by an absence of aristocratic patronage and of anyone willing to pick up the pieces. Baker's substitute leadership was ineffectual. Quarterly Communications were irregular and problematic, and formal set piece events, including the annual Grand Feast, absent. Press coverage, let alone positive coverage, was nonexistent.

John Jesse

John Jesse (__?–1753), a second member of the St Paul's Head lodge and a Grand Steward in 1735 was elected Grand Treasurer in January 1739. His predecessor, Nathaniel Blackerby, had resigned after seven years, piqued at a resolution that he now be required to provide security for the funds he held on behalf of the Grand Charity.

> The Treasurer then stood up & thanked the Brethren for the honour they had done him in continuing so long their Treasurer but told them that he could not be insensible of the Indignity offered him in the Resolutions & the ill treatment he had met with in the Debate & he resented the same in the highest manner And then resigned his Office of Treasurer & promised to send the next morning to the Grand Secretary a Draft on the Bank for the Balance in his hands.[88]

Although absent at the time of the meeting, John Revis, the Grand Secretary, was proposed as Blackerby's replacement. The proposal was agreed but at the next meeting Revis asked to be excused from holding both posts. His request was accepted and on 28 June at the next Quarterly Communication, Lord George Graham informed Grand Lodge that he had the Grand Master, Lord Carnarvon's command to propose John Jesse for the office. What occurred next provides an insight into the inner workings of Grand Lodge.

Jesse's nomination as prospective treasurer did not move as planned. Samuel Righton [Wrighton] handed up a written objection to proceeding to an immediate election and announced that he wished to propose an alternative. Asked to name the person, Wrighton initially prevaricated but 'after many times called upon for that purpose, proposed John Horne of Newport Market, poulterer, to serve the said office'.[89] Horne was divisive, and not merely because his proposal went against the wishes of the new Grand Master. In December 1730, when Horne had been Master of the lodge at the Crown & Sceptres in St Martin's Lane, No. 27 in the 1729 register of lodges, he had been one of five who had volunteered to serve as a Grand Steward. So small a number was thought to be inadequate to underwrite the cost of the Grand Feast, and it was instead proposed that the six junior stewards who had served the previous year should attend the Deputy Grand Master (Nathaniel Blackerby) at the Horn tavern 'who is desired to fix this affair in such manner as he shall think fit'.

At that meeting, Horne and two others who had volunteered were excluded from the new list of prospective Grand Stewards that was presented to the next meeting of Grand Lodge on 29 January 1731. The amended list was headed by James Chambers, a City banker, who had been asked to encourage volunteers and had invited five members of his own lodge to join him. Not only was Horne aggrieved at being excluded, he had also been insulted by Chambers' somewhat gratuitous assertion that 'the stewards would not have such a fellow amongst them'. The aspersion led to the Crown & Sceptres lodge refusing to attend the Grand Feast; they instead dined separately. Grand Lodge's minutes record the debate that followed and the dispute between Horne and Chambers was referred to the Charity Committee to be resolved. In the meantime, it was agreed that in future no lodge should arrange a dinner that coincided with the Grand Feast. However, perhaps inevitably, no report from the Charity Committee was ever minuted as having been presented to Grand Lodge; and only two months later in March 1731, Chambers was appointed Junior Grand Warden.

The declaration that Horne was willing to stand against Jesse resulted in 'great debates arising', a reflection that at least some of those present considered that he had an arguable case. Critically, Wrighton had stated that Horne 'would not only give land security of a sufficient value in the county of Middlesex for what he should be entrusted, but would also allow interest at the rate of four per cent per annum'. In short, should Horne be elected treasurer, he would agree to forego any personal financial benefits that might otherwise be obtained from holding the Grand Charity's funds. This was a considerable give up: holding such financial assets was a standard means of earning income and amassing capital. But rather than debate and deliberate, Graham ended the discussion and 'it being high twelve, the Lodge was closed without coming to any determination'.

The next Quarterly Communication was held on 31 January 1739 and the turnout was substantial. Carnarvon was present with his Grand Officers, who were accompanied by eight past Grand Masters and Grand Officers, together with the representatives of just under one hundred lodges. In a pre-arranged move, Desaguliers proposed that it should be the Grand Master's right to name the person to serve in the office of treasurer. It being agreed, Carnarvon named Jesse without further debate and ordered that the charity's funds be paid across. That the transfer of monies took place before any security had been provided by Jesse underlines the desire that the matter be resolved immediately. It was only at the following meeting that Fotherley Baker's bond was 'read, approved of and ordered to be engrossed and executed'. Jesse was re-elected annually and served as treasurer until his death in 1753. Horne's lodge, then meeting at Forrest's Coffee House in Charing Cross, ceased to attend Grand Lodge and was erased in March 1745.[90]

John Jesse was a minor bureaucrat who held a middle-ranking administrative position at the Post Office. He first appeared in the press in 1729 on succeeding to his father's position:

> we hear that Mr John Jesse, only Son to Mr John Jesse who died last Tuesday, will succeed his Father in the Post Office, said to be worth £100 per Annum.[91]

His father featured in the Post Office accounts in 1718 as an Assistant Comptroller of the Inland Office earning £75 per annum.[92] The 1723 edition of John Chamberlayne's *Magnæ Britanniæ notitia* noted that his salary had increased to £100 per annum five years later and that he was now occupied in 'overlook[ing] the mis-sent, overcharged and dead letters'.[93] His son's position and remuneration were similarly modest. However, the receipt of an inheritance in 1733 almost certainly accelerated his Masonic profile and his career. It was also sufficient to attract press comment:

> a few days since died at Deptford, Mrs Grace Jesse, a maiden lady, worth upwards of £10,000, the bulk of which she has left to her nephew and sole executor, Mr John Jesse of the General Post Office.[94]

A year later following the death of Charles Peal, his former superior, Jesse was promoted to the position of first clerk to the Postmaster General and under secretary to the Post Office, a position commanding a salary of around £200 per annum.[95] He became Deputy Cashier in 1737 and was later promoted to Cashier.[96] From this point onward, Jesse's profile rose as he became the signatory to numerous formal announcements issued by the Post Office and appeared at magistrates' courts and the Old Bailey to give evidence on behalf of his employer.[97] Jesse's involvement with the judiciary also took a more personal turn. In June 1747, suspecting a theft, Jesse took direct action, seized the suspect 'and dragged him into the lodge [at Newgate] . . . whereupon . . . six handkerchiefs were found in his pockets besides Mr Jesse's.

He was immediately charged in the custody of a constable, to be confined'.[98] Jesse was equally robust in the case of a courier who was charged and sentenced to two weeks hard labour for failing to deliver a letter. The justice trying the case in 1751 was Henry Fielding, then London's chief magistrate:

> Yesterday one Williams, a Porter, was committed to Bridewell for a fortnight to hard labour, by Justice Fielding, on the statute made in the 20th year of his present Majesty against labourers who are guilty of any misdemeanour in their employment for the following fact. He received eighteen-pence of John Jesse, Esq., of the Post Office to carry a letter to Mrs Jesse at Bayswater but instead of delivering it, thought proper to throw it away.[99]

Jesse was promoted again in 1747, succeeding Edmund Barham as Accomptant General, the second most senior position at the Post Office after that of Postmaster General, then as now a political appointment.[100] Coincidentally or otherwise, the joint Postmaster General from 1733 until his death in 1759 was another prominent freemason, Thomas Coke, Lord Lovell, a loyal supporter of Sir Robert Walpole. Coke had been raised to a peerage in 1729 and his political allegiance rewarded further with elevation to Viscount Coke and earl of Leicester in 1744. Lovell had succeeded the duke of Norfolk as Grand Master of English Grand Lodge in 1731. He had been initiated in the 1720s and was part of the duke of Richmond's social and Masonic set.

Until his marriage in 1744, Jesse lived in Clement's Lane, a small street off Eastcheap in the City, close by the Post Office's headquarters in Lombard Street, his office for some twenty-five years.[101] Stow's comment on the efficacy of the postal service in the eighteenth century reflects the respect in which the institution was held and its importance 'for the advancement of trade and commerce as well as the convenience of all other business'. In the light of modern postal and courier services, it demands repetition:

> The conveyance of all domestic letters is so expeditious that every 24 hours the Post goes 120 Miles . . . for a letter containing a whole sheet is conveyed 80 Miles for 2d, if a double letter for 6d, one ounce of letters for 10d; but if above 80 Miles, a single Letter 4d, if doubled 6d and an ounce 14d.

> The Post Days to send letters from *London* to any part of *England* and *Scotland* are *Tuesdays*, Thursdays, and *Saturdays*: and the returns certain on *Mondays*, *Wednesdays* and *Fridays* . . . to *Wales* and *Ireland*, the Post goes only twice a week; *viz* on *Tuesdays* and *Saturdays*, and comes from *Wales* every *Monday* and *Friday*; but from *Ireland* the Return is uncertain, because it (as all other foreign Letters do) depends upon Winds.

> For foreign Intelligence in Times of Peace, *Mondays* and *Thursdays* are the Posts for *France*, *Spain* and *Italy*; and *Tuesdays* and *Fridays* for *Holland*,

Germany, Denmark and *Sweden*. On *Mondays* and *Fridays*, the Post goes also for *Flanders* and from thence to *Germany, Denmark* and *Sweden* . . . for the further encouragement of trade and commerce, the late Queen Anne appointed boats to carry letters and pacquets from England as far as the West Indies . . . the rate for every letter is 9d a sheet.[102]

Jesse's marriage to Esther Wood, the daughter of Christopher Wood, described as a gentleman of Norton, Staffordshire, was reported in several newspapers, including the *Daily Post* of 1 October 1744. No dowry was mentioned and it is possible that his wife's family was even then in financial difficulty. The *Whitehall Evening Post or London Intelligencer* of 14 November 1749 recorded that Christopher Wood of Norton under Cannock in Staffordshire, now a 'dealer and chapman', had been declared bankrupt. He died soon after and a private act of parliament in 1750 ordered that his estate be sold to repay his debts.[103] The *General Advertiser* on 28 July 1752 set out the particulars of the estate which included several farms amounting to some 400 acres, pools and ponds, two-thirds of the manor of Norton and a further 3,000 acres 'with coal mines in them'. One of the four attorneys appointed to handle the sale was Fotherley Baker. The estate was almost certainly heavily mortgaged and no purchasers were forthcoming; in 1757, the Court of Chancery ordered that the estate be auctioned.[104]

Following his marriage, Jesse moved from the City, acquiring a house in Bayswater on a recently built development at Craven Hill on Lord Craven's estate. A similar property was advertised in March 1749, described as containing 'all sorts of conveniences' and considered entirely suitable for a middling family, being 'pleasantly situated at Craven Hill . . . adjoining to Kensington gravel pits, opposite Kensington Gardens and at a distance from the road'.[105] Jesse's affluence was marked not only by his new house but also the coach and staff that he maintained.[106]

His association with Fotherley Baker almost certainly originated within freemasonry. Both were successively members of *Philo-Musicae* and the St Paul's Head lodges; each was appointed a Grand Steward, Baker in 1733 and Jesse in 1735; and both served as Grand Officers throughout the 1740s and early 1750s. Over time, their relationship developed extra-masonically. Probably at Baker's invitation, Jesse became a director of the Amicable Society; he was first elected in 1746 and, with a statutory one-year gap, served two successive three years terms until 1752.[107] Jesse also became a governor of the London Infirmary in 1742, a life governor the following year and, in 1752, a trustee;[108] he also subscribed to become a governor of the Small Pox Hospital in 1750.[109]

Jesse served as Grand Treasurer until his death in 1753.[110] The minutes for 6 March that year note his inability to attend due to illness and those of 14 June record that 'the DGM acquainted the Brethren with the death of Bro John Jesse Esq'. His will was proved at the Prerogative Court of Canterbury on 13 June 1753.[111]

JOHN REVIS

In 1723, John Revis (__?–1765) was Junior Warden of the Crown & Anchor lodge close to St Clements Church, a few steps away from Jesse's house in Clement's Lane.[112] Two years later, the lodge had moved to the Star and Garter in Covent Garden and Revis had become Senior Warden.[113] In 1728, the lodge relocated to the Globe in the Strand and Revis had become its Master and a Grand Steward.[114] Revis also featured in the minutes of Grand Lodge three years later on 24 June 1731, described as the Master of the Queen's Head, Great Queen Street, in connection with a petition seeking relief for a fellow mason – North Stainer – who had been imprisoned for debt. Revis supported the petition and had 'taken the trouble of going to [Stainer's] creditors'; he reported that they would accept 2s 6d in the pound in full discharge of their debts.[115] An enthusiastic freemason, Revis was appointed Grand Secretary on 30 March 1734. He held the position for twenty-three years until 1757, when he was appointed DGM, serving until 1763. He held active office eighteen years longer than any of his peers.

Revis was born in Newport Pagnell, Buckinghamshire, the son of an apothecary.[116] He moved to London and worked, apparently successfully, as a lace and linen draper. However, he was not a member of the Drapers' Company. The electoral roll confirms his address near Charing Cross and that he voted for Sir George Vandeput, a candidate for the Independent Electors of Westminster in the 1749 elections.[117] Revis was also one of several signatories who testified to the effectiveness of 'Mr Godfrey's Fire Machines' in extinguishing a fire in Charing Cross on 2 August 1724; a certificate to the effect was published in the *London Gazette* on 8 and 11 August 1724. There is no record of a marriage. Obituary notices following his death on 3 September 1765 confirm his occupation, residence and charitable activities:[118]

> Tuesday night last died, at Rochester, [on] his way to London, John Revis, Esq.; formerly a linen draper at Charing Cross; much esteemed for his honesty and integrity while in business, and whose death will be severely felt by many people, as he always took delight in relieving the distressed, and has left the most convincing proof of his humane and charitable disposition towards the poor, having for many years since built alms houses at Newport Pagnell, Bucks., the place of his nativity, with a generous endowment: but too sensible will the poor in general be of the loss of so good a friend to enumerate his many other amiable qualities would exceed the bound of this paper.[119]

The seven almshouses in Newport Pagnell financed by Revis in the mid-1750s still stand and the charity he founded and endowed continues.[120] His bequest and the death of his mother and sisters are commemorated in the parish church of St Peter and St Paul and the underlying conveyances, trustees and value of the endowment, then some £3,700, are described in *A History of Newport Pagnell*.[121]

Unlike Baker, Jesse and other Masonic colleagues, Revis appears not to have engaged with any of the more popular London charities but instead maintained a low public profile. His freemasonry and business may have absorbed the majority of his time. Indeed, freemasonry may have become a substitute for family. Revis received no financial reward for his role as Grand Secretary and self-financed his expenses for nearly two decades, including paying the salary of an assistant. When in 1752, it was proposed somewhat belatedly that his costs be reimbursed, Revis declined, 'generously waiving all pecuniary advantages'. Nonetheless, it was agreed that he should be allowed a stipend of three guineas for each meeting, including the Grand Feast, in order 'to defray his expenses of an assistant secretary and the expenses of printing and sending out the Summonses together with every other incidental charge and or expense'.[122]

Within Grand Lodge, Revis appears to have been regarded as little more than a functionary, rather than a colleague on equal terms. It is difficult otherwise to explain how he came to be nominated for the post of Treasurer in 1738 while he was already Secretary without having been consulted, let alone the matter of his funding Grand Lodge's operating costs and expenses for twenty years. If this were so, he would have been out of step with many of his Moderns contemporaries who treated freemasonry as a continuation of their associational life. And it may explain his absence from the later membership list of the OKA which in the 1740s harboured many of Grand Lodge's leading figures. In 1728, when Revis was Master of the Globe, it was common for Grand Stewards and other senior freemasons to be members of more than a single lodge and he is listed as a member of the OKA, then lodge No. 43.[123] No minute books pre-dating 1731 survive and Revis is not mentioned in the list of members submitted to Grand Lodge in 1725 or 1730. Had he had been a member of the OKA in 1728, it would appear that he later ceased to attend. He would otherwise have been mentioned in the OKA minutes given his subsequent positions as Grand Secretary and Deputy Grand Master.[124] One reason may have been the shift in the character and membership of the lodge, which was becoming increasingly socially exclusive. Indeed, the OKA became so important in the 1740s, it was almost an inner core of Grand Lodge – a grand lodge within.

1 *1ˢᵗ Degree Tracing Board* (date unknown).

2 Antients *Grand Register*, Attendance List, extract.

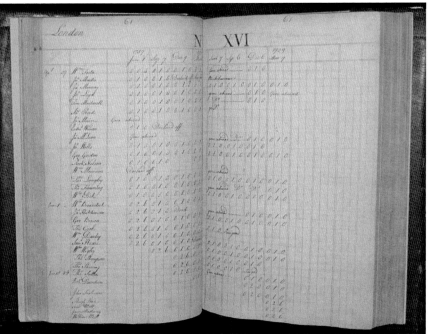

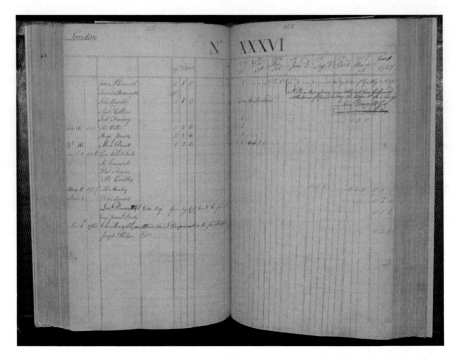

3 Antients *Grand Register*,
Membership List, extract.

4 'Ceremony of making a
Free-Mason'; engraving from
*Hiram, or The Grand Master
Key* (1764).

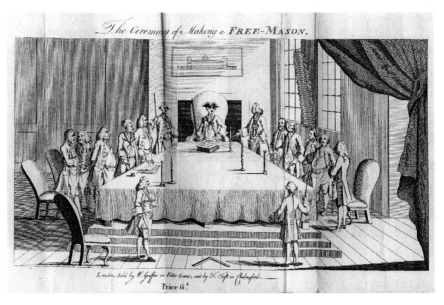

5 Early Moderns' Masonic Apron (date unknown).

6 John Senex, *Map of London* (1720).

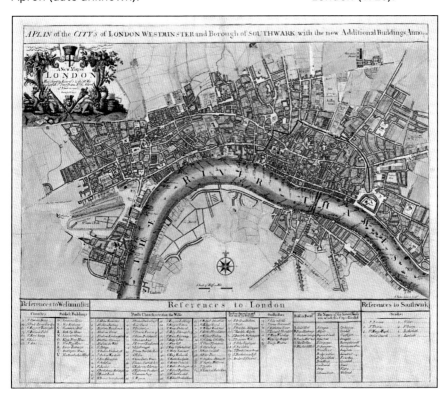

7 William Stewart, 1st earl of Blessington (1709–1769); oil painting by Stephen Slaughter (1744).

8 John Murray, 3rd duke of Atholl (1729–1774); engraving by unknown artist (undated).

9 Thomas Alexander Erskine, 6th earl of Kelly (1731–1781); engraving by Lizars after portrait by Robert Home (*c.* 1780).

10 Sir Cecil Wray (1734–1805); engraving (unknown artist) published by J. Walker of Paternoster Row (1784).

11 Robert Freke Gould (1836–1915); engraving by Chardon-Whitman, Paris (c. 1899).

12 Henry Sadler (1840–1911); cabinet print of a photograph by Burt Sharp, Brighton (1879).

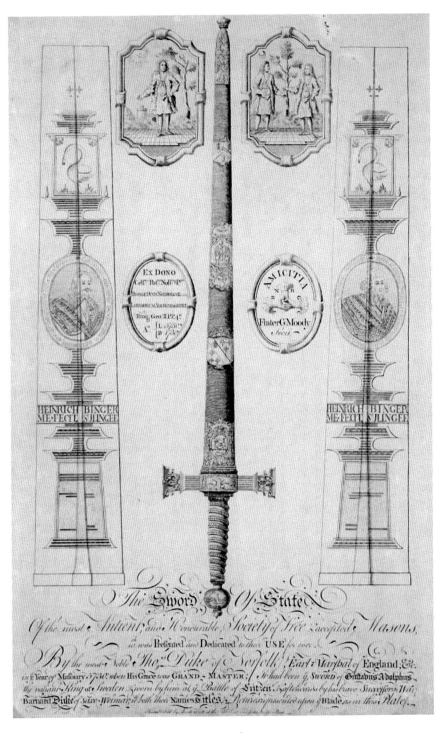

13 'Sword of State of the Moderns Grand Lodge'; engraving, printed and sold by Bro. Scott of Paternoster Road (undated).

14 'Reception des Compagnons';
engraving from L. Travenol, *Nouvea
Catechisme des Franc-Maçon* (1749).

CHAPTER SEVEN

The King's Arms Lodge

In the 1720s and early 1730s, the duke of Richmond's Horn tavern had dominated Grand Lodge and a few key members substantially controlled the direction of English freemasonry. By the late 1730s, the position had changed to the extent that within a decade, the Horn had ceased to be recognised as a 'regular' lodge. A catalyst was the appointment in 1735 of the 2nd viscount Weymouth as Grand Master of English freemasons.[1] Weymouth had been initiated into the OKA the prior year and in deference to his rank, if not to his age, he was 25, he was elected Master of the lodge in March 1735. Two short months later, Weymouth was installed as Grand Master.

Sir Cecil Wray, the Master of the OKA at whose invitation Weymouth had joined, had been Deputy Grand Master the prior year and was instrumental in arranging Weymouth's accession within Grand Lodge. The appointment cemented a connection between the OKA and Grand Lodge that would last more than fifteen years. In 1735, Martin Clare, who for many years had deputised for Wray at the OKA, was appointed Junior Grand Warden; in 1736, both Grand Wardens, Sir Robert Lawley and William Graeme, were sourced from the OKA. Other members of the lodge were also given grand rank over the next decade, including Benjamin Gascoyne and Edward Hody, who became Grand Wardens in the early 1740s. But perhaps most impressively, in virtually every year between 1738 and 1752, a member of the OKA occupied the pivotal position of Deputy Grand Master. By the mid-1740s, the lodge had established itself as London's best connected and most exclusive lodge. Indeed, if further evidence were required, Anthony Sayer, Grand Master in 1717, was employed as the lodge's tyler in 1735, a post he retained until his death in 1742.

Table 24 demonstrates the level of interconnectivity between the OKA and Grand Lodge. This had been orchestrated. Where in the early 1730s the OKA was positioned as one of the leading Enlightenment lodges, the lodge minute book hints that by the mid- and late 1740s the lodge operated almost as an exclusive outpost of Grand Lodge and a grand dining club. The lodge had a policy of inviting members of Grand Lodge to join and to attend its meeting and dinners. Eccleshall notes the OKA minutes of 15 March 1736, which record that the guests that evening included John Ward, the Deputy Grand Master and acting Grand Master; Sir Edward Mansell, the Senior Grand Warden; and Lord Loudon, the prospective Grand Master. On occasions such as this, the main emphasis was on dining and drinking, and

Table 24 The Members of the OKA Holding Grand Office, 1730–52

OKA Member	Grand Rank	Year(s)	OKA Rank	Year(s)	GSt
Sir Cecil Wray	DGM	1734	WM	1730–3, 1735	N/A
Lord Weymouth	GM	1735	WM	1735	N/A
Martin Clare	GW	1735	SW/WM	1730–5, 1737	1735
	DGM	1741			
Sir Robert Lawley	GW	1736–7	WM	1738	1735
	DGM	1742–3	WM	1741, 1745–7	
William Graeme	GW	1737	Member	1730	1735
	DGM	1738–40			
Benjamin Gascoyne	GW	1741	WM	1740	1736
Edward Hody	GW	1742–3	WM	1735, 1739	1736
	DGM	1745–6	WM	1744	
Lord (John) Ward	GM	1742–3	Member	1744	1733
Lord Cranstoun	GM	1745	Member	1747	N/A
Thomas Smith	GW	1745–6	Member	1735	1744
George Payne	GM	1746	Member	1747	N/A
			WM		1749
Fotherley Baker	DGM	1747–52	Member	1747	1734
			WM	1748	
Hon Robert Shirley	GW	1747–52	Member	1747	1745
Daniel Carne	GSwBr	1746–55	Member	1747	1741
			WM	1750–2	

'[Masonic] business was adjourned', albeit that 'the Society did not break up until after midnight'.[4] The practice continued into the 1740s. Edward Hody's year as Master concluded with the lodge entertaining the then Lord Ward, now Grand Master in his own right, and his principal officers. Eccleshall records that 'the lodge was clearly anxious to preserve its close contact with Grand Lodge' and in 1746 it was resolved that 'any former or present Grand Officer . . . shall be admitted (without the form of a ballot or the usual fee) by a majority of the brethren then present'.[5] That year, five Grand Officers joined: George Payne, the oldest and most senior surviving non-aristocratic Grand Master; Lord Cranstoun, the immediate past Grand Master; the Hon Robert Shirley, later Senior Grand Warden; Fotherley Baker, Deputy Grand Master; and Daniel Carne, the Grand Sword Bearer. Baker, Payne and Carne were elected Master of the OKA in 1748, 1749 and 1750, respectively. The association ceased to be positive for the OKA in the 1750s, once Lord Carysfort had replaced Byron as Grand Master and a new slate of Grand Officers had been appointed. Many members left or ceased to attend and the lodge regressed, beginning, in Eccleshall, words 'a much quieter period':

the great names of those who directed the lodge during its close association with Grand Lodge disappear from the minutes. The number of members declined, as did the attendance, most meetings being attended by 15–20 brethren [and often less] and on occasions the three principal officers were all marked *pro tem.*[6]

Of the handful of lodge minute books from the 1720s and 1730s that have survived, most are formulaic, detailing the names of attendees, the ritual undertaken but often little else. Covering the period from 1733 to 1756 and beginning at the time the lodge moved from the Cross Keys in Henrietta Street to the King's Arms tavern in the Strand, the first extant minute book of the OKA offers greater insight. In the 1730s, the OKA's members were primarily middling and professional, with a small number of landed gentry. At the time, the OKA was renowned as one of, if not the leading Enlightenment lodge in London and under Martin Clare's *de facto* leadership, members and guests gave lectures on a diversity of subjects in which they were either practitioners or hobbyists. The lodge encapsulated Edward Oakley's dictum that freemasonry should be at the forefront of education, providing 'proper lectures . . . in such of the sciences, as shall be thought to be most agreeable to the Society, and to the honour and instruction of the Craft'.[7] Indeed, the OKA in the 1730s provides one of the clearest examples of what Clare, its acting Master and Senior Warden, had termed 'useful and entertaining conversation' and under his guidance the OKA promoted rational analysis of the natural world: 'the grand design'.[8]

Some thirty-six lectures were given in the decade 1733–43, the majority in the early years. These included the practical application of recent scientific discoveries, with three lectures based on different industrial processes and nine that examined new scientific inventions, techniques and apparatus. Other talks explored architecture, art, ethics, history and mathematics. Speakers included Robert West, a portraitist, who spoke on 'some evident faults in the Cartoons of Raphael', and Isaac Ware, the architect and later Secretary of the Board of Works, on Andrea Palladio.[9] Ware, a member of James Thornhill's St Martin's Lane Academy, re-founded by Hogarth in 1735, gave his lecture immediately after he had been initiated, suggesting that this was the principal reason for him having joined.

At that time, the OKA combined Masonic ritual and dining with educational entertainment. The formula followed the approach pioneered by Desaguliers and other fashionable peripatetic lecturers who popularised science and gave it a cultural status.[10] Clare was one of their number. A successful educator and mathematician, he had established his Soho Academy in 1717 and his pupils were 'fitted for business' rather than given a purely classical education. Clare's textbook, *Youth's Introduction to Trade and Business*, around which the Soho Academy operated, was considered path breaking and ran to twelve editions through to 1791.[11] The school itself was regarded as one of England's leading educational establishments – 'one of the most celebrated and successful of private boarding schools'.[12]

Reflecting this, its students came from affluent and well-connected families. They included John Murray, later the 3rd duke of Atholl; John Christopher Smith, the composer; and sons of parliamentarians, including Arthur Onslow, then Speaker of the House of Commons.

Clare had been elected FRS in 1735, proposed by a raft of freemasons including Desaguliers and Sir Richard Manningham of the Horn; Dr Alexander Stuart of the Rummer in Charing Cross; and Robert Hart of the Mitre in Covent Garden. Support for his election was probably linked to the publication of *Motion of Fluids*.[13] Clare's aims were at one with Desaguliers and the scientific Enlightenment: to use 'experiments performed with accuracy and judgment' and to create

> principles . . . built on the strongest and most rational basis, that of experiment and fact; which cannot but be acceptable to those, who admire demonstration, and delight in truth.

The papers in *Motion of Fluids* had been given by Clare as lectures to the members of the OKA: 'a set of gentlemen who were so indulgent both to their matter and form as to encourage their publication'.[14] And the book was dedicated to Lord Weymouth, the then Master of the OKA and later Grand Master. Subscribers included members of the lodge and many other freemasons, and the second and third editions were dedicated respectively to Richard Boyle, Lord Burlington, and Henry Herbert, 9th earl of Pembroke, also freemasons.

Clare's standing in Masonic circles was underpinned further by his *Discourse*, a lecture given to the Grand Stewards' lodge and again at Grand Lodge, and its central message became a tenet of eighteenth-century freemasonry:

> The chief pleasure of society – viz., good conversation and the consequent improvements – are rightly presumed . . . to be the principal motive of our first entering into then propagating the Craft . . . We are intimately related to those great and worthy spirits who have ever made it their business and aim to improve themselves and inform mankind. Let us then copy their example that we may also hope to attain a share in their praise.[15]

Sir Cecil Wray, elected Master of the OKA in 1730, had agreed to accept the chair on the express understanding that Clare would act as his Senior Warden and preside in his place during Wray's regular absences from London. This Clare did, and the OKA's minutes record how the lodge attracted numerous applications for membership. A few were contentious and after several eminent prospective joiners had been blackballed, a new structure was introduced to allow 'members of ability and consequence . . . being generally acceptable to the lodge' to join with a lower risk of rejection. Thus from 4 March 1734, and in contrast to what was set out in the regulations issued by English Grand Lodge, three blackballs would be required for exclusion from the OKA. The following week, on 11 March, Viscount Weymouth and Viscount Murray, the 2nd duke of Atholl, were admitted members. Each gave six guineas towards the cost of the evening's entertainment.[16] Two weeks later on 27 March, Lord Vere Bertie and William Todd Esq., the latter a member of the Rummer, were made members. The evening was financed by Todd and the minutes note the cost at £8 4s 10d.[17]

It was from about this time that the lodge began to develop more as a dining club. The annual membership fee was increased to five guineas for gentlemen but remained at three guineas for artisans, notwithstanding that this was still high. The OKA also modified its admission rules further such that gentlemen would require the approval of a simple majority but a two-thirds majority would be required otherwise.[18] With an increasingly exclusive membership, the lodge began to consolidate its connections to Grand Lodge. Members promoted colleagues and enhanced the OKA's influence through invitations to other Grand Officers. The lodge's reputation was rising and many did join. But as the links to Grand Lodge grew stronger and its members more gentrified, the frequency with which lectures were given declined. On 2 February 1743, the minutes noted that the lodge had been disappointed by brethren failing to provide their promised lectures, and at the meeting on 7 December the same year, the Master 'called upon several brethren to oblige the lodge with a lecture upon any useful subject'. No-one complied and Sir Robert Lawley was prevailed upon 'to offer a further continuance of a lecture in Masonry either on the next or the succeeding lodge night'. By the end of the 1740s, the practice of offering lectures had atrophied and was largely discontinued, replaced principally by dining.

Among the visitors to the OKA and, in 1744, a joining member, John Ward, by then Lord Ward, was unique in being the first (later noble) mason to rise through the ranks to become Grand Master. Ward was an avid freemason: a founder, the first Master and sometime Secretary of Staffordshire's earliest recorded lodge, the Bell and Raven in Wolverhampton;[19] and a member of the aristocratic Bear and Harrow lodge in London, among others. He had been appointed a Grand Steward in 1732; was Junior Grand Warden and Senior Grand Warden from 1732–4; and sat as Deputy Grand Master from 1735–7.[20] He was to rise higher. In 1740, Ward succeeded his cousin to become 6th baron Ward of Birmingham and, two years later, he was selected as Grand Master.

Ward had inherited estates in Sedgeley and Willingworth in Staffordshire, to which his cousin's death in 1740 added property at Dudley as well as the title.[21] His marriage to Anna Maria Bourchier of Clontarf, Co. Dublin, produced a son, John, later 2nd viscount of Dudley & Ward. His wife died within a year of the birth and Ward married again in 1745. His second marriage to Mary Carver, heir to a Jamaican plantation fortune, brought another son, William, who later inherited the title from his half brother.[22] Ward was elected an MP for Newcastle-under-Lyme in 1727 but lost the seat in 1734.[23] This would have been a disappointment given that his father had been an MP for Staffordshire from 1710 to 1713 and again in 1715 until his death. Nonetheless, he was appointed Sheriff for Northampton in December 1729 and subsequently made Lord Warden of Birmingham, Recorder for Worcester and sworn to the privy council.[24] In common with many in freemasonry, Ward was also a magistrate, appointed to the bench in 1729.[25] Politically, he initially tended to the opposition, first a Tory, then a Country Whig, and later a Patriotic Whig and deemed ally of William Pitt.[26] However, before the 1745 rebellion, Ward may have been associated with the Jacobites and his name was communicated to the French and ostensibly noted as an influential and wealthy supporter. In the election of 1747, Ward campaigned against the Leveson Gowers, one of the more politically influential families in Staffordshire and then supporters of the administration, leading to a complaint from Lord Gower to the duke of Newcastle that Ward was undermining the family's interest in the county 'by all the little low dirty tricks you can imagine'.[27]

Ward's political and judicial activities reflected above all a self-interested desire to protect and add to his property and financial assets. The House of Commons' parliamentary papers mention him once, on 18 May 1733, and only then in relation to his own estate:

> a Complaint being made to the House, that Jonah Persehouse, of Wolverhampton, in the County of Stafford, John Green, William Mason, Daniel Mason, Thomas Mason, William Goston, Samuel Mason and Benjamin Whitehouse, of Sedgeley, in the said County, having sunk a coal pit adjoining to the Estate of John Ward, esquire, a member of this House, have entered upon his said estate, and taken coals therefrom; in breach of the Privilege of this House.[28]

Although the second viscount was more celebrated and successful as an industrialist and politician, Ward was aware of the commercial value of his inheritance which generated an annual income of around £10,000 and contained numerous broad coal seams interspersed with iron ore, brick clay and limestone. He maintained and expanded coal mining and iron smelting on his estate, especially at Dudley, which comprised one of the most significant holdings in the Black Country and had been one of the earliest to install a Newcomen engine. Ward also safeguarded his commercial interests in the House of Lords where he supported and promoted road construction.[29] But his son did more, sponsoring a succession of bills that advanced enclosures, facilitated extraction and connected the family's mines to the growing network of canals that served the area and in which he was a prominent shareholder.[30] During Ward's lifetime, the income generated from the Dudley & Ward estates increased more than fivefold.[31] However, they rose a further tenfold by the late nineteenth century.

Although motivated by the prospect of amassing more wealth, Ward's financial resources were also expended in social self-promotion. The development of his mines and natural resources in Staffordshire took second place to expenditure on the demolition of the family's mediaeval mansion at

Himley and its replacement with a large Palladian house within ornamental grounds. The scale of the development was such that the local village required relocation. In London, Ward's townhouse was in fashionable Upper Brook Street in Mayfair where he owned two houses, numbers 35 and 36.[32] But they too were considered insufficiently grand and, in the 1750s, construction began on the first Dudley House, one of the precursors to the later Park Lane palaces, completed in 1757.[33]

Ward's belief in wealth being the mark of a man and property as personal aggrandisement partly explains his doctrinaire approach as Grand Master. He understood the role of Grand Master principally to be to maintain and protect the authority of Grand Lodge, and thereby his own status. The developments taking place in society more widely were ignored or not understood. In this, Ward epitomised the unreconstructed agricultural landed interest to which his mining activities were an adjunct. Reflecting this, the large-scale development of the industrial aspects of his estate occurred only after the 1760s, when his agents and sons pursued the enclosures, turnpikes and canals that were to increase its value almost exponentially. For Lord Ward, mineral resources were the milk cow that supplied funding to support an ostentatious lifestyle; for his sons, they were the more the foundation of a commercial dynasty.

One of Ward's Staffordshire neighbours was Sir Robert Lawley (17__?– 1779), 4th Bt., of Canwell Hall in Staffordshire. He succeeded to the title and estates in 1730.[34] Lawley's marriage in 1726 to Elizabeth, the daughter of Sir Lambert Blackwell, with its £30,000 dowry, featured prominently in the society press.[35] Lawley also had political ambitions but failed in a bid to become MP for Bridgenorth. His appointment as high sheriff of the county a decade later in 1744 may have been part compensation. Lawley was close to Sir Cecil Wray and in the same social set in London. He joined the OKA at the time it transferred to the Cross Keys tavern when Wray became Master. Lawley became a Grand Steward in 1735 alongside William Graeme and Martin Clare and later that year became Master of the Stewards' Lodge. An avid attendee at Grand Lodge, Lawley sat as Senior Grand Warden from 1736–8, and as Deputy Grand Master from 1742–3. He was Master of the OKA in 1738, again in 1741, and from 1745 until 1747, when he consolidated the OKA's connections to Grand Lodge with the admission of the principal Grand Officers.

Other Grand Officers linked to the OKA during the 1740s were Robert Shirley, William Graeme and Edward Hody. The Hon Robert Shirley (1723–1787), was the son of the Hon Laurence Shirley, the fourth son of Robert, 1st earl Ferrers. The absence of any male heirs to succeed the 2nd and 3rd earls allowed Shirley's eldest brother, also Laurence, to inherit the title and estates in 1745. He is best known as the last peer in England to be hanged: tried and convicted for murder in 1760. The title passed to Washington Shirley and, at his death in 1778, to Robert. The family owned large estates in Derbyshire, Northamptonshire and Leicestershire, where their principal house was Staunton Harold Hall. Shirley was appointed a

Grand Steward in 1745–6 and served as Senior Grand Warden from 1747–51 under Baker's Deputy Grand Mastership.

William Graeme (1700–1745), a Scottish surgeon, was educated at Leyden (1720) and St Andrews (1724). He taught surgery in Edinburgh until 1726 but subsequently moved to London to practice and lecture. Other than with regard to freemasonry, Graeme had a modest public profile and his Masonic status at Grand Lodge appears to have been linked solely to the OKA's patronage. He was appointed a Grand Steward in 1735, promoted to Grand Warden the following year (1736–7) and sat as Deputy Grand Master in 1739 and 1740. In 1744, he was recalled to become SGW to Baker's JGW. Perhaps reflecting his modest social status, Graeme was not elected Master of the OKA. However, in April 1730, he was elected FRS, proposed by Martin Folkes, another former Deputy Grand Master and the leading figure at the Bedford Head lodge in Covent Garden. Graeme's other proposers included Alexander Stuart of the Rummer, Charring Cross, and John Ranby and Sir Edward Wilmot, two eminent surgeons.[36]

Graeme's introduction to the OKA may have been via Edward Hody (1698–1759), a fellow physician. Hody, specialised in the lucrative area of midwifery. Born at Spettisbury House in Dorset to a wealthy landed family, he was educated at Charterhouse and St John's, Cambridge, where he matriculated in 1716. He subsequently studied at Leyden (1719), where he may have met Graeme, and Rheims (1723), where he received his MD.[37] Hody's revision and publication of Giffard's *Cases in Midwifery* 'printed by subscription . . . for the benefit of the Widow and her Children' was advertised widely from 1732 and it was possibly a consequence of the more than thirty press advertisements for the book that his election as FRS in 1733 was considered newsworthy.[38] His main proposer was Thomas Pellet, a member of the Bedford Head lodge and later President of the Royal College of Physicians.[39]

Hody's election notice described him as 'a Gentleman well skilled in Physick, Anatomy and Natural Sciences' and he was in several ways an Enlightenment figure. A subscribing governor of St George's Hospital, Hody was subsequently appointed its chief physician.[40] His book subscriptions reveal non-medical interests that ranged from Martin Clare's *Motion of Fluids* to John Miller's *Poems on Several Occasions*, and he was an antiquarian and a member of Stukeley's Society of Antiquaries. Hody was additionally a governor of the Bridewell Hospital and, alongside Baker, a director of the Amicable Society. Masonically, he was appointed a Grand Steward in 1735, Senior Grand Warden in 1742 and 1743, and Deputy Grand Master in 1745 and 1746.[41] Hody was Master of the OKA in 1735 and again in 1739 and 1742. His association with Lawley and Clare was not limited to the OKA; all three had also been members of the Shakespeare's Head lodge in Little Marlborough Street.

CHAPTER EIGHT

The Anglo-Irish:
Ascendancy and Alienation

Our final chapter explores the economic and political alienation of the Anglo-Irish, an issue that motivated the earl of Blessington to agree to become the Antients' first noble Grand Master and politicised those in the Grand Lodge of Ireland at the loyalist heart of the Protestant Anglo-Irish community and persuaded them to recognise the Antients to the exclusion of the original Grand Lodge of England. The disaffection of the Anglo-Irish from Britain is not widely understood and this chapter explores the context and draws the development of patriotic nationalism from the end of the seventeenth century to the mid- and late eighteenth.

The Treaty of Limerick ended the Irish rebellion against William and Mary's accession to the English throne. But the settlement did more than conclude the Williamite-Jacobite War; it also entrenched the political dominance of Ireland's minority Protestant elite.[1] By the 1740s, the Anglo-Irish ascendancy had been in place for over fifty years. England's subjugation of Ireland was not new. Suppression dated back to the eleventh century and boasted an honour roll of subsequent English rulers. Henry VIII had declared himself king of Ireland in 1542; and James I, and later Elizabeth I, had consolidated English power with a campaign of repression that culminated in the 1594–1603 Nine Years' War. Another rebellion in 1641 triggered the Confederate Wars. On this occasion, Ireland's insurrection was halted by Cromwell's invasion and a four-year military campaign. The punitive sanctions that followed reinforced English domination: the colonial Plantations were extended; Catholic estates confiscated to compensate Cromwell's officers and soldiers; and Irish insurgents imprisoned, transported overseas or executed. Peace in Ireland was not negotiated; it was inflicted. And in the wake of the large-scale conveyance of land and assets to the Protestant minority came a further transfer of political authority through the introduction and application of a discriminatory anti-Catholic legal code. But Ireland's opposition was not destroyed; it was in abeyance. In 1689 and 1690, the Glorious Revolution that took William and Mary to the English throne triggered another conflict as James II's Irish Catholic supporters attempted to leverage the country into a base from which to launch his return to power. They failed. Irish Jacobitism was eviscerated at the Boyne in 1690 and buried at Aughrim in 1691. Subdued, disarmed and cowed, Ireland's

Catholic opposition was unable to recover and not even the Scottish risings of 1715 and 1745 triggered active Jacobite support for the Stuart Pretenders in Ireland, far less rebellion.

Regardless of the military reality, Ireland's Catholic majority continued to be viewed as a potential threat with the danger from its rebellious youth probably the source of greatest fear. In such a context, it is easy to understand why *de facto* permission to recruit in Ireland for service in foreign regiments remained substantially in place until 1745.[2] There were obvious positive benefits in allowing Ireland's otherwise unemployed young Catholics to emigrate to join French and Spanish regiments rather than remain at home where they could and would constitute a more immediate prospective problem. The same argument applied to the exiled 'Wild Geese', those Irish soldiers who had fought with the Jacobites against William. Under the terms of the peace treaty they had been transported to exile in France where many served in Louis XIV's Irish brigades.[3] The expatriate Irish also served in other continental armies, including Spain's, which mustered with five Irish regiments. Estimates vary but it is probable that during the course of the eighteenth century, at least several hundred thousand Irishmen were recruited and left for overseas service. Basil Williams has quoted one estimate of 450,000 in the period to 1745;[4] other commentators have put forward figures as high as 500,000.[5]

With London's acquiescence, Ireland's parliament executed a range of additional measures to reduce the risk of dissent, including active support for forcible impressment in the British army and navy. Three examples from three consecutive months in 1726 involving over five hundred Irishmen suggest the policy would have had a considerable cumulative impact.

On 8 March 'came in His Majesty's Ships, *Lively* and *Success*, Men of War from Ireland, having on board 220 impressed seamen for the fleet'.

On 13 April 'the *Drake*, Man of War, sailed from Cork for Portsmouth, with 130 men impressed for the service of the Navy'.

On 31 May 'came in the *Lively* Man of War, from Ireland, with 170 men impressed for Sir John Jenning's fleet'.[6]

Successive tranches of sometimes-savage anti-Catholic legislation were enacted and although legislation was in practice often enforced with some moderation, both old and new penal laws were deployed to reinforce the dominance – political and economic – of Ireland's minority ruling elite. Catholics and non-conforming dissenters who together represented more than 80 per cent of the population were disenfranchised and excluded from standing for parliament or public office.[7] Restrictions on access to mortgage funding and land ownership reduced by two thirds the acreage of estates held by Catholics from an already modest 25 per cent of aggregate landholdings to between 5 and 10 per cent. The prohibition of leases longer than thirty-one years intentionally limited Catholic security of tenure and, on inheritance, unless the eldest son abjured Catholicism and converted to the Church of Ireland, land would be divided equally among the deceased's heirs as a means of limiting the influence of any single landowner.

Other sanctions targeted the more middling, with Catholics being excluded from many professions and the magistracy and judiciary. The ability to access secondary and tertiary education was curbed:

> no person of the popish religion shall publicly teach school or instruct youth, or in private houses teach youth, except only the children of the master or mistress of the private house, upon pain of twenty pounds and prison for three months for every such offence,

with Catholics prohibited from matriculating at Trinity College, Dublin.[8]

Perhaps more intrusively and in an echo of the restrictions enforced on the Huguenots in France the previous century, the Irish parliament banned inter-marriage between the faiths:

> whereas many Protestant women, heirs or heirs apparent to lands or other great substances in goods or chattels, or having considerable estates for life, or guardianship of children entitled to such estates, by flattery and other crafty insinuations of popish persons, have been seduced to contract matrimony with and take to husband, papists, to the great ruin of such estates, to the great loss of many Protestant persons to whom the same might descend, and to the corrupting such Protestant women that they forsake their religion and become papists, to the great dishonour of Almighty God, the great prejudice of the Protestant interest, and the heavy sorrow of all their Protestant friends.[9]

A few loopholes nonetheless remained available. Affluent Catholic landed gentry were permitted to send their sons abroad to be educated in continental Europe; and although Catholics were prevented from possessing arms or owning horses suitable for cavalry use, defined as 'worth more than £5', 'papist gentlemen who can prove themselves comprised under the Articles of Limerick may have a sword, a case of pistols, and a gun for defence of their house or for fowling'.[10]

The suppression of Irish culture and Catholicism was considerable but it was not complete. In the face of sustained legal prejudice and widespread antipathy, many landed Catholic families ensured that at least one son would become a Protestant, even if only in name, in order to preserve the family's remaining estates intact. And Catholic worship continued, although priests were meant to be approved and registered; local 'hedge row' rural education failed to be wholly displaced by the new centrally funded Protestant schools that were becoming established across the country; and substantial elements of Gaelic culture and language survived, particularly in the west and north west of Ireland.

British colonial rule in Ireland was directed by an administration led by the Lord Lieutenant and his Chief Secretary. In formal terms, the Lord Lieutenant represented the crown – the king of Ireland – and in that capacity was head of both the executive and judiciary. In practice, the position was given in the name of the king to a prominent British politician, often one who was out of favour or seen as a potential political threat. Nonetheless, the Lord Lieutenant was generally a significant member of the government with a political remit to preserve stability in Ireland, keep London informed of domestic Irish politics (although there were multiple communication channels between the two countries) and ensure the smooth passage of the finance bills that allowed the Irish establishment to function.

From a Catholic standpoint, notwithstanding any laxity in enforcing the penal laws, the Protestant ascendancy would have been regarded as virtually absolute. But despite the form, the substance of political and administrative authority in Ireland was absent. It remained in London. Indeed, in recognition of the political and economic reality, many Irish landowners and merchants employed lobbyists to protect or advance their interests and frequently travelled to England or sent family members to live in London for the same purpose. Reflecting the lack of primacy of Ireland's domestic parliament and administration, and the pre-eminence of that in London, until 1767, the Lord Lieutenant was usually in occupation at Dublin Castle and resident in Ireland only during the two or three months of the biennial Irish parliamentary sittings.[11] In his absence, Ireland would be ruled by three lord justices, usually the Speaker of the Irish House of Commons, the Irish chancellor and one of Ireland's primates. Whichever authority was in place, the government of Ireland was undertaken in conjunction with the Irish privy council, the Irish parliament and devolved in part to a network of Anglo-Irish landed magnates appointed to oversee each of Ireland's counties. At least until the mid-eighteenth century, Ireland's aristocracy and ruling elite were in the main highly anglicised and regarded correctly as a virtual instrument of British imperialism.

Poynings' Act of 1495, known as Poynings' Law, had made Ireland subservient to England in matters of parliamentary legislation over two centuries earlier.[12] Instigated and encouraged by Sir Edward Poyning, then Lord Deputy of Ireland, Ireland's parliament had enacted a law voluntarily restricting its powers to the approval or rejection of bills drawn up in London.[13] Although by the seventeenth century, an informal procedure had evolved in which Dublin had the capacity to draft a summary of proposed legislation, or the 'heads of bills' as opposed to the actual bills or legal text, such documents remained subject to further amendment or rejection by the English privy council. The preparation of parliamentary propositions in Dublin allowed the Irish parliament some influence and encouraged a somewhat more meaningful political dialogue, but there were limits. Nonetheless, if Ireland's proposals were approved, and many were not, the formally drafted bills would then be returned by London for passage through the Irish parliament. The system more or less worked and, as James Kelly noted, post-restoration, parliamentary cooperation between London and Dublin developed to a point where such interaction was considered normal, reasonable and practical.[14] Moreover, despite the formal position set out in Poynings' Law, England's constitutional sovereignty was often more nuanced than absolute, and minor – and sometimes major – conflicts between London and Dublin had a habit of emerging. One of the more contentious issues concerned the entitlement of the Irish commons to initiate finance legislation. In 1692, the Ireland's parliament had rejected an English privy council money bill and the relevant parliamentary session had ended in failure with the issue unresolved. In response, an informal political trade-off emerged that allowed Ireland to take the lead in bringing forward revenue measures but with the English privy council retaining and exercising the right of amendment or rejection. The counterpart to the consensus was that Dublin was allowed greater leeway to proceed with its slate of domestic anti-Catholic legislation.

The compromise was viewed as representing a minimal risk to London's authority. After all, the Irish parliament was dominated by Protestant landowners and the Church of Ireland, whose bishops London appointed. In addition, parliamentary business was managed by usually dependable parliamentary 'undertakers': influential members of the Irish commons and lords who undertook to steer the required government legislation through to a successful conclusion. Their loyalty to successive administrations in London was bought and maintained via an extensive and expensive system of British and Irish government patronage and sinecures. The alternative to accommodation was the potential risk of a parliamentary stalemate and the possibility that necessary financial legislation could stall or fail. In broad terms, albeit with exceptions, this political cooperation lasted for much of the first half of the eighteenth century. But even before the 1750s' money bills crisis and 1760s' constitutional disputes discussed below, signs were emerging that Protestant Ireland was increasingly less willing to remain legislatively supine.

Throughout the eighteenth century, Anglo-Irish discontent was driven by antipathy to Britain's mercantilist legislation and compounded by concerns over Ireland's financial exploitation and what was viewed as administrative incompetence and corruption at Dublin Castle. Politically and economically, the seeds of Anglo-Irish unhappiness, Tony Stewart's 'grievances of the Protestant nation', were sown at the end of the seventeenth century and harvested in the eighteenth.[15] The starting gun to Anglo-Irish unease was the passage of the Wool Act in 1699, designed to shield English sheep farmers and woollen manufacturers from external competition:

> great quantities of . . . manufactures . . . [that] have of late been made and are daily increasing in the Kingdom of Ireland and in the English Plantations in America and are exported from thence to foreign market heretofore supplied from England which will inevitably sink the value of lands and tend to the ruin of the trade and woollen manufactures of this realm.[16]

From an Irish standpoint, the Act was ruinous. It became obligatory for wool and wool products to be exported via England, with excise duty levied at export and on re-export. The cost was onerous, Irish (and American) wool production was penalised and a brake placed on intra-colonial trade between Ireland, the Americas and the Caribbean. Before the Act, the price of Irish wool had been as much as a third below comparable prices in England, with both the raw material and processed woollen yarn at a significant competitive advantage given Ireland's lower labour costs. After the Act, although the overall volume of Irish woollen exports was broadly maintained, prices fell absolutely and potential profits and export markets evaporated. Neither was capable of offset either by the switch to linen exports, which remained free of excise duty, nor by what evolved into the widespread smuggling of fleeces to France and elsewhere.[17]

Although smuggling has been proposed by a number of historians as a (major) mitigating factor, it is doubtful that the illegal export of wool from Ireland successfully circumvented Britain's excise duties and trade restrictions, nor that the suffering experienced by Ireland's agricultural communities was significantly more moderate in practice than the level of tariffs would otherwise suggest. Although the eighteenth century has been referred to as a golden age in Irish smuggling, the statement demands qualification.[18] The very illegality of smuggling translates into an absence of reliable records and it is difficult, if not impossible, to assess either directly or accurately the extent to which smuggling occurred, let alone any possible financial contribution. Besides, notwithstanding the argument that smuggling will generally focus on products with a small volume in relation to their value, something not often encountered in agricultural goods, perhaps the most significant argument against its benefits to Ireland was its high attendant costs. Not the least of these included bribing customs and other officials, and the additional expenses associated with transporting goods illegally. Both would have reduced the profitability of smuggling to exporter and importer alike. However, any discussion that focuses on the relative effectiveness or otherwise of Irish smuggling as a means of alleviating Ireland's rural poverty risks missing the key point. Despite the ebb and flow of advantage in the war between customs evasion and enforcement, Ireland's economy suffered considerably and measurably as a result of British mercantilism. Moreover, even if smuggling was widespread, there was every chance that it would have had the perverse effect of increasing rather than reducing Irish resentment given the high risk of fines, imprisonment and the seizure or destruction of the goods involved. Indeed, it was a sign of how widely British trade policies were especially disliked in Ireland that unlike in England, the death penalty for smuggling was not provided for in Irish law until 1785.[19]

Further restrictive trade legislation was passed in the wake of the Wool Act. Irish enterprises came to be regulated across a spectrum from baking, curing and butter making, to salmon fishing and the control of street markets. Others laws levied additional duties on 'wine, silk, hops, china, earthen, japanned, or lacquered ware' and on 'beer, ale, strong waters, wine, tobacco, and other goods and merchandises'.[20] Although a small number of industries, including flax, hemp and linen, were encouraged and promoted with modest financial bounties from the Irish or British Treasury, whenever there was the prospect that Irish manufactured or agricultural products might out-compete their British counterparts, they were suppressed or contained and obliged by legislation to remain little more than nascent.[21]

Reinforcing Ireland's second tier status, in 1720, the emasculating Dependency of Ireland on Great Britain Act reversed Ireland's 1689 Declaratory Act. That Ireland was subordinate to the British crown, and that the king via the British parliament had 'full power and authority to make laws and statutes to bind the kingdom and people of Ireland', was neither contentious nor an issue for debate among many if not most within Ireland's Anglo-Irish elite.[22] But the Dependency of Ireland Act went further, legislating that the Irish House of Lords had no jurisdiction to judge, affirm or reverse any judgment made in any Court within Ireland. Instead, only the British House of Lords was to hold such authority. The lack of consideration with which Ireland was viewed in Britain was epitomised by the contrast in Britain's response to the Lisbon earthquake in 1755 and the Irish famines a decade earlier. Although public sympathy in Britain generated donations totalling an estimated £100,000 to relieve the survivors of Lisbon's earthquake, virtually nothing was raised to alleviate the Irish famines of the early 1740s, the result of which was to kill around a quarter of Ireland's rural population.[23]

✳ ✳ ✳

The first stirring of Protestant political opposition in Ireland was set out in William Molyneux's *Case of Ireland's being Bound by Acts of Parliament in England*.[24] His argument was contentious but based on the constitutional illegitimacy of England's legislative approach. However, despite its later popularity, with demand such that subsequent editions of the book were printed in 1705, 1706, 1720 and 1725, the prevailing view among the Anglo-Irish elite was for many years at odds with that of Molyneux. The majority of Irish Protestants considered Ireland a legitimate dependency and were fiercely loyal to the British (and Irish) Crown:

> The present Protestant Inhabitants are the descendants of Britons, either transplanted into Ireland as military adventurers, or allured over by the profits of employments and the prospects of trade, or else by misfortune in their own country. The Protestant interest of Ireland has thus grown under the wings of England and does now and ever must exist by her protection, consequently Ireland is a dependant Kingdom.[25]

Anglo-Irish hostility nonetheless for a short time became almost *de rigeur* in the 1720s, initiated by the furore over the corrupt grant of a patent to William Wood, a Wolverhampton iron manufacturer, to mint copper coinage for Ireland. Jonathan Swift's *Drapier's Letters* gave a powerful populist voice to Irish objections to 'Wood's Halfpence' and raised the spectre of independency, albeit under the rule of the Irish Crown and thus the British monarch.

> We, your Majesty's most dutiful subjects, the Commons of Ireland in parliament assembled, find ourselves indispensably obliged to represent to your Majesty our unanimous opinion that the importing and uttering of copper farthings and halfpence by virtue of the patent lately granted to William Wood, Esq. . . . will be highly prejudicial to your Majesty's revenue, destructive of the trade and commerce of this nation and of the most dangerous consequence.[26]

But despite Swift's eloquence, the upsurge in anti-British feeling among the Irish public at large was relatively brief and obviated by Walpole's replacement of the duke of Grafton as Lord Lieutenant by Lord Carteret and the withdrawal of Wood's patent in 1725. Nevertheless, the large-scale popular demonstrations that preceded the climb-down had a potent impact. And at the same time and more worryingly for London, there had also been effective opposition from within the Irish establishment. Both houses of parliament had passed condemnatory resolutions and the Irish privy council and even the lord justices and revenue commissioners had offered resistance. Walpole's response was to be tactically emollient but strategically to ensure that in future most of Ireland's key posts would be held by loyal placemen. The episode also demonstrated the importance to London of maintaining an effective parliamentary management system and underlined in bold the usefulness of Ireland's parliamentary undertakers.

Swift's stance against William Wood and other British impositions was echoed powerfully and almost as emotionally in the writing of Samuel Madden, Thomas Prior and other Protestant Irish patriots, who argued in defence of the country's economic interests and against unalloyed British mercantilism:

> it is notorious that . . . a great part of the Irish trade is carried on by English merchants, the profit of which, with the money paid for freight of most of our commodities in British bottoms, evidently centre in England.[27]

There was nevertheless a continuing philosophical and political problem in reconciling Anglo-Ireland's systemic need for military protection with its desire for economic self-determination. Although it was clear that trade restrictions were 'another cause of our poverty', in the light of English military support, there was almost an obligation to acknowledge that 'some limitations on the trade and manufactures of Ireland' could be considered just:

> when we consider that both the power and riches of England are owing to the flourishing of her trade and manufactures, and at the same time our

own state of dependency, we cannot with reason expect encouragement for any trade or manufacture which the English may apprehend to be injurious to their own staple; if they are mistaken, it is our duty, by fairly stating the case [to persuade them] that it is equally their interest to promote the trade and manufacture of Ireland as that of any city or shire of England.[28]

The justification for the subsidiarity of England's relationship with Ireland was outlined with some force from England's standpoint by John Cary in the mid-1690s.[29] Cary accepted that the economic threat from Ireland was potentially considerable, in his words, 'most injurious to the trade of this kingdom'. And he argued, as did others with a vested interest, that there was no reason to allow Ireland 'greater liberty than our other plantations', which were recognised as having the desire to trade free of constraints. However, in Cary's view, any such aspiration should and must fall at the first hurdle. The function of any colony was not to benefit the colonists, 'the first design . . . was to advance the interest of England'. Ireland was, in Cary's words, 'settled from England [and] supported and defended at England's expense'.[30] It should accordingly remain subordinate.

Cary's views were those of the mainstream, both in England and Ireland. At the time, almost no-one among Ireland's ruling Anglo-Irish elite leaned towards independence.[31] Irish dependency, the counterpart to English military protection, was considered essential to the survival of Protestant minority rule. Ireland's Anglo-Irish were also necessarily in favour of the Protestant succession, arguably more so than many in England, let alone Scotland. The Hanoverian dynasty provided a political bulwark against Jacobitism and Catholicism; without it stood the abyss. But as London's economic yoke of trade constraints and excise duties increasingly began to chafe, the Anglo-Irish slowly came to understand that dependency had an escalating cost. Ireland was prevented from operating freely. Domestic production, both agriculture and manufacture, was shackled and exports depressed. Indeed, Ireland suffered almost precisely in line with Charles Davenant's perceptive analysis written at the turn of the seventeenth century:

> the price of land, value of rents, and our commodities and manufactures rise and fall, as it goes with our foreign trade . . . for the profit of trade is not the advantage the merchant makes at home, but what the whole nation gets clear and net upon the balance in exchange with other countries of its commodities and manufactures.[32]

Compounding the predicament, Britain not unintentionally also depleted Ireland's capital surplus: 'the kingdom is quite drained of money . . . and where all this will end I cannot tell'.[33] Payments from the Irish Treasury that had originally been ordered by the Crown to finance the Irish military establishment alone were unilaterally expanded to cover contributions to the British navy, regiments posted overseas and to cover the salaries of an inflated number of absentee colonels and staff officers. An additional and possibly more onerous financial burden was imposed on Ireland by repeated extensions to the Irish pension list. Although a small proportion of those funded through the list lived in Ireland, including retired military officers and Huguenot refugees of rank who had settled in the country, the bulk was awarded as patronage by the Crown and lay in the hands of absentee English and foreign, mainly German, recipients. Added to payments to English-resident owners of Irish estates, which were understood to approach c.£1 million annually in a country whose total output was probably less than £5 million, the expatriation of civil and military payments overseas was abhorred in Ireland and recognised as key contributor to lower money supply and the meagre availability of domestic funding.[34] Adding to the melancholy, London appended political condescension, filling the most prestigious and lucrative civil, military and ecclesiastical positions in Ireland with British nominees.

For London none of these issues were seen as potential problems. Notwithstanding the protestations of otherwise loyal Anglo-Irish, successive British governments, when they considered Ireland, viewed it through a principally mercantilist lens and saw a subservient not a co-equal state. The Anglo-Irish might aspire emotionally to the entitlements and rights of free-born Englishmen in a sister country but in English eyes, Irish sovereignty had been compromised. Ireland could not be both a dependency under the protection of Britain and a sovereign nation (albeit with the same king) of equal economic standing within its empire. Viewed from London, Ireland could be seen as a colony and the Anglo-Irish Protestants simply colonists.[35] Most importantly and as Cary had proclaimed, colonialism served the commercial and political purposes of the colonial masters, not the colonists. There could be few reasons to advance solutions to political and financial problems that in England were considered irrelevant or barely existed.

In such a context, British disdain quickly became social and among the aristocracy and gentry, Irish accomplishments and titles commanded limited respect. Toby Barnard's comments that Sir John Perceval, 1st earl of Egmont, alongside other Irish peers, was callously 'shouldered aside' in the procession marking the wedding of the prince of Orange to George II's eldest daughter, and that Irish peers were unable to obtain proper recognition of the precedence due to their rank, encapsulates the position.[36] Simultaneously, the British view of the working-class Irish, whether in Ireland or Britain, became embedded in the caricature of a feckless and violent drunk. Ironically, Irish alienation led to greater self-reliance, one later expression of which was Antients freemasonry.

Despite the mounting financial and later social pressures on Ireland, an effective opposition took time to develop and resentment was initially 'kept within tolerable bounds'. Delay was a function of many causes, including the generational legacy of traditional Protestant Anglo-Irish loyalty to Britain and the power of British patronage. Nonetheless, over the first half of the eighteenth century, Britain's mercantilist policies slowly herded the once steadfast Anglo-Irish towards patriotic Irish nationalism. As the eighteenth century progressed, irritation at English condescension and revulsion at the opportunity cost of playing economic second fiddle began to translate into demands for greater self-determination.

The counterpoint to England's economic and financial success and London's mercantilist policies was Irish economic subservience. The cost of dependency, although once accepted, had become more stark:

> we are daily running in debt; our public funds prove deficient; our trade is diminished; our farmers are breaking condition; the value of land is lessened; money is scarce to a degree, and consequently our credit sinking.[37]

Indeed, by the 1750s, the patriotic faction in parliament could achieve a majority.[38] In what was or could be described as a period of economic Enlightenment, trade had become both a moral and a financial imperative. As Dobbs commented,

> a flourishing trade gives encouragement to the industrious . . . increases the power of the nation; [and] puts it in the power of every prudent and industrious man in it to enjoy more of the innocent pleasures of life.[39]

Different colonies would take their own routes to modify or escape Britain's mercantilist harness from the purchase of parliamentary seats by West Indian planters to the declaration of independence by the American colonies. However, all were looking at the same or similar goals: 'to promote the happiness of [their] nation . . . [and] to increase its power and wealth'.[40]

At first, the Irish argued that notwithstanding their need for military protection, their financial interests were and should be seen as inseparable from rather than subservient to those of England.[41] Indeed, Dobbs wrote that treating Ireland as a competitor to England was as unsophisticated as comparing 'the rest of England against London . . . as there are several trading towns in Britain very rich besides London . . . [and there is thus no reason] why Ireland might not have a share in the trade of the world, though never come into competition'.[42] But it was Dobbs who was politically naive and in England his words fell on barren ground.

Ireland nonetheless bristled. When Swift wrote of Lemuel Gulliver in Brobdingnag and his 'hope which never left me, that I should one day recover my liberty', he wrote of the inequity of the Anglo-Irish relationship.[43] Notwithstanding his Tory politics, Swift was at one with many of his Whig compatriots. Their frustrations were penned clearly in the *Drapier's Letters* and set an example to others who criticised the constitutional shackles that bound Ireland, denounced their unfairness and argued that the Protestant Anglo-Irish had a right to share the liberties enjoyed by their neighbours on the other side of the Irish Sea. But if Ireland could be regarded as a colony, it lacked any context for the claim 'that by the laws of God, of Nature, of Nations, and of your Country, you are, and ought to be as free a people as your brethren in England'.[44] What was perceived in Dublin as the exploitation of Ireland by a protectionist English administration was viewed through a different prism in London. The rights attributable to an independent state and freedom from external trade constraints were not on offer.

There were exceptions, albeit not many. Giles Earle, MP for Chippenham from 1715–22 and thereafter Malmesbury from 1722–47, appointed a commissioner of Irish revenue in 1728 and a lord of the treasury in 1737, was one of few who on 12 February 1734 supported a British parliamentary proposal for the duty on Irish yarn to be removed. Earle considered the matter 'an affair of the greatest consequence to the trade and well being of England; the laws are already as severe as can be, and make what other you will, the people of Ireland will not execute them, the penalties are so severe, no jury in Ireland will find a person guilty, as was the case in England when it was made death to run'. He continued, 'the only method to prevent it is to let Ireland into some small share of the trade, for their poor must be subsisted'.[45] Earle was unsuccessful.

The intellectual origins of England's mercantilist policies towards its colonies and the wider world lay in the new economic analysis that Charles Davenant developed and popularised at the end of the seventeenth century. Drawing on Gregory King's *Observations* and other contemporary work, Davenant built on King's fledgling theory of supply and demand and the positive impact of economic self interest.[46] His insights into the relationship between the responsiveness of the supply of goods to variations in price – price elasticity – allowed Davenant to set out an embryonic theory of comparative advantage in international trade a century before David Ricardo. It also marked him as a significant voice on tax and finance.[47] Notwithstanding the imperatives that flowed from war against the regime in France, a struggle he termed the obligation to defend 'this almost only spot of ground which seems remaining in the world to public liberty', Davenant argued that taxation could be ruinous for a nation's commercial health unless structured to reinforce or at least not harm management of the nation's economy.[48] But it was Davenant's insight that trade was the key component to a nation's commercial and financial well being that gave him later political influence. Davenant identified international commerce as the principal method of sustaining the war effort and, at the same time, a means of delivering economic growth and wealth creation through the application of comparative advantage: '[as] the price of land, value of rents and our commodities and manufactures rise and fall'.[49] Four years later, his *Essay upon the Probable Methods of Making People Gainers in the Balance of Trade* argued for and demonstrated the advantages of free trade, suggesting that duties should be reduced: 'with submission to better judgments, the trade thither can never hurt England'.[50] His arguments were repeated in other works that promoted British joint stock companies operating in India, Africa and elsewhere:[51]

gold and silver are indeed the measure of trade, but the spring and original of it in all nations, is the natural or artificial product of the country; that is to say, what their land, or what their labour and industry produces.[52]

Although expelled from his government positions under William and Mary as a suspected Jacobite sympathiser, Davenant returned to office in June 1703, when he was briefly secretary to the commission considering a union between England and Scotland. However, it was his subsequent appointment as Inspector General of Exports and Imports, a role with an annual salary of £1,000, that allowed him influence. Julian Hoppit has suggested, correctly, that Sydney Godolphin, the then Lord Treasurer, took account of Davenant in formulating Britain's subsequent trade policy and, over time, Davenant's theories and approach fed into the mainstream of political thought as successive governments followed his pragmatic trade-centric approach.[53] However, there was a problem: Ireland. Davenant's analysis provided a theoretical framework that suggested that all countries would benefit from extending trade, including Ireland. But given its climactic and other similarities to England and its lower wage rates, this would place Ireland in direct competition to England. Despite his theory of comparative advantage, for Davenant as for others, 'it is a very great question whether there are not weighty reasons to apprehend . . . the people of Ireland'. The issue was that:

Ireland abounds in convenient ports, it is excellently situated for trade, capable of great improvements of all kinds, and able to nourish more than treble its present inhabitants . . . its soil, sward and turf are in a manner the same with ours, and proper to rear sheep, all [of] which . . . beget a reasonable fear that in time they may come to rival us in our most important manufacture.[54]

However, despite the concerns, Davenant could not ignore the benefits of trade to both sides:

that they should increase in people, that their land should be drained and meliorated, that they should have trade, and grow wealthy by it, may not peradventure be dangerous to England; for it is granted, their riches will centre at last here in their mother kingdom.[55]

Indeed, he went further:

colonies that enjoy not only protection but are at their ease and flourish, will, in all likelihood, be less inclined to innovate or receive a foreign yoke than if they are harassed and compelled to poverty.[56]

Unsurprisingly, unreconstructed self-interest dominated London's political considerations, not economic and philosophical niceties. The planters of

Ireland would be encouraged to prosper but with the caveat that such prosperity would be permitted only in so far as was consistent 'with the welfare of England'. There were risks to this approach and Davenant noted that:

> if through a mistaken fear and jealousy of their future strength and greatness, we should either permit or contrive to let [Ireland] be dispeopled, poor, weak and dispirited, or if we should render them so uneasy as to incline the people to a desire for change . . . they must be prey to an invader.[57]

Ireland's 'invader' would not be the physical assault of a foreign power but rather the more insidious and powerful philosophy of patriotic nationalism. Ireland's deteriorating relationship with Britain spurred the development of Irish intellectual thought. Irish patriotism and nationalism, not always overt, was articulated through pamphlets, books and in the formation of organisations such as the Dublin Society, where its founders and members promoted national improvement and the Irish manufacture of goods to offset the nation's economic dependency. A new thesis was advanced by Madden, Dobbs, Prior, Berkeley and others in favour of an equal place for the Irish goods within Britain's imperial framework.[58] And support for domestic products and a common objection to English goods became synonymous with Irish patriotism, particularly during what were frequent periods of economic depression:

> A mob of weavers of the Liberty rose in order to rifle the several shops in the city for English manufactures, and stopped at the houses of Messrs Eustace and Lindsay, woollen drapers . . . They forced off the hinges of [the] shop windows with hammers and chisels . . . The army [was] brought against them, and a fight ensued, in which one of the weavers was killed.[59]

Going further, the climate changed to the extent that wearing Irish linen became a recognised political statement:

> Ye noblemen in place or out,
> Ye Volunteers so brave and stout,
> Ye dames that flaunt at ball or rout,
> Wear Irish manufacture.
>
> Thus shall poor weavers get some pence,
> From hunger and from cold to fence
> Their wives and infants three months hence,
> By Irish manufacture.[60]

Irish concerns percolated back to London through both formal and informal channels. Ireland may have been a relative backwater but it could not be ignored. The antipathy in relations between the two countries was recognised and Clark's argument that the lack of common political ground between the Irish and British establishments had an increasingly high political cost was correct.[61] Notwithstanding the self-interested rivalries of the Irish oligarchs, hostility to the Dublin Castle administration and its parliamentary allies developed into a succession of constitutional quarrels that dominated Irish politics throughout the latter half of the eighteenth century.

A second major constitutional crisis occurred in the 1750s, a generation after Wood's Halfpence, concerning the passage through parliament of a money bill dealing with the allocation of Ireland's tax surplus. Irish opposition to the bill hinged nominally on an arcane constitutional issue. The heads of bill as drafted in Dublin was considered to pose a challenge to the royal prerogative: the king's prior consent was required formally in order for surplus revenue to be applied to retiring public debt. The bill was returned by London for acceptance or rejection having had the appropriate new language inserted by the privy council. However, the amended language was unacceptable to Dublin and under Poynings' Law, since it was not open to the Irish parliament to amend the bill further, on 17 December 1753, it was rejected. Ireland's dispute with Britain's economic policies was gathering momentum.[62]

In her 2006 article, Jacqueline Hill pointed to the extra-parliamentary aspects of the money bills dispute and the manner in which the Irish press, pamphlets, open meetings and well-advertised dinners were used by the patriotic opposition to assemble and demonstrate widespread support within the Anglo-Irish elite and more extensively among middling Protestants across Ireland.[63] There were of course precedents to this approach, most notably in the mid-1720s, when Harding and Swift drove opposition to Wood's copper coinage and created a vehicle for Irish political nationalism and opposition to British parliamentary dominance. However, since that time, for almost three decades, opposition in the press and elsewhere had remained relatively dormant.

Until the 1720s, Irish newspaper content had been dominated by material reprinted from London and the continental gazettes of Amsterdam, Leiden, Paris and The Hague. But as the Irish press began to benefit from the more stable financial footing created by local advertisers and a larger and wealthier subscriber base, it grew more capable as a source of local news and independent editorial. Recognising this, the administration encouraged the press not to take an opposition line. Anti-British comment was considered treasonous and the threat of censorship and prison, compounded by parliamentary and Court investigations with their attendant fees and fines, provided an effective disincentive to newspaper proprietors and printers.[64] The administration's policy was complemented by the financial carrots offered to newspapers by government advertising and the direct and indirect sponsorship of Dublin Castle. Consequently, and with limited exceptions such as Harding's *Dublin Impartial News Letter*, the press was substantially pro-government and by the 1730s, largely because of such sanctions and incentives, dissent was contained. Indeed, even Tory-leaning papers were partly dependent on government advertising and correspondingly guarded in the views expressed. Others, such as *Pue's Occurrences*, slid from an opposition stance to support Dublin Castle as their proprietors shifted political allegiance, motivated by financial returns.

It is in the context of decades of press subservience that the impact and scale of newspaper and pamphlet opposition to the Castle faction in the 1750s should be viewed. Although the majority of anti-government articles and pamphlets were written anonymously, sedition still being a crime and Dublin Castle continuing to favour prosecution and imprisonment on conviction, dissent was widespread. In short, Irish patriotism appeared to have entered the mainstream. The dispute with Britain and its placemen was now at the heart of Irish public debate. *Honesty the Best Policy or, the History of Roger*, satirising the clash between Henry Boyle, then Speaker in the Irish parliament and a lord justice, and the Ponsonby family, a rival oligarchy, ran to seven editions in 1752 with massive sales: 'I am well assured over five thousand copies are gone off'.[65] But hostility to Dublin Castle did not equate to anti-monarchism among the Anglo-Irish. Irish patriotism and nationalism were fully compatible with and part of Irish loyalty to the Crown. Indeed, for the British government, one of the more worrying aspects of Irish patriotism was the espousal of loyalty to the king of Ireland and to Irish parliamentary rights as opposed to the exercise of power by Dublin Castle and the Church of Ireland on behalf of the London administration.

The character and composition of the Anglo-Irish elite and its political and social connections with England had evolved; and they were at the heart of change. That the relationship between Dublin and London had deteriorated over the course of the eighteenth century is axiomatic. It was a progression dictated by Britain's economic domination and the financial opportunity cost of restrictive trade legislation. In such a context, the parliamentary dispute over the money bills was a symptom rather than a cause of discontent. Indeed, as Beckett has commented, the Irish commons had a tendency to reject bills merely because they had been amended by the privy council in England rather than for any substantive reasons.[66] The issue was one of perception. But Beckett's observation that 'there was never any question of taxing Ireland by British legislation; and in even less vital matters ministers were very unwilling to [use] a British statute to over-ride the will of the Irish parliament' reflected a view from London's vantage point, not that of Dublin.[67] Britain may have considered its imposition of legislation as being principally administrative and economic, and not an exercise in political subjugation. But even if this had been objectively accurate from a British viewpoint, Ireland's perspective differed. Dublin saw an intolerable administrative straightjacket that reinforced a sense of national political and economic inferiority.

Pitt the Younger's later analysis of the issue in his correspondence with the duke of Rutland, then Lord Lieutenant of Ireland, contained insights that his predecessors lacked. And his statement of the necessity for any settlement or accommodation with Ireland to be reciprocal in nature was accurate:

In the relation of Great Britain with Ireland there can subsist but two possible principles of connection. The one, that which is exploded, of total subordination in Ireland, and of restrictions on her commerce for the benefit of this country, which was by this means enabled to bear the whole burden of the empire; the other is, what is now proposed to be confirmed and completed, that of an equal participation of all commercial advantages, and some proportion of the charge of protecting the general interest. If Ireland is at all connected with this country and to remain a member of the empire, she must make her option between these two principles, and she has wisely and justly made it for the latter . . . the great advantage that Ireland will derive is from the equal participation of our trade and of the benefits derived from our colonies.[68]

Albeit that Pitt was unwilling to relinquish any 'control on the executive government of the empire, which must reside here', he was willing to offer other concessions.[69] Earlier administrations had been less open to compromise and what was on offer in the 1780s was politically too little and too late. Before it was 'exploded', British subordination of Ireland had changed the political psychology of the Anglo-Irish, opening the gate to patriotic nationalism. The underlying terms of Ireland's dependency had become capable of challenge. The money bills crisis in the 1750s was followed in the 1760s and 1770s by effective resistance to Townshend's plans to reform the parliamentary undertaker system to the benefit of the British administration and the passionate and successful patriotic opposition of Henry Flood and Henry Grattan. Concerned that what had occurred in the Americas might also occur in Ireland, trade dispensations were eventually agreed by Britain, as was the new constitution of 1782, which largely removed Poynings' Law and repealed the 1720 Declaratory Act. Indeed, Britain became far more circumspect in its use of its parliamentary powers from the mid-1770s onward, and a large proportion of legislation was directed either to conferring benefits on Ireland or on repeal of restrictive legislation.[70] But despite British attempts to control and contain Irish disquiet, concessions would be short lived. Ireland's parliament would be subsumed by the Acts of Union less than two decades later and, in its wake, everything that followed became almost inevitable.[71]

Although understanding the political and economic context in which the leadership of Irish Grand Lodge operated provides a guide to the development of Irish freemasonry, something explored at greater length in Appendix V, it is also important to examine the composition of Irish freemasonry as a whole and its evolution over less than thirty years as it developed to encompass a broad social spectrum. Surviving lodge records, subscription lists for Masonic books and contemporary press reports confirm how the public profile of Irish freemasonry altered in the mid-eighteenth century from what had been a predominantly Protestant and relatively exclusive organisation in the 1730s, to become a more socially inclusive movement by the 1750s and 1760s with an increasingly interdenominational membership.

A range of factors drove the process. As in England, one motive for joining a Masonic lodge was the forum that freemasonry provided for association on a local level. For many, an invitation to fraternal drinking and dining would have been attractive as an end in itself, notwithstanding any potential benefits offered by networking opportunities. Freemasonry's tolerance towards different religious groups was another positive aspect that encouraged some men to join who may have been unable or unwilling to commit elsewhere. The spirituality of a quasi-religious ritual may also have had appeal, particularly in Ireland, where Catholic worship was relegated to a proscribed activity and nonconformist religious dissent penalised and discouraged. And there were other influences. Fraternal benevolence did not only equate to giving charity; it also included its receipt. Complete financial security may not have been on offer but lodge funds were available to assist distressed members and their families, particularly after the death or during the illness, incapacity or unemployment of a lodge member. The importance of this aspect of Irish freemasonry was reflected in the weight attached to Masonic funerals and underlined by the prominence of their reporting in the Irish press. And a similar if not identical approach was followed by the Antients in England:

> That upon the death of any of our worthy brethren whose names are or may be hereafter recorded in the Grand Registry &c., the Master of such lodge as he then belonged to shall immediately inform the Grand Secretary of his death and the intended time for his funeral, and upon this notice the Grand Secretary shall summon all the lodges to attend the funeral in proper order, and that each member shall pay one shilling towards defraying the expenses of said funeral or otherwise to his widow or nearest friend.[72]

In Ireland as in England, the patronage of prominent aristocrats provided political cover for freemasonry, which was far from being a secret society. Indeed, the pomp and ceremonial attached to its regular parades, dinners and public entertainments may have been a more effective draw than any supposed Masonic signs, tokens and other secrets that might be communicated privately in the lodge. Public Masonic processions accompanied by music, sometimes the military, and with all lodge members in full regalia, included not only the annual church parade to celebrate St John's Day but were often arranged to accompany the laying of civic foundation stones and would proceed or follow Masonic evenings at the theatre, where plays, concerts and other entertainments might be given a Masonic theme and be accompanied by Masonic verse and song.

Such events occurred regularly across Ireland, both in Dublin and at a local level:

Loughrea [Co. Galway], June 25th, 1755. Yesterday being St John's Day, the Patron Saint of the Most Antient and Honourable Fraternity of Free and Accepted Masons, the Free Masons of this Town, of lodge No. 248, met at some distance from the town from whence they marched in procession preceded by a band of music to the Fountain Tavern where they dined, and after dinner drank all the toasts peculiar to Masonry, the Royal Family, the Glorious Pious and Immortal Memory of King William, and other loyal toasts. At six in the evening, they marched to the Assembly Rooms where they gave an elegant Ball to the Ladies and Gentlemen. The Ball was opened by the Master; the first set consisted of twenty couple, the Men all Masons, and the Ladies (to do honour to the Fraternity), wore blue ribbons, and particularly a blue rose on each of their left breasts.[73]

At the dinner that followed, the lodge 'agreed unanimously to subscribe for a prize of fifty guineas, to be run for next August, at the course of Loughrea, by four year-old horses, etc., the property of Freemasons of any regular lodge whatsoever'.[74]

In Dublin, the more elevated social and financial status of those attending such Masonic events allowed the entertainments to be commensurately greater:

By Command of the Right Worshipful and Rt Hon Ford, earl of Cavan, Grand Master of Ireland. For the benefit of distressed Free and accepted Masons.

On Thursday the 22nd of June, will be a Grand Concert of vocal and instrumental music. The Grand Master, with the Grand Officers and brethren, will appear in their jewels and proper clothing, according to ancient customs; [Ranelagh Gardens] will be illuminated, and a large additional band of music provided to attend the grand procession round the gardens.[75]

In common with other Irish clubs and societies, Irish freemasonry afforded in John Money's words, 'a bridge between the different ranks of society'.[76] It would be appropriate to add 'and religious denominations', given that freemasonry included dissenting and conformist Protestants, Quakers and Catholics. Although the Irish freemasonry of the 1720s and early 1730s was dominated by the gentry, as it expanded across Ireland it absorbed a wide cross section of Irish society.

The membership of the Grand Lodge of Munster demonstrates the exclusive social characteristics of freemasonry in the 1720s.[77] The lodge met at the house of Herbert Phaire, a wealthy landowner, and among those holding office were Hon James O'Brien; Springett Penn, the grandson of William Penn, the founder of Pennsylvania; and Colonel William Maynard, JP, MP for Waterford, a past high sheriff of Cork and colonel of the county's militia dragoons. Other lodge members included Walter Gould, an attorney and land agent for the earl of Orrery; Samuel Boles, land agent for Lord Middleton; and two landowners, Robert Longfield and William Galway. Munster freemasonry was already interdenominational and its members included Quakers and wealthy Catholics. Indeed, English and Irish membership lists indicate that from the 1720s, a member's social and financial status and potential business relationships were, in the more exclusive lodges, a more important determinant for membership than religion.

By the latter part of the century Irish freemasonry had opened its doors more fully, and comprised both urban and rural lodges and members across the social and financial spectrum from Anglo-Irish landed gentry to the Protestant and Catholic working class. This is not to argue that every Masonic lodge was universally and uniformly open to all. In many lodges class remained an important divider and lodge fees and expenses, whether for admission, dress, dining or the annual levy, were used as a barrier to preclude and discourage the membership of those considered socially unsuitable. There is also evidence that religious discrimination remained an issue in certain lodges. Nonetheless, Irish freemasonry was far less socially stratified than elsewhere in Europe. And by the end of the eighteenth century it had become the most popular form of civil association in Ireland.

Two academic studies have shed light on this aspect of Irish freemasonry: Lisa Meaney's unpublished MA thesis and Petri Mirala's *Freemasonry in Ulster*.[78] Mirala's paper, published in *Clubs and Societies in Eighteenth-Century Ireland*, also provides a comparative analysis within a European context.[79] He suggests that in relation to its population, Irish freemasonry had a larger footprint than in any other European country with nearly four times as many members in proportion to its population as compared to England. A total of around seven hundred lodges were warranted in Ireland between 1730 and 1790, which encompassed an estimated forty thousand or more members in an adult male population of just over one million. The comparable figures for England were around 20–25,000 masons in an adult male population of about 2 million; France had roughly 50,000 masons in an adult male population of about 7 million.

Many Irish lodges tended to guard their independence jealously, especially those based some distance from Dublin and outside the immediate orbit of the influence of the Grand Lodge of Ireland. As a consequence, early attempts by the Irish Grand Lodge in Dublin to impose a federal structure over its notionally subordinate lodges failed. As Meaney observed, lodges in Munster resented interference from any central authority and often took an independent stance.[80] Some fifty-eight lodges were warranted in Munster between 1726 and 1760. The majority were in Co. Cork, which had twenty-two lodges. Limerick and Waterford had ten each; Tipperary nine; and Clare and Kerry one apiece. Several lodges may have pre-dated the establishment of Irish Grand Lodge in 1725 but even after 1730 when Grand Lodge was more fully operational, there is no evidence of anything other than a limited line of communication between Dublin and its outlying lodges for at least several decades. An instructive incident was the request in May 1748 that

John Calder, then Grand Secretary of Ireland, compile a report on the condition of the lodges in Munster (the province most closely allied to grand lodge) and that he collect the outstanding dues. The exercise was an attempt by Dublin to exert its authority. However, Calder's report the following year suggests that its authority was more likely to be exercised in the breach. Calder outlined the practical problems encountered in Dublin's attempts to exercise governance over the lodges it nominally regulated, including a comment from one provincial lodge that it would 'never pay any dues, except a shilling from each Master and sixpence from each Warden, on the commencement of their officers and secretary's fees for registry'.[81] In the event, an informal but effective accommodation was reached whereby Irish Grand Lodge chose largely to ignore most provincial irregularities and most dues went unremitted.

Evidence of a growing number of Irish Catholic freemasons from the mideighteenth century onward is apparent from the membership lists of individual lodges. The rise predated Catholic emancipation, which was then almost absent from the political agenda. Of course, Catholic freemasons were not present uniformly across Ireland and not all lodges were interdenominational. Indeed, some lodges excluded Catholics either formally or less formally. However, many were open to both religious communities and the Masonic practice of inter-visitation, that is, visiting different lodges within a given area, helped to expand the level of contact between the two. Given the restricted circumstances in which the Catholic Church operated in Ireland, the papal bulls of 1738 and 1751 and canon law against freemasonry were more or less ignored until Catholic emancipation was more firmly rooted in the second decade of the nineteenth century.[82] The rationale was clear. Irish Catholicism had been constrained by penal legislation for decades and any attempt to impose strict papal doctrine on freemasonry could have affected the Catholic Church's emergence from proscription. Perhaps more worrying for Rome, many Catholic priests were themselves freemasons, as were a number of bishops, and as Mirala noted, Ireland's archbishops even petitioned Pope Pius VI in 1788 to withdraw the penalty of automatic excommunication.[83]

With the acquiescence of the Irish episcopality, the popularity of freemasonry among Catholics expanded, most particularly in the last quarter of the eighteenth century. By the early 1790s, a number of lodges advertised openly that they welcomed both Protestant and Catholic members, and freemasonry was held up and publicised as an example of an inclusive and non-sectarian organisation.[84] Freemasonry was also popular in the non conformist and conformist Huguenot émigré community who, as in England, were well represented in the upper ranks of Irish Grand Lodge. George Boyde, originally from Bordeaux, was Grand Treasurer from 1732 until 1735; Captain John Arabin became Grand Treasurer in 1736; and Captain John Corneille was made JGW in 1735 and SGW the following year. Later, in the 1760s, David, Peter and John La Touche, the eminent Dublin-based Huguenot financiers, were elected Grand Wardens, and in 1767, David

La Touche became Deputy Grand Master. The commonality of interest in freemasonry across the religious and social divide in Ireland spoke to a key factor that promoted the Craft across Ireland as a whole in the latter half of the eighteenth century and was shared by aristocrat and artisan alike: the outrage and national patriotism that was the response to British mercantilism.[85]

Conclusion

In some ways, the creation of the Antients Grand Lodge in 1751 and the decades of internecine Masonic disaffection that followed can be traced back to the Glorious Revolution that exiled James II and brought William and Mary to the English throne. Ireland's Williamite-Jacobite war and the Treaty of Limerick that concluded the fighting crushed Irish Catholic opposition and brought in a century of Anglo-Irish Protestant minority government and punitive anti-Catholic legislation that only began to be repealed and amended in the 1780s. But it was not the opposition of the Irish Catholic majority that caused a rift to open between Dublin and London but the mercantilist legislation that was imposed with growing force and effect from the late seventeenth century and into the eighteenth. Until that time, no laws had regulated Ireland's foreign trade more onerously than that of England, and no duties or tariffs had been imposed that affected Ireland alone. In short, apart from the relatively benign Navigation Acts of 1663, until the introduction of the onerous Wool Act and the anti free trade legislation that followed, Ireland's exports and manufactures had been virtually free of restrictions. Moreover, although there was a long history of seasonal workers travelling to England from Ireland to work on the harvest, more permanent settlement was relatively uncommon, especially among the lower middling and working classes.

Mercantilism changed everything. As the financial and opportunity cost of trade controls became apparent, and as the tariffs and duties imposed on Irish agriculture and industry were sustained, Ireland was divided economically from Britain and forced into a subsidiary position. Irish alienation was reinforced by London's growing political and later social disdain, an attitude epitomised by the arrogant imposition of the Dependency of Ireland on Great Britain Act in 1720 and the massively unpopular grant to William Wood of a patent to coin Irish copper currency some two years later. Opposition Anglo-Irish commentators such as William Moylneux may have been lone voices in the 1690s but three decades later, Jonathan Swift was able to rouse Ireland to widespread resistance and the risk of Irish nationalism was forestalled only by Walpole's tactical retreat. By the 1750s, despite Dublin's parliamentary 'undertakers' and the waterfall of patronage and sinecures that lay at the heart of London's control of Ireland, the cost of economic repression, the draining of Ireland's capital and increasing British condescension combined to give Ireland's patriotic opposition a voice that would remain at the forefront of parliamentary debate until temporarily extinguished by the Acts of Union. With some irony, over little more than three or four generations, Britain's economic policies and political and social conceit pushed many of its most loyal Irish Protestant supporters from advocates of dependency and promoters of empire to staunch patriotic activists. It also triggered a near exodus of long-term economic migration from Ireland.

For Britain, mercantilism worked, but only in so far as its economic interests could be managed against those of its colonial dominions. In the Americas, arguments concerning citizens' rights and the appropriate responsibilities of government eventually led to insurgency. But the drive for political independence masked what was at its core more a commercial disagreement over the spoils of trade and competing pecuniary self interest. The same political and financial imperatives drove West Indian plantation owners and merchants to purchase British parliamentary seats and the Irish and others to finance extensive lobby interests in London.

Despite colonial disquiet, in the second half of the late eighteenth century Britain was approaching industrial take-off. An expanding empire and burgeoning global companies sustained growth in international trade which transformed the prospects and realities of economic growth at home and abroad, symbiotically feeding and being fed by revolutions in agriculture, demography, finance and science. But there was an exception: Ireland. In contrast to Britain, the Caribbean and the Americas, trade benefited few in Ireland. The country's economic prospects remained lean and its treatment by Britain was punctuated by domestic resentment. Dobbs' comment that 'a flourishing trade gives encouragement to the industrious . . . increases the power of the nation; [and] puts it in the power of every prudent and industrious man in it to enjoy more of the innocent pleasures of life' had become a global theme of empire, adopted by Britain and its colonies and dependencies alike. In effect, trade was recognised as both a moral and a financial imperative. For politicians in London to seek to prevent or curtail Ireland from trading was to dismember the intellectual basis on which economic and political policy was founded and to ride against what might be termed the economic Enlightenment. The Irish railed. In Swift's words:

> Ireland is the only kingdom I ever heard or read of, either in ancient or modern story, which was denied the liberty of exporting their native commodities and manufactures wherever they pleased, except to countries at war with their prince or own state, yet this privilege by the superiority of mere power is refused us in the most momentous parts of commerce – beside an Act of Navigation, to which we never consented, pinned down upon us and rigorously executed, and a thousand other unexampled circumstances as grievous as they are invidious to mention.[1]

As Britain and the bulk of its empire benefited with agriculture and industry no longer geared simply to meet local demand but directed towards both national and international markets, Ireland was largely excluded. Constraints on trade and the expatriation of domestic capital overseas impeded Irish agriculture and hampered its emergent industries. It was recognised at the time. For Swift, Irish economic inefficiency was not a function of the lack of any 'industry of the people';[2] Ireland's 'misfortune is not altogether of our own fault, but to a million of discouragements'.[3] Spurred by vested interests at home, Britain would not accept competition from Ireland in either agriculture or industry. But where this might have been justified in the late seventeenth century as appropriate retribution against what was popularly portrayed as Ireland's papist Jacobite-supporting majority, it was perhaps less appropriate for Ireland's pro-Hanoverian Anglo-Irish Protestants. Indeed, as the century progressed, the Anglo-Irish gradually came to perceive that Britain's attitude had transitioned to disdain towards Ireland and the Irish as a whole, whether Catholic or Protestant.

Although one might argue whether Swift's analysis of British economic policy was essentially correct or otherwise, this is less important than the intellectual and emotional schematic that he and others imposed on Irish thinking. The rapid evolution of trade in eighteenth-century Britain laid the foundations for industrialisation and a concomitant social transformation. Technological progress transformed what had once been relatively isolated sectors. Practical inventions such as the Newcomen engine and hydraulic pump multiplied labour productivity and drove down costs and prices; and the impact on economic growth rippled out to become a continuous and self-reinforcing process. Over time, labour, especially segments of the urban workforce, benefited, as primary production was substituted in part by value added manufactured goods and an emerging service economy.

The contrast with Ireland was extensive, obvious and unfortunate. Revisiting Swift once again:

> I would be glad to know by what secret method it is that we grow a rich and flourishing people without liberty, trade, manufactures, inhabitants, money or the privilege of coining, without industry, labour or improvement of land, and with more than half the rents and profits of the whole kingdom annually exported for which we receive not a single farthing, and to make up all this, nothing worth mentioning except the linen of the north, a trade casual, corrupted, and at mercy, and some butter from Cork. If we do flourish, it must be against every law of nature and reason.[4]

Ireland foundered. And as William Hewins noted, its failure was a direct consequence of the 'narrow conception of national interests which then ... dominated English economic policy'.[5] Swift's polemic was on balance correct and his arguments resonated within his Anglo-Irish audience in Ireland – both Whig and Tory – and echoed elsewhere, including among the Catholic majority. Even allowing for exceptions in the textile industries and in small-scale paper and glass making, Irish commerce was strangled by legislation and made uncompetitive by excise duties.

Under-invested, over-regulated and unable to export freely, Ireland's agriculture was incapable of taking up the economic slack or even providing adequately for the domestic market. Despite the endeavours of the Dublin Society and other organisations that hoped to improve Ireland's cultivation, husbandry and manufacture, potential success on anything like the necessary scale was penalised by insecurity of land tenure, the excessive rents demanded by landowners and onerous British tariffs. Ireland's core agriculture – dairy, grain and wool production – all suffered. Where in Britain agricultural output tripled between 1700 and 1800 and industrial output accelerated from the 1760s, in Ireland neither occurred. And in the light of the failed harvests that resulted in dislocation and despair across almost the whole of the country, it was ironic that the victualling yards that supplied the British navy and the Caribbean colonies – Swift's 'butter from Cork' – gave rise to a conceit that Ireland as a whole produced a food surfeit.

Using Alice Murray's well-placed adjective, British mercantilism gave rise to 'melancholy' in Ireland and famine and economic hardship drove both Catholic and Protestants to seek alternatives, including enlistment in the British and foreign armies and emigration.[6] Those that were able to do so left for the Americas and other colonies. But many of the more impoverished and desperate made their way to England and Scotland, in Ruth-Ann Harris' memorable phrase, 'the nearest place that wasn't Ireland'.[7] That the St Giles rookery was built on the site of a former leper colony offers an allegory that is in many ways only too obvious. The London slums represented not only social exclusion and economic deprivation but were also a testament to the consequences of famine and the political and trade policies that proscribed or prevented alternative employment in Ireland. The entry ports of Bristol, Liverpool and Glasgow, and emerging industrial towns in the north and midlands, including Bradford, Leeds and Manchester, all had their own small or large Irish ghettos. But it was the slums of St Giles, St Martin's, Rosemary Lane and the Ratcliffe Highway that embodied the initial and often enduring poverty of the Irish émigré. Many lived in what became dystopian Irish ghettos, lodged in insanitary and overcrowded tenement houses where eighty or more beds might be let out at 3*d* or 4*d* a night, or a shilling or two per week. Roger Swift's characterisation of this swathe of migrants as the 'outcast Irish' was apposite and life for most would have been unforgiving.

In comparison to the avalanche of studies of the nineteenth- and twentieth-century working class, research into the condition of the London Irish in the mid-eighteenth century has been sparse. There are occasionally hints that the Irish had a presence beyond the minority of affluent middling traders, merchants, artists and lobbyists that were at the heart of recognised Irish society in the British capital. Eoin Kinsella's work on hurling in London in the eighteenth century, for example, opens a window on the popularity of the Gaelic game in London which appears to have attracted both gentlemen players and large audiences of working class and lower middling Irish spectators.[8] In August 1733, for example, 'a game called hurling was played for 50 guineas a side in Hyde Park by gentlemen of Ireland, the county of Kildare, against the county of Meath'.[9] Its popularity suggests a relatively large expatriate Irish population in London willing to pay for traditional entertainment; indeed, a second match took place the same month at the Bell Inn in Paddington with a combined Meath and Queen's County side taking on Wicklow and Wexford.[10] By the mid-century, hurling matches were regularly held elsewhere, including the Artillery Grounds to the north of the City of London, an area marked by a large Irish colony. In 1748 and in 1749, Munster took on Leinster;[11] and two years later, demand within London's Irish community was apparently sufficient to justify a pair of back-to-back matches between the counties.[12]

Traditionally, historical analysis of the London Irish has spoken to the upper and middling segments of that population. With respect to the far larger number of Irish working class in the many rookeries across the city and the aspirational lower middling seeking to climb out of poverty – and succeeding in so doing – there is relative silence. Some progress has been made in recent years. The digitisation of trial records and sessions' papers of the Old Bailey, the Central Criminal Court and the magistrates' courts of Middlesex and Westminster, provide accessible source material. And there are other data sources, including the primary records of the Antients Grand Lodge and its constituent Masonic lodges. This material offers a unique and informative testimony that opens up for review the different dimensions of the urban working class and most especially details of residence, occupation and association.

Although Antients freemasonry and the formation of the Antients Grand Lodge can be viewed, if one dimensionally, as a function of the alienation of the London Irish from mainstream English freemasonry, there were other more important economic, political and social drivers. Unlike the original Whiggist Grand Lodge of England established in 1717, Antients freemasonry and its Grand Lodge were moulded chiefly by working class and lower middling freemasons from London's Irish diaspora. However, although the two grand lodges were largely at opposite ends of the social spectrum, there were similarities in their development. Most notably, each was controlled in its formative years by a small group of dynamic and highly effective principals. In the 1720s until the early 1730s, John Theophilus Desaguliers was the primary driving force at English Grand Lodge, albeit supported by a core group of like-minded men including George Payne, Martin Folkes, William Cowper and others from their circles in the magistracy, the professions and among parliamentarians and the Court. Within the Antients, Laurence Dermott was dominant for three decades from the early 1750s into the 1780s. Both Desaguliers and Dermott set their marks on their respective organisations and each propelled it forward in their image. However, where Desaguliers and his colleagues retired in the late 1730s and early 1740s to be replaced a bureaucratic leadership that presided over Masonic stagnation and decline, Dermott's influence was longer, positive and far more indelible.

As the original Grand Lodge of England succumbed to a 'Masonic malaise', membership of the Antients grew rapidly, particularly once it enjoyed the patronage of the 1st earl of Blessington and other members of the

Anglo-Irish and Scottish gentry. The imprimatur of recognition by the Grand Lodge of Ireland followed.

Despite earlier opposition to Wood's Halfpence and the money bills dispute of the 1750s, relatively few of Ireland's oligarchs and Anglo-Irish aristocracy and gentry were willing to oppose British policy overtly. London's patronage and power were too substantial to be countered head on. Indirect and more oblique resistance was preferable, whether expressed through the Dublin Society or via support for and recognition of Antients freemasonry. And although perhaps superficially inconsequential when viewed in a broader framework, in the light of the proximity of association between the original Grand Lodge and London's political establishment, the subtext of a cessation of fraternal Masonic relations should not be underestimated.

Ireland's Masonic break with Britain was followed by a *volte face* by members of the Scottish aristocracy and, in the early 1770s, Scottish Grand Lodge recognised the Antients as the only legitimate Masonic authority in England. The joint recognition of the Irish and Scots was particularly important in consolidating the Antients' reputation and facilitating membership growth overseas, especially in the Americas and other colonies where military expansion and trade had introduced and embedded freemasonry into the local culture. Dermott was able to take advantage. His public promotion of Antients freemasonry and overt control of news management was similar to the strategy adopted by Desaguliers some three decades earlier. And as the Antients developed a higher profile and attracted patrons, Antients Grand Lodge posed an unequivocal challenge to the authority of the now derogatorily termed 'Moderns' and to the prestige of those in its senior ranks.

Members of Masonic lodges in dispute with the original Grand Lodge of England had an alternative course open to them. And even where there was no difference of Masonic opinion, the Antients beckoned as a preferred alternative, offering a supposedly more traditional form of ritual to that of the Moderns, equal aristocratic provenance, active mutual support and the frisson of an establishment yet anti-English establishment organisation.

The background to the schism in English freemasonry and to Ireland's crucial support was the politicisation and alienation of the Anglo-Irish elite and of the middling Irish more widely. But although such support may have been a key factor, Antients freemasonry had a more immediate British context. It was a direct response to the prejudice and intolerance of the English 'Moderns' towards not only the London Irish but also many among its own ranks. Freemasonry was a product of its milieu. The associational culture of the early eighteenth century had previously been restricted principally to the upper and middling classes and was encapsulated by the fraternal drinking, dining and self-improving conversation that was at the heart of many Moderns lodges. But towards the middle of the eighteenth century the socio economic environment was changing. By the late eighteenth century, perhaps a third or more of the five hundred or so Masonic lodges in England lay within the orbit of Antients freemasonry and had predominantly lower middling and working-class members. And with that impetus, Britain's associational culture metamorphosed to extend towards the lower strata of society.

From the early 1750s, Antients freemasonry and lodge activity moved beyond simple Masonic ritual to incorporate a broadly based form of mutual financial assistance. In doing so, it helped to set the foundations for working-class self-help in England's urban and industrial communities.

The schism in English Freemasonry was a consequence of the deterioration in England's economic and political relationship with Ireland and of the social condescension with which Ireland and the Irish were viewed. The split was also a metaphor for Irish alienation and their burgeoning disaffection. But it was more. Antients freemasonry was integral to the economic and social development of both the London Irish and a significant minority of the urban working class and lower middling. Masonic lodges carried forward and extended the concept of mutual benefit societies, provided a fraternal social nexus beyond the church and alehouse, and offered social access to many otherwise excluded. Of course, Antients freemasonry also fulfilled emotional and spiritual needs, but beyond this, it reflected and contributed to the transformation taking place within urban society and to the changing relationship between labour and capital. Above all, it was a symbol of aspiration and, over time, would mark what was a period of transition from alienation to assimilation.

List of Abbreviations

1723 Constitutions	James Anderson, *Constitutions of the Freemasons* (London, 1723).
1738 Constitutions	James Anderson, *The new book of constitutions of . . . free and accepted masons* (London, 1738).
Antients Grand Lodge	The Antients Grand Lodge of England, established 1751.
Antients Grand Lodge Minutes	Minutes of the Antients Grand Lodge, 1752–60, reprinted as *QCA*, vol. XI (London, 1958).
Burney	The Burney newspaper collection at the British Library, London.
CC Transactions	Transactions of the Lodge of Research, No. 200, Ireland.
CUP	Cambridge University Press.
DGM	Deputy Grand Master.
DIB	Dictionary of Irish Biography.
ed(s)	Editor(s).
edn.	Edition.
FCP	Four Courts Press.
FRS	Fellow of the Royal Society.
Grand Lodge of England	The Grand Lodge of England (formerly 'of London', later the 'Moderns'), established 1717, also 'Grand Lodge'.
Grand Lodge of England Minutes	1723–39: reprinted as *QCA*, vol. X (London, 1913). 1740–58: reprinted as *QCA*, vol. XII (Margate, 1960).
GM	Grand Master.
GS	Grand Secretary.
GSt	Grand Steward.
GT	Grand Treasurer.
HC	House of Commons.
HL	House of Lords.
HRI	Humanities Research Institute.
IHR	Institute of Historical Research.
JW	Junior Warden.
JGW	Junior Grand Warden.

LMA	London Metropolitan Archives, London.
MS(S)	Manuscript(s).
MUP	Manchester University Press.
SPCK	Society for Promoting Christian Knowledge.
ODNB	Oxford Dictionary of National Biography.
OKA	Old King's Arms Lodge, No. 28.
OUP	Oxford University Press.
QC	Quarterly Communication of Grand Lodge.
QCL	Quatuor Coronati Lodge, No. 2076.
QCL Transactions	Transactions of the Quatuor Coronati Lodge, No. 2076.
QCA	Quatuor Coronatorum Antigrapha.
QUB	Queen's University, Belfast.
RCP	Royal College of Physicians, London.
rev.	revised.
RS	The Royal Society, London.
Sackler Archives	The Sackler Archive of the Royal Society .
SW	Senior Warden.
SGW	Senior Grand Warden.
UGLE	United Grand Lodge of England.

Appendix

Antients Grand Lodge, Principal Grand Officers, 1751–1780

Pages 192–194

Year	Grand Master	Deputy Grand Master	Grand Wardens	Grand Secretary	Grand Treasurer
1751	NA	NA	NA NA	John Morgan	NA
1752	NA	NA	NA NA	Laurence Dermott	NA
1753	Robert Turner	William Rankin	Samuel Quay Lachlan McIntosh	Laurence Dermott	NA
1754	Hon Edward Vaughan	William Holford	Samuel Quay John Abercromby	Laurence Dermott	NA
1755	Hon Edward Vaughan	William Rankin	John Jackson Samuel Galbraith	Laurence Dermott	NA
1756	William Stewart, 1st earl of Blessington	William Holford	John Abercromby James Nisbett	Laurence Dermott	NA
1757	William Stewart, 1st earl of Blessington	William Holford	James Nisbett John Abercromby	Laurence Dermott	NA
1758	William Stewart, 1st earl of Blessington	Robert Goodman	Robert Goodman William Osborne	Laurence Dermott	NA
1759	William Stewart, 1st earl of Blessington	Robert Goodman	William Osborne David Fisher	Laurence Dermott	NA
1760	Thomas Erskine, 6th earl of Kellie	William Osborne	David Fisher William Dickey	Laurence Dermott	NA
1761	Thomas Erskine, 6th earl of Kellie	William Osborne	David Fisher William Dickey	Laurence Dermott	NA
1762	Thomas Erskine, 6th earl of Kellie	William Osborne	David Fisher William Dickey	Laurence Dermott	NA
1763	Thomas Erskine, 6th earl of Kellie	William Osborne	William Dickey David Garnault	Laurence Dermott	NA
1764	Thomas Erskine, 6th earl of Kellie	William Dickey	William Dickey James Gibson	Laurence Dermott	Matthew Beath

1765	Thomas Erskine, 6th earl of Kellie	William Dickey	James Gibson / Richard Swan	Laurence Dermott	Matthew Beath
1766	Hon Thomas Mathew	William Dickey	James Gibson / Richard Swan	Laurence Dermott	Matthew Beath
1767	Hon Thomas Mathew	William Dickey	William Clarke / Peter Duffy	Laurence Dermott	Matthew Beath
1768	Hon Thomas Mathew	William Dickey	Hon Edward Butler / Henry Allen	Laurence Dermott	Matthew Beath
1769	Hon Thomas Mathew	William Dickey	William Clarke / John Christian	Laurence Dermott	John Starkey
1770	Hon Thomas Mathew	William Dickey	William Clarke / John Christian	Laurence Dermott	Thomas Smith
1771	John Murray, 3rd duke of Atholl	Laurence Dermott	William Clarke / John Christian	William Dickey	Thomas Smith
1772	John Murray, 3rd duke of Atholl	Laurence Dermott	William Clarke / John Christian	William Dickey	Thomas Smith
1773	John Murray, 3rd duke of Atholl	Laurence Dermott	John Christian / Peter Shatwell	William Dickey	John Peck/ William Clarke
1774	John Murray, 3rd duke of Atholl	Laurence Dermott	John Christian / Peter Shatwell	William Dickey	William Clarke
1775	John Murray, 4th duke of Atholl	Laurence Dermott	William Tindall / Thomas Carter	William Dickey	William Clarke
1776	John Murray, 4th duke of Atholl	Laurence Dermott	William Tindall / Thomas Carter	William Dickey	John Ryland
1777	John Murray, 4th duke of Atholl	Laurence Dermott	Thomas Carter / Robert Davy	William Dickey	John Ryland
1778	John Murray, 4th duke of Atholl	William Dickey	Robert Davy / George Stewart	James Jones	John Ryland

| 1779 | John Murray, 4th duke of Atholl | William Dickey | Robert Davy
George Stewart | James Jones | John Ryland |
| 1780 | John Murray, 4th duke of Atholl | William Dickey | George Stewart
James Jones | Charles Bearblock | John Ryland |

Note: The above dates do not always correspond to calendar years; appointment and election to officer was often mid- or part way through a year.

Grand Lodge of Ireland, Principal Grand Officers, 1725–1770

Pages 195–198

Year	Grand Master	Deputy Grand Master	Grand Wardens	Grand Secretary	Grand Treasurer
1725	Rt Hon Richard, 1st earl Rosse	Hon Humphrey Butler	Sir Thomas Prendergast Marcus Morgan	Thomas Griffith	NA
1730	Rt Hon Richard, 1st earl Rosse		Not known	Thomas Griffith	NA
1731	Rt Hon James, 4th lord Kingston	Rt Hon Nicholas, 5th viscount Netterville	Hon William Ponsonby Dillon Pollard Hampson	Thomas Griffith	NA
1732	Rt Hon 5th viscount Netterville	Rt Hon Henry Benedict, 4th viscount Barnewall of Kingsland	James Brennan M.D. Robert Nugent	John Pennell	George Boyde
1733	Rt Hon 4th viscount Barnewall of Kingsland	Rt Hon Marcus Bereford, 1st earl Tyrone[1]	James Brennan M.D. Capt. William Cobbe	John Pennell	George Boyde
1734	Rt Hon 4th viscount Barnewall of Kingsland	James Brennan M.D.	Capt. William Cobbe John Baldwin	John Pennell	George Boyde
1735	Rt Hon James, 4th lord Kingston	James Brennan M.D.	John Baldwin Capt. John Corneille	John Pennell	George Boyde
1736	Rt Hon Marcus Bereford, 1st earl Tyrone	James Brennan M.D.	Capt. John Corneille William Stanford	John Pennell	Capt. John Arabin
1737	Rt Hon Marcus Bereford 1st earl Tyrone	James Brennan M.D.	Capt. John Corneille John Putland	John Pennell	Capt. John Arabin
1738	Hon Sir William Stewart, 3rd viscount Mountjoy[4]	Cornelius Callaghan	John Putland[2]/Kane O'Hara[3] Robert Callaghan/Edward Martin	John Pennell	Thomas Mills
1739	Hon Sir William Stewart, 3rd viscount Mountjoy	Cornelius Callaghan	Edward Martin Charles Annesley	John Pennell John Baldwin[5]	Thomas Mills
1740	Rt Hon Arthur St Leger, 3rd viscount Doneraile	Cornelius Callaghan	Edward Martin John Morris	John Baldwin	Thomas Mills
1741	Rt Hon Charles Moore, 2nd baron Tullamore	Cornelius Callaghan	Edward Martin John Morris	John Baldwin	Thomas Mills
1742	Rt Hon Charles Moore, 2nd baron Tullamore	Cornelius Callaghan	Edward Martin John Morris	John Baldwin[6] Anthony Relham M.D.	Thomas Mills
1743	Rt Hon Thomas Southwell, 2nd baron Southwell	Cornelius Callaghan	Edward Martin Keane Fitzgerald	Edward Spratt	Edward Martin
1744	Rt Hon John Allen, 3rd viscount Allen	Cornelius Callaghan	Hamilton Gorges Richard Houghton	Edward Spratt	Edward Martin

Year					
1745	Rt. Hon, James King, 4th lord Kingston	Cornelius Callaghan	Hamilton Gorges / Richard Houghton	Edward Spratt	Edward Martin
1746	Rt. Hon, James King, 4th lord Kingston	Cornelius Callaghan	Hamilton Gorges / Richard Houghton	Edward Spratt	Edward Martin
1747	Sir Marmaduke Wyvill, 6th Bt.	John Putland[7]	Boyle Lennox / Ald. Hans Baillie	Edward Spratt	Edward Martin
1748	Sir Marmaduke Wyvill, 6th Bt.	John Putland	Boyle Lennox / Ald. Hans Baillie	Edward Spratt	Edward Martin
1749	Rt Hon Robert King, 1st baron Kingsborough	John Putland	Boyle Lennox / Hon Roderick MacKenzie	Edward Spratt	Edward Martin
1750	Rt Hon Robert King, 1st baron Kingsborough	John Putland	Boyle Lennox / Hon Roderick MacKenzie	Edward Spratt	Edward Martin
1751	Rt Hon Lord George Sackville[8]	Hon Thomas George Southwell	Hon Roderick MacKenzie / Hon Brinsley Butler	Edward Spratt	Edward Martin
1752	Rt Hon Lord George Sackville	Hon Thomas George Southwell	Hon Roderick MacKenzie / Hon Brinsley Butler	Edward Spratt	Edward Martin
1753	Hon Thomas George Southwell[9]	Hon Brinsley Butler[10]	Charles, Viscount Moore / John Bury	Edward Spratt	Edward Martin
1754	Hon Thomas George Southwell	Hon Brinsley Butler	Charles, Viscount Moore / John Bury	Edward Spratt	Edward Martin
1755	Hon Thomas George Southwell	Brinsley Butler, Lord Newtown-Butler	Charles, Viscount Moore / John Bury	Edward Spratt	Edward Martin
1756	Hon Thomas George Southwell	Brinsley Butler, Lord Newtown-Butler	Charles, Viscount Moore / John Bury	John Calder	Edward Martin
1757	Brinsley Butler, Lord Newtown-Butler	Charles Moore, Viscount Moore[11]	John Bury / Capt. George Clarges	John Calder	Edward Martin
1758	Charles Moore, Viscount Moore	John Bury	Major Edward Windus / Rt Hon Charles Gardiner	John Calder	Edward Martin
1759	Charles Moore, 6th earl of Drogheda	Edward Martin	Ald. Hans Baillie / Capt. Christopher Parker	John Calder	Edward Martin
1760	Rt Hon Charles Moore, earl of Charleville	Edward Martin	Capt. Christopher Parker / William Marshall	John Calder	Edward Martin
1761	Rt Hon Sir Edward King, 5th Bt.	Edward Martin	William Marshall / Major Holt Waring	John Calder	Edward Martin

1762	Rt Hon Sir Edward King, 5th Bt.	William Marshall	Major Holt Waring Rt Hon Henry King	John Calder	Major Holt Waring
1763	Rt Hon Thomas Nugent, 6th earl of Westmeath	John Putland	Rt Hon Henry King Ald. Matthew Baillie	John Calder	Major Holt Waring
1764	Rt Hon Thomas Nugent, 6th earl of Westmeath	John Putland	Ald. Matthew Baillie David La Touche jr.	John Calder	Major Holt Waring
1765	Rt Hon Edward, 1st lord Kingston	Major Holt Waring	David La Touche jr. George Hart	John Calder	Major Holt Waring
1766	Rt Hon Ford Lambart, 5th earl of Cavan	Major Holt Waring	George Hart Peter La Touche	John Calder	Major Holt Waring
1767	Rt Hon Ford Lambart, 5th earl of Cavan	David La Touche jr.	Peter La Touche John La Touche	John Jones	Major Holt Waring
1768	Rt Hon Ford Lambart, 5th earl of Cavan	George Hart	John La Touche John Jones	Maj Charles Vallance	Major Holt Waring
1769	Rt Hon Edward King, 1st earl Kingston	William Ruxton	John Jones Joseph Keen	Vernon Hawley	Major Hart Waring
1770	William Robert, Marquess of Kildare	Joseph Keen	Ald. Francis Fetherston Henry Morris	Ald. Henry Hart	Major Holt Waring

Note: The above dates do not always correspond to calendar years; appointment and election to officer was often mid- or part way through a year.

Grand Lodge of England, Principal Grand Officers, 1717–1770

Pages 199–203

Appendix 3: Grand Lodge of England, Principal Grand Officers, 1717-1770

Year	Grand Master	Deputy Grand Master	Grand Wardens	Grand Secretary	Grand Treasurer
1717	Anthony Sayer	NA	John Elliot / Jacob Lambell	NA	NA
1718	George Payne	NA	John Cordwell / Thomas Morris	NA	NA
1719	J.T. Desaguliers	NA	Anthony Sayer / Thomas Morris	NA	NA
1720	George Payne	NA	Thomas Hobby / Richard Ware	NA	NA
1721	John Montagu, 2nd duke of Montagu	John Beale	Josias Villeneau / Thomas Morris	NA	NA
1722	Philip Wharton, 1st duke of Wharton	J.T. Desaguliers	Joshua Timpson / William Hawkins/James Anderson	William Cowper	NA
1723	Francis Scott, 5th earl of Dalkeith	J.T. Desaguliers	Francis Sorrel / John Senex	William Cowper	NA
1724	Charles Lennox, 2nd duke of Richmond	Martin Folkes	Francis Sorrel / George Payne	William Cowper	NA
1725	James Hamilton, Lord Paisley	J.T. Desaguliers	Col. Daniel Houghton / Sir Thomas Prendergast	William Cowper	NA
1726	William O'Brien, 4th earl of Inchiquin	William Cowper	Alexander Choke / William Burdon	Edward Wilson	NA
1727	Henry Hare, 3rd baron Coleraine	Alexander Choke	Nathaniel Blackerby / Joseph Highmore	William Reid	NA
1728	James King, 4th baron Kingston	Nathaniel Blackerby	Sir Joseph Thornhill / Martin O'Connor	William Graeme	NA
1729	Thomas Howard, 8th duke of Norfolk	Nathaniel Blackerby	Col. Hon George Carpenter / Thomas Batson	John Revis	NA
1730	Thomas Howard, 8th duke of Norfolk	Nathaniel Blackerby	Col. Hon George Carpenter / Thomas Batson	John Revis	Nathaniel Blackerby
1731	Thomas Coke, Lord Lovell	Thomas Batson	Dr George Douglas / James Chambers	John Revis	Nathaniel Blackerby

Year					
1732	Anthony Browne, 7th viscount Montagu	Thomas Batson	George Rooke / James Smythe	John Revis	Nathaniel Blackerby
1733	James Strathmore, 7th earl of Strathmore	Thomas Batson	James Smythe / John Ward	John Revis	Nathaniel Blackerby
1734	John Lindsay, 20th earl of Crawford	Sir Cecil Wray	John Ward / Sir Edward Mansell	John Revis	Nathaniel Blackerby
1735	Thomas, 2nd viscount Weymouth	John Ward	Sir Edward Mansell / Martin Clare	John Revis	Nathaniel Blackerby
1736	John Campbell, 4th earl of Loudoun	John Ward	Sir Robert Lawley / William Graeme	John Revis	Nathaniel Blackerby
1737	Edward Bligh, 2nd earl of Darnley	John Ward	Sir Robert Lawley / William Graeme	John Revis	Nathaniel Blackerby
1738	Henry Brydges, Marquis of Carnarvon	William Graeme	Lord George Graham / Capt. Andrew Robinson	John Revis	John Jesse
1739	Robert Raymond, 2nd lord Raymond	William Graeme	J. Harvey Thursby / Robert Foy	John Revis	John Jesse
1740	John Keith, 3rd earl of Kintore	William Graeme	James Ruck / William Vaughan	John Revis	John Jesse
1741	James Douglas, 14th earl of Morton	Martin Clare	William Vaughan / Benjamin Gascoyne	John Revis	John Jesse
1742	John Ward, Viscount Dudley & Ward	Sir Robert Lawley	Edward Hody / Samuel Berrington	John Revis	John Jesse
1743	John Ward, Viscount Dudley & Ward	Sir Robert Lawley	Edward Hody / Samuel Berrington	John Revis	John Jesse
1744	Thomas Lyon, earl of Strathmore	William Vaughan	William Graeme / Fotherley Baker	John Revis	John Jesse
1745	James Cranstoun, 6th lord Cranstoun	Edward Hody	Fotherley Baker / Thomas Smith	John Revis	John Jesse
1746	James Cranstoun, 6th lord Cranstoun	Edward Hody	Fotherley Baker / Thomas Smith	John Revis	John Jesse
1747	William Byron, 5th lord Byron	Fotherley Baker	Hon Robert Shirley / Thomas Jeffries	John Revis	John Jesse
1748	William Byron, 5th lord Byron	Fotherley Baker	Hon Robert Shirley / Thomas Jeffries	John Revis	John Jesse

Year					
1749	William Byron, 5th lord Byron	Fotherley Baker	Hon Robert Shirley / Thomas Jeffries	John Revis	John Jesse
1750	William Byron, 5th lord Byron	Fotherley Baker	Hon Robert Shirley / Thomas Jeffries	John Revis	John Jesse
1751	William Byron, 5th lord Byron	Fotherley Baker	Hon Robert Shirley / Capt. Thomas Jeffreys	John Revis	John Jesse
1752	John Proby, Lord Carysfort	Thomas Manningham	Hon James Carmichael / Sir Richard Wrottesley	John Revis	John Jesse
1753	John Proby, Lord Carysfort	Thomas Manningham	Sir Richard Wrottesley / Francis Blake Delaval	John Revis	George Clarke
1754	James Brydges, Marques of Carnarvon	Thomas Manningham	Fleming Pinckstan / Arthur Beardmore	John Revis	George Clarke
1755	James Brydges, Marques of Carnarvon	Thomas Manningham	Hon Horatio Townshend / James Dickson	John Revis	George Clarke
1756	James Brydges, Marques of Carnarvon	Thomas Manningham	James Nash / Edward Joachim Boetefeur	John Revis	George Clarke
1757	Sholto Douglas, Lord Aberdour	John Revis	William Chapman / Alexander Valdevelde	Samuel Spencer	George Clarke
1758	Sholto Douglas, Lord Aberdour	John Revis	James Dickson / Thomas Singleton	Samuel Spencer	George Clarke
1759	Sholto Douglas, Lord Aberdour	John Revis	James Dickson / Thomas Singleton	Samuel Spencer	George Clarke
1760	Sholto Douglas, Lord Aberdour	John Revis	Caspar Schombart / Charles Massey	Samuel Spencer	George Clarke
1761	Sholto Douglas, Lord Aberdour	John Revis	Caspar Schombart / Charles Massey	Samuel Spencer	George Clarke
1762	Washington Shirley, 5th earl Ferrers	Col. John Salter	Col. John Salter / Robert Groat	Samuel Spencer	George Clarke
1763	Washington Shirley, 5th earl Ferrers	Col. John Salter	Robert Groat / Thomas Edmonds	Samuel Spencer	George Clarke
1764	Cadwaller Blayney, 9th lord Blaney	Col. John Salter	Hon Thomas Shirley / Thomas Alleyne	Samuel Spencer	George Clarke
1765	Cadwaller Blayney, 9th lord Blaney	Col. John Salter	Richard Ripley / Capt. Charles Tuffnal	Samuel Spencer	George Clarke

1766	Henry Somerset, 5th duke of Beaufort	Col. John Salter	Peter Edwards Horatio Ripley	Samuel Spencer	Rowland Berkeley
1767	Henry Somerset, 5th duke of Beaufort	Col. John Salter	Hon Charles Dillon Capt. Alasdair Campbell	Samuel Spencer	Rowland Berkeley
1768	Henry Somerset, 5th duke of Beaufort	Hon Charles Dillon	Rowland Holt Henry Jaffray	Thomas French	Rowland Berkeley
1769	Henry Somerset, 5th duke of Beaufort	Hon Charles Dillon	Rowland Holt Charles Taylor	James Heseltine	Rowland Berkeley
1770	Henry Somerset, 5th duke of Beaufort	Hon Charles Dillon	Rowland Holt Sir Watkins Williams Wynne	James Heseltine	Rowland Berkeley

Note: The above dates do not always correspond to calendar years; appointment and election to officer was often mid- or part way through a year.

1. Later Earl of Tyrone.
2. Until 24 June.
3. From 24 June.
4. Created Earl of Blessington in 1745. Sworn a Privy Councillor (Ireland) in 1748 and made Governor of Co. Tyrone.
5. Succeeded Pennell on his death
6. Resigned, succeeded by Anthony Relham
7. Sometimes written as 'Pentland'.
8. Later 1st viscount Sackville. Sackville was the son of the 1st duke of Dorset, Lord Lieutenant of Ireland, 1751-5, and served as his father's Chief Secretary.
9. Succeeded as the 3rd baron Southwell in 1766.
10. Succeeded as 2nd earl of Lanesborough in 1768; honorific title from 1755.
11. Later 6th earl of Drogheda; subsequently 1st earl of Charleville.

Military Lodges Warranged by the Irish and Antients Grand Lodges

Pages 204–212

Irish Warranted Military Lodges

	Lodge Numbers and Warrant Dates
Cavalry	
2nd The Queen's Bays	960 (1805–34)
4th Royal Irish Dragoon Guards	295 (1757–96)
5th (Princess Charlotte of Wales) Dragoon Guards	277 (1757–1818)
	570 (1863–...)
6th Dragoon Guards, the Carabiniers	577 (1780–99)
	exchanged for 876, (1799–1858)
7th (Princess Royals) Dragoon Guards – the Black Horse	305 (1758)
	exchanged for 7, (1817–55)
1st or Blue Irish Horse, later 4th Dragoon Guards	295 (1758–...)
2nd or Green Irish Horse, later 5th Dragoon Guards	277 (1757–1818)
	570 (1780–1824)
	44 re-issued (1863–...)
3rd or Irish Horse, later 6th Dragoon Guards	577 (1780)
	876 issued 1799
	in lieu of 577, lost 1794
4th or Black Irish Horse, later 7th Dragoon Guards	305 (1758
	exchanged for No. 7, 1817)
4th Dragoons – Queen's Own Hussars	50 (1815)
	exchanged for No. 4, 1818
	cancelled 1821
5th Dragoons – Queen's Own Hussars	289 (1757–96)
	297 (1758–1818)
5th Royal Irish Lancers	595 (1914–1922)
8th Dragoons – Kings Royal Irish Hussars	280 (1757–1815)
	646 (1932–80)
9th Dragoons – Queen's Royal Lancers	158 (1747–1815)
	356 (1760–1818)

12th Dragoons – Royal Lancers (Prince of Wales)	179 (1804–17)
	exchanged for 12 (1817–27)
	179 (1868–91)
	255 (1755–1815)
13th Dragoons – Hussars	234 (1752–1815)
	400 (1791–1849)
	607 (1782–89)
14th Dragoons – King's Hussars	273 (1756–1827)
16th Dragoons – Queen's Lancers	929 (1803–21)
17th Dragoons – Lancers (Duke of Cambridge Own)	218 (1873–83)
	478 (1769–1801)
18th Lord Drogheda's Light Dragoons – 1st Squadron	388 (1762–1813)
18th Lord Drogheda's Light Dragoons – 2nd Squadron	389 (1762–1821)
20th Jamaica Light Dragoons	759 (1792–1815)
23rd Light Dragoons (1794–1802)	873 (1799–1802)
23rd (26th) Light Dragoons (1802–1817)	164 (1808–17)

Artillery Regiments

7th Battalion, Royal Artillery	68 (1813–34)
	226 (1810–25)
9th Battalion, Royal Artillery	313 (1823–28)
Royal Irish Artillery	374 (1761–1818)
	528 (1781–87)
Corps of Artillery Drivers	241 (1811, but not issued)

Regiments of the Line

1st Foot, Royal Scots 1st Battalion	11 (1732–1847)
	381 (1762–1814)
1st Foot, Royal Scots 2nd Battalion	74 (1737–1801)
2nd Foot, Queen's Royal Regiment (West Surrey)	2 (1818)
	in lieu of 244 (1754–1825)
	390 (1762–1815)
4th Foot, King's Own Royal Regiment (Lancaster)	4 (1818) in lieu of 50
	91 (1857–1876)
	522 (1785–1823)
5th Foot, Royal Northumberland Fusiliers	86 (1738–1815)
6th Foot, Royal Warwickshire	45 (1735–1801)
	643 (1785–1800)
	646 (1785–1818)
7th Foot, Royal Fusiliers (City of London)	231 (1752–1801)
9th Foot, Royal Norfolk	246 (1754–1817)
10th Foot, Lincolnshire	177 (1748–55)
	299 (1758–1803)
	378 (1761–1815)
11th Foot, Devonshire	604 (1782–94)
13th Foot, Somerset Light Infantry	637 (1784–1818)
	661 (1787–1819)

14th Foot, West Yorkshire (Prince of Wales Own)   211 (1750–1815)

15th Foot, East Yorkshire   245 (1754–1801)

16th Foot, Bedfordshire & Hertfordshire   293 (1758–1817)
300 (1758–1801)

17th Foot, Leicestershire   136 (1743–1801)
921 (1802–1824)
258 (1824 in lieu of 921, 1847)

18th Foot, Royal Irish   168 (1747–1801)
351 (1760–1818)

19th Foot, Green Howards   156 (1747–1779)

20th Foot, Lancashire Fusiliers, 1st Battalion   63 (1737–1869)

20th Foot, Lancashire Fusiliers, 2nd Battalion   263 (1860–1907)

21st Foot, Royal Scots Fusiliers   33 (1734–1801)
936 (1803–1817) in exchange for
33 (1817–1864)

22nd Foot, Cheshire   251 (1754–1817)

23rd Foot, Royal Welsh Fusiliers   738 (2) (1808–1821)
revived (1882–1892)

25th Foot, King's Own Scottish Borderers   92 (1738–1815)
250 (1819–1823)
exchanged for 25 (1823–1839)

26th Foot, 1st Battalion, The Cameronians   309 (1758)
exchanged for 26 (1823)
26 (1810–1823 and 1823–1922)

27th Foot, 1st Battalion, Royal Inniskilling Fusiliers   24 (1734–1801)
205 (1750–1785)
528 (1787–1815)
692 (1808–1818)

28th Foot, 1st Battalion, Gloucestershire   35 (1734–1801)
510 (1773–1858)

28th Foot, 2nd Battalion, Gloucestershire   260 (1809–15)

29th Foot, 1st Battalion, Worcestershire   322 (1759–...)

30th Foot, 1st Battalion, East Lancashire 85 (1738–1793 exchanged for No. 30,
1805–1823),
535 (1776–...)

32nd Foot, 1st Battalion, Duke of Cornwall's Light Infantry   61 (1736–1801)
617 (1783–1815)
524 (1921–37)

33rd Foot, 1st Battalion, Duke of Wellington's   12 (1732–1817)

35th Foot, 1st Battalion, Royal Sussex   205 (1749–90)

36th Foot   542 (1770–80)
559 (1778–...)

38th Foot, 1st Battalion, South Staffordshire   38 (1734–1801)
441 (1765–1840)

39th Foot, 1st Battalion, Dorsetshire	128 (1742–1886)
	290 (1758–1815)
40th Foot, 1st Battalion, Prince of Wales Volunteers	
(South Lancs.)	204 (1810–1813)
	284 (1821–1858)
42nd Foot, 1st Battalion, Black Watch (Royal Highlanders)	42 (1809–1840)
	195 (1749–1815)
44th Foot, 1st Battalion, Essex	788 (1793–...)
45th Foot, 1st Battalion, Sherwood Foresters	445 (1766–1815)
46th Foot, 2nd Battalion, Duke of Cornwall's Light Infantry	174 (1896–1921)
	227 (1752–1847)
47th Foot, 1st Battalion, The Loyal Regiment (North Lancs)	147 (1810–1823)
	192 (1748–1823)
48th Foot, 1st Battalion, Northamptonshire	86 (1738–1784)
	218 (1750–1858)
	631 (May–Aug 1784)
	reissued (Oct. 1784–1818)
	982 (1806–17)
49th Foot, 1st Battalion, Royal Berkshire	354 (1760–1851)
	616 (1783–1817)
50th Foot, 1st Battalion, Queen's Own Royal West Kent	58 (1857–1876)
	113 (1763–1815)
51st Foot, 1st Battalion, King's Own Yorks. Light Infantry	94 (1761–1815)
	690 (1788–96)
52nd Foot, 2nd Battalion, Oxford and Bucks Light Infantry	244 (1832–1845)
	370 (1761–1825)
53rd Foot, 1st Battalion, King's Shropshire Light Infantry	236 (1773–1815)
	950 (1804–24)
56th Foot, 2nd Battalion, Essex	420 (1765–1817)
58th Foot, 2nd Battalion, Northamptonshire	466 (1769–1816)
	692 (1789–1808)
59th Foot, 2nd Battalion, East Lancashire	219 (1810–1819)
	243 (1754–1815)
62nd Foot, 1st Battalion, Wiltshire (Duke of Edinburgh)	407 (1763–86)
63rd Foot, 1st Battalion, Manchester	512 (1774–1814)
64th Foot, 1st Battalion, North Staffordshire	
(Prince of Wales)	130 (1817–58)
	686 (1788)
	exchanged for No. 130, 1817
65th Foot, 1st Battalion, York and Lancaster	631 (1784–1818)
66th Foot, 2nd Battalion, Royal Berkshire	392 (1763–1817)
	538 (1777–1811)
	580 (1780–1817)
66th Foot, 2nd Battalion, Royal Berkshire	656 (1808) (not confirmed)
67th Foot, 2nd Battalion, Royal Berkshire	388 (1762–1813)

68th Foot, 1st Battalion, Durham Light Infantry	714 (1790–1815)
69th Foot, 2nd Battalion, The Welsh	174 (1791–1821)
	983 (1807–36)
70th Foot, 2nd Battalion, East Surrey	770 (1871–75)
71st Foot, 1st Battalion, Highland Light Infantry	895 (1801–58)
72nd Foot, 1st Battalion, Seaforth Highlanders	65 (1854–60)
75th Foot, 1st Battalion, Gordon Highlanders	292 (1810–25)
76th Foot, 2nd Battalion, Gordon Highlanders	359 (1760–1763)
77th Foot, Atholl Highlanders	578 (1780–1818)
82nd Foot, 2nd Battalion, Prince of Wales Volunteers	138 (1817–58)
83rd Foot, (1758 – 1763)	339 (1759–64)
83rd Foot, 1st Battalion, Royal Ulster Rifles	435 (1808)
	exchanged for 83, (1817)
83rd Foot, 16th Service Battalion, Royal Irish Rifles	420 (1915–21)
87th Foot, 7th Service Battalion, Royal Irish Fusiliers	415 (1915–1924)
88th Foot, 1st Battalion, Connaught Rangers	19 (1907–20)
	176 (1821–71)
89th Foot 2nd Battalion, Royal Irish Fusiliers	538 (1811–15)
	863 (11798–1818)
92nd Foot, Donegal Light Infantry	364 (1761–63)
96th/97th Foot, Queen's Germans	984 (1807–1818
	exchanged for 176, (1818–19)
103rd Foot, Bombay European Regiment	292 (1834–56)
112th Foot, Lord Donoughmore's	815 (1795–1815)
4th Foot, Garrison Battalion	986 (1810–15)
5th Foot, Garrison Battalion	125 (1808–14)
7th Foot, Garrison Battalion	992 (1808–15)
8th Foot, Garrison Battalion	995 (1808–14)
4th Foot, Veteran Battalion	988 (1808–15)
Commissariat Corps	203 (1809–15)
West Africa Regiment	157 (1908–28)
West India Regiment	390 (1905–27)
Colonel Pool's Regiment	177 (1748–55)
Colonel Folliott's Regiment	168 (1747–01)
Hon Brigadier Guise's Regiment	45 (1801), but no GLI record.
Colonel Hamilton's Regiment	23 (1733–1801)
Colonel Lascelle's Regiment	192 (1749–1823)

Militia Regiments

Antrim	289 (1796–1856)
Armagh	888 (1800–45)
Carlow	903 (1801–16)

Cavan	300 (1801–16)
South Cork	495 (1794–15)
City of Cork	741 (1806–17)
Donegal	865 (1798–1821
Downshire	212 (1795–1813)
South Down	214 (1810–15)
City of Dublin	62 (1810–21)
Fermanagh	864 (1798–1830)
Kerry	66 (1810–29)
Kildare	847 (1797–1825)
Kilkenny	855 (1797–1825)
King's County	948 (1804–16)
Leitrim	854 (1797–1868)
Longford	304 (1807–26)
Louth	10 (1809–49)
Mayo South	79 (1810–30)
	81 (1812–25)
Meath	50 (not issued)
	898 (1801–49)
Monaghan	200 (1801–16)
	552 (1796–1816)
Queen's County	398 (1805–10)
	857 (1797–1832)
Roscommon	242 (1808–17)
Sligo	837 (1796–1835)
South Lincoln	867 (1799–1813)
Tipperary	856 (1797–1825)
Tyrone	225 (1808–14)
	562 (1797–1817)
	846 (1796–1818)
Waterford	961 (1805–16)
Westmeath	50, 791 (1793–1826)
Wexford	935 (1803–24)
Wicklow	848 (1796–1815)
	877 (1800–18)
Royal Independent Dublin Volunteers	620 (1783–...)

Fencible Regiments

1st Fencible Light Dragoons	384 (1799–1802)
Ulster Provincial Regiment of Foot	612 (1783–...)
Breadalbane	907 (1801–13)
Elgin	860 (1798–1813)
Essex	852 (1796–1813)

Fife	861 (1798–1804)

Sources:
Grand Lodge of Ireland, Register of Warranted Lodges.
Gould, *Military Lodges.*
Lane, *Masonic Records.*

Antients Warranted Military Lodges

	Lodge Numbers and Warrant Dates
Cavalry	
3rd Dragoons, R A Union	197 (1806–...)
6th Dragoons	123 (1763–...)
6th Dragoons	311 (1797–1837
7th Dragoons	262 (1807–24)
9th Dragoons	284 (1794–1813)
11th Dragoons	339 (1807–10)
17th Dragoons	285 (1794–1828)
Artillery Regiments	
1st Battalion Royal Artillery, Scotland	134 (1764–74)
1st Battalion Royal Artillery, Chatham	187 (1774–77)
1st Battalion Royal Artillery, Gibraltar	230 (1785–...)
2nd Battalion Royal Artillery, Perth	148 (1767–...)
4th Battalion Royal Artillery, New York	213 (1781–...)
4th Battalion Royal Artillery, New York	144 (1804–...)
4th Battalion Royal Artillery, Gibraltar	209 (1779–...)
4th Battalion Royal Artillery, Gibraltar	345 (1809–27)
5th Battalion Royal Artillery, Eastbourne	101 (1812–23)
6th Battalion Royal Artillery, Ceylon	329 (1802–30)
9th Battalion Royal Artillery, Gibraltar	187 (1812–22)
10th Battalion Royal Artillery, South Africa	354 (1812–51)
10th Battalion Royal Artillery, Gibraltar	356 (1813–21)
Royal Horse Artillery, Colchester	156 (1809–28)
RHA, Woolwich	86 (1761–...)
Capt. Webdell's Company	183 (1773–...)
Quebec, St John	241 (1787–...)
Port Royal, Jamaica	262 (1790–1805)
Calcutta	317 (1798–...)
Quebec	40 (1804–14)

Infantry Regiments

3rd	170 (1771–92)
5th, St George	353 (1812–62)
7th	153 (1804–...)
9th	183 (1803–29)
11th	72 (1758–67)
11th	313 (1798–1813)
13th	153 (1768–76)
14th	58 (1759–1813)
14th, Union	338 (1807–30)
14th, Officers' Lodge	347 (1810–13)
17th	237 (1787–92)
18th	335 (1806–13)
23rd	252 (1788–1822)
33rd	90 (1761–1813)
34th	340 (1807–32)
37th	52 (1756–1813)
40th	42 (no date)
45th	272 (1792–1807)
50th	112 (17763–1830)
51st, Orange	94 (1763–1805)
52nd	309 (1797–1801)
52nd	170 (1801–13)
57th	41 (1755–...)
58th	332 (1805–23)
65th	191 (1774–...)
67th	175 (1772–...)
68th, Durham Light	348 (1810–44)
72nd	75 (1759–64)
76th	248 (1788–1828)
78th	322 (1801–30)
79th, Waterloo	191 (1808–38)
85th	298 (1801–46)
91st, Argyle	321 (1799–1828)
92nd	333 (1805–32)
96th	170 (no date)

Royal Engineers

Artificers, Jersey	293 (1795)
RM Artificers, Jersey	350 (1810)

Sources:
Grand Lodge of Ireland, Register of Warranted Lodges.
Gould, *Military Lodges*.
Lane, *Masonic Records*.

An Introduction to Eighteenth-Century Irish Freemansonry

The popularisation of modern freemasonry and its introduction into eighteenth-century Ireland lagged developments in England by around four years. The Dublin press first mention the subject in 1721, when the duke of Montagu's decision to accept the position of Grand Master of the Grand Lodge of England pushed freemasonry into the public's consciousness and led to its renaissance. At the time, London freemasonry appears to have attracted broad interest in Ireland and featured across the political spectrum in articles in both pro-government and opposition newspapers. John Whalley's loyalist *Dublin News Letter* carried a typical description of Montagu's installation in July 1721; and the following month, John Harding's opposition-leaning *Dublin Impartial News Letter* wrote an account of the initiation of Viscount Hinchingbroke, Sir George Oxenden and Sir Robert Rich at the King's Arms tavern at St Paul's Churchyard 'where they had a very handsome entertainment'.[1] However, it was probably reports of the mercurial and sometime pro-Jacobite duke of Wharton's decision to join the Craft later the same year that catalysed a more widespread interest among the Irish gentry and middling class.

Many Irish newspapers reproduced accounts carried in the London press that the duke of Wharton had become a freemason, alerting their readers that

> his Grace, the duke of Wharton, was admitted into the Society of Freemasons; the ceremonies being performed at the King's Arms Tavern in St Paul's Churchyard,

and that Wharton ostentatiously 'came home to his house in the Pall Mall in a white leather apron' having been initiated.[2]

One Irish newspaper to feature the story was Thomas Hume's *Dublin Courant*. Its target readership included Dublin's Anglo-Irish gentry and middling professionals and Hume probably believed Wharton's involvement with the organisation to be of interest to both. The following year, the *Courant* featured Wharton's own elevation to the Grand Master's chair in London:

yesterday the Grand Meeting of the most noble and ancient Fraternity of Free-Masons was kept at Stationers' hall where they had a most sumptuous Feast, several of the nobility, who are Members of the Society, being present, and his Grace the duke of Wharton was then unanimously chosen Governor of the said Fraternity.[3]

Philip, duke of Wharton (1698–1731), had been made and declared a freemason at the age of 22. He was most probably inspired by Montagu's installation as Grand Master only a few months earlier and the extensive and positive publicity that the event generated.[4] Wharton had been brought up in a wealthy, well-connected and strongly Whiggist family. His father, Thomas, had been honoured for his opposition to James II and support for the accession of William and Mary and was sworn a privy councillor, made comptroller of the royal household and created earl of Wharton and Viscount Wichendon. In later years, he was appointed to the lord lieutenancy of Ireland and thereafter made Lord Lieutenant of Oxfordshire and Buckinghamshire and Lord Privy Seal. As a capstone, shortly before his death in 1715, Thomas Wharton was granted five additional titles as Marquess of Catherlough, earl of Rathfarnam and Baron Trim in the Irish peerage, and Marquess of Wharton and Marquess of Malmesbury in the English.

Philip Wharton inherited the titles and estates aged 17.[5] His relationship with his father had been fractious and Wharton now had the freedom and opportunity to rebel. Although obliged to meet a proviso in his father's will that he continue his religious education in Geneva, Wharton abandoned his Huguenot teacher in Switzerland and diverted to Paris where he corresponded with the exiled duke of Mar, John Erskine, and visited James Stuart, the Old Pretender, at Avignon. Wharton was a potential catch for Stuart and his gift of a thoroughbred horse was reciprocated by Stuart with Wharton being invested duke of Northumberland.

Wharton's actions were treasonous and could have been politically and personally disastrous; however, they were overlooked on his return to Britain and intentionally regarded as a misdemeanour of youth. Wharton was now nineteen and despite being two years under the necessary minimum age, was permitted to sit in the Irish parliament and sworn to the Irish privy council. As a further encouragement and an inducement to secure his loyalty, Wharton was created a duke on 28 January 1718.[6] The letters patent announced that 'as it is to the honour of subjects who are descended from an illustrious family to imitate the great example of their ancestors, we esteem it no less a glory as a king, after the example of our ancestors, to dignify eminent virtues by similar rewards'. However, it is more likely that the English dukedom was intended to displace Wharton's affection for his Jacobite title.

As duke, Wharton took his seat in the British House of Lords on reaching his majority in December 1719 and immediately attracted considerable press interest.[7] He appeared initially to have matured and his speeches were Whiggist and pro-government. Indeed, Wharton's political reconfiguration appeared to be such that he was even invited to attend a meeting of 'gentlemen of the Whig interest' at the George Inn at Aylesbury in Buckinghamshire.[8] But any change was superficial. Wharton's principal political focus was his own self-interest. Unhappy with his seeming political trajectory and the manner in which he considered he had been overlooked for a suitable sinecure or office, Wharton launched an attack on the administration over its handling of the South Sea Company, condemning it as 'dangerous bait which might decoy unwary people to their ruin'.[9] Although arguably correct, his comments were neither prescient nor altruistic. Wharton was reported to have invested and lost £120,000 in the company's stock.[10] Nevertheless, his political assault was effective and struck pointedly at the web of dishonest relationships between the City, the government and the Court. Unsurprisingly, it made Wharton few friends in any of the three.

Rebellious in his youth, Wharton retained the same mercurial attitude as a young adult. Outside of politics, his chief interests were those of an aristocratic rake and involved amusing himself and his friends in a flurry of whoring, gambling, drinking and general mischief making. It was in this context that he founded the first Hell Fire club and, in 1721, was proscribed for blasphemy by the Lord Chancellor, a charge he denied. Wharton's interest in freemasonry may have been sparked by curiosity but is likely to have fanned by the opportunity he may have considered it offered for further self promotion and the drunken amusement and entertainment of his friends. In typical style, Wharton sought to usurp rather than succeed Montagu as Grand Master of England and commandeer what he could have viewed as a potentially influential organisation. An alternative is that he may simply have wished to cause a nuisance and, as a wealthy aristocrat, a duke and one of the hundred or so most affluent and best-connected men in England, there were few who would or could stand in his way:

> Philip, duke of Wharton lately made a Brother, tho' not the Master of a Lodge, being ambitious of the Chair, got a number of others to meet him at Stationers Hall 24 June 1722. And having no Grand Officers, they put in the Chair the oldest Master Mason . . . and without the usual decent ceremonials, the said oldest Mason proclaimed aloud Philip, duke of Wharton, Grand Master of Masons . . . but his Grace appointed no deputy nor was the lodge opened and closed in due form. Therefore the noble Brothers and all those that would not countenance irregularities disowned Wharton's authority, till worthy Brother Montagu healed the Breach of Harmony by summoning the Grand Lodge to meet 17 January 1723 at the King's Arms aforesaid, where the duke of Wharton promising to be true and faithful, Deputy Grand Master Beale proclaimed aloud the most noble Prince and our Brother Philip duke of Wharton, Grand Master of Masons, who appointed Dr Desaguliers the Deputy Grand Master and Joshua Timson and James Anderson Grand Wardens.[11]

The description of Wharton's installation was written by the Rev. James Anderson and appears in his *1738 Constitutions*. The record was slanted and designed to avoid the perception of any fraternal 'breach of harmony'. Nonetheless, this is precisely what occurred and although Wharton was accepted as Grand Master and a formal dinner held at the Stationers' livery hall to celebrate the installation, as a counter-balance to his suspect politics, Desaguliers, a leading Whiggist freemason and former Grand Master, was appointed his deputy. The event was reported extensively in the press. One newspaper remarked in passing that membership of the freemasons at the time was some four thousand. If accurate, this would have represented around a fifth of London's gentry and middling adult male population.[12]

Given freemasonry's pro-Hanoverian and Whiggist associations, Wharton was a divisive figure. The issue came to the fore when the musicians performing at the feast were instructed or encouraged to play the Jacobite anthem, 'Let the King enjoy His own again'.[13] Lawrence Smith has suggested that Wharton sang the song rather than simply permitting it to be played at dinner.[14] But regardless of whether he encouraged the musicians or participated by singing, Wharton was making what would have been considered an overtly offensive political point among a gathering of predominantly loyal Hanoverian Whigs. David Stevenson, quoting from a record of the event, commented that the musicians, and thus by implication Wharton, were 'immediately reprimanded by a person of great gravity and science'.[15] There should be little doubt that this was Desaguliers. Following Wharton's public censure:

> Hanoverian decorum was restored – and indeed emphasized. The bottle went merrily about and toasts were made to king, royal family and the established churches . . . other toasts were drunk to prosperity to Old England "under the present Administration" and "Love, Liberty and Science".[16]

At the end of his year in office, Wharton waived his right to name a successor, perhaps expecting that he would be re-elected. Instead, Grand Lodge voted narrowly to appoint the earl of Dalkeith as the new incumbent. The election had been orchestrated by Desaguliers who had arranged for himself to be named Dalkeith's deputy, and two loyal lieutenants, Francis Sorrel and John Senex, to be made the new Grand Wardens.[17] Wharton was not content to let matters go uncontested. His hostility to Desaguliers provoked an unsuccessful attempt to hold the vote again and to declare Desaguliers' appointment invalid. Despite withdrawing with his supporters in protest against the proceedings, Wharton failed to have the vote overturned and left 'without ceremony'.

The episode prompted Desaguliers to continue his strategy of promoting trustworthy friends to key positions. The most notable was William Cowper, selected as the first Grand Secretary and later Deputy Grand Master. The appointment passed control of the minutes to a staunchly Whiggist fellow member of the duke of Richmond's Horn tavern lodge and placed another ally in a key organizational position.[18] Cowper was at the time Clerk to the

Parliaments, the most senior administrative position in the House of Commons and Lords; he was also chairman of the Westminster magistrates' bench. To consolidate power further, Desaguliers instigated new rules to prevent or at least delay any future attempt at Masonic subversion. Shortly after Wharton's departure Grand Lodge resolved that 'it was not in the power of any body of men to make any alteration or innovation in the body of masonry without the consent first obtained of the annual Grand Lodge'. The restriction became so ingrained that it continues to this day to be repeated as part of the installation ceremony each time a new Master is elected in a lodge. Six months later the absolute entitlement of the Grand Master to nominate and appoint his deputy was confirmed, thereby establishing Desaguliers' formal authority as deputy to act as pro Grand Master and to exercise authority in his name. Wharton's departure from Grand Lodge ensured that freemasonry's relationship with the Hanoverian establishment would endure for at least the next decade under Desaguliers' influence and that of a loyalist inner circle.[19]

The early 1720s offered a difficult backdrop against which to demonstrate publicly Grand Lodge's pro-Hanoverian and Whiggist stance. In addition to Wharton's opposition sympathies and Jacobite tendencies, the Atterbury Plot in 1721–2 had accompanied the possibility of another Jacobite rising and was marked by heightened security across London with troops recalled from Ireland and encamped in Hyde Park as a show of force. In such a febrile environment, the government was openly suspicious of secret societies and Grand Lodge reportedly sent emissaries to the secretary of state, Lord Townshend, requesting his consent to the June meeting. The *London Journal* described the event:

> a select body of the Society of Freemasons waited on the Rt Hon the Lord Viscount Townshend, one of his principal Secretaries of State, to signify to his Lordship, that being obliged by their constitutions to hold a General Meeting now at midsummer, according to ancient custom, they hoped the administration would take no umbrage at their convention as they were all zealously affected to His Majesty's person and government.[20]

It is telling that there is no reference to such a meeting in the domestic State Papers. Indeed, given the close relationship between Townshend and freemasonry, it is possible that the meeting may not have occurred in any formal sense and that the press report was fabricated to demonstrate freemasonry's loyalist political credentials to the public at large rather than to the government. Indeed, that freemasonry could be relied upon was probably considered by the government to be axiomatic. Two of many examples suggest why this was almost certainly the case. Townshend's eldest son, Charles, a Whig MP for Great Yarmouth, was a member of the lodge at the Old Devil tavern in Temple Bar. Second and more significantly, Charles Delafaye, Townshend's under secretary of state, the principal figure in the government's anti-Jacobite spy network and a civil servant of unquestionable political loyalty, was himself a leading freemason and, together with Desaguliers and Cowper, a member of the duke of Richmond's Horn tavern lodge.

Perhaps unhappy with his enforced departure from Grand Lodge and probably wishing to retaliate against freemasonry, Wharton founded an alternative society, an event satirised by Hogarth in *Masonry Brought to Light by the Gormogons*. The first reference to the new organisation was in the *Daily Post* on 3 September 1724. It was followed by an anti-Masonic article in the *Plain Dealer* on 14 September and a note in the *British Journal* that also confirmed Wharton's involvement:

> we hear that a peer of the first rank, a noted member of the Society of Freemasons, hath suffered himself to be degraded as a member of that society, and his leather apron and gloves to be burnt, and thereupon entered himself a member of the Society of Gormogons, at the Castle-Tavern in Fleet Street.[21]

That the press reported the affair extensively indicates the public's interest in both freemasonry and Wharton. However, apart from Hogarth's print, little more was heard of the Gormogons and Wharton's attention was captured quickly by new interests. He formed a second society the same year, 'the Schemers', a club that met at Lord Hillsborough's London house 'for the advancement of that branch of happiness which the vulgar call whoring'.[22] In Lady Montagu's words, 'twenty very pretty fellows (the duke of Wharton being president and chief director) have formed themselves into a committee of gallantry, who call themselves Schemers; and meet regularly three times a week to consult on gallant schemes'.[23]

Despite selling his Irish estates to fund his investment in South Sea Company stock, Wharton continued to have a following in Ireland and several close friends within the Anglo-Irish aristocracy, particularly Lord Hillsborough, whose family had large landholdings in Co. Down. And despite his financial decline and departure for continental Europe in 1725, Wharton was a celebrity aristocrat whose personal and political activities commanded attention in both Dublin and London. Indeed, Richard Parsons, 1st earl of Rosse (1696–1741), the first Grand Master of the Grand Lodge of Ireland, may well have looked to Wharton as well as the dukes of Montagu and Richmond, as his primary role models as Grand Master.

In Ireland as in England, freemasonry was led publicly by the aristocracy. Born in Twickenham to the west of London, Rosse succeeded his father as the 2nd viscount Rosse in the Irish peerage in 1702 and, aged 22, was created earl by George I, like Wharton, to encourage and reward his political loyalty. He was appointed Grand Master of Ireland in 1725. There is no extant information on those holding office at Irish Grand Lodge between 1726 and 1730 and Rosse may have remained the titular head of Irish freemasonry until 1731, when Lord Kingston succeeded him in the chair. Lepper & Crossle's *History of the Grand Lodge of Ireland* contains virtually nothing on Rosse's Masonic activities but instead provides an outline of his family history and political connections.[24] Rosse matriculated at Christ Church, Oxford, in 1713, and built a reputation as an impressive drinker and sometime wit. There is no record of his graduation.[25] His family wealth was enhanced by dowries from two successive marriages: in 1714, to Mary, the eldest daughter of Lord William Paulet, the second son of the 1st duke of Bolton, MP for Winchester; and in 1719, following Mary's death the prior year, to Frances, the daughter of Thomas Claxton, an affluent Dublin merchant. However, Rosse's finances received a more substantial boost with his inheritance in 1731 of close to £1 million on the death of his grandmother, Fanny (Frances) Talbot, the older sister of Sarah, the duchess of Marlborough. The inheritance was equivalent to perhaps £100–200 million in current terms. Fanny's first husband, Rosse's grandfather, was Sir George Hamilton. But it was her subsequent marriage to Richard Talbot, an Irish Jacobite created 1st duke of Tyrconnell by James II, that created her fortune. Tyrconnell died in 1691 and forfeited his assets leaving Fanny in poverty. But following the accession of Queen Anne, the Talbot estates were for the most part restored by act of parliament and at her death the *Dublin Weekly Journal* recorded that 'her Grace left near a million of money, which mostly now is possessed by the Rt Hon the Lord Rosse, her grace's grandson'.[26]

Rosse was chosen to become Grand Master as a function of his rank, celebrity and extensive political connections, which could be traced back to the family's association with and patronage received from Richard Boyle, 1st earl of Cork. The Parsons, Rosse's ancestors, had been in Ireland and active in its administration since Elizabeth I, having come over as colonists in the late sixteenth century. William Parsons was granted a baronetcy in 1620 and later served as a lord justice of Ireland and, briefly, as lord president of Munster.[27] Rosse's grandfather, the 3rd baronet, had been created the 1st viscount Rosse in 1681.

Earl Rosse had a superficially similar background and character to the aristocrats who had consented to become the figureheads for the Grand Lodge of England and English freemasonry. Its early Grand Masters were also young, affluent and predominantly Whig noblemen who acted as beacons to prospective members and imbued freemasonry with a combination of social celebrity, exclusivity and political protection. Like them, Rosse was handsome, wealthy, witty and a clubbable celebrity. However, whereas John, duke of Montagu, Charles, duke of Richmond, and other English Grand Masters (with the notable exception of Wharton) embraced the Enlightenment and latitudinarianism, and can be argued to have had a sense of moral integrity, Rosse was culturally a libertine whose fortune was directed principally towards personal pleasure. Following his grand tour of Europe and Egypt from 1731 to 1735, Rosse, emulating Wharton, established a Hell Fire club in Dublin where wealthy young Protestant rakes including Lord Irnham, Lord Santry and Colonel Henry Ponsonby, drank, whored and gamed. One of the several properties at which they were reported to meet, Montpelier Hill, about ten miles south of Dublin, had been owned originally by Wharton.

Chetwode Crawley, a Masonic historian, depicted Rosse as a man whose 'ideas of morals were inverted' and whose 'skill shone most in the management of the small-sword and the dice-box'.[28] Whether correct or otherwise, Rosse was nonetheless also attuned to the prevalent political mood and was one of many signatories protesting alongside Swift against Wood's patent to produce copper coinage in Ireland. Moreover, notwithstanding his libertinism, something not uncommon and echoed in the activities of other aristocrats in Dublin, London and elsewhere, Rosse was a loyal Hanoverian and his Grand Officers, the Hon Humphrey Butler (DGM), Sir Thomas Prendergast (SGW), Marcus Anthony Morgan (JGW) and Thomas Griffith (GS), similarly and uniformly Whiggist. This is significant given that others have argued that the Grand Lodge of Ireland between 1725 and 1731 was the subject of a struggle for political dominance between Irish Jacobites and pro-Hanoverian Whigs, and that Irish freemasonry was split between the supporters of each camp. The evidence supporting such a contention is slight, if not non-existent.[29] Indeed, the opposite appears to have been the case. Irish freemasonry was dominated by and reflected the ascendancy of the Protestant pro-Hanoverian Anglo-Irish elite. Although the political outlook of Ireland's Grand Officers changed over time, this was not a function of religion or anti-Hanoverian political opposition but of economic self-interest.

An analysis of those at the head of Irish Grand Lodge reinforces the point. Humphrey Butler (*c.*1700–1768), Rosse's deputy, was the son of Brinsley Butler, 2nd baron Newtown-Butler, created 1st viscount Lanesborough in 1728. Butler succeeded his father in the Irish parliament, sitting as MP for Belturbet from 1725 until 1736, albeit that his participation in debates appears to have been minimal.[30] Tangentially, his co-MP for the constituency until 1727 was Charles Delafaye, Townshend's ultra loyal under secretary of state at the Northern Department and thereafter under secretary at the Southern Department under the duke of Newcastle.

Aside from Swift's satirical description of Butler in *The Public Spirit of the Whigs* as 'Prince Butler, a splenetic madman, whom everyone may remember about the town', there is comprehensive evidence of Butler's pro-Hanoverian political loyalties and establishment credentials.[31] Not the least is that he served as captain in the Lord Lieutenant's Battle Axe Guards, a unit modelled on the Yeomen of the Guard, which provided personal protection to the sovereign's representatives in Ireland.[32] Butler was also appointed high sheriff and the Crown's chief judicial representative for Co. Cavan in 1727, and served in the same capacity for Co. Westmeath in 1728. That year, following his father's elevation to viscount, Butler gained the honorific title of Lord Newtown-Butler. Butler received his own title in 1756, when he was created 1st earl of Lanesborough.

Sir Thomas Prendergast, (*c.*1702–1760), was elected Senior Grand Warden of the Grand Lodge of Ireland in June 1725. He was appointed Junior Grand Warden in the Grand Lodge of England six months later in December.[33] The latter position was obtained on the recommendation of the duke of Richmond. However, his membership of the duke's Horn tavern lodge and his robust Anglo-Irish connections would also have spoken strongly in favour of his selection as Senior Grand Warden in Ireland. Like the members of the Ship behind the Royal Exchange discussed in the following Appendix, Prendergast provides an excellent example of the connections between English and Irish freemasonry in the 1720s.

Prendergast divided his time between Ireland and London, where he had been admitted to the Inner Temple in 1721 following two years at Clare College, Cambridge. His mother was Penelope Cadogan and Prendergast was first cousin to the duke of Richmond's wife, Lady Sarah Cadogan. Prendergast wrote repeatedly to Richmond seeking patronage.[34] The family had originally been Catholic supporters of James II and Prendergast's father, a landowner in Co. Tipperary, had been a captain of horse in the Irish Jacobite army. However, having joined William III after the Treaty of Limerick, he is best known for having cautioned Whitehall of a plot to assassinate the king for which warning he received a £2,000 grant, the Gort estate in Galway and other Irish landholdings. Following his conversion from Catholicism to the Church of Ireland, Prendergast's father was created a baronet and later represented Monaghan in the Irish House of Commons from 1703–9. His reputation and standing was sufficient for his newly granted estates to be excluded from the Act of Resumption in 1700, which cancelled and redistributed many of William's earlier land grants.[35]

Prendergast succeeded his father as the second baronet at the age of seven. A core member of the Anglo-Irish gentry, he later represented Clonmel in the Irish parliament from 1733, where he was active in the Irish legislature and involved in debates across a spectrum of issues over six sessions of parliament to 1759.[36] Separately, in 1733, Richmond arranged for Prendergast to sit in the British commons as MP for Chichester. However, Walpole ensured that he lost his seat at the general election the following year for failing to support the Excise Bill. This was a dysfunctional decision by Prendergast less than a week after being elected but followed Walpole's non-committal response to a request that Prendergast be appointed Irish Postmaster General. Prendergast was nonetheless made an Irish privy councillor in August 1733 and eventually obtained the coveted and lucrative post of Postmaster General in 1754. Despite being described as an 'Irish blockhead' by George II over his opposition to the Excise Bill, Prendergast was nevertheless a loyal Hanoverian.[37] Swift satirised and vilified him as such in *On Noisy Tom*: 'the spawn of him who shamed our isle, traitor, assassin, and informer vile!'.[38] Swift's characterisation was more cruel in *The Legion Club*, where Prendergast was drawn as a servile government supporter, 'Sir Tom, that rampant ass', the 'offspring of a shoe boy, footman, traitor, vile seducer, perjured rebel, bribed accuser . . . from papist sprung'.[39]

The driving force behind the formation of Irish Grand Lodge and the participation of Prendergast and others among the aristocracy, gentry and professional classes in Dublin was a general desire to emulate the success and celebrity of the new English Grand Lodge. London freemasonry had expanded dramatically under successive well-known noble Grand Masters and its popularity in the 1720s and 1730s reflected their celebrity as much if not more than the achievements and influence of Desaguliers and its other Grand Officers.

The Irish press continued to publish regular reports on English freemasonry throughout the period noting the appointment of Richmond as Grand Master in 1724, Martin Folkes, a vice president of the Royal Society, as his deputy, and Frances Sorrell and George Payne, officials in the tax office, as his Grand Wardens.[40] And there were other indications of Dublin's interest, notably the publication in mid-1724 of *A Letter from the Grand Mistress of Female Free-Masons*, printed by Harding and probably written by Swift. An obvious conclusion is that it would have been pointless for Swift to satirise an unfamiliar or unpopular subject. *The Grand Mystery of the Free-Masons Disclosed* was published in Dublin the same year, as was a riposte, *The Free-Masons Vindication, being an Answer to a Scandalous Libel.*[41] At the same time, Anderson's *1723 Constitutions* remained widely advertised by Dublin's booksellers and on sale throughout the late 1720s and into the following decade.[42]

The first direct evidence of an Irish Grand Lodge appeared in June 1725 in *The Dublin Weekly Journal*, which published a lengthy account of Rosse's appointment as Grand Master.[43] The report covered nearly a full page and described the Masonic procession, installation ceremony and subsequent Grand Feast. It recorded that 'above a 100 gentlemen' met at the Yellow Lion in Warborough [Werburgh] Street and 'after some time putting on their aprons, white gloves and other parts of the distinguishing dress of that Worshipful Order, they proceeded over Essex bridge to the Strand and from thence to the King's Inns'. The Grand Officers were accompanied by the masters and wardens of 'six lodges of gentleman freemasons . . . under the jurisdiction of the Grand Master'. After 'marching round the walls of the great hall . . . the grand lodge, composed of the Grand Master . . . Grand Wardens and the masters and wardens of the lodges, retired to the room prepared for them where . . . they proceeded to the election of a new Grand Master etc'.[44] The article also noted that following dinner, 'they all went to [a] play, with their aprons etc., the private brothers sat in the pit, but the Grand Master, Deputy Grand Master and Grand Wardens, in the government's box.'[45]

The press report was written in a style and with a content that implied that the Grand Lodge of Ireland had been in existence for some time. However, the opposite was more probably correct. The procession to the King's Inn, apparently on foot rather than by carriage, and the subsequent installation and Grand Feast were modelled on the same pattern as that used in London. This would have been familiar to many of those involved in Dublin, Prendergast included, and had been widely written up in the London and Dublin press. There were nonetheless points of difference between the English and Irish ceremonies, most notably the election of the Grand Officers by the members of Irish Grand Lodge as a whole rather than their direct appointment by the Grand Master as in England.[46] This may suggest either a relatively new organisation with a consequent need for consensus or the legacy of past working masons' practices.

The most decisive argument against the Grand Lodge of Ireland having existed prior to 1725 is the absence of any named predecessor Grand Master or Grand Officers. The implication is that those who were appointed as such were the first to occupy the positions, regardless of what was written. In short, the article was disingenuous and designed to deceive by emphasising tradition and continuity with the past. The same approach had been adopted by Desaguliers and Anderson in the *1723 Constitutions* where the traditional history of freemasonry was designed to place English Grand Lodge in a similarly artificial but lengthy historical timeline. Support for such an interpretation is given indirectly by Lepper and Crossle in *History*, where they suggest that the editor of the *Dublin Weekly Journal*, James Arbuckle, who probably wrote the report, was a freemason and therefore suggestible to such a ruse.[47]

Mark Anthony Morgan (1703–1752), Prendergast's fellow Grand Warden, was MP for Athy, Co. Kildare, from 1727 until 1752, and high sheriff for adjoining Co. Meath in 1726.[48] The family came from Anglo-Irish landed gentry and held extensive property interests in Cottelstown in Co. Sligo, Cork Abbey in Co. Dublin and Balleyvalley in Co. Meath, in addition to their townhouse on St Stephen's Green.[49] Morgan graduated from Trinity College Dublin at 17 and was quickly entrenched as an establishment figure and active parliamentarian. Swift satirised him savagely for his pro-government leanings. Morgan had the misfortune to be chairman of a parliamentary committee dealing with a petition against the 'tithe agistment', a tax for the benefit of the Church of Ireland levied on cattle and other pasturage products to which Swift and others took exception. Swift decried Morgan: 'art thou there, man? bless mine eyes! art thou the chairman? chairman to yon damn'd committee! . . . will you, in your faction's phrase, send the clergy all to graze; and to make your project pass, leave them not a blade of grass?'[50]

Rosse's last Grand Officer was Thomas Griffith (1680–1744), an Irish actor and sometime theatre owner who was made Grand Secretary in 1725 and reappointed in 1731. Thomas Southwell, Grand Master of Ireland in 1743, had procured Griffith the position of tide waiter, an excise officer, at Dublin's port. Griffith executed the job personally rather than appoint an alternate at lower pay. The role entailed ensuring that vessels unloaded their cargoes at the correct docks under proper supervision and that they pay excise duties. Griffith was also responsible for gathering and passing on intelligence on any returning Wild Geese and Irish Jacobite sympathisers.[51] Lepper and Crossle commented that 'he discharged his duties . . . with an intrepid courage for one of so small a stature, being often exposed to armed men attempting to embark for the continent, or in the act of smuggling contraband'.[52] A press report supports their view:

> Dublin, June 7th. This morning . . . persons were apprehended at the end of the north wall on the Strand by Mr Thomas Griffith and Mr Hamilton belonging to His Majesty's Revenue as they were upon their duty. A guard

of soldiers was, by Order of the government immediately dispatched thither, who conducted up to the Castle, in order to their being examined, it seems they have already confessed they were going to the Pretender, and had arms and other necessaries for that purpose.[53]

There are no further references to the Grand Lodge of Ireland and few others regarding Dublin freemasonry until March 1731, when the *Dublin Weekly Journal* published a report of a lodge meeting that had been held on 6 March the prior week. This had also taken place at the Yellow Lyon tavern in Warborough Street.[54] The *Journal* recorded that Earl Rosse, Grand Master, the Hon William Ponsonby, worshipful master, and his two wardens, William Cooper and Rowly Hill, were present.[55] Others attending included Lord Kingston, the past Grand Master of the Grand Lodge of England; the earl of Drogheda; Lord Southwell; John White; Abraham Creyton; Henry Plunket; Lawrence Toole; and William Moseley. William Dobbs, John Haley and Thomas Griffith, the Grand Secretary, were also present. The *Journal* went on to note that 'upon proper application, the Rt Hon the Lord Tyrone, the Rt Hon the Lord Netterville, the Hon Tho. Bligh, Esq.; and the Hon Henry Southwell, Esq.; were in due form, admitted members of that Ancient and Right Worshipful Society'.[56]

An analysis of those in attendance once again provides confirmation of the pro-Hanoverian and pro-establishment nature of the meeting. William Ponsonby was the second (but first surviving) son of Brabazon Ponsonby, later 1st earl of Bessborough, one of the most ambitious and powerful politicians in Ireland. The Ponsonby family's influence dated from Cromwell's grant of extensive Irish estates in return for military services; the arrangement was later confirmed by the Act of Settlement in 1662. Ponsonby represented Newtownards in Co. Down, from 1725 until 1727 and thereafter Co. Kilkenny from 1728 until 1758. In 1739, he married Lady Caroline Cavendish, the eldest daughter of the 3rd duke of Devonshire, then Lord Lieutenant of Ireland. Devonshire had been appointed to the position in 1737. Ponsonby became his private secretary and political advisor and was also sworn a member of the Irish privy council. In each capacity he advanced a firmly pro-Protestant political agenda.[57] Following his marriage, Ponsonby sat in the British commons in the Devonshire interest as MP for Derby (1742–54), Saltash (1754–6) and Harwich (1756–8).[58] Devonshire patronage also gave him the positions of lord of the admiralty (1746–56), lord of the treasury (1756–9) and joint-Postmaster General (1759–62). He was sworn to the British privy council in 1765.

With William spending most of his time in England, Brabazon vested his Irish political ambitions in John (1713–87), his younger son, to whom he transferred the parliamentary seat at Newtownards in 1739 and, in 1741, the post of secretary to the Irish revenue commissioners, where Brabazon had secured the position of first commissioner for himself. John was encouraged to emulate his brother and ally himself with Devonshire and in 1743 he married Elizabeth Cavendish, Caroline's younger sister. Strengthening his political influence, he succeeded his father as first revenue commissioner the following year. John was also positioned as a potential successor to Henry Boyle, the Speaker of the Irish commons, and despite several setbacks and much politicking, was elected to the position in 1756.[59] The Ponsonby's embraced the Hanoverian succession and all three were leading government supporters, albeit while it remained in their interest to remain so. By the 1740s and 1750s, the family had become one of the most powerful political families in Ireland and one of the principal undertakers who managed Ireland's parliament on behalf of the British.[60]

Among others present at the Yellow Lyon tavern was Edward Moore, the 5th earl of Drogheda (1701–1758). He had inherited the title in 1727 and that year married Lady Sarah Ponsonby, William and John's sister. Their son, the 6th earl and later 1st marquess of Drogheda (1730–1822), continued the family's Hanoverian allegiance and in 1746 carried the British colours at Culloden. He also inherited his father's interest in freemasonry and was from 1758–60, Grand Master of Irish Grand Lodge.

Thomas Southwell, 2nd baron Southwell (1698–1766), an Irish privy councillor, appointed in June 1726, was governor of Co. Limerick. He became Grand Master of Ireland in 1743. Southwell was a Fellow of the Royal Society in London, elected in 1735, a member of the Dublin Society (1733–40) and founder and the first president of the Physico Historical Society, an antiquarian club formed in 1744 whose objectives included 'removing 'the prejudices' under which Irish history laboured and of doing justice to the country'.[61]

Southwell travelled to England in June 1731.[62] He had been appointed Master of Horse to the Princess Royal on her marriage to the Prince of Orange and his wife made a Lady of the Bedchamber to the princess.[63] Although Lord Lovell's installation as Grand Master of English Grand Lodge took place at the end of June, Southwell was not among those attending. However, the minutes of English Grand Lodge note his presence, 'the Rt Hon Lord Southwell', on 23 November 1732, where he is described as 'Provincial Grand Master in Ireland'. Newspaper reports at the time record him as 'late Grand Master of Ireland' or as 'late Provincial Grand Master of Ireland'.[64] Neither description can be substantiated by extant records, however, if accurate, his election as Grand Master could only have occurred prior to 1731 and after 1726, a period when Rosse was overseas.

The following year on 7 June 1733, the minutes of English Grand Lodge show that Southwell acted as proxy for the earl of Strathmore at the latter's installation as Grand Master. The annual procession to the Grand Feast at the Mercers' Hall set off from Southwell's London town house in Little Grosvenor Street and Southwell on Strathmore's behalf personally installed the incoming Grand Officers.[65] Southwell also attended the next Grand Lodge meeting on 13 December. Both demonstrate the strong connection between Irish and English freemasonry and suggest that the Irish and English grand lodges at the time regarded each other and their respective Grand Officers as equals.

James King, 4th baron Kingston (1693–1761), Grand Master of the Grand Lodge of England in 1729, also attended the lodge at the Yellow Lyon. King became Grand Master of Ireland in 1731, and sat again in 1735, 1745 and 1746. The baronetcy had been granted to Sir John King (*d*.1676) in 1660. He had commanded Boyle Castle at the time of the Irish uprising and later fought against the Irish Catholic army. He was subsequently sworn to the Irish privy council, made governor of Connaught and colonel of Lord Kingston's cavalry. His political loyalty and military service were rewarded with the Mitchelstown estate, around 100,000 acres across the counties of Cork, Limerick and Tipperary.[66] Although Robert King, the 2nd baron (1659–1693), fought for William III, his younger brother, John (1664–1728), supported James II and followed him into exile, converting to Catholicism. He was later outlawed. When he unexpectedly succeeded to the title following Robert's death, with his estates forfeit, John sought a pardon and this was granted by privy seal in 1694. Despite opposition from within parliament, John recovered Mitchelstown in 1708 and swore an oath of loyalty in 1715, taking his seat in the Irish House of Lords. It is probable that the division of religious loyalty within the family had been manufactured to insure against the loss of Mitchelstown and John's reconversion was equally pragmatic.

James King was John's sole surviving son. Born in France during his father's exile, he petitioned for naturalisation as a child 'born out of her Majesty's allegiance, but [a] good Protestant' when his father returned to Mitchelstown.[67] James inherited both the estate and the baronetcy on his father's death and although often referred to as a Jacobite sympathiser, there is little or no substantiating evidence. The family's history suggests political realism rather than idealism as their principal tenet. King was sworn an Irish privy councillor in 1729, the same year he became Grand Master of the pro-Hanoverian English Grand Lodge. His connections with freemasonry are well documented and he is recorded as having been initiated at the Swan & Rummer on 8 June 1726, 'admitted into the Society of Free Masonry and made by [Dr Desaguliers] the Deputy Grand Master'.[68] The lodge was aristocratic with links to both the Irish and Scottish gentry. Among those present on that occasion was William O'Brien, the 4th earl of Inchiquin, Grand Master of England in 1727, a guest of Martin O'Connor, the Master of the lodge, who was appointed Junior Grand Warden of English Grand Lodge the following year. Three others were initiated the same day: Gerald de Courcy, 24th lord Kingsale, Ireland's most ancient baronetcy; Sir Winwood Moffat, a Scottish baronet; and Michael O'Bryan (O'Brien), possibly the Irish lawyer of that name then studying at Gray's Inn.[69]

King's connection with Irish freemasonry extended to Munster, a county dominated by large Anglo-Irish estates created through the mass confiscation of Irish Catholic landholdings and the establishment of the Plantations in the sixteenth century. King was Grand Master of Munster in 1731, the same year that he was appointed Grand Master of Ireland in Dublin. A Masonic lodge existed in Cork since at least 27 December 1726, when its proceedings were first recorded. As in Dublin, freemasonry in Cork was substantially an expression of Anglo-Irish solidarity.[70] The Master of the lodge at Munster from 1726 to 1728 was the Hon James O'Brien (1695–1771), the younger brother of William O'Brien, the 4th earl of Inchiquin. He sat as MP for Charleville from 1715 until 1727 and thereafter for Youghal until 1760. Both constituencies were in Co. Cork where the family had extensive estates. The third son of the 3rd earl, O'Brien also held the lucrative position of collector of customs for Drogheda. The family were Hanoverian loyalists and firm supporters of Walpole. Not coincidentally, Thomas Southwell was invited to become a godfather to O'Brien's daughter.[71]

Despite the title, the Grand Lodge of Munster functioned principally as the chief lodge for the province and there are no records of any Munster Grand Lodge after 1731, most probably at James King and Dublin's behest as they sought to replicate England's federal Masonic governance structure. King's election as Grand Master of Munster in 1731 may have been designed to consolidate Munster into Dublin's fold. King's principal Irish estates were at Mitchelstown and the first warrant in the county was issued there by the Grand Lodge of Ireland the following year. In common with others members of Munster freemasonry, O'Brien had strong links to its English counterpart. Indeed, he may have been a member of the lodge at the Rummer in Charing Cross, where a 'James Bryan' is recorded. Other relationships are more easily identified: Springett Penn, O'Brien's deputy and the heir and grandson of William Penn, Pennsylvania's founder, was a member of the Ship behind the Royal Exchange, as was Nathaniel Gould, an English merchant and a principal associate of Walter Gould, Munster's Senior Grand Warden, with whom he held mortgages over land in Munster. Penn and Gould both had extensive landholdings in Co. Cork and Lepper and Crossle note multiple family, social and business connections between both them and other lodge members.[72]

Of the others present at the Yellow Lyon lodge, Sir Marcus Beresford (1694–1763), represented Coleraine until 1720, when he was raised to the Irish peerage as Viscount Tyrone. He took his seat the following year and in 1746, was created 1st earl of Tyrone. Beresford was appointed Grand Master of Irish Grand Lodge in 1736, serving for two years. Lord Netterville was Nicholas Netterville, the 5th viscount (16_?–1750), Grand Master in 1732. Unusually for Irish freemasonry, the family were Anglo Catholics and traced their origins to the Norman conquest. Netterville was the nephew of earl Rosse and had sat in the Irish parliament since 1728 after succeeding his father, having taken the oath of loyalty. The Hon Thomas Bligh (1685–1775), was probably the second son of Thomas Bligh of Rathmore, Co. Meath. If so, he served as lieutenant colonel of Napier's Horse, later the 2nd Irish Horse.[73] Bligh was appointed colonel of the 20th Foot in 1740 and served in Flanders in the War of Austrian Succession. He was promoted brigadier general in 1745 and major general in 1747, when he obtained the colonelcy of the 2nd Irish Horse. Lastly, the Hon Henry Southwell (1700–1758), Thomas Southwell's younger brother, was MP for Limerick from

1729 until his death; he served as deputy governor for the county under his brother.[74]

Lepper and Crossle explain the absence of meetings of the Grand Lodge of Ireland between 1726 and 1730 as a function of Ireland's economic depression. Whether the explanation is correct or not, a severe famine in the late 1720s had affected virtually the whole country. Successively disastrous harvests, a lower demand for linen and the higher rents imposed on tenant farmers by land agents acting for often absentee landlords led to scarcity, poverty and increased emigration from Ireland, particularly to colonial America. Irish poverty was exacerbated by British protectionism and trade restrictions. Irish lobbying eventually brought some relief.[75] Although in practice this was only modest, any adjustment to British policy in favour of the Irish and West Indian lobbies was seen as a significant victory.[76] The political reversal in Dublin's favour was also positive for the duke of Dorset who replaced Carteret at Dublin Castle a few months later in June 1730; Dorset's more constructive approach towards Irish development was marked by his acceptance of the presidency of the Dublin Society in 1731.

Since Lepper and Crossle's argument did not apply to the even more dire famine of 1740–41, a more likely explanation for the absence of any Irish Grand Lodge meetings in the late 1720s is that they were undocumented rather than non-existent and the absence of key figures probably reduced their number.[77] Rosse was away from Dublin for part of the period from 1726 until mid-1729 and Griffith, the Grand Secretary, was seriously ill in 1727 and 1728. Nonetheless, the registration in 1727 by Ireland's Grand Lodge of lodge No. 2 in Dublin indicates that the organisation was functioning, if only in part. Moreover, repeated Irish press reports on English freemasonry, its initiations, feasts, processions and charitable activities, suggests that the subject remained of interest. The 1730 publication of Pennell's Irish version of Anderson's *Constitutions* similarly confirms freemasonry's popularity. Pennell had advertised the prior year in *Faulkner's Dublin Chronicle* for a minimum of two hundred subscribers and achieved this goal without any evident difficulty.[78] Tangentially, Pennell's *Constitutions* contained a number of slight differences in Masonic ritual when compared to the form practiced in London and these may have reflected the then current practice in Ireland.[79] Variations included the form of prayer at initiation, a system of three degrees (rather than the two thought then to have been practiced in London) and the role of deacons, effectively lodge stewards. Over time, these and other relatively minor discrepancies became to be treated as more substantive issues.

On 10 April 1731, *Faulkner's Dublin Journal* reported a meeting of the 'masters and wardens of the lodges of freemasons in the City of Dublin, assembled at the Bull's Head in Fishamble Street'. The meeting had been called 'to consider some of the regulations for the good of that ancient and right Worshipful Society' and to elect Lord Kingston Grand Master for the ensuing year.[80] Kingston's installation on 7 July was reported in due course;[81] as was the succession of Netterville, his deputy, the following year:

last Tuesday being the 1st of August, a Grand Lodge of Free Masons was held at the Two Black Posts in Sycamore Alley. The Rt Hon the Lord Viscount Netterville being Grand Master, and the Rt Hon the Lord Viscount Kingsland Deputy Grand Master, James Brennan, M.D. and Robert Nugent, Esq.; were chosen Grand Wardens by the said Grand Lodge.[82]

Within this group, one figure stands out. Unusually among the Anglo-Irish elite that led Irish Grand Lodge, Henry Benedict (1708–1774), 4th viscount Barnewall of Kingsland, DGM in 1732 and GM in 1733–4, was a Catholic from a prominent family who had settled within the Pale. Like Netterville, Barnewall was also related to Earl Rosse, his second cousin. Barnewall's mother was the youngest daughter of Sir George Hamilton and Fanny Talbot, countess of Tyrconnel.[83] Barnewall's father, the 3rd viscount, like many in the Catholic gentry had fought for James II and been outlawed. His position and estates were restored under the Treaty of Limerick but upon being summoned to William III's first Irish parliament in 1692, although he took an oath of allegiance, he refused as a Catholic to take a further oath against transubstantiation and reject the spiritual authority of the Pope. Accordingly, he was refused his seat in the Irish House of Lords.[84] His son inherited in 1725 and emulated his father both politically and religiously, swearing allegiance but forswearing a seat.[85]

Barnewall was related to another Grand Officer, Robert Nugent(1702–1788), of Carlanstown, Co. Westmeath, JGW in 1732 and the second son of Michael Nugent (*d.*1739) of Carlanstown, and Mary (*d.*1740), the fifth and youngest daughter of Robert Barnewall, 9th lord Trimlestown, another branch of the same family. As in England, one faction within Ireland's Grand Lodge can be identified with the patriotic opposition associated with Frederick, prince of Wales; and one of the more prominent figures in that camp was Nugent.

Unlike Barnewall, Nugent was a convert from Catholicism. Described as 'a jovial and voluptuous Irishman who had left popery for the Protestant religion, money and widows', Nugent inherited a modest estate worth around £1,500 per annum but added to it vastly by marrying successively three wealthy widows.[86] Following the death in childbirth of his first wife, his second marriage to the twice-widowed daughter of the affluent but disgraced James Craggs (*c.*1657–1721), Postmaster General, brought extensive properties, including the borough of St Mawes in Cornwall, which Nugent represented from 1741 until 1754.[87] Nugent was a firm ally and important creditor of the prince of Wales and was rewarded for his loyalty by being appointed comptroller of the prince's household in 1747. Nugent's loans were later redeemed in kind by George III with positions and sinecures. Nugent was elevated to the Irish peerage as Viscount Clare (1757) and Earl Nugent (1776); he also obtained prominent and lucrative positions as a lord of the treasury (1754–9), privy councillor (1759), president of the board of trade (1766–8) and vice-treasurer of Ireland (from 1759–65 and 1770–82).[88]

Anecdotally, the financial aspect of Nugent's marital activities had such notoriety that they were granted the honour of an adjective by Horace Walpole:

> Lord Middlesex is going to be married to Miss Boyle, Lady Shannon's daughter; she has thirty thousand pounds, and may have as much more, if her mother, who is a plump widow, don't happen to *Nugentize*.[89]

Arthur Mohun St Leger, 3rd viscount Doneraile (1718–1750), Grand Master in 1740 at the age of 22, was another in the prince of Wales' camp. St Leger was MP for Winchelsea from 1741 until 1747 and in the latter year became a Gentleman of the Bedchamber to the prince. English and Irish freemasons were disproportionately represented in the role and their influence may have been a factor in the prince's embrace of freemasonry. It was one of several avenues he pursued in taking a stand against his father. William O'Brien, 4th earl of Inchiquin, served as a Gentleman of the Bedchamber to the prince from 1744 to 1751; Edward Bligh, 2nd earl of Darnley, English Grand Master in 1737, was appointed from 1742–45; Henry Brydges, Marquess of Carnarvon and 2nd duke of Chandos, Grand Master in 1738, held the role for 13 years from 1729–42; Charles, Lord Baltimore, served for 18 years from 1731–49; and Lord Villiers for 5 from 1733–38.[90]

> Friday last, being St John's Day the Grand Lodge of Free-Masons met at their Hall in Smock-Alley; there were present several noblemen, gentlemen, and the masters and wardens of the several Lodges in and about the City of Dublin; where they elected the Right Hon the Lord Viscount Tyrone Grand Master for the year ensuing, who appointed James Brenan M.D. for his deputy; Cornellius Callaghan, junior, Esq.; and John Purland, Esq.; were chose Grand Wardens. After several acts of charity, regulations settled, and other business done, the masters and wardens adjourned to their several lodges, dined in splendour, and spent the day in mirth and pleasure.[91]

It can be stated with some certainty that throughout the 1730s and into the 1740s, Irish Grand Lodge was dominated by Whiggist Grand Officers. Sir Marcus Beresford (1694–1763), Grand Master in 1736 and 1737, sat as MP for Coleraine from 1715 until 1720. He was the only son of Sir Tristram Beresford who had commanded a Protestant regiment in the Williamite Wars. Beresford's own loyalty was returned with elevation to the Irish peerage as Baron Beresford and Viscount Tyrone in 1720 and promotion to 1st earl of Tyrone in 1746, a resurrection of his father-in-law's title.[92]

Beresford was succeeded in 1738 by Sir William Stewart, 3rd viscount Mountjoy (1709–1769), who inherited the title in 1728 and was created 1st earl Blessington in 1745, his mother having been the sister and heir of the 2nd and last viscount Blessington. First mentioned as a freemason in 1731 when a member of Viscount Montagu's Bear and Harrow lodge in Butcher

Row near Temple Bar in London, Mountjoy was Grand Master of Ireland from 1738 until 1740.[93] However, perhaps more significantly, he later gave his imprimatur to the Antients Grand Lodge, where he acceded to become their first noble Grand Master in 1756, remaining as such until 1760.

The Mountjoy family had settled in Ulster from Scotland in the sixteenth century and been loyal undertakers in the Irish parliament for six generations. Mountjoy's grandfather, the 2nd Bt., (1653–1692), had fought against the Irish rebellion as commander of a foot regiment and had been created Viscount Mountjoy in 1682 as a reward. A Protestant, he was suspected of disloyalty by Lord Tyrconnel, the Catholic commander of James II's army in Ireland, and sent on a false diplomatic mission to Paris where, as intended, he was arrested and imprisoned in the Bastille. Joining William's army on his release in 1692, he was killed at Steenkerque later the same year. Mountjoy's father, the 2nd viscount (1625–1728), was another talented soldier. Like his own father, he had command of a foot regiment and was advanced successively to brigadier general, major general and lieutenant general. In 1714, he was promoted Master General of the Ordnance, given the colonelcy of a regiment of dragoons and made Keeper of the Great Seal.[94]

In 1728, Mountjoy inherited his titles and estates in Ireland, at Newton-Stewart, Co. Tyrone, and Blessington, Co. Wicklow, together with property in England. The latter included an estate at Silchester in Hampshire and town houses successively in Grosvenor Square and Hill Street, Mayfair.[95] He was one of many absentee property owners criticised by Thomas Prior in his *List of absentees of Ireland*, who accused Mountjoy of an annual expenditure abroad of £2,500.[96] It is unclear whether the figure was valid or otherwise: the data was unchanged in the third edition published in 1745, sixteen years later. Despite the criticism, Mountjoy was nonetheless an active contributor to charities in Ireland and Britain, where he was a prominent supporter of the Middlesex Hospital, among other institutions.[97] In 1748, consolidating his position as a person of quality and one of the great and good, the now Earl Blessington was appointed governor of Co. Tyrone and sworn a member of the Irish privy council.[98] He was reappointed to the privy council in 1761 following the succession of George III and received the governorship of Carlisle Castle in 1763.[99] His political loyalty to the Hanoverian dynasty – although not to its government – was absolute. His strong support for Irish agriculture and manufacture and for the right to trade freely was also notable and noted, not least by the London agents and representatives of the West Indies merchant community who sought his backing to promote the cause of free trade both in parliament and more widely.[100] And despite Prior's criticism, Blessington was also faithful to the Irish interests. This was expressed not only in his support for the Antients but in membership of organisations ranging from the Incorporated Society for the Promotion of Protestant Working Schools in Ireland to the Dublin Society, where he was a member until 1762.

Given the many interconnections between freemasonry and the Royal Society in London, it is interesting to note the parallels in Ireland with the

Dublin Society.[101] In addition to Blessington and among other senior members of Irish Grand Lodge, Humphrey Butler, the first Irish DGM, was a member of the Dublin Society from 1731 and thereafter a vice president from 1750 until 1758.[102] Thomas Prendergast and Marcus Morgan, the first two Grand Wardens, were also members, from 1731–54 and 1733–40, respectively. And other influential freemasons who were also members included at least three more Grand Masters: Viscount Netterville; Baron Tullamore; and Viscount Allen; and several Grand Officers, James Brennan; Capt. William Cobbe; John Baldwin; John Putland; Robert Callaghan; and Hamilton Gorges.

Supported by the Irish parliament, the Dublin Society was an expression of hope that Ireland might reduce its dependency on England. More than a provincial counterpart to London's Royal Society or the French Royal Academy of Science, the Society represented an attempt to improve national wealth through the practical application of science to agricultural and manufacturing. Experimentation, the assessment of different agricultural techniques and the subsequent promotion of best practice, placed it at the vanguard of scientific advancement. And prizes or 'bounties' were established to encourage and reward Irish culture and the arts. Support for both the sciences and the arts reflected the Society's position as an Irish champion offering a new vision of nation.[103] In 1733, two years after its formation, it had 267 members, including sixteen peers and their sons; five members of the judiciary, including the lord chancellor; parliamentarians, including the speaker of the commons; as well as baronets, army officers, barristers, doctors, academics and 'men holding high positions in the world of commerce'.[104] A royal charter was awarded in 1750 and in 1820, under the patronage of George IV, it was renamed the Royal Dublin Society.

Among Ireland's Grand Officers in the 1740s was the loyalist Charles Moore, 2nd lord Tullamore (1712–1764), Grand Master from 1741 to 1742, an Irish privy councillor and the governor of King's County. He was elevated in the peerage in 1758, becoming 1st earl Charleville. Moore also held the position of Muster Master General of Ireland, as had his father. John Allen, 3rd viscount Allen (*bap.* 1708–1745), was MP for Carysfoot from 1732 until 1741, and Co. Wicklow until 1742, when he succeeded his father and took his seat in the Irish House of Lords. He was Grand Master from 1744 until his death the following year. This followed an altercation in Dublin during which he was wounded:

> His Lordship was at a house in Eustace Street. At twelve in the night, three dragoons making a noise in the street, he threw up the window and threatening them, adding as is not unusual with him a great deal of bad language. The dragoons returned it. He went out to them loaded with a pistol. At the first snapping of it, it did not fire. This irritated the dragoon who cut his fingers with his sword, upon which Lord Allen shot him.[105]

Lord Kingston returned to the chair on short notice to succeed Allen and was succeeded in turn by Sir Marmaduke Wyvill, 6th Bt., (1692–1754).

Wednesday last the 24th Inst. being the feast of St John the Baptist, the Grand Lodge of Free and Accepted Masons met according to ancient custom, with their usual ceremony, at their lodge room in Smock Alley, where Sir Marmaduke Wyvill, Bt., Postmaster General, was installed and proclaimed Grand Master of Masons in the Kingdom of Ireland for the ensuing year. The evening was concluded with ringing of bells, and the greatest demonstrations of joy that could be expressed on that occasion, among the true and worthy brethren of that antient and honourable fraternity.[106]

Wyvill remained Grand Master until 1749 and was unique among Irish Grand Masters in that he was English rather than Anglo-Irish. His father had been a Tory with strong Stuart connections through his wife, who had been maid of honour to Catherine of Braganza and Mary of Modena. Despite this, he had taken the oath of allegiance in 1691 and following the accession of Queen Anne, was rewarded for his dependability and was granted the sinecures of commissioner of the excise at an annual salary of £800 and commissioner of salt duties at £500. Even if not a Whig, he supported the Hanoverian succession in 1714 and remained in post until his death in 1722. His son was less successful in holding on to office and was only briefly MP for Richmond in Yorkshire in 1727. The election was contested and the obvious voting irregularities, 412 votes in a borough with 273 electors, resulted in its being re-run and Wyvill and his fellow MP, Charles Bathurst, were dismissed.[107]

Wyvill's principal estates were at Constable Burton in north Yorkshire, which were best known for the family's successful stud farm. As with many in the gentry, Wyvill was often in the press in connection with both horseracing and horse breeding.[108] Like his father, he was also considered a loyal Hanoverian and appointed clerk to the Irish privy council in 1735 and vice chamberlain to the Queen.[109] In 1716, he had married Carey Coke, the sister of Thomas Coke, later ennobled as Lord Lovell and subsequently created 1st earl of Leicester. As Lovell, Coke became Grand Master of English Grand Lodge in 1731. Coke was both Walpole's neighbour and one of his strongest supporters and was recompensed with the sinecure of joint-Postmaster General in England in 1725. As such, in 1736, Lovell was able to lever Wyvill into the position of Postmaster General for Ireland, a position he retained until his death. Although his wife, Carey, died in 1734, Wyvill's relationship to Lovell may have also contributed to the former's elevation to the Grand Master's chair in Dublin, although the patronage and influence available to the Postmaster General's office may have been the more important factor.

Robert King, 1st baron Kingsborough (1724–1755), to whom Edward Spratt's 1751 Irish *Constitutions* were dedicated, was Grand Master from 1749–50. He succeeded as baronet in 1740, was MP for Boyle from 1745 until 1748, when he was made a peer. King also served as *Custos Rotulorum* for Co. Roscommon. He was followed by Lord George Sackville, the youngest son of the duke of Dorset, then Lord Lieutenant.

Irish Grand Lodge in the 1750s was dominated by Sackville's successors: the Hon Thomas George Southwell (1721–1780); the Hon Brinsley Butler (1728–1779), later Lord Newtown-Butler; and Charles, Viscount Moore (1730–1822). Thomas Southwell came from a deeply Masonic family. His father had been Grand Master in 1743, a notable attendee at the lodge meeting at the Yellow Lion tavern in 1731 at which his brother had been initiated into freemasonry, and active at a senior level in English Grand Lodge. Southwell himself was Deputy Grand Master during Sackville's Grand Mastership and Grand Master in his own right from 1753–6.[110] The family were patriotic Whigs. His grandfather, the 1ˢᵗ baron, had been closely involved with settling Huguenot refugees in Ireland and in promoting the Irish linen industry. All were active parliamentarians, his grandfather, father and uncles representing Co. Limerick in the Irish parliament. Southwell himself represented Enniscorthy from 1747–61 and his family's seat for Limerick from 1761–7. The family's Irish nationalism was underlined by their opposition to the oppressive Declaratory Act and they expressed similar sympathies in subsequent parliamentary debates.[111]

Brinsley Butler, styled Lord Newtown-Butler from 1756 and 2ⁿᵈ earl Lanesborough from 1768, was MP for Co. Cavan from 1751 until succeeding. He was elected a Grand Warden in 1751–2, Deputy Grand Master from 1753–6 and made Grand Master in 1757. Within parliament he remained a government loyalist and voted in favour of the money bills in the crisis of 1753. His support for the administration was rewarded with appointment as a revenue commissioner in 1761 and he was sworn a privy councillor in 1765. However, Butler's later opposition politics saw him removed from both positions in 1770, albeit that he was later reinstated to the council by Lord Harcourt in December 1774 and received an annual pension of £1,200 to compensate for the loss of his place on the revenue board. Butler was mentioned by Pope as that 'sober Lanesb'row dancing with the gout'. He married Jane Isabella, the only daughter of the less than fortunate 1ˢᵗ earl of Belvedere.[112] His eldest son, Robert, later married the daughter of the Huguenot banker David La Touche, another Irish freemason, to whom Butler sold the borough of Belturbet. It is hard to determine whether Butler's support for and recognition of the Antients Grand Lodge was an act of defiance calculated carefully not to upset the political apple cart in Ireland, however, it might be considered indicative of his later opposition to the government.

Charles Moore, Viscount Moore, later 6ᵗʰ earl of Drogheda, was Grand Master from 1758 to 1760. He had been Deputy Grand Master in 1757 and prior to that a Grand Warden from 1753. A second son, Moore had joined the 12ᵗʰ dragoons as a cornet at 14 and carried the regimental colours at Culloden. He was promoted successively to captain in 1750 and major in 1752, but saw no further active service.[113] On the death of his older brother in 1752, he became heir to the title and obliged to become more closely involved in Irish politics, sitting as MP for St Canice in Co. Kilkenny (1757–8) and nominated to serve on nineteen parliamentary committees. Moore inherited in 1758 and took his seat in the lords. He was a consistent if self-interested government supporter, appointed governor of Co. Meath in 1759 and sworn to the Irish privy council the following year. Given the colonelcy of the 18th light dragoons in 1762, a regiment he raised, Moore led the repression of the Whiteboys, an amalgam of tenant farmers and agricultural workers in southern Ireland whose initially peaceful protests against enclosures, evictions and excessive rents and tithes had morphed into violence and insurgency, partly in response to the aggressive reaction of the authorities to their activities.

Moore's militia and regular dragoons arrested hundreds of suspects in Munster, Limerick and Tipperary. In their wake, some locals formed vigilante groups and in parts of the country an effective state of martial law existed. In Dublin, there was a sense that matters had been allowed to go too far and Lord Halifax, then Lord Lieutenant, expressed his concern that the flight or arrest of so many agricultural workers might result in a famine. The press agreed and reported that 'the county of Tipperary, near the county of Cork . . . is almost waste, and the houses of many locked up, or inhabited by women and old men only; such has been the terror the approach of the light dragoons has thrown them into'.[114]

Moore succeeded William Hamilton as chief secretary to the Lord Lieutenant on the appointment of Hugh Percy, 2nd earl of Northumberland in 1763 and in 1766, during the absence of the 1st marquess of Hertford, was appointed a lord justice. Tangentially, and with Moore's consent if not at his instigation, two regimental warrants were issued to the light dragoons within a year of his colonelcy of the regiment. These were warrant numbers 388 and 389, issued on 2 December 1762 to lodges formed by the 1st and 2nd squadrons.

The First Irish Lodge in London – the Ship behind the Royal Exchange

Eighteenth-century London was a confluence of competing pressure groups. American colonists, West Indian planters, the great international trading companies and numerous other foreign and domestic interests all contended with the Irish and Anglo-Irish to influence British government policy. In Westminster and the City, parliamentary legislation affecting Ireland was promoted and contested, something increasingly necessary after the passage of the Dependency of Ireland on Great Britain Act; lawyers were instructed, other advisers consulted and funds sourced and deployed. As today, the combination of financial and professional resources and the political connections available in London were often of fundamental importance to business success and instrumental in making or breaking personal reputation.

London was awash with rival lobbyists and the Irish lobby – perhaps lobbies would be more appropriate – was one of many competing for influence. The importance of local representation was such that it became customary for Irish merchants and the gentry to send a younger son to London to safeguard their family's interests. Influence could also be sought and bought through the agencies of professional lobbyists resident in London or by trading through well-positioned English merchant houses with appropriate political and commercial links. Other Irish conducted business personally, with a mixture of aristocrats, members of the gentry and the more middling travelling to London for the purpose. The city was in any case an attraction in its own right. London was the capital of the British Empire, the largest metropolis in Europe and an entertainment, social and intellectual hub with a spectrum of attractions to suit the highest and lowest brow. Aside from merchants, traders and those seeking influence, employment or education, London also attracted ambitious artists and authors hoping to make use of social, family or more distant relationships and to build the right connections with potential patrons. A minority made their names and rose to success and popularity. Most did not. But for Ireland's elite and middling classes, despite the extended journey and often dangerous passage across the Irish Sea, a visit to London was necessary and commonplace, both a means to an end and an end in itself.

Located behind Edward Jerman's elegant cloistered Royal Exchange building, the lodge at the Ship tavern is the first documented Irish Masonic lodge in London.[1] The setting may have been significant. The Royal Exchange was a principal meeting place for the City of London's cosmopolitan trading community and a hub for commerce. The Ship's membership reflected this and included a selection of wealthy and respectable Irish-connected and Irish merchants, traders and bankers. Lane's *Masonic Records* notes that the lodge, number 18 in the 1729 list, was constituted on 5 May 1723 and erased just over two decades later in 1745.[2] In the intervening years it relocated in 1727 to the St Paul's Head in Ludgate Street and thereafter, in 1729, to the Crown at Ludgate Hill and to the Sun in Holborn in 1736.

The register of members compiled in 1723 and submitted to Grand Lodge later that year points to many having business and personal relationships outside of freemasonry, at least some of which were cemented through marriage. It suggests that the lodge offered a convenient locus for personal interaction and perhaps a less formal but equally confidential social and business space adjacent to but apart from the Royal Exchange.

Most members were likely to have been initiated into freemasonry in London; others may have been made masons in Irish lodges. There are few confirmatory records either way. Regardless, the lodge's register contains a unique cross-section of the middling London Irish and those doing business with Ireland – merchants and professionals – and crosses the religious divide from Protestant conformists and dissenters, to Catholics and Quakers. As with Munster freemasonry, the lodge's composition suggests, if not corroborates, that secular considerations of affluence and influence were probably more significant criteria for membership than religious denomination, and that potential social and business networking opportunities trumped differences of faith.

English freemasonry in the eighteenth century was unusual in providing a space where its members could be free of some of the religious and social constraints that existed elsewhere; specifically, many other clubs and societies excluded the Irish, particularly Catholics. However, despite its interdenominational characteristics and professed tolerance, the raising of financial and commercial interests above religion was found extensively elsewhere in the City of London and was far from limited to the Masonic lodge. As Voltaire, later himself a freemason, noted:

> take a view of the Royal Exchange in London, a place more venerable than many courts of justice, where the representatives of all nations meet for the benefit of mankind. There the Jew, the Mahometan and the Christian transact together, as though they all professed the same religion and give the name of infidel to none but bankrupts.[3]

Philip Crossle undertook a first exercise in analysing the composition of the lodge at the Ship tavern nearly a century ago in the early 1920s. His partly annotated list of members was outlined in a short appendix to the 1923 *CC Transactions* and this chapter makes use of and extends Crossle's tentative biographical notes and, where appropriate, offers alternatives.[4] The chapter

Table 25 The Members of the Ship behind the Royal Exchange, 1723[5]

John Leigh Esq. (Master)

Mr Cloud Stuart (SW)	Mr Nathaniel Gould (JW)
Mr Johvn Gascoyne	Mr John Hope
Mr Albert Nesbitt	Mr William Bently
Mr John Mason	Henry Cunningham Esq.
Mr Joseph Gascoyne	Mr Henry Hope
Mr John Bourne	Sir James Tobin
Mr Ralph Knox	Mr Bearc. Stonehewer
Richard Warburton Esq.	Robert Allen Esq.
Mr Peter Webb	William Spaight Esq.
William Worth Esq.	Mr Benjamin Lambert
Benjamin Dry Esq.	Abraham Sharigley Esq.
Gerard Bourne Esq.	Captain Patrick Trahee
Mr Jonas Morris	Captain Lionel Beecher
Mr Row Hill	Mr Richard Fitzgerald
William Moreton Esq.	Leon Hatfield Esq.
Mr Springett Penn	Paul Minchell Esq.
Mr Thomas Watts	Mr John Pringle
William Hoar Esq.	Tiss. [Sisson] Putland Esq.
Mr Robert Waller	Mr William Richardson

comprises a series of brief biographical sketches that provide an outline of the Ship tavern's membership. It explores a selection of important overlapping relationships and presents a uniquely Masonic aspect to eighteenth-century sociability among this stratum of the London Irish and their circle.

In certain instances, this appendix identifies members of the lodge for the first time. There is, of course, an important caveat to any study of the eighteenth century, that is, the difficulty of identifying specific individuals from contemporary documents. This is a function of the phonetic spelling variations that were commonly used to write individual names. Additionally, a further complication arises where more than one person has the same or a similar name. Nonetheless, for the reasons specified, there is reasonable certainty about the identity of the majority of those detailed below.

THE MASTER OF THE LODGE

Philip Crossle suggested that the Master of the lodge, **John Leigh**, was probably from Greenhills in Co. Louth and a member of the Inner Temple. He also noted that a John Leigh had attended a lodge in Dublin in 1731 and 1733.[6] However, given the commercial and trading context of the lodge's membership, it is perhaps more probable that the Master was John Leigh of Rosegarland in New Ross, Co. Wexford. Leigh would later become MP for New Ross in the Irish Parliament, sitting as the second member from 1727 until 1758.[7] The Leigh family were joint patrons of the seat and John's son, Robert, inherited the constituency in 1759.

In the early and mid-eighteenth century, New Ross was a strategically located and prosperous port town with extensive trading connections to England, the continent and the Americas. The manor of Rosegarland had been granted to Leigh's uncle, Robert, by Charles II following the restoration of the monarchy, together with a mid-size estate of more than 3,300 acres of productive and accessible land in Wexford and Kildare. John inherited the estate at his father's death in 1727.[8] At the time the membership returns to Grand Lodge were compiled in May 1723, Leigh may have been representing the family's interests in London while his father remained in Ireland managing the estate; this would have been a common practice among the Irish gentry.[9]

There is a third alternative identity that might be explored: that John Leigh may have been the Irish born actor and playwright of that name, a member of the New Play House and the Lincoln's Inn players' company. There are two reasons to believe that this was not the case. First, there is no obvious connection to other lodge members whose affluence and social status would have been considerably higher than that of a jobbing actor. Second and more conclusively, such a man would have been unlikely to have had 'Esq.' appended to his name.[10] Nonetheless, freemasonry attracted a number of prominent actors, dramatists and theatrical managers, including Colley Cibber and his son, Theophilus. Leigh, the actor, is known to have had a connection through the stage to Cibber, which may have mirrored a Masonic friendship: 'Cibber Jr.' was later a member of the influential Bear & Harrow lodge in Butcher's Row. Indeed, many actors, artists and other entertainers later became freemasons in order to be close to their current or potential patrons.

THE WARDENS

Cloud Stewart – Senior Warden
Crossle was unsuccessful in identifying 'Cloud Stuart'. However, the lodge's Senior Warden was most probably **Cloudesley Stewart**, a descendant of the Stewart family of Athenry in Co. Tyrone. The forename is unusual and probably an abbreviation or nickname derived from Sir Cloudesley Shovel (1650–1707), a popular English naval officer who was promoted to become Admiral of the Fleet in 1705.[11] Although it has not been possible to determine definitively Cloud Stewart's identity, there is strong evidence that the Stewart family was associated with Admiral Shovel.

Originally from Scotland, Captain Andrew Stewart had migrated to Ireland in the 1620s:

Andrew Stewart, commonly called Captain Andrew Stewart, who, with Lord Castle Stewart, to whom he was related, and his (Andrew's) brother James . . . went from Scotland to Ireland about the year 1627. On his marriage, he obtained from Lord Castle Stewart the greater part of the manor of Castle Stewart, but afterwards built and resided on another seat near Stewart's Town, Co. Tyrone.[12]

Captain Stewart had four sons. The third, James, was a naval officer, later killed in battle. The connection to Admiral Shovel was noted in *Debrett's Baronetage* which recorded that he married one of the Admiral's daughters: 'James, an officer of the Royal Navy, married —-, daughter of Admiral Sir Cloudesley Shovel, and died gallantly in battle'.[13] The claim was repeated in later editions of *Debrett's* and expanded in 1893 in *Notes & Queries.*[14] Contemporary newspaper articles also note that a Captain Stewart, possibly the same man, served alongside Admiral Shovel.[15]

Unfortunately, the *ODNB* entry for Admiral Shovel contradicts *Debrett's.*[16] John Hattendorf states that Shovel's second daughter, Anne (1696–1741), married first, the Hon Robert Mansell (*d.*1723), and second, John Blackwood, a West India merchant.[17] However, it is possible that the *ODNB* entry is incomplete. Although there is transparent evidence that Anne Shovel married Mansell in 1718, it is also feasible that she had been widowed by that date.[18] Offering tentative support for this argument is her description in a press report as 'Mrs Shovel, daughter to the late Sir Cloudesley Shovel', as opposed to 'Miss Shovel'.[19] Nonetheless, later press reports omit any mention of an earlier marriage and the obituary of Lady Shovel, the Admiral's widow, refers only to Mansell and Blackwood as being her younger daughter's successive husbands.[20]

In contrast, the Stewart family's records indicate that James Stewart and Anne Shovel had a daughter, also named Anne. It is possible that they also had a son. A pair of oval portraits painted in the eighteenth century in the style of Sir Godfrey Kneller supports *Debrett's* contention of an earlier relationship and the birth of a son and daughter. The portraits depict 'Anne Stewart and Cloudesley Stewart'. They were sold by Christies in London in 1995.[21] The sitters may have been James and Anne's children. Naming a son and daughter after a parent or grandparent was common practice. Nonetheless, there are other options. It is possible that James and Anne Stewart did not marry and that Cloudesley Stewart was a natural son. It is also feasible but less likely that *Debrett's* and *Notes & Queries* are both incorrect and that 'Cloud Stewart' was unrelated to the Shovel family and to the Stewart family of Athenry.

Nathaniel Gould – Junior Warden

Nathaniel Gould (1697–1738), the Ship's Junior Warden, is more readily identified. He was a successful merchant with extensive trading interests in the Baltic, Ireland, continental Europe, Turkey and later the West Indies. The family were prominent non-conformists. Gould's banking and investment connections with Ireland and his relationship with Walter Gould of Munster have been mentioned in association with Munster freemasonry. Gould's father and uncle were prominent City figures: directors of the Bank of England and East India Company and members of parliament. With their sons, they were also partners in Gould & Co., 'one of the largest suppliers of hemp, pitch and tar to the Navy' and active in the profitable, oligopolistic tobacco trade with Russia.[22] Following his uncle and father's death in 1728, Nathaniel Gould and his older brother, John (*d.*1740), previously junior partners, took over Gould & Co. and invited **Albert Nesbitt**, a member of the Ship and another successful and 'eminent Irish trader', to join the partnership.[23] In addition to their business relationship and obvious connection through the lodge, the invitation would have been spurred by Nesbitt's marriage to Nathaniel and John's sister, Elizabeth, in 1729.[24] The partnership was afterwards renamed 'Gould & Nesbitt'; it developed into one of the most successful merchant trading and banking houses in London.[25]

Like his uncle, Nathaniel Gould later became a director of the Bank of England. He also purchased a seat in parliament and was elected MP for Wareham at a by-election in 1729 following the death of the incumbent, **Joseph Gascoyne**, another lodge member (see below). Gould retained the seat and represented Wareham until 1734.

Members of the Lodge

Albert Nesbitt (*d.*1753), a younger son, had been sent to London from Ireland in 1717. On his arrival in the City he established Nesbitt & Co. and entered into business on his family's account as a Baltic merchant. He lived at Cattle's Court on College Hill, just north of Thames Street, west of London Bridge. In Ireland, the family had built up large estates at Brenter and Malmusoy in Co. Donegal, which were later inherited by his brother, Thomas. Nesbitt's success in London allowed him later to acquire the estates for himself.

A study by Craig Bailey of the 'Nesbitts of London and their Networks', underscores Nesbitt's strong business links with Ireland:

> the Nesbitts never abandoned their Irish circles. Indeed, Irish connections appear to have been vital for the house at all times it was active in trade. The need for access to Irish markets as well as political and social favours from Irish contacts in London were factors that kept the Nesbitt's 'Irish' and involved in ethnic networks.[26]

In establishing his own trading house and subsequently joining forces to create 'Gould & Nesbitt', the family was doing what many others among the Irish gentry and merchant classes had done before. Despatching a son to London to act as the family's agent to found or join a trading house had become an established formula and an effective mechanism for the Irish gentry to pursue their commercial objectives. The network of expatriate Irishmen created both formal and informal Irish associations in London that encompassed a range of competing and complementary business and social circles and extended into the political sphere. In all three, freemasonry played a part.

Nesbitt used his connections in Cork and Kinsale to facilitate Admiralty provisioning at those ports and it may be no coincidence that **Jonas Morris** of the prominent Cork trading family of that name was a member of the lodge. Similarly, Nesbitt also worked closely with the Dublin bankers, Hoare & Arnold, of which house **William Hoar** (see below), another lodge member, was a probable scion.[27]

In common with other Irish expatriate traders, the Nesbitt's developed extensive non-Irish connections to advance their trading activities. Albert's marriage to Elizabeth Gould can in part be viewed in such a light as can his willingness to ignore religion in the pursuit of profit, trading with Jewish, Catholic and Protestant houses. The importance of government provisioning contracts may have been an important factor in Nesbitt's support for Walpole and his political connections to Newcastle. He entered parliament in 1741, gaining a seat at a by-election at Huntingdon, where he sat as a government supporter until 1747. The constituency was within the influence of Lord Sandwich who wrote to Pelham in 1747 commenting 'as for Mr Nesbitt, my only objection to him is that I can't choose him for Huntingdon without hurting if not endangering, my interest in that borough'.[28] Nesbitt was subsequently nominated to represent Mitchell, a Cornish pocket borough with around 40 electors, where he sat from 1747 until his death in January 1753.

Albert Nebitt's financial success can be measured by the extent of his personal and real estate. In addition to property in London, Sussex and Ireland, he left legacies of over £20,000 and an £800 annual annuity to his wife.[29] In all, three successive generations of the Nesbitt family traded from London until the death of John Nesbitt in 1817. The family's interests included the Caribbean trade in rum and sugar; provisioning British naval and military forces in the Americas, Ireland and elsewhere; iron and coal production; banking; and the continental wine trade. Perpetuating the dynasty, Nesbitt was succeeded by his nephew, Arnold, who had himself become a partner in Gould & Nesbitt.

Richard Fitzgerald was a nephew of George Fitzgerald who founded another thriving London trading house that carried the family name. They were active in both the Anglo-Irish trade and that with North America, the Caribbean and the continent, exporting linen and importing sugar, wine and tobacco. Louis Cullen has commented that George Fitzgerald & Co. cooperated with Nesbitt & Co. and Gould & Nesbitt, and both the Fitzgeralds and Nesbitts had an array of complementary relationships in the Caribbean trade, naval and military provisioning in the West Indies, in the trade with France and elsewhere.[30]

The Fitzgeralds were a landed Catholic family from Co. Waterford who despite losing land after the Williamite War, retained and recovered sufficient estates to maintain their status as members of the Irish gentry. They also developed extensive mercantile interests.[31] George Fitzgerald had moved to London in 1718 having previously been a partner with Bernard Walsh in a Canary Islands trading house. Although his uncle, brother and the majority of the family remained faithful to the Catholic Church, Richard conformed in 1735, most probably to protect the family's assets from legal challenge on inheritance, a path followed by many other affluent Irish Catholic families. He nonetheless had a Catholic wife and remained on excellent terms with his family, despite their being regarded as papists.

In his study of the period, Thomas Truxes noted that London's Irish merchants such as the Fitzgeralds and Nesbitts, represented not only the interests of Irish exporters and importers, but also those of expatriate Irishmen and other clients across continental Europe, the Americas and the Caribbean.[32] The Irish merchant community had grown strongly and internationally from the end of the seventeenth century and by the mid-eighteenth, formed a large emigrant community. Within the City, the number of Irish trading houses had risen to over fifty by the 1760s, to which figure can be added many non-Irish houses that specialised in the Irish trade. Despite a wide spread of religious affiliations, including Quakers, conformist Protestants, non-conformists and Roman Catholics, there appears to have been no division along sectarian lines but rather a strong affiliation based on common Irish interests. An identical pattern is reflected in the membership of the Ship.

Many of the Irish merchant houses were geographically close to each other in the City, with around 40 located in the Cateaton Street district close to St Lawrence Jewry to the north of Cheapside. The area had originally been dominated by the cloth trade and was a natural home to firms that had and continued to specialise in Irish linen.[33] The 1745 Linen Bounty Act provided a small additional impetus to London's Irish merchant community, partly liberalising the way in which the parliamentary bounty was applied and setting more attractive rates for exported Irish and British linen, albeit that the Irish bounty was limited to coarse linens that did not compete with those from England. The mechanics of receiving the bounty, 'that no Irish Linen exported from Great Britain shall be entitled to the Bounty, unless the property of some person resident in Great Britain or America', served to reinforce the importance of the Irish merchant houses and cemented the financial links between Ireland and London.[34]

The significance of the transatlantic route to the Fitzgerald family was such that at least one family member was resident on a virtually permanent basis in the Canary Islands, a waypoint for transatlantic navigation. Other merchant families did the same and it was common for agents to be stationed in Cadiz, Lisbon and other key continental ports. From there they provided market intelligence, monitored or arranged transhipments, supervised the re-provisioning of vessels and ran or oversaw local trading operations. Accurate information was critical to both trading and the banking businesses of merchants providing short-term working capital and clearing and issuing bills of exchange, an increasingly important aspect of their business. They also procured or provided insurance and sourced equity capital. Indeed, over time, the Irish-connected merchant houses became integral to the commercial success of their correspondents, both in Ireland and North America.

Sir James Tobin was another merchant and an Irish Catholic.[35] Originally from Kilkenny, he was described in his obituary as 'formerly a captain of a ship in the United East India Company's service; but on some disgust went to Germany, and became there the chief projector of the Ostend East India Company, for which he obtained the honour of knighthood from his imperial majesty.'[36] Highly successful, Tobin was reported to have left an estate worth some £40,000, equivalent to £4–8 million today.[37]

Other merchants in the lodge included **Henry Hope; Benjamin Dry**, the vintner; and **Ralph Knox**, who, with Samuel Mercer, was a partner in Knox and Mercer, a house that specialised in the transatlantic trade.[38] Knox later became a director of the London Assurance Company and of Royal Exchange Assurance.[39] The two companies had a number of freemasons on their respective boards, including several members of the Ship, as well as several prominent Irish traders. The latter included George Fitzgerald, William Snell and **John Bourne**, seventh on the Ship's membership list, whose directorship of the Royal Exchange pre-dated 1720.[40] It is likely that **Gerard Bourne** was his brother. Crossle commented that the two may have been younger sons of the Bourne family of Burren in Co. Cork, or possibly Cournallane in Co. Carlow.

Brearcliffe Stonehewer was another City luminary, a well-known merchant with a strong connection to the Irish trade in a business inherited from his father. Stonehewer was a member of the Skinners Company and another director of Royal Exchange Assurance and of the London Assurance Company.[41] He also sat on the Court of the City-run Bridewell Hospital, a house of correction and penitentiary for petty offenders.[42]

William Moreton, a barrister, was a member of the Middle Temple who later sat as a Recorder. A prominent City figure, he was another governor of the Bridewell, as was **John Gascoyne**, third on the membership list, a merchant and a director of the Royal Africa Company.[43] Crossle noted that Gascoyne's father, Benjamin, also a merchant, owned a large estate in Ireland; both would have had regular business contacts and connections with Ireland. **Joseph Gascoyne** was John's brother, as was Sir Crisp Gascoyne (1700–61), later elected Alderman, Sheriff and the City of London's Lord Mayor (in 1752). All three were linked to **Thomas Watts**, who married the Gascoynes' sister, Susannah, in the mid-1720s. Crossle noted that **John Mason**, fifth on the membership list and yet another City merchant, was a witness at the wedding.[44]

Joseph Gascoyne (*d.*1728), held a lucrative post in Minorca. He defeated the sitting Tory member of parliament at Wareham in 1722, notwithstanding that 'he was a stranger', and sat as a government supporter until his death in 1728.[45] Gascoyne was succeeded as MP for the borough by **Nathaniel Gould**, who was elected 'without opposition'.[46]

Thomas Watts (*c*.1695–1742), was renowned as a mercurial entrepreneur, lecturer, educationalist and mathematician, with whom Desaguliers had given a joint scientific lecture course at Richard Steele's 'Censorium' at the York Buildings off the Strand in 1719. Watts' *Essay on the Proper Method of Forming the Man of Business*, published in 1716, ran to four editions.[47] It was written at the same time that he founded a school in Abchurch Lane in the City at which he used the methodology he publicised. The school – the 'Accountant's Office' – specialised in basic business administration and achieved considerable financial success, moving to larger premises in Little Tower Street to accommodate the growing demand.

> Young Gentlemen are completely qualified for any Manner of Business, free from the interruption and loss of time in Common Schools, at the Accomptant's Office, erected for that purpose in Little Tower Street, at the house lately Sir John Fleet's, where they are taught to perfection, writing, arithmetic, and merchant's accounts, from the Methods of use in real Business, by Thomas Watts, author of the Essay on the proper method for forming the Man of Business. Where also all parts of Mathematics are taught, and Courses in Experimental Philosophy performed, by Benj. Worster, MA, and Thomas Watts.[48]

In the preface to the fourth edition of his *Essay*, Watts set out that his objective was to teach a business education to 'young gentlemen . . . from about thirteen or fourteen upwards . . . such as are immediately designed for trades, merchandise, the Sea, Clerkships in Offices, or to Attorneys, or any other Employments in Business'.[49] The school was still functioning successfully in 1730, when Benjamin Worster, Watts' partner, published his own *Course of Experimental Philosophy*. This advertised that the teaching would now be 'performed by Benj. Worster, AM, and Tho. Watts at the Accomptant's Office for qualifying young Gentlemen for Business.'[50] However, Watts and Worcester's lectures were not confined to the school at Little Tower Street. They also presented at the York Buildings on the Strand where, in common with Desaguliers and other eminent peripatetic lecturers, their talks and demonstrations fed a growing appetite for education as entertainment and the desire to profit from the practical application of the new scientific Enlightenment.

In another parallel with Desaguliers, Watts also enjoyed the patronage of James Brydges, the duke of Chandos, who part financed the move to Little Tower Street and for whom Ruth Wallis has suggested Watts provided insider stock market intelligence and acted as agent for Chandos and others involved in the takeover of Sun Fire insurance.[51] Certainly, Watts became closely involved with Sun Fire following the acquisition of a significant holding by Royal Exchange Assurance. Indeed, according to Relton, Watts became Sun Fire's 'ruling genius'.[52] There is no doubt that he had influence. He was Company Secretary from 1727 until 1734, when he appointed his brother to succeed him, and thereafter Cashier until his retirement in 1741. The position propelled him into a leading figure in the City of London.

In 1725, at around the time of his marriage to Susannah, John Gascoyne, her brother, was given a job at Sun Fire and later succeeded Watts' brother, William, as the Company Secretary. Crisp Gascoyne, Susannah's youngest brother, was given a sinecure from 1749 until 1761. And Thomas Watts' sons, Thomas and Hugh, were handed jobs at the company and each successively became Secretary. Such nepotism was common and of greater interest are the interlocking commercial relationships between the different members of the lodge. The most obvious are the several common directorships with respect to the Royal Exchange and Sun Fire, but the members' joint influence extended elsewhere and to other organisations. The arrangements epitomised a growing level of sophistication and nepotism in eighteenth-century finance.

Watts prospered. He was awarded government sinecures through the influence of his political patron, Lord Falmouth, and in 1734, was elected MP for the pocket borough of Mitchell in Cornwall, the parliamentary seat later occupied by Albert Nesbitt. Watts was Falmouth's candidate for the seat and sat as an opposition Whig in the prince of Wales' parliamentary faction. In 1741, he was elected for the equally venal borough of Tregony, another pocket constituency.[53] With around 150 electors, the 'principal customers were the Treasury, who usually bought one seat, and wealthy London merchants, who competed for the other.'[54] Watts died in 1742 having retired from Sun Fire the prior year. He had been awarded an annuity at the time, the company recognising that:

> many of the good regulations made in this office and more particularly the scheme and success of the subscription stock (from which era we may date the establishment and good fortune of the office) were owing in a great measure to the contrivances and good services of Mr Thomas Watt.[55]

Crossle suggests that **John Hope** may have been the Ulster Quaker of that name. Hope (*d*.1740), was a successful merchant and linen draper who had inherited a profitable business from his father.[56] He became one of the wealthiest members of the Quaker community in Lurgan, if not in Ulster, and cultivated and benefited from strong commercial relationships within the Quaker community across Ireland and particularly in Dublin. Hope maintained accounts with bankers and merchants in Bristol, Manchester and London, where he would have been a regular visitor.[57] Crossle's identification of Hope, although the most probable, is not definitive and there were two other relatively prominent 'John Hopes' living in London at the time. The first, a brewer, was based in Shoreditch; the second was a merchant and a director of the East India Company.

William Worth (1698–1725), of Rathfarnham in Co. Dublin, eleventh in the list of members, was the grandson of his namesake who from 1681–6 held office as Baron of the Irish Exchequer. Following the Williamite Wars, the family's fortune was established through a commission to manage the duke of Ormonde, the Lord Lieutenant's, Irish estates. In 1723, Worth would have been representing the family's business interests in London. Two years later he married Jane Saunders (1704–47), of Saunders Court, Kilpatrick in Co. Wexford, in August 1725, 'a lady of a considerable fortune.'[58] Unfortunately, Worth died in November the same year, aged only 27.[59] He was related by marriage to Robert Callaghan who in 1738 became SGW of Irish Grand Lodge, and to William Newenham, who was JGW of Munster in 1731.

William Spaight, a barrister, had an estate at Six-mile Bridge, Co. Clare, where he subsequently sat as a magistrate. In 1723, he may have been attending the Inns of Court in London in order to qualify for the Irish bar, a requirement for Irish barristers. The Irish comprised a relatively large part of the judicial community with certain chambers known for their strong Irish relationships.[60] Even Catholics had a presence. Although prohibited from practicing as solicitors or barristers, they specialised in conveyance and property where a legal qualification was not a formal requirement.

Peter Webb, tenth on the list, is a relatively common name. It is possible but unlikely that he was a linen draper whose premises were at the Wheat Sheaf in Henrietta Street, Covent Garden.[61] The occupation and location would connect him with Ireland and with others in the lodge. However, it is more probable that Webb was the Irish jeweller and banker of that name, who was at the time at the apex of his profession. He had many Irish customers.[62] Crossle noted that Webb had lent money to one of **John Gascoyne**'s business associates, James McCulloh, and that the debt was subsequently recovered through the intermediation of Andrew Crotty of Lismore, Co. Waterford. McCulloh, a gentleman of the King's Chamber, was employed in the procurement of goods for the Crown but also traded on his own account.

Benjamin Lambert, another merchant or high-end tradesman, was probably a Huguenot.[63] There were at least seven Lamberts among London's freemasons. Edward Lambert, a member of the Crown at Acton; George, a member of the Fountain in the Strand; John Lambert, the Ship tavern on Fish Hill; Philip, of the Crown at Acton and the Fountain in the Strand; Thomas, the Three Cranes in Poultry, later the Ship behind the Royal Exchange; and William, the Swan Tavern, Fish Street Hill. Another (or the same) Edward Lambert, was recorded in Grand Lodge's *Minutes* as a confectioner in Pall Mall. The last named was deputy Grand Steward to John Heidegger in 1725 and a Grand Steward in his own right in 1727. Tangentially, Crossle noted that members of the Lambert family living in Cregclare, Co. Galway had leased land from **Joseph Gascoyne**.

Henry Cunningham was from Mount Charles, Co. Donegal. A friend of **Albert Nesbitt** and **Nathaniel Gould**, he was probably connected to Greg, Cunningham & Company, a trading house with offices in New York and Belfast. Interestingly, one of the most important Irish American firms trading in Philadelphia in the mid- and late 1700s was Conyngham and Nesbitt. Its senior partner was Redmond Conyngham, who had originally migrated from Co. Donegal. There is also a connection to Cloud Stewart: Captain Andrew Stewart's second son, Hugh, married Margaret Morris of Mountjoy Castle. Their eldest son, also Hugh, married the daughter and heiress of William Cunningham of Castle Conyngham in Donegal.[64] A James Cunningham, described as a merchant and possibly related, was listed in Kent's *London Directory* for 1740.

Richard Warburton was probably the Irish MP of that name (1674–1747), then chairman of the Accounts Committee in the Irish Commons. MP for Portarlington from 1715–27 and Ballykanill from 1727–47, Warburton took an active role in the Irish parliament where he was involved with bills concerning the militia and trade. If not the MP, Warburton may have been another member of the same family despatched to London to look after their commercial and financial interests.[65] The Warburtons had lived at Garryhinch in Queens County since the early seventeenth century and had had representatives in the Irish parliament almost continuously since that time. Crossle stated that Warburton was 'well-known about town – a keen business man in vested land interests'.

Jonas Morris (*d*.1734), had been sent to London to monitor and manage his family's political and mercantile interests. On his return, he was elected to the Commons where he sat as the second member for Cork from 1730 until his death.[66] The Morris family were Quaker traders and merchants who had settled in Cork at least a century earlier.[67] A Jonas Morris had been mayor of the city in 1659; his mayoral seal had the mark of a ship between two towers. A descendant, Theodore Morris, became mayor in 1699; and another, Jonas Morris, was High Sheriff for the county in 1769.[68] Their political achievements across two centuries point to the family's financial success and influence; and the marriage of their daughters into prominent Irish political families indicates that their wealth had given them access to and membership of the local gentry, a view validated by James Morris becoming SGW of Munster's socially exclusive grand lodge in 1731. Jonas Morris' relationship with **Albert Nesbitt** is commented on above in connection with the provision of naval supplies at Cork and Kinsale. The political lobbying of the Quakers in London at the turn of the seventeenth century has been studied by John Bergin, who places them in the 'vanguard of political lobbying'.[69] He noted, tellingly, that their lobbying techniques were copied by their Irish counterparts and that both groups retained permanent lobbyists in London.[70]

It is likely that **William Hoar**, alternatively written as 'Hore' and 'Hoare', was the MP for Taghmon in the Irish parliament. The Hoare family were prominent merchants and bankers, based predominantly in Cork and with a large scale interest in shipping, victualling and brewing. They were unrelated to the English banking family of the same name. Over time, the Hoares acquired substantial landholdings in Cos. Cork, Kerry and Limerick, and built a series of alliances within Ireland and England through marriage and trading relationships. The family had robust Quaker connections. Joseph

Hoare (*d*.1729) married into the Rogers family, another prominent Cork Quaker merchant family, and his son, Samuel Hoare (1716–96) married the daughter of another London Quaker merchant with solid Irish connections.[71] It is unclear whether William was a direct descendant of Edward Hoare (*d*.1690), the principal founder of the Irish dynasty in the seventeenth century. However, Edward had six brothers and at least three sons and a direct or indirect connection is a reasonable assumption. As an alternative identification, Crossle proposed that William Hoar may have been from Harperstown in Co. Wexford, who held a variety of lucrative government sinecures in Ireland.[72] Bergin has suggested that it is unlikely that the two families – Cork and Wexford – were connected.[73]

William Richardson (*c*.1690–1755), from Somerset in Coleraine, Derry, was MP for Augher, which he represented in the Irish Commons from 1727–55, a position connected directly to his employment as agent for The Honourable The Irish Society. The organisation had been created by royal charter at the beginning of the seventeenth century as a means of obliging the City of London livery companies to co-finance Londonderry's plantations and to expedite English colonisation. It designed and financed the initial construction of the cities of Londonderry and Coleraine.[74] As agent, Richardson represented and was appointed by the society's governing board, an institution whose directors were nominated by the livery companies.

John Pringle may either have been the parliamentarian of that name (*c*.1674–1754), MP for Selkirkshire from 1708 until 1729, or more probably and as Crossle suggests, Mr John Pringle of Caledon, Co. Tyrone, the father of Major General Henry Pringle, later colonel of the 51ˢᵗ Foot. If the MP, Pringle was a Whig loyalist who from 1715, voted with the administration in all recorded divisions at which he was present. His Selkirkshire constituency was in the pocket of its hereditary sheriff, John Murray, Pringle's brother-in-law. Pringle was created Lord Haining in 1729 and appointed a justice on the bench in the Court of Session, the supreme civil court in Scotland. If the latter, Pringle (*d*. 1741) would have been descended from Scottish immigrants. He lived at Lyme Park, Caledon, an estate close to the border with Armagh, where he was a local justice of the peace and land agent for John Hamilton and then his daughter, Margaret, who inherited the Caledon estate in 1713. As such, Pringle would have been present in London in his capacity as agent to the estate.

Robert Waller was perhaps the person of that name commissioned as a cornet in 1723 and promoted to adjutant in the 1ˢᵗ Regiment of Foot in 1725, a prestigious position in a premier regiment that could only have been purchased at a significant cost.[75] Although the regiment was normally on the English Establishment, in 1713 it had been detached to Ireland on garrison duty. A Robert Waller was in 1736 made sheriff for Roscommon.[76] Crossle suggests that Waller may have been the eldest son of Robert Waller of Allenstown, Co. Meath.[77]

The other member of the lodge holding military rank was **Captain Lionel Beecher**, who later served as 1ˢᵗ lieutenant in Colonel John Wynyard's

Regiment of Marines, which was raised in November 1739. Crossle noted that the family lived at Sherhin in Co. Cork.

Captain Patrick Trahee, also written as 'Trehee', was not an army or naval officer but a merchant seaman and the son of James Trehee (*d*.1709), who had captained the merchant ship 'Crocodile'.[78] Like his father, Patrick Trehee worked the Caribbean and Atlantic trade. A press report in 1709 recorded the following from Deal in Kent:

> March 10. Yesterday morning the Guildford, Captain Patrick Trehee, of 327 Tuns [sic] and 22 Guns, homeward bound from Jamaica, but last from Lisbon, was unfortunately cast away on the flats between the Downs and the River, but all the men saved. Her cargo, which consisted chiefly of sugar, indigo etc., was valued at £25,000.[79]

The ship was recovered and Trehee continued to captain her on the Jamaica route. Press reports featuring Trehee occur throughout the early decades of the eighteenth century and a classified advertisement from 1722 provides evidence of the profits from the trade.[80]

> Lost, on Thursday . . . between London Bridge and Aldermanbury, a black pocket book in which was a Bank Note No. 385 for £120 payable to Capt. Patrick Trehee dated May 31st 1722 with several other Bills and Notes of no use to any other Owner, payment being stopped at the Bank and other places. Whoever brings it to the Portugal Coffee House near the Royal Exchange shall have Five Guineas reward and no questions asked.81

Trehee was still sailing in 1730, with the press noting his excursions to and from Rotterdam.[82] He was at this time a director of Royal Exchange Assurance alongside other members of the lodge. A press notice shows him as such in 1729, although his first appointment to the board would have been earlier.[83] Trehee remained a director of the Royal Exchange for many years.[84] His Will was proved at the Prerogative Court of Canterbury on 24 October 1737, where he was described briefly as a merchant, resident in London.

'Tiss. Putland' is a misspelling of or abbreviation for Sisson Putland, the son of Thomas Putland, whose nephew was John Putland, JGW of Irish Grand Lodge in 1737, SGW in 1738, and DGM 1747–50 and 1763–4. Thomas Putland and his eldest son, Sisson's brother, also named Thomas, had been successful London merchants who had earlier emigrated to Ireland where they settled in Dublin.[85] Tiss lived in Spring Gardens, close to Charing Cross, and acted as the family's London agent with oversight of their business affairs. The *Gentleman's Magazine* described him succinctly at the time of his death as 'very rich'.[86] His obituary in the *London Evening Post* was slightly more informative:

> Yesterday Morning died, very much lamented, after a long illness, in Spring Gardens, Charing Cross, Sisson Putland, Esq. We hear he has left the bulk

of his estate, which is very considerable, to his brother George Putland, Esq.,[87] and a very handsome legacy with his coach and horses to Miss Lindar, and to his man, a hundred pounds.[88]

A second obituary in the *London Evening Post* a few days later placed the value of Miss Lindar's bequest at £2,000, together with 'all the furniture of his house'.[89]

It is not known whether Thomas Putland, Sisson's father, died in Dublin or London. However, a Will for a Thomas Putland was proved at Canterbury in July 1723 and referred to a merchant who had resided at Chelsea. Marriage announcements for Thomas Putland's daughters in 1728 and 1733, also referred respectively to 'a late eminent Merchant of this City' and to 'the late Thomas Putland . . . of Paradise Row, Chelsea, Esq.[90]

'Leon. Hatfield' may have been the Rev. Leonard Hatfield who in 1751 was given the livings of Stradbally and Moyana in Queens County by the Anglo-Irish Cosby family of Stradbally Hall.[91] However, it is more probable that he was the better-known appellant who appeared before the House of Lords in 1725. Hatfield *versus* Hatfield was an attempt by Leonard Hatfield to overturn a decree made by the Court of Exchequer in Ireland relating to his father's estate. A judgment in the Irish Courts had been issued the prior year in favour of his mother (or stepmother), Jane Hatfield, described as 'widow and relict of Leonard Hatfield, gentleman, deceased'. Leonard Hatfield's appeal was described in a counter-petition to the House of Lords as 'scandalous, impertinent and greatly reflecting on the petitioner, charging her with crimes not contained in the pleadings and wholly improper and indecent to be mentioned or suggested.'[92] Leonard Hatfield's claim failed; his appeal was dismissed and the decree confirmed.[93] A notorious rather than celebrated litigant, Crossle commented that Hatfield was 'well-known in the Dublin law courts'. The family came from Killinure in Co. Westmeath.

Alongside **Nathaniel Gould** and **Albert Nesbitt**, probably the wealthiest member of the lodge was **Springett Penn** (*d.*1731), a Quaker and the principal heir and grandson of William Penn, who founded the Pennsylvania colony. Penn had inherited substantial land holdings in Pennsylvania and in England, principally at Worninghurst, Sussex. However, he also had extensive land holdings in Ireland where he lived on the family's large Shanagarry estate. Shanagarry had originally been granted to his great-grandfather, Admiral Sir William Penn, by Charles II, in exchange for the market town of Macroom and its castle, which Admiral Penn had in turn been granted by Cromwell. In 1723, Springett Penn was almost certainly in London in connection with his estates and the legal obligations he retained in connection with Pennsylvania.[94] Despite being a Quaker, together with his mother, Hannah, Penn had inherited the right to govern the colony under the auspices of the Crown and as such his and his mother's formal consent was required periodically in connection with the colony's administration. For example, in 1725, the *Calendar of State Papers Colonial, America and West Indies*, record:

1 March. Declaration by Mrs. Penn that the royal approbation of Patrick Gordon to be Deputy Governor of Pennsylvania and the Three Lower Counties upon Delaware River, shall not be construed to diminish the right claimed by the Crown to the said Three Lower Counties. Signed, Hannah Penn, in the presence of S. Clement and Will. Penn.[95]

1 March. Similar Declaration. Signed, Springett Penn. Endorsed as preceding

11 March. St James's. Order of King in Council. Approving of appointment of Major Patrick Gordon as Deputy Governor of Pennsylvania, provided he qualify himself as the law directs and give security as proposed, and that Springett and Hannah Penn make the declaration proposed.

June 1726. Order in Council approving draught of instructions for Major Gordon:
Order in Council of the 18th of April, 1726, approving the draught of instructions relating to the Acts of Trade for Springett Penn, Esquire, and Hannah Penn, widow, to be by them given to Major Gordon, Deputy Governor of Pennsylvania.[96]

Springett Penn was twenty-one in 1723 when a member of the Ship, four years below the stated minimum age to be accepted as a freemason. However, exceptions were often made for those of sufficient wealth and social standing and he was in good company. The duke of Wharton was 24 when installed as English Grand Master; the duke of Richmond, 23; and the earl of Darnley, 22. Penn was appointed or elected DGM of Munster in 1726 and 1727, under the Grand Mastership of the Hon James O'Brien, GM of Munster from 1726 to 1728. O'Brien was the brother of the 4th earl of Inchiquin, himself GM of England in 1727.

The associational overlap between Penn's commercial and social/Masonic networks can be seen not only in his membership of the Ship behind the Royal Exchange but also in his leasing of land on the Shanagarry estate to many recognisable Munster freemasons. Lepper and Crossle in their *History* note that among others, Thomas Wallis, Munster's Grand Warden, leased eight townships from Penn; Edward Webber of Cork held nine; and John Longfield of Castlemary, who succeeded Penn as DGM, leased one. **Nathaniel Gould**'s extensive mortgage holdings in Co. Cork, with which Walter Gould was linked, speak similarly to a blurring of business, social, family and Masonic connections.[97] Support for the argument is also suggested by Penn and Walter Gould's business relationships with Richard Longfield, Munster's DGM in 1728, and John Gamble, Munster's JGW in 1730, from whom Penn borrowed on the security of Gamble's mortgages on Shanagarry.[98]

Paul Minchell may have been a relation of and London agent for the

Chester merchants and mercers of that name. The head of family who died in 1741, was described as 'the most eminent Mercer in the whole city of Chester'.[99] Crossle suggests that the name may have been misspelled and referred to Paul Minchin of Ballynakill in Co. Tipperrary.

Of the remaining members of the lodge, '**William Bently**' is presently unidentified; '**Mr Row Hill**' was probably Rowley Hill, described by Crossle as Junior Warden for a Dublin lodge in 1731 whose relations were from Ballkelly in Co. Derry. The family had been granted lands in Armagh, Antrim, Derry and Tyrone in the 1640s when Samuel Hill had been appointed Treasurer in Ireland under Cromwell.[100] Rowley Hill is however probably better known masonically as one of William Ponsonby's wardens at the lodge at the Yellow Lion tavern on 6 March 1731. **Abraham Sharigley** was, in Crossle's words, a 'well-known man about town in Dublin.'

Notes

INTRODUCTION

1 Desaguliers was ordained a deacon in 1710, a year after graduating from Christ Church, Oxford. He received an MA in 1712 and was awarded a doctorate in 1719, incorporated LLD at Cambridge in 1726. He was elected FRS in 1714 and 'in consideration of his great usefulness to the Royal Society as Curator and Operator of Experiments . . . excused from paying his Admission money, signing the usual bond and Obligation and paying the weekly contributions': RS Minutes of the Council, II, 29 July 1714.

2 Cf., *1723 Constitutions*. Article 10 (p. 61), for example, stated that a 'majority of every particular Lodge, when congregated, shall have the privilege of giving instructions to their Master and Wardens . . . because the Master and Wardens are their representatives'.

3 Cf. R.A. Berman, *Foundations of Modern Freemasonry* (Brighton: Sussex Academic Press, 2011).

4 Cf., Simon Schaffer, *Natural Philosophy and Public Spectacle in Eighteenth Century England* in *History of Science* (Cambridge, 1983), vol. XXI.

5 Larry Stewart, 'A Meaning for Machines: Modernity, Utility, and the Eighteenth-Century British Public', *Journal of Modern History*, 70.2 (1998), 259–294, esp. 269; and 'James Brydges to William Mead, 16 June 1718', Huntington Library: Stowe MS, ST 57, XV, 252.

CHAPTER ONE **Laurence Dermott and Antients Grand Lodge**

1 John Ward was created Lord Ward, Baron of Birmingham in 1740. He was appointed GM (1742–4), following his elevation to the peerage.

2 Grand Lodge of England *Minutes*, 1723–39, pp. 259–60.

3 Ibid., p. v.

4 Ibid., pp. 259–60.

5 Cf., Berman, *Foundations*.

6 John Heron Lepper & Philip Crossle, *History of the Grand Lodge of Free and Accepted Masons of Ireland* (Dublin: Lodge of Research, CC, 1925), vol. I, p. 232.

7 Anonymous, *Hiram: or the Grand Master Key* (London: W. Griffin, 1766), 2nd edn.

8 R.F. Gould, *History of Freemasonry* (London, 1882–7), (6 vols), vol. 2, ch. 4; and Henry Sadler, *Masonic Facts and Fictions* (London, 1887), ch. 3–5.

9 J.R. Dashwood (ed.), *Early Records of the Grand Lodge of England According to the Old Institutions* (London: Quatuor Coronati Lodge, 1958), QCA, vol. XI, p. v.

10 Cf., Grand Lodge of England *Minutes*, 24 July 1755.

11 Antients Grand Lodge *Minutes*, 1 June 1774.

12   Laurence Dermott, *Ahiman Rezon* (London, 1756), *Dedication*.

13   1723 *Constitutions*.

14   Dermott, *Ahiman Rezon*, pp. vi–xvi.

15   There are no satisfactory biographies of Laurence Dermott. However, cf., Witham Matthew Bywater, *Notes on Laurence Dermott* (London, 1884); and Dudley Wright (rev.), *Gould's Freemasonry Throughout the World* (New York: Charles Scribner's Sons, 1936), vol. 2, pp. 145–95.

16   Dermott succeeded John Morgan who resigned in February 1752 'he being lately appointed to office on board one of His Majesty's ships [had] received orders to prepare for his departure'.

17   Antients Grand Lodge *Minutes 1752–60*, reprinted as QCA Antigrapha XI, pp. 7, 29–30, 39. Hagarty is also described as a 'painter' in the *General Register*.

18   Seán Murphy, 'Irish Jacobitism and Freemasonry', *Eighteenth-Century Ireland/Iris an dá chultúr*, 9 (1994), 75–82.

19   Six MacDermotts from Co. Roscommon (Owen and Michel [Michael] MacDermott and Charles, Dudley, James and Laurent [Laurence] Macdermot[t]), are recorded as serving in France's Irish brigades in the eighteenth century. The total number of MacDermotts listed is thirty-eight. In seventeen instances the county of origin was not stated. Cf., National University of Ireland, *The Irish in Europe Project*. Twenty-three other MacDermotts or Macdermot[t]s appear in the records of Irish soldiers who saw service in Spain. In aggregate, *The Irish in Europe Project* lists seventy-one MacDermotts, including two clerical students at Leuven University in Belgium.

20   I am indebted to Joseph McIlveen, Irish Lodge of Research, No. 200, for this information.

21   Thomas Dermott, Laurence's father, traded from premises in Frances Street and/or New Row, its northern extension.

22   The McDermott's, a sister branch of the family, were associated with other lodges including No. 355 in Co. Sligo, whose warrant was issued on 4 December 1760.

23   Lepper and Crossle, *History*, pp. 236–42.

24   Dermot MacDermot, *MacDermott of Moylurg* (Manorhamilton, Ireland: Drumlin, 1996), pp. 313–31, cites *Collectonea Hibernica*, 34–5 (1992–3). He also mentions the merchant house of Dermott and Paine which traded from Rue de la Savonniere in Rouen in the early 1700s. A Michael McDermott later lived at Rue des Jacobins in St Sauveur, Rouen. It is likely that this branch of the family was Catholic and that the trading house had been founded after the Treaty of Limerick. The National University of Ireland, *The Irish in Europe Project*, also lists several merchants named MacDermott living in Spain. A Pedro (Peter) MacDermott was recorded in Cadiz in the eighteenth century, as was a Hugo MacDermott. A Juan MacDermott was also listed as living in Madrid.

25   A copy of Christopher Dermott's will was made available to the author by Joseph McIlveen. Cf. also Lepper and Crossle, *History*, p. 238.

26   Cf., the *Daily Gazetteer (London Edition)*, 8 December 1738, which noted the loss of 'warehouse and a large quantity of paper belonging to Mr Dermott', the consequence of a fire at Usher's Quay in Dublin.

27   Cf., for example, *Dublin Mercury*, 10–13 June 1769 and later issues, in which Anthony and Owen Dermott are among the signatories to a letter from the 'merchants of the city of Dublin'; and the *Public Register or The Freeman's Journal*, 11–13 December 1770 et al. Anthony Dermott was also a signatory to

an open letter addressed to the Irish parliament, published in the *Public Advertiser*, 22 July 1784, complaining against the unjust duties levied by Britain.

28 *Public Register or The Freeman's Journal*, 24–27 November 1770.

29 *Gazetteer and New Daily Advertiser*, 26 May 1780; *London Courant and Westminster Chronicle*, 26 May 1780.

30 Cf., for example, *Dublin Mercury*, 25–27 May and 3–6 June 1769 and successive issues, in relation to an imported consignment of Antigua rum.

31 *Lloyd's Evening Post and British Chronicle*, 13–15 August 1760.

32 *London Evening Post*, 15–18 November 1766; cf., also, *Public Advertiser*, 19 November 1766.

33 *Public Ledger*, 29 November 1765. Spelt variously as 'Windall', 'Windle', 'Windel' and 'Windell'.

34 *St James's Chronicle or the British Evening Post*, 27–29 December 1763.

35 *London Chronicle*, 27 February–1 March 1766; also, *London Evening Post*, 27 February 1766.

36 Cf., for example, *London Gazette*, 12–16 June 1759; *General Advertiser*, 19 February 1752 and 4, 7, 9, 11 March 1752; and *Daily Advertiser*, 21 January 1752: a meeting of the 'Master Taylors and Staymakers of the Cities of London and Westminster'.

37 Cf., *London Daily Advertiser*, 9 April 1752 and *Gazetteer and London Daily Advertiser*, 30 May 1763.

38 *London Evening Post*, 30 December 1766–1 January 1767; *London Chronicle*, 6–9 June 1767; *Public Advertiser*, 22 June 1768.

39 *Public Advertiser*, 26, 27 & 28 March 1754.

40 No Wills appear to have been recorded for probate purposes for either William or Mary Windall [Windle].

41 *Report on the Charities of the Haberdashers' Company Part II* (London: City of London Livery Companies Commission, 1884), vol. 4, pp. 457–77.

42 *Gazetteer and New Daily Advertiser*, 3 November 1769.

43 Antients Grand Lodge *Minutes*, 1752–60, p. 90.

44 *AQC*, 38, p. 154.

45 William Smith, *A Pocket Companion for Freemasons* (Dublin, 1735).

46 Cf. Antients' *General Register*.

47 Valerie Rumbold, *The Dunciad in Four Books* (Harlow: Pearson, 2009), rev. ed., p. 4.

48 UK Data Archive: *Wills 1790–91*. Proved at the Prerogative Court of Canterbury, 15 July 1791.

49 http://www.londonlives.org/static/StBotolphAldgate.jsp accessed 17 August 2012.

50 Antients Grand Lodge, *General Register*.

51 *Daily Advertiser*, 24 February 1773 et al.

52 Rebuilt in c. 1740 to a design by Henry Flitcroft.

53 Cf., MacDermot, *MacDermott of Moylurg*.

54 Anthony Dermott (1700–1784) had one daughter and four sons. Three sons, Owen (*d*.1787), Francis (*d*.1788) and Anthony (*d*.1786), also became merchants, trading from 15 Usher's Quay, 30 Arran Quay and 19 Usher's Island, respectively.

55 *Parker's General Advertiser and Morning Intelligencer*, 23 May 1782.

56 *Parker's General Advertiser and Morning Intelligencer*, 24 September 1782; *Morning Herald and Daily Advertiser*, 25 September 1782 et al.

57 Dermott, *Ahiman Rezon* (London, 1756).

58 Albert Gallatin Mackey, *An encyclopaedia of freemasonry and its kindred sciences* (Philadelphia: Moss & Co., 1874), p. 46.

59 A 2nd edn. was published in 1764; a 3rd in 1778; and the 4th, 5th and 6th in 1779, 1780 and 1782, respectively. Other known editions were published in 1795, 1797, 1800, 1801, 1807 and 1813.

60 William Alexander Laurie, *The History of Free Masonry and the Grand Lodge of Scotland* (Edinburgh: Seton & MacKenzie, 1859), fn. p. 60.

61 Mackey, *An Encyclopaedia of Freemasonry*, p. 214.

62 Ibid.

63 Wright (rev.), *Gould's Freemasonry Throughout the World*, vol. 2, p. 151.

64 William James Hughan, *Memorials of the Masonic Union* (Leicester, 1913), rev. ed., p. 8.

65 Sadler, *Masonic Facts and Fictions*, pp. 110–2.

66 Dermott, *Ahiman Rezon* (London, 1764), 2nd edn., pp. xxix–xxxi.

67 Ibid.

68 *Gazetteer and New Daily Advertiser*, 21 September 1765 et al.

69 Wright (rev.), *Gould's Freemasonry Throughout the World*, vol. 2, p. 168.

70 Dermott, *Ahiman Rezon*, 'Explanation of the Frontispiece'.

71 Ibid., p. xv.

72 Grand Lodge of England *Minutes*, 29 November 1754.

73 Ibid., 24 July 1755.

74 Ibid.

75 Ibid.

76 It is now Fortitude and Old Cumberland, No. 12.

77 Dermott, *Ahiman Rezon* (London, 1778), 3rd edn., pp. xvi–xvii.

78 Ibid., p. xviii. A cynic might suggest that one reason for the 1762 edition being silent on the matter was that Dermott's presentation of the events in 1755 might have been open to challenge. In 1778, the events were more than two decades in the past.

79 *Middlesex Journal or Chronicle of Liberty*, 9–11 April 1772.

80 Smith, Captain George, HC 8/F/35 *15 October 1776*: UGLE Library. The 4th duke had succeeded on his father's death in 1774.

81 *Morning Herald*, 29 December 1786. Author's italics.

82 Antients Grand Lodge *Minutes*, 14 September 1752.

83 Ibid., 6 December 1752.

84 Charles visited Florence in 1733 and became master of an Irish Masonic lodge established there. He is associated with what became known as the Sackville Medal, the first known example of a Masonic medal, struck to commemorate his mastership.

85 Antients Grand Lodge *Minutes*, 5 December 1753,

86 *Gazetteer and New Daily Advertiser*, 23 September 1766.

87 John Murray, 3rd duke of Atholl (1729–1774) was GM Antients (1771–4) and GM Scotland (1773–4); and John Murray, 4th duke of Atholl (1755–1830) was GM Antients (1775–81 & 1791–1812) and GM Scotland (1778–80).

88 Blessington's mother was the sister and heir of the second and last Viscount Blessington.

89 The membership of the Bear & Harrow lodge included a number of former and current Grand Officers, including Montagu, GM; Thomas Batson, DGM;

Desaguliers, formerly GM and DGM; George Rook and James Smythe, GWs; James Chambers, a former GW; and George Moody, the Grand Swordbearer.

90 Cf. Francis Nichols, *The Irish Compendium* (London: J. Knapton, 1756), 5th ed., pp. 233–6.

91 *Jacobite's Journal*, 13 August 1748; *London Daily Advertiser and Literary Gazette*, 20 April 1751. Mountjoy also owned a house at Blackheath: *Gazetteer and New Daily Advertiser*, 4 August 1768.

92 Thomas Prior, *A list of the absentees of Ireland* (Dublin: Richard Gunne, 1729), p. 6. Cf. also the 3rd edn. (Dublin, 1745), p. 6.

93 *Public Advertiser*, 4 May 1757.

94 The date is sometimes given as 1746, but cf. for example, *General Advertiser*, 6 September 1748. He was reappointed to the Privy Council in 1761 following the succession of George III.

95 *Public Advertiser*, 10 June 1763.

96 *St James's Chronicle or the British Evening Post*, 10–12 September 1761.

97 Toby Barnard, *Improving Ireland?* (Dublin: FCP, 2008), p. 123.

98 The Mathew family had settled in Co. Tipperary in the seventeenth century and had considerable estates around Thomastown. Thomas' son, Francis, was created 1st earl of Llandaff in 1797. Cf. National University of Ireland, Galway: Landed Estates Database: http://landedestates.nuigalway.ie:8080/LandedEstates/jsp/family-show.jsp?id= 2785 accessed 21 September 2012.

99 *St James's Chronicle or the British Evening Post*, 18–20 February 1762 et al. Cf. obituary in *General Evening Post*, 8–11 November 1777; and *Gazetteer and New Daily Advertiser*, 10 November 1777.

100 Randall MacDonnell, 6th earl of Antrim (1749–1791), was created 1st marquess of Antrim in 1789.

101 D'Assigny's *Serious and Impartial Enquiry into the Cause of the present Decay of Freemasonry in the Kingdom of Ireland* (Dublin: Edward Bates, 1764).

102 Dermott, *Ahiman Rezon*, p. 47 (1st edn.).

103 Antients Grand Lodge *Minutes*, 16 December 1759.

CHAPTER TWO **Antients Freemasonry and the London Irish**

1 http://www.oldbaileyonline.org/static/Irish.jsp, accessed 15 April 2012. Roger Swift estimates that the total Irish-born population in the whole of England, Wales and Scotland rose from 415,000 in 1841 to a peak of just over 800,000 in 1861. Cf., Swift, 'The Outcast Irish in the British Victorian City: Problems and Perspectives', *Irish Historical Studies*, 25.99 (1987), 264–76.

2 Charles Dickens, *Gin Shops: Sketches by Boz* (London: John Macrone, 1836), vol. I.

3 *Registers of the Grand Lodge of the Antients, 1751–1813*. The unpublished primary data is held at the Library and Museum of Freemasonry, Great Queen Street, London. Cf., also, J. R. Dashwood (ed.), *Early Records of the Grand Lodge of England according to the Old Institutions* (London: QC, 1958), published as *Quatuor Coronatorum Antigrapha*, vol. XI.

4 Freemasonry also grew strongly in Ireland itself, where the proportion of the adult male population who were freemasons was greater than in any other European country, including England. Between 1732 and 1789, over 700 lodges were warranted in Ireland; and by the 1790s, Irish freemasonry has a member-

ship estimated at 35–40,000 within an adult male population of around a million. Cf. Petri Mirala, 'Masonic sociability and its limitations: the case of Ireland' in James Kelly & Martin J. Powell (eds.), *Clubs and Societies in Eighteenth-Century Ireland* (Dublin: FCP, 2010), pp. 315–31.

5   Cf. Lodge No. 20 (A), *Minutes*, 9 July 1753: 'Constituted after the Antient Manner and form of York Masons by the Master of No. 16'.

6   Unfortunately, given variations in spelling, streets in different parts of London with the same name, and partial or part-illegible addresses, the place of residence cannot be regarded as definitive. Where possible, street names and locations have been verified using contemporary data sources including W. Stow, *Remarks on London being an Exact Survey* (London, 1722); John Motley, *A Survey of London & Westminster* (London, 1753); Carrington Bowle, *Reduced Plan of London* (London, 1775); John Hinton, *New and Accurate plan of the cities of London and Westminster and Southwark* (London, 1761).

7   Lodge No. 20, *Minutes*, 2 December 1754.

8   Antients Grand Lodge *Minutes*, 7 August 1754.

9   Ibid., 17 September 1755.

10 The *General Register* numbered members by their date of joining. Any subsequent move to another lodge was recorded and numbered separately.

11 Frank McLynn, *Crime and Punishment in Eighteenth Century England* (Abingdon: Routledge, 1989), p. 5; McLynn was correct, *Burney* contains over 4,000 instances of attacks by footpads in the period 1740–80 alone.

12 Mirala, 'Masonic sociability and its limitations', 327–30.

13 Sarah Knott, review of James Livesey, *Civil Society and Empire: Ireland and Scotland in the Eighteenth Century Atlantic World* in *American Historical Review*, 115.2 (2010), 608–9.

14 'John Gillum (1698–1776), Will, proved at London, 2 June 1777 before William Compton, DL, for Sir George Hay, DL, of the Prerogative Court of Canterbury': http://www.natgould.org/will_of_john_gillum_1698–1776, accessed 10 May 2012.

15 Near Golden Lane, Barbican.

16 Written as 'Welto'.

17 Spitalfields.

18 Written as 'Boling Row'.

19 Resident at Mr Thomas Greenwood, Shoemakers.

20 Near Brick Lane, Old Street.

21 Near Goodman's Fields

22 Lodge No. 20 (Antients), *Visitors*.

23 W. J. Songhurst, 'Lodge No. 20, Antients', *Transactions* (London: QC, 1919), vol. 32, pp. 114–40.

24 Ibid.

25 Cf., www.measuringworth.com; also, www.nationalarchives.gov.uk/currency.

26 Lodge No. 20 (Antients), *Minutes*, 17 November 1755.

27 Grand Lodge of England *Minutes*, 24 October 1751.

28 Cf., R.F. Gould, *Atholl Lodges* (London: Spencer's Masonic Depot, 1879).

29 Cf., *List of Lodges*, Antients General Register.

30 Antients Grand Lodge *Minutes*, 2 October 1754.

31 A similar application to acquire a vacant lodge number was recorded on 1 December 1756, when a fee of 'one guinea towards the relief of distressed freemasons' was paid by the Master of lodge No. 54 to 'take rank as No. 12'.

32 Cowen is noted as having 'gone abroad' after April 1755.

33 Buss is shown as having been 'declared off' in 1754.

34 Enoch Lodge, Minute Book, 1770–1801.

35 The address is unclear in the minutes.

36 On 7 January 1771, Patrick Murphy was proposed as Master of the lodge for the ensuing half year and was installed on that day.

37 Excluded for non-attendance and non-payment of lodge dues.

38 Not minuted but cf., *Gazetteer and New Daily Advertiser*, 21 June 1774.

39 Not minuted but cf., *Public Advertiser*, 13 September 1763. Later of Petticoat Lane, Spitalfields: cf., *Whitehall Evening Post*, 22–24 March 1781.

40 Bearblock was Grand Secretary of the Antients, 1779–82.

41 The entry is referenced 'N1'.

42 The entry is referenced 'N2'.

43 The membership list is dated 1773. The first page contains 35 names, after which several pages are missing.

44 Antients Grand Lodge *Minutes*, 6 June 1759. St George's merged with Corner Stone Lodge (previously No. 63 of the Moderns) on 6 December 1843.

45 Lewis Namier, John Brooke (eds.), *The House of Commons 1754–1790* (London: Martin Secker & Warburg, 1984), p. 672.

46 Domestic service would, of course, remain a key component of national employment until the early twentieth century.

47 Cf., Daniel Defoe, *The Great Law of Subordination Considered* (London, 1724); also, E.P. Thompson, 'Patrician Society, Plebeian Culture', *Journal of Social History*, 7.4 (1974), 382–405.

CHAPTER THREE **The Antients'** *General Register*

1 'Town Spy' quoted in Carol Houlihan Flynn, 'Where the Wild Things Are: Guides to London's Transgressive Spaces', in Regina Hewitt and Pat Rogers (eds.), *Orthodoxy and Heresy in Eighteenth Century London* (Cranbury, N.J.: Associated UP, 2002), p. 37.

2 Anon., *A Trip through London: containing observations on Men and Things* (London, 1728), 8th edn.

3 Anon., *A second part of A view of London and Westminster: or, the town spy* (London, 1725).

4 Randolph Trumbach, *Sex and the Gender Revolution: Heterosexuality and the Third Gender in Enlightenment London* (Chicago, 1998), pp. 112–20.

5 Trumbach, *Sex and the Gender Revolution*, p. 121. Cf. also, Timothy Erwin, 'Parody and Prostitution', *Huntington Library Quarterly*, 68.4 (2005), 677–84.

6 Cf., *London Lives*, e.g., http://www.londonlives.org/browse.jsp?div=WCCD EP35826EP358260343; cf., also, maps generated at oldbaileyonlin.org, e.g. http://www.oldbailey online.org/maps.jsp?map=green&map_item_id= 7216.

7 *Reports from Committees, Fever, Ireland, Courts of Justice*; Session 27 January–10 June, 1818 (London: House of Commons Papers), vol. 7, p. 17.

8 Thomas Beames, *The Rookeries of London* (London: Frank Cass, 1852).

9 John Times, *Club Life of London* (London, 1866), p. 197.

10 Alexander Pope, *Sober Advice from Horace* (London, 1737).

11 Cf. John Mottley, *A history and survey of the cities of London and Westminster* (London, 1733–5), vol. 2, p. 756.

12 Ibid.

13 D.A. Kent, 'Ubiquitous but Invisible: Female Domestic Servants in Mid-Eighteenth Century London', *History Workshop*, 28 (1989), 111–28.

14 Isaac Maddox, Bishop of Worcester, *The Expediency of Preventive Wisdom, a Sermon* (London, 1750).

15 Kent, 'Ubiquitous but Invisible: Female Domestic Servants in Mid-Eighteenth Century London', 114.

16 Peter Clark, 'The 'Mother Gin' Controversy in the Early Eighteenth Century', *Transactions of the Royal Historical Society*, 5th series, 38 (1988), 63–84.

17 William Maitland, *The History and Survey of London from its Foundation to the Present* (London, 1756), 2 vol.s, ii, pp. 718–9, 735–6.

18 Clark, 'The 'Mother Gin' Controversy', 67.

19 *Daily Journal*, 18 December 1735.

20 Cf., among many examples, *Read's Weekly Journal Or British Gazetteer*, 14 June 1735 and 3 January 1736.

21 Old Bailey Proceedings, 2 July 1735. HUL, reference LL t17350702–42. Cf., also, *Daily Journal*, 7 July 1735.

22 John Strype, *A Survey of the Cities of London and Westminster* (London, 1720).

23 *British Medical Journal*, 2.664 (1873), 355.

24 Charles Dickens, *Sketches by Boz* (1839).

25 *Whitehall Evening Post or London Intelligencer*, 31 July 1760–2 August 1760.

26 *Lloyd's Evening Post*, 13–15 May 1765.

27 *London Morning Penny Post*, 7–9 August 1751.

28 Frederick Engels, *The Condition of the Working-Class in England in 1844* (London: Allen and Unwin, 1943), p. 27. Originally published 1887.

29 Also No.s 81 & 207.

30 Also No. 481.

31 Roger Swift, 'Heroes or Villains?: The Irish, Crime, and Disorder in Victorian England', *Albion*, 29.3 (1997), 408. It is possible that the belief in the widespread availability of poor relief was influenced by the Antients' support structure.

32 3&4 Will & Mar, c 11. The 1692 Act extended the Poor Relief Act of 1662 (14 Car 2 c 12). In general terms, the Poor Laws required a recipient to have lived in the parish for forty days without complaint; paid local rates and taxes; held a parish office for a year; served a full apprenticeship; or be employed for at least a year.

33 *St Martin's Pauper Examinations*, 1725–1773: Christopher Dallmange, examined 7 January 1740. *London Lives*: smdsset_112_58664, accessed 9 July 2012.

34 *Whitehall Evening Post or London Intelligencer*, 27–29 November 1750.

35 Cf., J.M. Feheney, 'Delinquency among Irish Catholic Children in Victorian London', *Irish Historical Studies*, 23.92 (1983), 319–29.

36 *London Daily Advertiser*, 22 January 1752.

37 *Read's Weekly Journal Or British Gazetteer*, 9 February 1751.

38 *Penny London Post or The Morning Advertiser*, 15–18 February 1751.

39 Also No. 360.

40 Mottley, *Survey*, vol. 2, pp. 770–5, passage from p. 774.

41 Wych Street.

42 Also No. 220.

43 Also No. 217.

44 St Mary Spital was erected in the twelfth century and demolished in the sixteenth following the reformation.

45   Phyllis Deane and W.A. Cole, *British Economic Growth, 1688–1959* (Cambridge: CUP, 1969), 2nd ed., pp. 98–104.
46   Ibid., 115–20.
47   A brewery owned by Thomas Bucknall occupied the site in 1669.
48   William Page (ed.), *A History of the County of Middlesex* (London: Victoria County History, 1911), vol. 2, pp. 168–78.
49   Ibid.
50   Walter Thornbury, *Old and New London* (London, 1878), vol. 2, pp. 149–152.
51   Also No. 115: moved to Mr Rottenbury's, Quaker Street, Spitalfields.
52   Also No. 116: moved to Mr Rottenbury's, Quaker Street, Spitalfields.
53   Also No. 427
54   Also No. 825.
55   Also No. 372
56   Also No. 423.
57   Also No. 592.
58   Beames, *The Rookeries of London*, pp. 94–6.
59   Berkeley Hill, 'Illustrations of the Working of the Contagious Diseases Act', *British Medical Journal*, 1.386 (1868), 505–6.
60   HL Sessional Papers, *Report from the Select Committee of the Health of Towns* (London, 1840), vol. XXVIII, pp. 244–8; p. v.
61   Also No. 567.
62   Alexander Pope, *The Dunciad with Notes* (London: Lawton Gilliver, 1729), book 1, pp. 55–6.
63   Ibid.
64   Quoted in Gordon Williams, *A Dictionary of Sexual language and Imagery in Shakespearian and Stuart Literature* (London: Athlone Press, 1994), vol. 1, p. 794.
65   *Read's Weekly Journal Or British Gazetteer*, 2 August 1755.
66   *London Chronicle*, 14–16 February 1758.
67   Surgeon.
68   Also No. 202.
69   Also No. 193.
70   Also No. 466.
71   Stow, *Survey of London*, Appendix.
72   Strype, *Survey*.
73   The Surrey gaol was replaced in 1791 by the Horsemonger Lane gaol to the south of Southwark at St George's Fields.
74   Probably the Marshalsea Tap House in Marshalsea Road, which was geographically closer to Borough than Southwark.
75   Also No. 376
76   G.H. Gater & F.R. Hiorns (eds.), *Survey of London* (London: English Heritage, 1940), vol. 20, pp. 95–100.
77   Mottley, *Survey*, vol. 2, pp. 664–5.
78   Ibid.
79   Gater & Hiorns, *Survey of London*, vol. 20, pp. 89–94.
80   Edward Walford, *Old and New London* (London: Centre for Metropolitan History, 1878), vol. 4, pp. 326–38.
81   Mottley, *Survey*, vol. 2, p. 666.
82   Ibid., p. 669. Cf. John Senex (rev'd), 'A Plan of the City's of London,

Westminster and Borough of Southwark, with the new additional buildings' (1720).

83 Mottley, *Survey*, vol. 2, p. 669–70

84 Ibid., p. 670.

85 Lodge No. 1 in Ireland was issued to Mitchelstown lodge in Cork by Lord Kingston (GMI) in 1731.

86 Dashwood has suggested that the warrant was held back until it could be signed by a member of the nobility. Cf., *QCA XI*, p. ix.

87 Constituted on 17 July 1751. Cf., also, W.J. Hughan, 'A Unique Engraved List of Lodges, 'Antients' A.D. 1753', *QCL Transactions* (1906), pp. 94–5.) Lodge numbers 3–6 were similarly constituted formally on 17 July 1751. Declared vacant 4 June 1783. Warrant later purchased by No. 32.

88 Constituted 7 July 1751.

89 Constituted 7 July 1751.

90 Constituted 17 July 1751.

91 Constituted 17 July 1751.

92 Constituted 29 July 1751; erased for disobedience 27 December 1752.

93 Formerly No. 8. Constituted 29 January 1752.

94 Formerly No. 9. Constituted 30 January 1752.

95 Formerly No. 11. Constituted 12 June 1752.

96 Constituted 5 February 1751; erased for disobedience 27 December 1752.

97 Formerly No. 12. Constituted 15 September 1752.

98 Formerly No. 13. Constituted 13 November 1752.

99 Formerly No. 14. Constituted 4 November 1752.

100 Formerly No. 15. Constituted 7 December 1752.

101 Formerly No. 16. Constituted 11 December 1752.

102 Constituted 9 January 1753.

103 Constituted 10 January 1753.

104 Constituted 4 May 1753.

105 Constituted 15 May 1753.

106 Constituted 9 July 1753.

107 Constituted 10 July 1753.

108 Constituted 12 July 1753.

109 Constituted 10 October 1753.

110 Constituted 17 October 1753.

111 Constituted 17 October 1753.

112 Constituted 8 November 1753.

113 Constituted 9 November 1753.

114 Constituted 15 November 1753.

115 Constituted 15 November 1753.

CHAPTER FOUR **London's Magistracy and the London Irish**

1 Berman, *Foundations*, chapter 3.

2 Nathaniel Blackerby, *The Speech of Nathanial Blackerby* (London, 1738), p. 18.

3 William Cowper, quoted in *Pasquin*, 17 January 1723.

4 There were of course exceptions. The Irish gentry and merchants, both Catholic and Protestant, employed Irish agents, brokers and parliamentary lobbyists in London. Many were highly effective and men such as Matthew Duane, Denis

Moloney and Peter Sexton became wealthy, influential and respected. Other Irish émigrés became prominent doctors and surgeons or were skilled in property conveyance, a branch of the legal profession heavily populated by Catholics.

5   Cf., Richard Kirkland, 'Reading the Rookery: The Social Meaning of an Irish Slum in Nineteenth Century London', *New Hibernia Review*, 16.1 (2012), 16–30.

6   *London Lives 1690–1810: Crime, Poverty and Social Policy in the Metropolis* at www.londonlives.org.

7   Ibid.

8   Adam Crymble, 'Identifying the Irish in electronic text: surname analysis and Irish defendants in the Old Bailey Online', *The London Irish in the Long Eighteenth Century* (conference: University of Warwick, 13 April 2012).

9   Cf. *House of Commons Parliamentary Papers, Judicial Statistics, England & Wales, 1858*, Part 1, pp. xxii–iiii, and *1859*, Part 1, p. xxv'; Irish prisoners represent over 13 per cent of the total prison population in 1858 and over 14 per cent in 1859. A prisoner's place of birth was recorded for the first time in 1857.

10 Swift, 'Heroes or Villains?: The Irish, Crime, and Disorder in Victorian England', 399–421.

11 Ibid., 399.

12 Flora Tristan, *Promenades dans Londres* (Paris, 1840), pp. 134–6.

13 *Old Bailey Proceedings Online*, 3 September 1740: LL ref.: t17400903-31; accessed 10 November, 2011.

14 Ibid., 15 October 1740: LL ref.: t17401015-10; accessed 10 November, 2011.

15 Ibid., LL ref.: t17460702-26; accessed 24 April 2012.

16 Ibid., LL ref.: t17520116-28: accessed 24 April 2012.

17 Ibid., LL ref.: t17550702-19: accessed 24 April 2012.

18 Cf. Grand Lodge of England *Minutes*, 23 July 1740, for an example of a charity petition rejected on the grounds of less than five years membership of a regular lodge.

19 Grand Lodge of England *Minutes*, 30 November 1752.

20 Cf., John Chamberlayne, *Magnae Britanniae* (1736), p. 160; *Daily Gazetteer*, 6 April 1738. Blackerby was appointed to the bench in 1719.

21 Nathaniel Blackerby, *The Speech of Nathanial Blackerby* (London, 1738), p. 18.

22 *Pasquin*, 17 January 1723.

23 William Cowper, *The Charge delivered . . .* (London, 1730), pp. 5–6.

24 *1723 Constitutions*, p. 50.

25 5 Eliz. c.4 (1562).

26 Cf., 7 Geo I st 1 c.13 (1720) and 12 Geo I c.34 (1725), which concern tailoring and the woollen trade, respectively. Other statutes include 9 Geo. I c.27 (1722); Geo. II c.36 (1729); 13 Geo. II c.8 (1740); 20 Geo. II c.19 (1747); and 22 Geo. II c.27 (1749). Employment legislation dealt both with employee breaches and at a granular level with trade regulation, including the terms of apprenticeships, setting wages, employee theft and embezzlement etc.

27 Douglas Hay, 'Paternalism, and Welfare: Masters, Workers and Magistrates in Eighteenth-Century England', *International Labor and Working-Class History*, 53 (1998), 27–48.

28 Cf., Marie Mulvey-Roberts, 'Hogarth on the Square: Framing the Freemasons', *Journal for Eighteenth Century Studies*, 26.2 (2003), 251–70. *Night*, the last

painting, later an engraving, in the series, *Four Times of the Day*, was completed in 1736 and published in 1738. Cf. also Sugden, 'Sir Thomas de Veil', *ODNB*.

29 Philip Sugden, 'Sir Thomas de Veil (1684–1746)', *ODNB*.

30 Ruth Paley (ed.), *Justice in eighteenth century Hackney: The Justicing notebook of Henry Norris* (London, 1991).

31 Ibid., pp. ix–xxxiii.

32 Ibid.

33 Ibid.

34 LMA: London and Westminster *Sessions' Papers*.

35 Paley, *Justice in eighteenth century Hackney*, pp. ix–xxxiii.

36 *Evening Journal*, 4 December 1727.

37 Nicholas Rogers, 'Money, Land and Lineage: The Big Bourgeoisie of Hanoverian London', *Social History*, 4.3 (1979), 437–54, esp. 448–9.

38 John Noorthouck, *A New History of London* (London, 1773), vol. I, pp. 889–93.

39 http//www.oldbaileyonline.org: *Proceedings of the Old Bailey*, 16 April 1740.

40 *London Evening Post*, 10–12 March 1737.

41 *Daily Journal*, 15 December 1721; *Weekly Journal or British Gazetteer*, 13 January 1722; *Evening Post*, 8 March 1722, et al.

42 London Lives: *Middlesex Sessions: Sessions Papers – Justices' Working Documents*: 31 March 1733. LL ref.: LMSMPS502900004.

43 Op. cit.

44 Ibid., pp. 75–94.

45 LMA, London.

46 Ibid.

CHAPTER FIVE An Age of Decline – English Grand Lodge, 1740–1751

1 The lodge was warranted in 1736 and had met initially at Lord Cardigan's Head at Charing Cross before transferring to Little Marlborough Street. The minutes can be found within the minute book of the Lodge of Friendship, No. 6, at the UGLE Library.

2 The lodge met at the King's Arms in the Strand from 1733 to 1742 and thereafter at the Cannon at Charing Cross (1742–6) and Bear & Rummer (1746–58).

3 The Royal Society, Sadler Archives: EC/1735/05: GB 117.

4 Martin Clare, *A Defence of Masonry* (London, 1730).

5 *Discourse* given by Clare to the Quarterly Communication of Grand Lodge on 11 December 1735.

6 Lodge of Friendship, No. 6, *Minutes*.

7 Corner Stone Lodge, *Minutes*, 1735–1748. Cf. St George's and Corner Stone Lodge, No. 5, *Minutes*.

8 Grand Lodge of England *Minutes*, 1740–58, pp. 164, 167 and 191. The other lodges were, respectively, the Rose Tavern in Cheapside, Three Kings in Spitalfields and St Paul's Head in Ludgate Street

9 Colin Dyer, *Grand Stewards' Lodge* (London, 1985), published privately, pp. 32–7.

10 Grand Lodge of England *Minutes*, 1740–58, p. 38.

11 *Daily Advertiser*, 15 April 1745.

12 *Daily Advertiser*, 25 April 1745.

13 *Daily Advertiser*, 5 May 1745.

14   *The Complete Freemason: or Multa Paucis for Lovers of Secrets* (London, 1764), p. 104.
15   1738 *Constitutions*, p. 117.
16   Ibid., p. 124.
17   Ibid., p. 125.
18   *Daily Post*, 22 January 1730.
19   1738 *Constitutions*, p. 125.
20   *London Evening Post*, 28 April 1737.
21   *Daily Advertiser*, 29 April 1737.
22   *London Daily Post*, 20 March 1741.
23   Cf., *Freemasons Magazine*, 1858.
24   *Whitehall Evening Post or London Intelligencer*, 30 April–2 May 1747. The event had not been held in public the prior year. The feast and parade had been cancelled with the excuse that 'many brethren, as well of the Nobility as others, [were] in Flanders and several retired into the country': Grand Lodge of England *Minutes*, 14 April 1746.
25   *London Evening Post*, 24 March 1747; the following edition, 28 March 1747, downgraded the fortune to £60,000.
26   *General Evening Post*, 7–9 June 1748.
27   *General Advertiser*, 30 October 1749. Two daughters were born in 1751 (died an infant) and 1755. All of Byron's children predeceased him.
28   *London Daily Post and General Advertiser*, 6 October 1743.
29   *General Evening Post*, 20 April 1745.
30   *London Evening Post*, 6 September 1746.
31   For example, *London Evening Post* 29 August 1752; 7 October 1752; and 19 July 1753.
32   *The Complete Freemason*, p. 105.
33   *General Advertiser*, 11 May 1747.
34   *General Advertiser*, 16 May 1747.
35   *General Advertiser*, 8 July 1747.
36   Chaworth had been a member of the lodge at the Wool Pack in Warwick. He appears in the lodge register as 'Cornet William Chaworth'.
37   Quoted in R.F. Gould (rev. Frederick Crowe), *The Concise History of Freemasonry* (London, 1951), p. 244.
38   Alphonse Cerza, *Anti-Masonry: Light on the Past and Present Opponents of Freemasonry* (Fulton, 1962), Appendix A, pp. 193–211.
39   *General Advertiser*, 21 August 1751.
40   Mulvey-Roberts, 'Hogarth on the Square: Framing the Freemasons', 251–70.
41   *The Complete Freemason*, p. 105.
42   Cf. Grand Lodge of England *Minutes*, 1740–58, p. 61, fn. (d).

CHAPTER SIX **Masonic Misrule, Continued**

1   The name is spelt variously as 'ffotherley', 'Fotherley' or 'Fotherby'.
2   Grand Lodge of England *Minutes*, 1723–39, pp. 234–5.
3   Ibid., pp. 249–50.
4   Ibid., p. 230.
5   Ibid., p. 229. The petition was presented in May 1733.
6   British Library, Add. MS. 23202.
7   Cf. Andrew Pink, 'A music club for freemasons: *Philo-musicae et -architecturae*

societas Apollini, London, 1725–1727', *Early Music*, 38.4 (2010), 523–36, published on-line 30 September 2010.

8 Grand Lodge of England *Minutes*, 21 November 1724.

9 Those named by Grand Lodge represented a fraction of those at *Philo-Musicae* known to have been members of other masonic lodges.

10 William Jones was initiated on 22 December 1724. It is possible but, in the author's view, not probable that the William Jones of *Philo-Musicae* was not the same person as William Jones, the mathematician, a member of the Vine Tavern lodge in Holborn and Senior Warden of the Queen's Head, Hollis Street. Andrew Pink has posed a counter argument.

11 Knevit was from a prosperous landed family of Buckenham Castle, Norfolk.

12 *Daily Post*, 11 October 1729.

13 Grand Lodge of England *Minutes*, 1723–39, p. 40.

14 Francesco Geminiani (1687–1762), trained under Alessandro Scarlatti and Carlo Abrogio. His patrons in London included William Capel, 3rd earl of Essex, and George I, for whom he first played in 1715.

15 Bedford was a riding master based in Windmill Street north of Piccadilly. Cf. *Evening Post*, 6–8 October 1726. Thomas Harbin was a bookseller and stationer with premises at New Exchange on the Strand. He was initiated in September 1721 at the Cheshire Cheese in Arundel Street by John Beale, DGM under the Duke of Montagu. Cf., *Applebee's Original Weekly Journal*, 9 September 1721.

16 Hordern, a vintner, was based at Watling Street in the City. The *London Gazette*, 29 July–2 August 1729, recorded that he became insolvent and applied for relief in 1729.

17 Andrew Pink, *The Musical Culture of Freemasonry in Early Eighteenth-century London* (London: Goldsmith's College, 2007), unpublished PhD Thesis, Appendix 7, pp. 319–23.

18 Gould, *History of Freemasonry Throughout the World*, p. 81.

19 Pink, *The Musical Culture of Freemasonry*, Appendix 5, pp. 312–17.

20 Rawlinson was appointed a Grand Steward in 1733, the same year as Fotherley Baker, and in the 1730s was master of the lodge at the Oxford Arms in Ludgate Street and a member of three others. Although Rawlinson was characterised as an 'opposer of our established religion' and 'abuser of the present government', he was also held in sufficient esteem to be elected a Vice President of the Society of Antiquaries under Martin Folkes' Presidency as late as 1753 and at his death laudatory obituaries described him as the 'Worshipful and Learned Dr Rawlinson'. Cf., *Public Advertiser*, 8 April and 21 April 1755.

21 They included William Gulston, Coort Knevit, William Jones, Papillon Ball, Joseph Murden, William Grant, Richard Mason, Richard Cock, Joseph Samson, Fotherley Baker and John Revis.

22 Grand Lodge of England *Minutes*, 1723–39, p. 251.

23 Grand Lodge of England *Minutes*, 1723–39, p. 314.

24 *London Evening Post*, 24–26 February 1741. Cf. also *Daily Gazetteer*, 25 February 1741; and *Weekly Miscellany*, 28 February 1741.

25 Bishop Burnet, *History of His Own Time* (London: Thomas Ward, 1723), vol. 1. Also, *Daily Courant*, 14 February 1724.

26 *London Gazette*, 14–17 June 1740.

27 Joseph Reddington (ed.), *Calendar of Treasury Papers, 1720–1728* (London: IHR, 1889), vol. 233, *12 January–31 March 1721*, p. 41. Cf. also, William A

Shaw (ed.), *Calendar of Treasury Papers, 1696–1697* (London: IHR, 1933), vol. 11, *27 November 1696*, p. 322. *Post Man and the Historical Account*, 26–28 June 1707.

28 *Universal Spectator and Weekly Journal*, 24 October 1741. The *London Morning Advertiser*, 23 October 1741, noted that his election was by 39 votes to 34, and that he stood against a Mr Deputy Kenyon. The senior twelve livery companies in order of precedence are known as the 'Great Twelve'. The Haberdashers' Company ranks eighth.

29 Cf. *Daily Gazetteer*, 21 October 1741; *London Evening Post*, 20–22 October 1741; and *London Morning Advertiser*, 23 October 1741.

30 Grand Lodge of England *Minutes*, 1740–58, p. 25.

31 I am indebted to the archivist of the Drapers' Company for this information, *5 September 2011*.

32 Information provided by David Bartle, Archivist, The Haberdashers' Company, 23 August 2011.

33 Baker's death was reported in the *London Evening Post*, 9–11 May 1754. Cf. for example, *London Daily Advertiser and Literary Gazette*, 3 May 1751 and *London Evening Post*, 9–11 January 1753.

34 *Daily Post*, 14 November 1737.

35 Noorthouck, *A New History of London*, pp. 894–7; cf. also *Evening Post*, 31 January 1721–2 February 1721.

36 *Evening Post*, 23–25 July 1724.

37 *Daily Courant*, 15 September 1729; *Monthly Chronicle*, October 1729; also Noorthouck, *A New History of London*, Addenda: The Mayors and Sheriffs of London, pp. 889–93.

38 *City of London Sessions Papers*, LMA.

39 Tim Hitchcock, 'Review of J.M.Beattie's *Policing and Punishment in London, 1660–1750* (New York: OUP, 2001)', *Albion*, 35.1 (2003), 127–9.

40 *Post Boy*, 26–28 January 1721. *Evening Post*, 18–20 June 1723.

41 The London Infirmary, renamed the London Hospital in 1748, was first located at a house in Featherstone Street in Moorfields in November 1740. In May the following year, the hospital moved to rented premises in Prescot Street, near the Tower of London, where it remained until 1757. It was the forerunner of the Royal London Hospital, renamed in 1990, its 250th anniversary year. Cf. Edward Morris, *A History of the London Hospital* (London: E. Arnold, 1910) 2nd ed., pp. 25–6.

42 *An Account of the Rise, Progress and State of the London Infirmary* (London, 1742), p. 11.

43 Grand Lodge of England *Minutes*, 15 April 1736. Cf. also, *London Daily Post and General Advertiser*, 11 March 1743. Thomas Boehm was also a director of the London Assurance Corporation (cf., *Daily Gazetteer*, 10 July 1741) and a governor of the Corporation for the Relief of Seamen in the Merchant Service.

44 London Infirmary, *Annual Account of Receipts and Payments, 1742–9*.

45 Morris, *A History of the London Hospital*, p. 293.

46 Isaac, Lord Bishop of Worcester, *A Sermon Preached before His Grace, Charles, Duke of Richmond* (London: J. Brotherton & J. Stagg, 1744).

47 *London Daily Post and General Advertiser*, 11 March 1743; *London Evening Post*, 17–19 March 1743; *Daily Advertiser*, 22 March 1743.

48 Cf. Bishop of Worcester, *A Sermon Preached before His Grace, Charles, Duke of Richmond*, pp. 32–8: a 'List of Governors and Contributors to the London

Infirmary'. Cf. also, the 'List of Governors and Contributors' contained in the *Sermon* published in 1745 and 1747, respectively.

49 *General Advertiser*, 28 April 1744; 9 May 1746; 18 May 1747; 28 April 1749; 28 June 1751; 15 May 1752; and *London Evening Post*, 26–28 June 1750.

50 The *General Advertiser*, 2 April 1747, notes Lowther's contribution of £50 at the Anniversary Feast that year.

51 J.V. Beckett, 'Lowther, Sir James, fourth baronet (*bap*. 1673, *d*. 1755)', rev. *ODNB* (Oxford: OUP, 2004; accessed 27 Sept 2011). In his closet at his death were bank notes to the amount of £30,000 'which not being mentioned in his Will, are supposed to have escaped his recollection': *Whitehall Evening Post or London Intelligencer*, 1–4 February 1755. Cf. also, obituary in *Public Advertiser*, 4 January 1755.

52 Peter Du Cane was descended from Jean du Quesne, a Flemish Huguenot who had migrated to England in the 1560s. The family were merchants and bankers and included John Houblon, the first governor of the Bank of England, later Lord Mayor of London, and James, his brother, an MP and director of both the Bank of England and the Hon East India Company. Cf. also, *London Daily Post and General Advertiser*, 6 January 1743; and *General Advertiser*, 14 March 1746.

53 Du Cane rented 14 St James's Square from 1749–1767 in preference to his townhouse in St Pancras. Cf. F.H.W. Sheppard (ed.), *Survey of London* (London: IHR, 1960), vols 29 & 30, pp. 139–42.

54 *London Evening Post*, 27 March 1735–29 March 1735. Peter Du Cane, his wife and their children were painted in 1747 by Arthur Devis (1712–87) in a triptych, now at the Harris Museum in Preston, Lancashire.

55 *A List of the Members of the Corporation of the Amicable Society for a Perpetual Assurance* (London, 1730).

56 The Amicable's constitution limited directors to a maximum three-year term. Most served for three years, resigned and were reappointed a year later. It was a common practice.

57 Martin Clare was also a member. Cf., *General Advertiser*, 11 July 1752.

58 *Whitehall Evening Post or London Intelligencer*, 5–7 May 1747.

59 Aviva Archives, Norwich, Norfolk. Lists of directors sworn in at the Annual General Meeting of the Society: NU 2343 & 2344: *Amicable Society Order of Court Book, 21 August 1735–20 September 1743*; and *Amicable Society Directors Minute Book 22 September 1743–15 January 1755*.

60 The Amicable allowed each person on whom an assurance had been put in place to have one or more shares in the Society and to become a member either for his own benefit and that of his estate or on behalf of the contributor paying the premiums: 'Corporation of the Amicable Society for a Perpetual Assurance Office (on Lives): (plan, tables and rules)', *LSE Selected Pamphlets* (1844).

61 The Amicable remained an independent mutual company until 1886, when an act of parliament authorised its merger with the Norwich Union Life Insurance Society; the resulting company was the Norwich Union, now Aviva.

62 W. Whiston, *An Account of the Past and Present State of the Amicable Society for a Perpetual Assurance Office; With the Occasions of the low Condition it is now in; and Proposals in Order to recover its former Prosperity* (London, 1732). Probably William Whiston (1667–1752), the mathematician and former Lucasian professor at Cambridge, later expelled for religious heterodoxy.

63   Cf., among many press reports and advertisements, *Evening Post*, 11 August 1730.

64   *A short account of the rise and present state of the Amicable Society for a Perpetual Assurance-Office* (London, 1742).

65   Geoffrey Clark, 'Life insurance in the society and culture of London, 1700–75', *Urban History*, 24 (1997), pp. 17–36.

66   Ibid.

67   *A List of the Members of the Corporation of the Amicable Society.*

68   Gary Salzman, 'Murder, Wagering, and Insurable Interest in Life Insurance', *Journal of Insurance*, 30.4 (1963), 555–62.

69   Life Assurance Act 1774 (14 Geo 3 c.48, also known as the Gambling Act, 1774).

70   *Whitehall Evening Post or London Intelligencer*, 1–4 August 1747.

71   Philip Yonge, *A sermon preached before his Grace George, Duke of Marlborough* (London, 1764), p. 1; and *General Advertiser*, 8 March 1750.

72   *General Advertiser*, 19 October 1751; and *Read's Weekly Journal Or British Gazetteer*, 28 March 1752.

73   *A General Abstract of Receipts and Disbursements, from the first institution of the Small Pox Hospital, 26 September 1746 to 24 March 1763.*

74   *London Daily Advertiser*, 6 March 1752; and *The London Magazine; or Gentleman's monthly intelligencer* (London: J. Wiford, 1752), vol. 21.

75   *General Advertiser*, 15 February 1752.

76   Ibid.

77   *London Daily Advertiser*, 6 March 1752.

78   *The London Magazine; or Gentleman's monthly intelligencer*, vol. 21.

79   Brudenell was invested KG in 1752 and created 1st duke of Montagu in 1766. He had assumed the name Montagu on his father-in-law's death in 1749.

80   Parker was President of the Royal Society from 1752–64, succeeding Martin Folkes. He was a member of the lodge at the Swan in Chichester, most probably at the invitation of the duke of Richmond.

81   Beauchamp had been created a baronet in 1745; he changed his name by Act of Parliament to 'Beauchamp-Proctor' after inheriting the Langley Park estate in Norfolk from his maternal uncle.

82   Lesley Richmond & Alison Turton (eds.), *The Brewing Industry: a guide to historical records* (Manchester: MUP, 1990), p. 104.

83   *London Evening Post*, 25–27 April 1732; also *The Gentleman's Magazine*, 22 October 1733, and *Daily Courant*, 29 October 1733.

84   Mendes was one of the first Jewish freemasons, a member of the lodge at Braund's Head in New Bond Street and appointed a Grand Steward in 1738: cf., Thomas N. McGeary, 'Moses Mendez (1690?–1758)', *ODNB* (Oxford: OUP, 2004; online ed. Jan. 2008). Mendes purchased estates in Norfolk and Surrey before becoming a poet and dramatist. A relative, Solomon Mendes, was a member of the lodge at Daniel's Coffee House in Lombard Street and a Grand Steward in 1732.

85   *Public Advertiser*, 17 February 1753. He appears in the register of St Michael's Church, Cornhill, having been baptised on 13 December 1719.

86   *London Daily Advertiser*, 3 March 1753.

87   *Public Advertiser*, 5 April 1754.

88   Grand Lodge of England *Minutes*, 6 April 1738.

89   Ibid., 28 June 1738.

90 John Lane, *Masonic Records, 1717–1894* (London: UGLE, 1895), 2nd edn. (rev.). Published online (Sheffield: HRI, 2011) version 1.0: http://www.hrionline.ac.uk/lane.

91 *London Evening Post*, 12–14 June 1729; *Daily Post*, 14 June 1729; et al.

92 William A. Shaw and F. H. Slingsby (eds),'Declared Accounts: Post Office', *Calendar of Treasury books, Volume 32: 1718* (IHR, 1962), p. ccclv.

93 John Chamberlayne, *Magnæ Britanniæ notitia: or, the present state of Great Britain* (London: B. & S. Tooke et al., 1723), part II, p. 524.

94 *Read's Weekly Journal Or British Gazetteer*, 29 September 1733. The legacy would have been worth around £2 million in current money.

95 *Grub Street Journal*, 6 June 1734.

96 *Weekly Miscellany*, 15 January 1737; and John Chamberlayne, *Magnæ Britanniæ notitia: or, the present state of Great Britain* (London: D. Midwinter et al., 1741), part II, p. 82.

97 For example, *London Daily Post and General Advertiser*, 7 September 1738; *Daily Gazetteer*, 11 September 1738. There were upwards of sixty such announcements over the next three years. Also cf. Middlesex Sessions: Justices' Working Documents – deposition on 1 October 1737; and signature appended to affidavit 13 October 1737. Cf. also, City of London Sessions: Justices' Working Documents – signature on deposition at Justice Hall in the Old Bailey, 4 September 1746; and 15 October 1746.

98 *Whitehall Evening Post or London Intelligencer*, 9–11 June 1747.

99 *London Evening Post*, 6–8 June 1751; *General Advertiser*, 7 June 1751.

100 *Whitehall Evening Post or London Intelligencer*, 1–3 October 1747. Also, *Penny London Post or The Morning Advertiser*, 2–5 October 1747. The position of Receiver General was regarded as of equal status to that of Accountant General.

101 *Daily Gazetteer*, 1 October 1744. The thoroughfare remains best known for 'oranges and lemons, ring the bells of St Clement's'.

102 Stow, *Remarks on London*, pp. 130–1.

103 Parliamentary Archives, London: *Private Act*, 24 George II, c. 40 HL/ PO/PB/1/1750/24G2n99 *1750*.

104 *London Gazette*, 9 July 1757, et al.

105 *General Advertiser*, 16 March 1749.

106 Bridewell Royal Hospital, *Minutes of the Court of Governors*, 12 July 1746.

107 Aviva Archives, op. cit. Cf. also, *Whitehall Evening Post or London Intelligencer*, 5–7 May 1747; and *London Daily Advertiser*, 1 May 1752.

108 Cf., *An Account of the . . . London Infirmary* (London, 1742), p. 12; also, *Alexander's feast . . . set to music by Mr Handel* (London: J. & R. Thomson, 1753), p. 22; *A Sermon Preached before the governors of the London Infirmary* (London: London Infirmary, 1743), p. 34; and *London Evening Post*, 18–21 July 1752.

109 *General Advertiser*, 19 May 1750.

110 From 1741, the office of Treasurer had become elective by those attending the Quarterly Communication. Adopting what had been the position in practice, the Treasurer, Secretary and Sword Bearer were declared automatic members of every meeting of Grand Lodge.

111 It is possible that Jesse was a Huguenot, a group represented disproportionately among freemasons. The surname was relatively common both in the Low Countries and France, where the family may have descended from 'de Jessé

Lévas' who emigrated from Languedoc to England after the revocation of the edict of Nantes. The Huguenot connection is supported by contemporary records, including an 'Abraham Jesse' in William and Susan Minet (eds.), *Register of Churches of the Tabernacle, Glasshouse Street and Leicester Fields, 1688–1783* (London: Huguenot Society, 1926), vol. XXIX, p. 100.

112 Grand Lodge of England *Minutes*, 1723–39, p. 19.

113 Ibid., p. 35.

114 Ibid., p. 92.

115 Ibid., p. 208.

116 His father's will was proved at probate on 22 May 1703.

117 Westminster Poll Books, 1749.

118 *St James's Chronicle or the British Evening Post*, 3 September 1765–5 September 1765. His will was proved at the Prerogative Court of Canterbury on 17 September 1765.

119 *Gazetteer and New Daily Advertiser*, 5 September 1765. Other notices appeared in the *Public Advertiser*, 5 September 1765 and *St James's Chronicle*, 3 September 1765.

120 John Revis, registered charity number 206841: 'almshouses for the needy, single men and women who are not less than fifty-five years of age resident in . . . Newport Pagnell'. Cf., also, William Page (ed.), *A History of the County of Buckinghamshire* (London: IHR, 1927), vol. 4, pp. 409–22.

121 Frederick William Bull, *A History of Newport Pagnell* (Kettering: W.E. & J. Goss, 1990), pp. 261–5.

122 Grand Lodge of England *Minutes*, 18 June 1752.

123 George Eccleshall, *A History of the Old King's Arms Lodge, 1725–2000* (London: published privately, 2001) *Appendix*. No source is stated.

124 Eccleshall, *History*, p. 11.

CHAPTER SEVEN **The King's Arms Lodge**

1   Weymouth (1710–1751), inherited his title and the Longleat estate in 1714, together with extensive estates in Dorset, Gloucestershire and Wiltshire.

2   Clare and Wray joined in 1730.

3   Payne sat as acting Grand Master in 1746.

4   Eccleshall, *History*, p. 23.

5   Ibid., p. 13.

6   Ibid., p. 33.

7   Edward Oakley, 'Speech at the Carpenter's Arms, Silver Street, 31 December 1728', in Benjamin Cole, *Constitutions* (London, 1731), 2nd ed., pp. 25–34.

8   OKA *Minutes*, 6 August 1733.

9   Eccleshall, *History*, p. 20.

10 Cf. Berman, *Foundations*, esp. chapters 2 & 6.

11 Martin Clare, *Youth's introduction to Trade and Business* (London, 1720).

12 F.H.W. Sheppard (gen ed.), *Survey of London* (London, 1966), vol. 33, *No. 8 Soho Square*, pp. 60–1.

13 Martin Clare, *Motion in Fluids, Natural and Artificial* (London: Edward Symon, 1735).

14 Ibid., *Advertisement*.

15 Clare's *Discourse* was given to the Quarterly Communication of Grand Lodge on 11 December 1735.

16 OKA *Minutes*, 11 March 1734.

17 Ibid., 1 April 1734. The custom of new members paying for dinner and otherwise defraying lodge costs was part of a tradition that dated back to the mediaeval guilds. Cf. Berman, *Foundations*, pp. 21–5 et al.

18 Ibid., 5 May 1735. That the OKA rules contradicted Grand Lodge's Regulation VI, which demanded the unanimous consent of 'all the members of that lodge then present', is self-evident.

19 Constituted on 28 March 1732.

20 Weymouth did not attend Grand Lodge as GM other than at his installation; John Ward (DGM) deputised.

21 He was created 1st viscount Dudley and Ward in 1763.

22 Cf., among several reports, *Universal Spectator and Weekly Journal*, 5 January 1745.

23 *Weekly Journal or British Gazetteer*, 17 February 1728. Ward's father, William, had been MP for Staffordshire from 1710 to 1713 and again in 1715 until his death.

24 *London Gazette*, 20 January 1730; *Annual Register for the Year 1774* (London, 1801), 6th edn., p. 192.

25 *Flying Post or The Weekly Medley*, 12 July 1729.

26 Cf. Paul Langford, 'William Pitt and Public Opinion, 1757', *English Historical Review*, 88.346 (1973), 54–80, esp. 63.

27 Quote from R. Sedgwick (ed.), *The History of Parliament: the House of Commons, 1715–1745* (London, 1970): online at www.historyofparliamentonline.org/volume/1715–1754/member/ward-john-1704-74, accessed 12 August 2012.

28 *Journals of the House of Commons*, Seventh Parliament of Great Britain: 6th session, p. 155, *18 May 1733*.

29 Cf. for example, *Journals of the House of Lords*, Ninth Parliament of Great Britain: 3rd session, p. 464, *21 March 1744*; 5th session, p. 51, *24 February 1747*; 6th session, p. 93, *3 April 1747*; Tenth Parliament of Great Britain: 1st session, p. 220, *26 April 1748*; and General Index, vols XX–XXXV, p. 855.

30 Cf., T.J. Raybould, 'The Development and Organization of Lord Dudley's Mineral Estates, 1774–1845', *Economic History Review*, 21.3 ns (1968), 529–44.

31 Cf., George J. Barnaby, 'Review – The Economic Emergence of the Black Country by T.J. Raybould', *Economic History Review*, 27.3 n.s. (1974), 475–6.

32 He had held an interest in land elsewhere on the Grosvenor estate since 1737.

33 F.H.W. Sheppard, *Survey of London* (London: English Heritage, 1980), vol. 40, pp. 210–21. The new building was constructed on land to the rear of numbers 30–36 Upper Brook Street.

34 *Daily Post*, 2 January 1730.

35 Cf. for example, *British Journal*, 11 June 1726.

36 Sackler Archives.

37 He became a licentiate of the RCP in 1740; the College's archives confirm his deposit of a £50 surety to observe its statutes, by-laws and orders etc.: RCP, London, RCP-LEGAC/ENV 67, *3 September 1740*.

38 For example, *St James's Evening Post*, 22–24 March 1733.

39 Ibid.

40   Cf., Sackler Archives, EC/1732/12; also *An Account of the proceedings of the Governors of St George's Hospital* (London, 1733).

41   Cf. William Giffard, rev. Edward Hody, *Cases in Midwifery* (London: William Hody, 1734).

CHAPTER EIGHT   **The Anglo-Irish: Ascendancy and Alienation**

1   The Acts of Union with Scotland in 1707 joined the kingdoms of England and Scotland to create the single kingdom of Great Britain. Ireland remained a separate kingdom, albeit under the same monarch as England, then Great Britain, until the Acts of Union in 1800 gave rise to the United Kingdom of Great Britain and Ireland.

2   An 'Act for the more effectual preventing his Majesty's Subjects from entering into Foreign Service' ending foreign military recruitment in Ireland was passed in 1745 at the time of the second Jacobite scare: 19 George II, c. 7. Before 1745, government policy swung between encouraging and prohibiting recruitment for service overseas partly as a function of Anglo French relations.

3   In the 1690s, the Irish contingent in the French army comprised ten regiments of foot, two of horse and two horse troops under the command of the exiled James II, together with three regiments in Lord Mouncashel's brigade, the latter being under direct French command. The total strength was c. 18,000 men. A database of Irish nationals who served in the French army is maintained at the National University of Ireland. Cf. *The Irish in Europe Project, Irish Regiments in France Database*: www.irishineurope.com/about/research/irish-regiments-france. Cf., also, J.C. Callaghan, *History of the Irish Brigades in the service of France* (Glasgow: Cameron & Ferguson, 1885).

4   Basil Williams, *The Whig Supremacy, 1714–1761* (Oxford: OUP, 1997), 2nd edn., p. 291.

5   Sean McCann, *The Fighting Irish* (London, 1972); Maurice Hennessey, *The Wild Geese: The Irish Soldier in Exile* (London, 1973). Also cf., Peter Kartsen, 'Irish Soldiers in the British Army, 1792–1922: Suborned or Subordinate?', *Journal of Social History*, 17.1 (1983), 31–64.

6   Cf., *Evening Post*, 10–12 March 1726; *Daily Post*, 29 April 1726; and *Daily Journal*, 4 June 1726.

7   Until 1728, Catholics of sufficient affluence retained the franchise and Catholic peers who had taken a loyal oath of allegiance were permitted to sit in the Irish House of Lords. Cf. 'Disenfranchising Act (Ireland)' (1727).

8   Cf., for example, 'An Act to prevent Papists being Solicitors': 10 Will. III c.13 (1698); and 'An Act to Restrain Foreign Education': 7 Will. III c.4 (1695).

9   'An Act to prevent Protestants intermarrying with Papists': 9. Will III c. 3 (1697).

10   'An Act for the better securing the government, by disarming papists': 7 Will III c.5 (1695).

11   Sunderland and Townshend remained in England for the entire period of their respective lord lieutenancies.

12   10 Henry VII c.22.

13   Poynings' Law was not repealed until 1782.

14   Cf. James Kelly, *Poynings' Law and the Making of Laws in Ireland, 1660–1800* (Dublin: FCP, 2007).

15 A.T.Q. Stewart, *A Deeper Silence: Hidden Origins of the United Irishmen* (London: Faber & Faber, 1993), p. 27.

16 'An Act to prevent the Exportation of Wool out of the Kingdoms of Ireland and England into Foreign Parts and for the Encouragement of the Woollen Manufactures in the Kingdom of England': 11 Will III c.13 (1699). The quoted text is from the Act's preamble.

17 Louis M. Cullen, *Anglo-Irish Trade, 1660–1800* (Manchester: MUP, 1968).

18 F.G. James, 'Irish Smuggling in the Eighteenth Century', *Irish Historical Studies*, 12.48 (1961), 299–317.

19 Ibid., 311–12.

20 Cf., 3 Geo. II c.2, 5 Geo. II c.1 & c.2, 7 Geo. II c.2 & c.7, 9 Geo. II c.2 et al.; also, among many examples, cf. 12 Geo. I c.7 (1725) and 7 Geo. II c.11 (1737); 1 Geo. II c.16 (1727); 15 Geo. II c.1 (1741); and 21 Geo. II c.1 & c.2 (1747).

21 Examples include iron, paper and glass manufacture, all of which were restricted until later in the eighteenth century.

22 6. Geo. I c.5.

23 David Dickinson, *Arctic Ireland: the Extraordinary Story of the Great Frost and Forgotten Famine of 1740–41* (Belfast: White Row Press, 1997).

24 William Molyneux, *The Case of Ireland's being Bound by Acts of Parliament in England, Stated* (Dublin: Joseph Ray, 1698).

25 Anonymous, *An Inquiry into Some of the Causes of the Ill Situation of the Affairs of the Irish* (Dublin: George Grierson, 1731), p. 7.

26 The Hibernian Patriot [Jonathan Swift], *A Collection of the Drapier's Letters to the People of Ireland* (Dublin: A. Moor, 1730), pp. B 2–3.

27 Anonymous, *An Inquiry*, p. 9.

28 Ibid.

29 John Cary, *An Essay on the State of England in relation to its trade, its poor and its taxes* (Bristol, 1695).

30 Ibid.

31 Indeed, even Jacobites were loyal to the crown of the three kingdoms – albeit with a different king.

32 Charles Davenant, *An Essay upon Ways and Means of Supplying the War* (London, 1695), p. 82.

33 William Connolly to the duke of Grafton, 18 October 1720, quoted in Patrick Walsh, '"The Sin of With-Holding Tribute", contemporary pamphlets and the professionalisation of the Irish Revenue Service in the early eighteenth century', *Eighteenth-Century Ireland/Iris an dá chultúr*, 21 (2006), 48–65.

34 Cf. A.P.W. Malcolmson, *Nathaniel Clements: Government & the Governing Elite in Ireland* (Dublin: FCP, 2005); also, Alice E. Murray, *A History of the Commercial & Financial Relations between England & Ireland from the Period of the Restoration* (New York: Burt Franklin, 1970), reprint, first published 1903.

35 Cf. Curtis Nettels, 'The Menace of Colonial Manufacturing 1690–1720', *New England Quarterly*, 4.2 (1931), 230–69, esp. 235–8.

36 Toby Barnard, *Improving Ireland?* (Dublin: FCP, 2008), p. 123.

37 Anonymous, *An Inquiry*, p. 3.

38 Kelly, *Poynings' Law*, p. 157.

39 Arthur Dobbs, *An Essay on the Trade and Improvement of Ireland* (Dublin: J. Smith & W. Bruce, 1729), p. 3.

40 Ibid., p. 2.

41 Ibid., p. 3.

42 Ibid., pp. 27–8.

43 Jonathan Swift, *Travels into the Several Remote Nations of the World by Lemuel Gulliver* (London: Benj. Motte, 1726), vol. 1, part II, p. 35.

44 Swift, *A Letter to the Whole People of Ireland* (Dublin: Harding, 1724). Cf. commentary in Temple Scott (ed.), *The Prose Works of Jonathan Swift* (London: Bell, 1903), vol. VI, 'The Drapier's Letters', letter IV.

45 Earl of Egmont, *Diary of the 1ˢᵗ earl of Egmont* (London: HMSO, 1923), vol. 2, p. 27.

46 Cf. Richard Stone, *Some British Empiricists in the Social Sciences, 1650–1900* (Cambridge: CUP, 1997), pp. 71–115, who categorised King as 'the first great economic statistician'. The quote is from the *Prologue*, p. xxii.

47 Cf., Gregory King, *Natural and Political Observations and Conclusions upon the State and Condition of England* (London, 1696).

48 Charles Davenant, *An Essay upon Ways and Means of Supplying the War* (London, 1695).

49 Ibid., p. 82.

50 Charles Davenant, *The Political and Commercial Works of Charles D'Avenants*, collected and revised by Sir Charles Whitworth (London, 1771), vol. II (of five), esp. p. 102.

51 Davenant, *An Essay on the East-India Trade* (London, 1696); *A clear demonstration, from points of fact, that the recovery, preservation and improvement of Britain's share of the trade to Africa* (London, 1709); *Reflections upon the constitution and management of the trade to Africa* (London, 1709); and *An account of the trade between Great-Britain, France, Holland, Spain, Portugal, Italy, Africa, Newfoundland* (London, 1715). *An Essay on the East-India Trade* was written when Davenant was seeking employment with the Company.

52 Davenant, *Political and Commercial Works*, vol. I, p. 354.

53 Julian Hoppit, 'Charles Davenant', *ODNB* (Oxford: OUP, 2004; online edn, May 2006, accessed 29 Oct. 2011).

54 Davenant, *Political and Commercial Works*, vol. II, p. 236.

55 Ibid.

56 Ibid.

57 Ibid., p. 237.

58 Cf., in particular, James Livesey, 'The Dublin Society in Eighteenth Century Political Thought', *Historical Journal*, 47.3 (2004), 615–40.

59 Quoted in Sarah Foster, 'Buying Irish: Consumer Nationalism in Eighteenth Century Dublin', *History Today*, 47.6 (1997).

60 'Irish manufacture – A New Ballad', quoted in Henry Grattan, *Memoirs of the Life and Times of Henry Grattan* (London: Henry Colburn, 1839), vol. 2, p. 136.

61 J.C.D. Clark, 'Whig Tactics and Parliamentary Precedent: The English Management of Irish Politics, 1754–1756', *Historical Journal*, 21.2 (1978), 275–301.

62 Cf. Thomas Bartlett (review), 'A New History of Ireland', *Past and Present*, 116 (1987), 206–19.

63 Jacqueline Hill, 'Allegories, Fictions, and Feigned Representations: Decoding the Money Bill Dispute, 1752–6' *Eighteenth-Century Ireland*, 21 (2006), 66–88.

64 Cf. Robert Munter, *The History of the Irish Newspaper 1685–1760* (Cambridge: CUP, 1967).

65 Anonymous [Rev. Peter Bristow], *Honesty the Best Policy or, the History of Roger* (London, Dublin: T. Freeman, 1752).

66 J.C. Beckett, 'Anglo-Irish Constitutional Relations in the Later Eighteenth Century', *Irish Historical Studies*, 14.53 (1964), 20–38. Beckett (23) gives an example in December 1773: Harcourt to Rochford, 30 December 1773 (*Calendar of Home Office Papers, 1773–5*, 121–3), where reference is made to earlier instances.

67 Ibid., 21.

68 Pitt to Rutland, 6 January 1785, in William Pitt, *Correspondence between William Pitt and Charles, Duke of Rutland, 1781–1787* (Edinburgh: W. Blackwood, 1890), pp. 72–3.

69 Ibid., pp. 87–8.

70 Cf., Beckett, 'Anglo-Irish Constitutional Relations in the Later Eighteenth Century'.

71 'Union with Ireland Act, 1800' (39 & 40 Geo. III c.67), passed by the British parliament, and 'Irish Act of Union (Ireland) Act, 1800' (40 Geo. III c.38).

72 Antients Grand Lodge *Minutes*, 1 July 1752.

73 *Dublin Gazette*, 24–28 June 1755. Cf., also, *Faulkner's Dublin Journal*, 28 June–2 July 1757.

74 *Pue's Occurrences*, 25–28 June 1757.

75 *Dublin Mercury*, 17–20 June 1769.

76 John Money, *Experience and Identity: Birmingham and the West Midlands, 1760–1800* (Manchester: MUP, 1977), pp. 98–102.

77 Moses W. Redding, *Illustrated History of Freemasonry* (Whitefish, Montana: Kessinger Publishing, 1997), p. 367. Originally published New York: Redding & Co, 1910.

78 Lisa Meaney, *Freemasonry in Munster, 1726–1829* (Mary Immaculate College, Ireland: 2005), unpublished. Petri Mirala, *Freemasonry in Ulster, 1733–1813: A Social and Political History of the Masonic Brotherhood in the North of Ireland* (Dublin: FCP, 2007).

79 Mirala, 'Masonic sociability and its limitations', pp. 315–31.

80 Meaney, *Freemasonry in Munster*, Introduction.

81 Lepper and Crossle, *History*, pp. 113–14.

82 Clement XIII, *In Eminenti*, 28 April 1738; Benedict XIV, *Providas*, 18 May 1751.

83 Mirala, *Freemasonry in Ulster*, pp. 135–6. Also, *Irish Clubs and Societies*, pp. 327–8.

84 Ibid., pp. 136–40.

85 D'Assigny's *Serious and Impartial Enquiry* does not provide a reference point to explore eighteenth-century Irish freemasonry. The book is largely a fictional history of freemasonry '[tracing] antiquity even unto its infant state [to] our parent Adam' and argues that 'a [masonic] house divided against itself cannot stand'.

CONCLUSION

1 Jonathan Swift, *A Short View of the State of Ireland* (Dublin, 1728), in *The Works of Jonathan Swift* (London: Henry Washbourne, 1841) vol. II, p. 80. The

second Navigation Act, 'An Act for the Encouragement of Trade', was passed in 1663, prohibited the use of foreign ships in trade between England and its colonies and taxed a range of 'enumerated' products.

2   Swift, *A Short View of the State of Ireland*.

3   Ibid.

4   Ibid.

5   William A.S. Hewins in Murray, *History of the Commercial and Financial Relations between England and Ireland, Preface*.

6   Murray, *History of the Commercial and Financial Relations between England and Ireland*.

7   Ruth-Ann Harris, *The Nearest Place That Wasn't Ireland: Early Nineteenth Century Labor Migration* (Iowa State UP, 1994).

8   Eoin Kinsela, 'Hurling in Eighteenth Century London', unpublished paper, given at 'The London Irish in the Long Eighteenth Century' conference, University of Warwick, 13–14 April 2012.

9   *St James's Evening Post*, 14–16 August 1733.

10   *Daily Post*, 20 August 1733.

11   *London Evening Post*, 23–25 June 1748; *General Advertiser*, 12 May 1749.

12   *London Evening Post*, 25–27 July 1751; *General Advertiser*, 29 August 1751.

APPENDIX V **An Introduction to Eighteenth-Century Irish Freemasonry**

1   *Dublin News Letter*, 10 July 1721; *Dublin Impartial News Letter*, 15 August 1721. Cf., also, for example, the London *Post Boy*, 5 August 1721.

2   *Weekly Journal or British Gazetteer*, 5 August 1721.

3   *Dublin Courant*, 2 July 1722.

4   The event was reported in *Applebee's Original Weekly Journal*, 5 August 1721, and replicated elsewhere.

5   Thomas Wharton's death occurred shortly after Philip married against his father's wishes, which was believed to be a contributory cause.

6   Lawrence B. Smith, 'Philip Wharton, duke of Wharton and Jacobite duke of Northumberland', *ODNB* (Oxford: OUP, 2004; online edn, Jan. 2008), accessed 29 August 2012.

7   *Burney* includes over 500 references to Wharton over the period 1718–24.

8   The Centre for Buckinghamshire Studies: D-LE/A/2/4/j, *29 November 1721*.

9   Lewis Benjamin, *South Sea Bubble* (Manchester, New Hampshire, 1967), p. 49; also, Noorthouck, *A New History of London*, vol. I, pp. 306–25.

10   Lewis Melville, *South Sea Bubble* (London, 1921), p. 157.

11   *1738 Constitutions*, p. 114; also discussed in R.F. Gould, *History of Freemasonry*, vol. 2, p. 289.

12   *London Journal*, 30 June 1722. Cf. also, *Compleat Set of St James's Journals*, 28 June 1722, et al.

13   'Then let us rejoice, With heart and voice, There doth one Stuart still remain; And all sing the tune, On the tenth day of June, That the King shall enjoy his own again.'

14   Lawrence B. Smith, 'Wharton, Philip James, duke of Wharton and Jacobite duke of Northumberland (1698–1731)', *ODNB* (Oxford: OUP, 2004; online edn, Jan. 2008), accessed 25 August 2012.

15   David Stevenson, 'James Anderson: Man & Mason', *Heredom*, 10 (2002), 93–138, quote from 107.

16 Ibid., 108.

17 Francis Scott, 5th earl of Dalkeith and 2nd duke of Buccleuch (1695–1751).

18 Charles Lennox, 2nd duke of Richmond & Lennox (1701–1750). Richmond succeeded Dalkeith as Grand Master in 1724.

19 Grand Lodge of England *Minutes*.

20 *London Journal*, 16 June 1722.

21 *British Journal*, 12 December 1724.

22 Trumbach, *Sex and the Gender Revolution*, p. 83.

23 'Letter to the Countess of Mar, February 1724', in Lady Mary Wortley Montagu, Lord Wharcliffe (ed.), *The Letters and Works of Lady Mary Wortley Montagu* (New York, 1893), vol. 1, p. 477. The correspondence was previously published by Richard Bentley (London, 1837).

24 Lepper & Crossle, *History*, vol. I, pp. 130–2. The present day Freemason's Hall in Dublin was constructed in Molesworth Street in 1868 on the site of Rosse's house.

25 Turlough O'Riordan, 'Richard Parsons', *DIB* (Cambridge: CUP, 2009; online edn, accessed 19 October 2011).

26 *Dublin Weekly Journal*, 13 March 1731.

27 The position of lord president of Munster was similar to that of a military governor, with control of civil, judicial and military affairs.

28 W.J. Chetwode Crawley, *Caementaria Hibernica* (London: William McGee, 1895), Fas., II, p. 12, quoted in Lepper and Crossle, *History*, vol. I, p. 61.

29 The argument is advanced by Baigent and Leigh, however, the relevant chapter, 'The Masonic Jacobite Cause', contains several errors, for example, a statement that the duke of Montagu was Ireland's first Grand Master: Michael Baigent & Richard Leigh, *The Temple and the Lodge* (London: Jonathan Cape, 1989), ch. 13.

30 QUB, *Irish Legislation Database*: http://www.qub.ac.uk/ild; sourced 10 October 2011.

31 Jonathan Swift, *The Works of the Rev. Jonathan Swift* (London: J. Johnson et al, 1808), 19 volumes, vol. V, p. 237.

32 The Battle Axe Guards consisted of a captain, lieutenant, two sergeants and sixty men. The unit was stationed at Dublin Castle. Cf. Cæsar Litton Falkiner, 'The Irish Guards, 1661–1798', *Proceedings of the Royal Irish Academy*, 24 (1902–1904), 7–30. Also, Francis Elrington Ball, 'Some Notes on the Judges of Ireland in the Year 1739', *Journal of the Royal Society of Antiquarians of Ireland*, 5th series, 34.1 (1904), 6.

33 Prendergast was appointed JGW of English Grand Lodge in December 1725 by James, Lord Paisley, GM, Richmond's successor.

34 Cf. West Sussex Record Office: Goodwood/42, 43 *12 September 1737*, for relevant correspondence. Also, Lord March, *A Duke and His Friends*, pp. 206–7, 323–9.

35 Cf., Paul Hopkins, 'Sir Thomas Prendergast, 1st Baronet (*c*.1660–1709)', *ODNB* (Oxford: OUP, 2004; online edn, Jan. 2008, accessed 17 October 2011); also, John Bergin, 'Sir Thomas Prendergast', *DIB* (Cambridge: CUP, 2009; online edn, accessed 17 October 2011).

36 QUB, *Irish Legislation Database*: http://www.qub.ac.uk/ild; accessed 10 October 2011.

37 John Hervey, *Memoirs of the Reign of George II* (Philadelphia: Lea & Blanchard, 1884), vol. 1, p. 194.

38 Jonathan Swift, *On Noisy Tom* (1733).
39 Jonathan Swift, *A Character, Panegyric and Description of the Legion Club* (1736).
40 *Needham's Dublin Postman*, 6 July 1724.
41 Anonymous, *The Grand Mystery of the Free-Masons Disclosed* (London: T. Payne, 1724).
42 *Dublin Journal*, 27 April 1725; *Dublin Journal*, 29 April 1725; *Dublin Journal*, 22 June 1725 et al.
43 *The Dublin Weekly Journal*, 26 June 1725. No extant minutes, personal correspondence or other documents have been identified; primary material is restricted to newspaper reports.
44 Ibid.
45 Ibid.
46 The distinction between the two Grand Lodges with regard to this practice persists today.
47 Lepper and Crossle, *History*, p. 54.
48 Morgan's father also represented Athy between 1692 and 1712.
49 John Burke, *A Genealogical and Heraldic history of The Commoners of Great Britain and Ireland* (London: Henry Colburn, 1838), vol. IV, pp. 13–14.
50 Swift, *The Legion Club*.
51 The 'Wild Geese' was the name given to Irish Jacobite soldiers permitted to leave Ireland under the Treaty of Limerick; it was also used to refer to those seeking to leave for France and Spain and to returning Jacobite sympathisers.
52 Lepper and Crossle, *History*, p. 135.
53 *Hume's Courant*, 8 June 1726.
54 *Dublin Weekly Journal*, 13 March 1731.
55 Rowly (or Rowley) Hill was a member of the Ship behind the Royal Exchange in London. See below.
56 *Dublin Weekly Journal*, 13 March 1731.
57 Gerard O'Brien, 'William Ponsonby, 2nd earl of Bessborough (1704–1793)', *ODNB* (Oxford: OUP, 2004, online article 22504, accessed 10 Oct. 2011).
58 Patrick M. Geoghegan, 'William Ponsonby', *DIB* (Cambridge: CUP, 2009; online edn, accessed 17 October 2011).
59 James Kelly, 'John Ponsonby', *DIB*, *ibid.*
60 Cf., P.J. Jupp, 'William Brabazon Ponsonby 1st baron Ponsonby (1744–1806)', *ODNB* (Oxford: OUP, 2004, online article 22506, accessed 10 Oct. 2011).
61 Charles O'Conor, 'George Faulkner and Lord Chesterfield', *Irish Quarterly Review*, 25.98 (1936), 292–304.
62 *London Journal*, 12 June 1731.
63 *London Journal*, 29 September 1733; *London Evening Post*, 4 October 1733. Mary Coke, his wife, was the daughter of Thomas Coke (1674–1727), a pro-Hanoverian country Tory MP and privy counsellor (1708–death) under both Anne and George I; her mother was the daughter of Philip, Earl of Chesterfield.
64 *Universal Spectator*, 25 November 1732; *Daily Post*, 11 June 1733; *London Evening Post*, 15 December 1733.
65 *Daily Journal*, 25 May 1733; *Fog's Weekly Journal*, 2 June 1733; *Read's Weekly Journal Or British Gazetteer*; *Daily Post*, 9 June 1733 et al.
66 Cf. Bill Power, *White Knights, Dark Earls: The Rise and fall of an Anglo-Irish Dynasty* (Cork: Collins Press, 2000).

67 G.E. Cokayne et al. (eds), *The Complete Peerage, new ed.* (Gloucester: Alan Sutton Publishing, 2000), vol. VII, p. 298.

68 William J. Hughan, 'The Three Degrees of Freemasonry', *QCL Transactions*, X (1897), p. 134.

69 Chetwode Crawley, 'Discussion', *QCL Transactions*, p. 143.

70 Ibid. An example of his pro-Hanoverian stance was the celebration of victory over the Jacobites in 1746: a masonic banquet 'of such magnificence that it was chronicled in the public journals of the day'.

71 *London Evening Post*, 31 January–2 February 1734

72 Lepper and Crossle, *History*, pp. 141–6. Also cf. the following chapter.

73 Napier (1702–1773), the colonel of the regiment, was Bligh's uncle.

74 Matthew Kilburn, 'Thomas Southwell, 1ˢᵗ baron Southwell (c.1665–1720)', *ODNB* (Oxford: OUP, 2004), accessed online 10 Oct. 2011.

75 4. Geo. II, c. 15.

76 Cf. Thomas M. Truxes, *Irish American Trade, 1660–1783* (Cambridge: CUP, 2004), esp. pp. 29–32.

77 James Kelly, 'Harvests and Hardship: Famine and Scarcity in Ireland in the Late 1720s', *Studia Hibernica*, 26 (1992), 65–105.

78 *Faulkner's Dublin Journal*, 8–11 February 1729.

79 John Pennell, *Book of Constitutions* (Dublin: Grand Lodge of Ireland, 1730).

80 *Faulkner's Dublin Journal*, 10 April 1731.

81 *Faulkner's Dublin Journal*, 10 July 1731.

82 *Daily Journal*, 12 August 1732.

83 Deidre Bryan, 'Frances Talbot (c.1649–1731), Duchess of Tyrconnell', *DIB*, online edn., accessed 27 October 2011.

84 Patrick Fagan, 'Nicholas Barnewall, 3ʳᵈ viscount Barnewall of Kingsland (1668–1725)', *ODNB* (Oxford: OUP, 2004 online edn.), accessed 27 October 2011.

85 John Lodge (rev. Mervyn Archdall), *The Peerage of Ireland* (Dublin: James Moore, 1789), vol. V, p. 53.

86 Richard Glover (Richard Duppa, ed.), *Memoirs by a Celebrated Literary and Political Character* (London: John Murray, 1814), 2ⁿᵈ edn., p. 64. Cf. also, A.P.W. Malcomson, *The Pursuit of the Heiress: Aristocratic Marriage in Ireland, 1740–1840* (Belfast: Ulster Historical Foundation, 2006), pp. 23–5.

87 Nugent later represented Bristol (1754–74), before returning to sit for St Mawes from 1774 until 1784.

88 Sean P. Donlan, 'Robert Craggs Nugent', *DIB*, online edition sourced 12 October 2011.

89 Horace Walpole (Lord Drover, ed.), *Letters of Horace Walpole, Earl of Orford, to Sir Horace Mann* (New York: George Dearborn, 1833), vol. I, p. 299.

90 Mr Villers, a member of the Rummer at Charing Cross.

91 *Daily Gazetteer*, 5 July 1737.

92 Beresford married Catherine, the only daughter of the 3ʳᵈ earl of Tyrone, in 1717. Tyrone had served as governor of the city and county of Waterford from 1695 to 1704.

93 The membership of the Bear & Harrow included a range of former and current Grand Officers, including Montagu, GM; Thomas Batson, DGM; Desaguliers, formerly GM and DGM; George Rook and James Smythe, GWs; James Chambers, a former GW; and George Moody, the Grand Swordbearer.

94 Cf. Francis Nichols, *The Irish Compendium* (London: J. Knapton, 1756), 5ᵗʰ ed., pp. 233–6.

95 *Jacobite's Journal*, 13 August 1748; *London Daily Advertiser and Literary Gazette*, 20 April 1751. Mountjoy also owned a house at Blackheath: *Gazetteer and New Daily Advertiser*, 4 August 1768.

96 Thomas Prior, *A list of the absentees of Ireland* (Dublin: Richard Gunne, 1729), p. 6. Cf. also the 3rd edn. (Dublin, 1745), p. 6.

97 *Public Advertiser*, 4 May 1757.

98 The date is sometimes given as 1746, but cf. for example, *General Advertiser*, 6 September 1748.

99 *Public Advertiser*, 10 June 1763.

100 *St James's Chronicle or the British Evening Post*, 10–12 September 1761.

101 Up to around 40 per cent of FRSs are thought to have been freemasons: cf. Berman, *Foundations*, p. 107; the comparable figure for Ireland's Dublin Society cannot be determined given the almost complete lack of masonic membership data outside of a small number of lodges and the senior levels of Irish Grand Lodge.

102 Berry, *History of the Royal Dublin Society*, p. 24. Cf., also, the membership records of the Royal Dublin Society: http://www.rds.ie/cat_historic_member_detail.jsp?itemID=1098672&item_name=lanesborough.

103 Cf., James Livesey, *Civil Society and Empire: Ireland and Scotland in the Eighteenth-Century Atlantic World* (New Haven: YUP, 2009).

104 Henry Berry, *A History of the Royal Dublin Society* (London: Longmans, Green & Co., 1915), p. 31.

105 *Faulkner's Dublin Journal*, 25 May 1745.

106 *Faulkner's Dublin Journal*, 23 June 1747; cf., also, *General Advertiser*, 6 July 1747.

107 They were replaced as MPs by the rival D'arcy family. Following parliament's determination that voting rights should be linked to grazing rights, the D'arcys purchased a majority of the relevant properties which gave them effective ownership of the borough. Cf., *House of Commons Parliamentary Papers*, 6th parliament of Great Britain: 5th session (17 January 1727–15 May 1727), 15 March 1727.

108 Examples include *London Evening Post* on 1 August, 1 September and 3 September 1730. Cf. also, John Cheny, *An historical list of horse-matches run and of plates and prizes run for in Great Britain and Ireland* (London, 1731 et al). Wyvill was renowned as the breeder of three champions: 'Coalition Colt', 'Scarborough Colt' and 'Volunteer'.

109 *General Evening Post*, 19–22 April 1735; *Weekly Miscellany*, 10 May 1735.

110 He succeeded as the 3rd baron Southwell in 1766 and was created 1st viscount Southwell in 1776.

111 D.W. Hayton, 'The Stanhope/Sunderland Ministry and the Repudiation of Irish Parliamentary Independence' *English Historical Review*, 113.452 (1998), 610–36.

112 The earl believed that he had been cuckolded by his brother. He imprisoned his wife, who went insane, and sued his brother, whom he bankrupted and who later died in a Dublin debtors' prison.

113 Patrick M. Geoghegan, 'Charles Moore', *DIB* (Cambridge: CUP, 2009). Cf., also, *Irish Legislation Database*, QUB.

114 *Lloyd's Evening Post and British Chronicle*, 19–21 April 1762. Cf., also, *Dublin Journal*, *London Evening Post* and *Public Advertiser*.

APPENDIX VI **The First Irish Lodge in London – the Ship behind the Royal Exchange**

1   Edward Jerman's Royal Exchange was the second on the site and replaced an Elizabethan building destroyed in the 1666 Great Fire. The new Royal Exchange opened in 1669 and survived until it burned down in 1838.

2   Lane, *Masonic Records, 1717–1894*.

3   Voltaire, *Letters Concerning the English Nation* (London: C. Davies, 1733), p. 44.

4   Philip Crossle, CC *Transactions* (Dublin: Lodge of Research No. 200, 1923), pp. 109–12.

5   The list was compiled on 15 May 1723. Lane's *Masonic Records* gives the warrant date as 5 May 1723. The latter may be the date on which the lodge was recognised by English Grand Lodge rather than the date of its inception.

6   Ibid., p. 109.

7   *Daily Journal*, 21 November 1727.

8   Sir Bernard Burke, *The Landed Gentry of Ireland* (London: Harrison & Sons, 1912), pp. 395–6: *Leigh of Rosegarland*.

9   A John Leigh, possibly the same man, lived at the Black Boy tavern in Leather Lane, a second tier area popular with the London Irish. Cf., *London Journal*, 3 June 1727.

10   Cf. Roland Metcalf, 'John Leigh (*c*.1689–1726?)', *ODNB*, OUP, 2004, online ed. accessed 19 April 2012.

11   Admiral Shovel was drowned off the Isles of Scilly in 1707. The inability to calculate longitude led to a navigational error. Four ships of the line were lost together with their crews, a total of about 2,000 men.

12   John Debrett (ed.), *The Baronetage of England* (London: F.C. & J. Rivington, 1831), 3rd ed., p. 1120.

13   Ibid., p. 1121.

14   William White, *Notes & Queries* (Oxford: OUP, 1893), vol. 87, p. 255. Cloudesley Stewart is described as 'probably a descendant of James Stewart, a naval officer killed in battle (third son of Captain Andrew Stewart)'.

15   *Post Boy*, 6–8 August 1702.

16   John B. Hattendorf, 'Sir Cloudesley Shovel (*bap.* 1650, *d.* 1707)', *ODNB* (OUP, 2004; online edn, Jan. 2008), accessed 10 October 2012.

17   Cf., also, *Daily Journal*, 30 July 1726. John Blackwood was the son of Sir Robert Blackwood.

18   *Weekly Journal or British Gazetteer*, 26 April 1718.

19   *Original Weekly Journal*, 12–19 April 1718.

20   *London Evening Post*, 20–22 April 1732.

21   Christie's catalogue entry for sale 6867, 8 June 1995. Portrait of Anne Stewart, head and shoulders, wearing a green dress with a pale pink wrap; and Portrait of Cloudesley Stewart, head and shoulders, wearing an embroidered coat with a white cravat, inscribed 'Anne Stewart and Cloudesley Stewart'; ovals 30 × 25in; a pair.

22   D.W. Jones, 'Sir Nathaniel Gould (1661–1728)', *ODNB* (OUP, 2004; online edn, Jan. 2008), accessed 5 May 2012.

23   *Daily Journal*, 26 April 1729.

24   Ibid. Cf., also, Henry Kent, *Directory* (London: Henry Kent, 1740).

25 Gould & Nesbitt operated from offices in Coleman Street in the City of London until the early 1750s.

26 Craig Bailey, 'The Nesbitts of London and their Networks', in David Dickinson et al, *Irish and Scottish Mercantile Networks in Europe and Overseas in the Seventeenth and Eighteenth Centuries* (Gent: Academica Press, 2006), pp. 231–50. Quote from p. 233.

27 Ibid., p. 236.

28 25 May 1747 (N.S.), Newcastle (Clumber) MSS. Quoted in *The History of Parliament*: http://www.historyofparliamentonline.org/volume/1715–1754/member/nesbitt-albert-1753.

29 Bailey, 'The Nesbitts of London', p. 235.

30 Louis Cullen, 'The Two George Fitzgerald's of London, 1718–1759', in Dickinson et al, *Irish and Scottish Mercantile Networks*, pp. 251–70, esp. 253–5.

31 Crossle's suggestion that Richard Fitzgerald was 'perhaps youngest brother and eventual heir of John Fitzgerald, Knight of Glyn, who attended a Dublin Lodge in 1739' is less persuasive.

32 Thomas Truxes, 'London's Irish Merchant Community and North Atlantic Commerce in the Mid-Eighteenth Century', in *Irish and Scottish Mercantile Networks*, pp. 271–310.

33 Ibid., 274.

34 Thomas Truxes, *Irish–American Trade, 1660–1783* (Cambridge: CUP, 2004), esp. pp. 176–9.

35 He was buried at the Catholic and non-conformist St Pancras cemetery. Cf., Walter H. Godfrey and W. McB. Marcham (eds.), *Survey of London, vol. 24: The parish of St Pancras, part 4: King's Cross Neighbourhood* (1952), pp. 147–51. I am indebted to John Bergin at QUB for his assistance.

36 *Read's Weekly Journal or British Gazetteer*, 14 June 1735. Crossle's suggestion of 'James Tobin, well known in Dublin in the 1740s as treasurer of the Charitable Music society', may be wide of the mark.

37 Ibid.

38 Cf., *London Evening Post*, 27–30 June 1730.

39 *London Evening Post*, 26–28 June 1729; *Daily Journal*, 28 June 1732.

40 *Daily Courant*, 1 July 1720; 29 June 1723.

41 Stonehewer is first mentioned in 1724 although he was a director prior to this date; his name also appears in the *Daily Journal*, 31 October 1727. Cf. also, *London Evening Post*, 26–28 June 1729 and 29 June 1732–1 July 1732.

42 *London Lives* online database, accessed 19 April 2012. Stonehewer sat on the board of the Royal Bridewell through to the 1740s.

43 A magistrate named John Gascoyne was possibly the same person. Cf. also Kent's *Directory*.

44 Crossle appears to have an incorrect date for Thomas Watts' marriage to Susannah Gascoyne.

45 *History of Parliament*: http://www.historyofparliamentonline.org/volume/1715–1754/member/gascoigne-joseph-1728 accessed 12 July 2011.

46 *London Evening Post*, 13–15 February 1729.

47 Thomas Watts, *Essay on the Proper Method of Forming the Man of Business* (London: George Strahan, 1716). A second edition was published in 1716, a third in 1717 and the fourth in 1722.

48 *Daily Courant*, 16 January 1719.

49 Watts, *Essay*, 4th edn., pp. ii–iii.

50 Benjamin Worster, *A Course of Experimental Philosophy* (London: *c*.1730)

51 Ruth Wallis, 'Thomas Watts (*d*. 1742)', *ODNB* (Oxford: OUP, 2004; online edn, May 2009).

52 F.B. Relton, *An Account of the Fire Insurance Companies, Associations, Institutions, Projects and Schemes Established and Projected in Great Britain and Ireland during the Seventeenth and Eighteenth Centuries, including the Sun Fire Office* (London, 1893), p. 286.

53 http://www.historyofparliamentonline.org/volume/1715–1754/constituencies/tregony, accessed 20 April 2012.

54 Ibid.

55 Edward Baumer, *The Early Days of the Sun Fire Office* (London: Causton, 1910), p. 51.

56 Crossle, *CC Transactions*, p. 109.

57 Hoope's principal correspondents were James Bolt in Bristol; Jonathan Patton and Robert Fielding in Manchester; and Jonathan Gurney and Robert Hales in London. Cf., W.H. Crawford, *The Impact of the Domestic Linen Industry in Ulster* (Belfast: Ulster Historical Foundation, 2005), pp. 35–6. Also, Richard L. Greaves, *Dublin's Merchant Quaker: Anthony Sharp and the Community of Friends, 1643–1707* (Stanford: Stanford UP 1998), pp. 107, 128.

58 *Dublin Weekly Journal*, 21 August 1725.

59 *Dublin Weekly Journal*, 13 November 1725

60 Cf., John Bergin, 'The Irish Catholic interest at the London inns of court, 1674–1800', *Eighteenth-Century Ireland/Iris an dá chultúr*, 24 (2009), 36–61.

61 *Daily Post*, 23 January 1724.

62 I am grateful to Toby Barnard for this observation.

63 The name derives from 'de Lambert'; both were relatively common Huguenot names.

64 *Debrett's Baronetage of England* (London, 1815), vol. 2, p. 1121.

65 *Daily Courant*, 7 December 1725.

66 *Read's Weekly Journal Or British Gazetteer*, 28 November 1730.

67 John Windele, *Historical and Descriptive Notices of the City of Cork* (Cork: Luke H. Bolster, 1839), p. 100.

68 John Fitzgerald, *The Cork Remembrancer* (Cork: J. Sullivan, 1783), pp. 146, 186: *Protestant Mayors & Sheriffs of Cork*. There is also anecdotal evidence that he was mayor of Cork in 1651 during the Cromwellian wars.

69 John Bergin, 'The Quaker Lobby and Its Influence on Irish Legislation, 1692–1705', *Eighteenth-Century Ireland/Iris an dá chultúr*, 19 (2004), 9–36.

70 With respect to other political lobbyists, cf. also, Kenneth Morgan, 'Bristol West India Merchants in the Eighteenth Century', *Transactions of the Royal Historical Society*, 6th series, 3 (1993), 185–208, esp. 202.

71 John Bergin, Edward Hoare (*d*.1690), *DIB* (Cambridge: CUP & RIA), http://dib.cambridge.org, accessed 2 August 2012.

72 Crossle, *CC Transactions*, p. 112.

73 John Bergin, Queens University Belfast, private communication.

74 Cf., James Stevens Curl, *The Honourable The Irish Society and the Plantation of Ulster, 1608–2000: The City of London and the Colonisation of County Londonderry in the Province of Ulster in Ireland. A History and Critique* (Chichester: Phillimore & Co., 2000).

75 *British Journal*, 18 December 1725.

76 *London Daily Post and General Advertiser*, 20 January 1736.

77 Crossle, *CC Transactions*, p. 112.

78 'Captain, late Commander of the Ship Crocodile but bound for the Canaries': Will Proved at the Prerogative Court of Canterbury, 6 June 1709.

79 *Post Man and the Historical Account*, 10–12 March 1709.

80 Cf., for example, *British Mercury*, 28 October 1713.

81 *Daily Courant*, 8 June 1722.

82 *Daily Journal*, 30 July 1730; *Weekly Journal or British Gazetteer* , 1 August 1730.

83 *London Evening Post*, 26–28 June 1729.

84 *London Evening Post*, 29 June 1732–1 July 1732.

85 Thomas Putland, Sisson's elder brother, stayed in Ireland. The membership records of the *Incorporated Society in Dublin for Society for Promoting English Protestant Schools in Ireland* show him as a member as late as 1737: *An abstract of the proceedings of the Incorporated Society in Dublin, for Promoting English Protestant Schools in Ireland: from the opening of His Majesty's Royal Charter, on the 6th day of February, 1733 to the 25th day of March, 1737* (Dublin, 1737), p. 35.

86 *The Gentleman's Magazine*, vol. 8, March 1738, p. 165.

87 In 1723, a George Putland was the Master of the Star and Garter lodge in Covent Garden.

88 *London Evening Post*, 21–23 March 1738.

89 Ibid., 25–28 March 1738.

90 *Daily Journal*, 12 July 1728 and *The London Magazine or Gentleman's Monthly Intelligencer*, 1733, vol. 2., p. 425.

91 *General Advertiser*, 30 March 1751.

92 *Journal of the House of Lords*, 1722–1726, vol. 22, 21–31 March 1725.

93 Ibid., 1–10 April 1725.

94 Cf., for example, *British Journal*, 23 February 1723.

95 Cecil Headlam (ed.), *Calendar of State Papers Colonial, America and West Indies* (London: IHR, 1936), vol. 35, *America and West Indies*, 1 & 11 March 1726, pp. 29–43.

96 K.H. Ledward (ed.), *Journals of the Board of Trade and Plantations* (London: IHR, 1928), vol. 5, January 1723–December 1728, pp. 270–7.

97 Lepper and Crossle, *History*, p. 142.

98 Ibid., pp. 143–4

99 *London Evening Post*, 13–15 August 1741.

100 Cf. Robert Bashford, *History of Union Lodge of St Patrick, No. 367, Downpatrick*, sourced at www.irishfreemasonry.com/index.php?p=1_40_History-of-Lodge-367–Downpatrick: accessed 10 October 2011.

Selected Bibliography

Principal Manuscript Collections

London Metropolitan Archives, London
Middlesex Sessions of the Peace, Justices of the Peace: Sessions Papers.
Westminster Sessions of the Peace, Justices of the Peace: Sessions Papers.
Quarter Sessions of the Peace for the City and Liberty of Westminster, *1618–1844*.

The Royal Society Archives, London
The Raymond and Beverley Sackler Archive Resource.

United Grand Lodge of England, Library & Archives, London
Minutes of the Grand Lodge of England, 1723–31 and 1731–50.
Minutes of the Antients Grand Lodge of England, 1752–1813.
Historic Correspondence.
Other lodge files, MSS and publications, including:
  Minute Book of the Lodge of Antiquity, No. 2.
  Minute Book of the Shakespeare's Head lodge.
  Minute Book of the Old King's Arms lodge.
  Minute Book of St George's and Corner Stone Lodge, No. 5.
  Minute Book of lodge No. 4 (Antients).
  Minute Book of lodge No. 6 (Antients).
  Minute Book of lodge No. 20 (Antients).
  Minute Book of lodge No. 55 (Antients).
  Treasurer's Book of lodge No. 4 (Antients).

British and Irish Parliamentary Papers

Calendar of State Papers, Domestic (George I and George II).
Calendar of State Papers Colonial, America and West Indies .
Calendar of Treasury Books.
House of Lords & House of Commons' Parliamentary Papers.
House of Lords & House of Commons' Journals.
Statutes of the Realm.
Irish Legislation Database (Queen's University Belfast).

Selected IHR & Victoria County History Publications

Davies, K.G. *Calendar of State Papers Colonial, America and West Indies*. Volume 44. London, 1969.
Headlam, Cecil. *Calendar of Sate Papers Colonial, America and West Indies*. Volume 33, London, 1934.
Ledward, K.H. *Journals of the Board of Trade & Plantations*. London, 1925.
Page, William (ed.). *A History of the County of Middlesex*. London, 1911.

Sainty, J.C. *Office-Holders in Modern Britain*. Volumes 2 & 3. London, 1973 & 1974.

Shaw, William A. *Calendar of Treasury Books*. Volumes 1–26. London, 1897–1954.

Calendar of Treasury Books and Papers. Volumes 1–5. London, 1897–1903.

Shaw, William A., and Slingsby, F.H. *Calendar of Treasury Books*. Volumes 27–32, London, 1955–62.

Masonic Constitutions etc.

Anderson, James. *The Constitutions of the Freemasons* (London, 1723).

—— *The Ancient Constitutions of the Free and Accepted Masons* (London, 1731).

—— *The New Book of Constitutions*. (London, 1738).

Dashwood, J.R. *Early Records of the Grand Lodge of England according to the Old Institutions*, QCA vol XI (London, 1958).

—— *The Minutes of the Grand Lodge of Freemasons of England 1740–58*, QCA vol. XII. (London, 1960).

Dermott, Laurence. *Ahiman Rezon* (London, 1756) and later (London, Dublin) editions.

Entick, John. *The Pocket Companion and History of Freemasons*. (London, 1759).

—— *The Constitutions of the Ancient and honourable fraternity of Free and Accepted Masons* (London, 1756).

Lane, John. *Masonic Records 1717–1894* (Sheffield, 2009).

Pennell, John. *Book of Constitutions* (Dublin, 1730).

Smith, William. *A Pocket Companion for Freemasons* (London, 1735).

—— *A Pocket Companion for Freemasons* (London, 1759).

Songhurst, W.J. *The Minutes of the Grand Lodge of Freemasons of England 1723–1739*, QCA, vol. X. (London, 1913).

CC Transactions (Dublin, published annually, 1922–2002)

QCL Transactions (London, published annually, 1886–2009).

Newspapers (1700–1790)

Applebee's Original Weekly Journal

British Journal

British Mercury

Country Journal or The Craftsman

Daily Courant

Daily Journal

Dublin Courant

Dublin Mercury

Dublin Weekly Journal

Evening Post

Flying Post or The Postmaster

Fog's Weekly Journal

Gazetteer and London Daily Advertiser

General Advertiser

Gentleman's Magazine

Guardian

Athenian Gazette or Casuistical Mercury

British Journal or The Censor

Caledonian Mercury

Daily Advertiser

Daily Gazetteer

Daily Post

Dublin Gazette

Dublin News letter

Evening Journal

Faulkner's Dublin Journal

Flying Post or The Weekly Medley

Freeholder's Journal

Gazetteer and New Daily Advertiser

General Evening Post

Grub Street Journal

Hume's Courant

Lloyd's Evening Post and British Chronicle

London Courant & Westminster Chronicle

London Daily Post and General Advertiser

London Daily Advertiser

London Chronicle

London Evening Post

London Gazette

London Journal

London Morning Penny Post

London Spy Revived

Middlesex Journal or Chronicle of Liberty

Mist's Weekly Journal

Monthly Chronicle

Morning Herald

Needham's Dublin Postman

New England Courant

Old Whig or The Consistent Protestant

Original Weekly Journal

Parker's General Advertiser and Morning Intelligencer

Parker's London News or the Impartial Intelligencer

Pasquin

Penny London Post or Morning Advertiser

Plain Dealer

Poor Robin's Intelligence

Post Boy

Post Man and the Historical Account

Public Advertiser

Public Ledger

Public Register or The Freeman's Journal

Pue's Occurrences

Read's Weekly Journal or British Gazetteer

St James's Chronicle or British Evening Post

St James's Evening Post

St James's Journal

The Censor

The Evening Post

The Spectator

The Tatler

The True Briton

Universal Spectator and Weekly Journal

Weekly Journal or British Gazetteer

Weekly Journal or Saturday's Post

Weekly Miscellany

Weekly Packet

Whitehall Evening Post or London Intelligencer

Other Selected Primary Sources

Anonymous. *The Grand Mystery of the Free-Masons Disclosed* (London, 1724).

—— *An Inquiry into Some of the Causes of the Ill Situation of the Affairs of the Irish* (Dublin, 1731).

—— *A Trip through London: containing observations on Men and Things* (London, 1728).

—— *A second part of A view of London and Westminster: or, the town spy* (London, 1725).

—— [Rev. Peter Bristow]. *Honesty the Best Policy or, the History of Roger* (Dublin, 1752).

Blackerby, Nathaniel. *The Speech of Nathanial Blackerby* (London, 1738).

Briscoe, Sam. *Secret History of the Freemasons* (London, 1724).

Cheny, John. *An historical list of horse-matches run and of plates and prizes run for in Great Britain and Ireland* (London, 1731 et al.).

Churchill, Sarah. *Private correspondence of Sarah, Duchess of Marlborough, volume II* (London, 1838).

Clement XII. Papal Bull, *In Eminenti* (Vatican, 1738).

Cowper, William. *Humble Address* (London, 1715).

—— *The Charge delivered* (London, 1730).

D'Assigny's *Serious and Impartial Enquiry into the Cause of the present Decay of Freemasonry in the Kingdom of Ireland* (Dublin, 1764).

Davenant, Charles. *An Essay upon Ways and Means of Supplying the War* (London, 1695).

—— *The Political and Commercial Works of Charles D'Avenants*, collected and revised by Sir Charles Whitworth (London, 1771).

—— *An Essay on the East-India Trade* (London, 1696).

—— *A clear demonstration, from points of fact, that the recovery, preservation and improvement of Britain's share of the trade to Africa* (London, 1709).

—— *Reflections upon the constitution and management of the trade to Africa* (London, 1709); and *An account of the trade between Great-Britain, France, Holland, Spain, Portugal, Italy, Africa, Newfoundland* (London, 1715).

de Veil, Sir Thomas. *Observations on the practice of a justice of the peace intended for such gentlemen as design to act for Middlesex and Westminster.* (London, 1747).

Dobbs, Arthur. *An Essay on the Trade and Improvement of Ireland* (Dublin, 1729).

Egmont, Earl of. *Diary of the 1st Earl of Egmont* (London, 1923).

Grattan, Henry. *Memoirs of the Life and Times of Henry Grattan* (London, 1839).

McCann, Timothy. *The Correspondence of the Dukes of Richmond & Newcastle 1724–50* (Lewes, 1984).

Macky, John. *Memoirs of the secret services* (London, 1733), 2nd edn.

Molyneux, William. *The Case of Ireland's being Bound by Acts of Parliament* (Dublin, 1698).

Morgan, William. *Morgan's map of the whole of London in 1682* (London, 1682).

Nichols, Francis. *The Irish Compendium* (London, 1756), 5th edn.

Noorthouck, John. *A New History of London* (London, 1773).

Pitt, William. *Correspondence between William Pitt and Charles, Duke of Rutland, 1781–1787* (Edinburgh, 1890).

Prior, Thomas. *A list of the absentees of Ireland* (Dublin, 1729 & 1745).

Richmond, Charles. *A Duke and His Friends* (London, 1911).

Stow, John. *Survey of London.* London: Nicholas Bourn, 1633.

Swift, Jonathan. *Gulliver's Traverls* (London, 1726).

—— *A Letter to the Whole People of Ireland* (Dublin, 1724).

—— *A Character, Panegyric and Description of the Legion Club* (Dublin, 1736).

—— *On Noisy Tom* (Dublin, 1733).

Voltaire, *Letters Concerning the English Nation* (London, 1733).

Walpole, Horace. *Reminiscences.* (London, 1788).

—— *Letters of Horace Walpole, Earl of Orford, to Sir Horace Mann* (New York, 1833).

Watts, Thomas. *Essay on the Proper Method of Forming the Man of Business* (London, 1716).

Wharcliffe, Lord (ed.). *The Letters and Works of Lady Mary Wortley Montagu* (New York, 1893).

Wharton, Philip. *The life and writings of the Duke of Wharton* (London, 1732).

Whiston, W. *An Account of the Past and Present State of the Amicable Society* (London, 1732).

Worster, Benjamin. *A Course of Experimental Philosophy* (London, 1730).

Selected Journal Articles

Ball, Francis Elrington. 'Some Notes on the Judges of Ireland in the Year 1739', *Royal Society of Antiquarians of Ireland*, 5th series, 34.1, (1904).

Bartlett, Thomas. 'A New History of Ireland', *Past and Present*, 116 (1987), 206–19.

Beckett, J.C. 'Anglo-Irish Constitutional Relations in the Later Eighteenth Century', *Irish Historical Studies*, 14.53 (1964), 20–38.

Bergin, John. 'The Irish Catholic interest at the London inns of court, 1674–1800', *Eighteenth-Century Ireland/Iris an dá chultúr*, 24, (2009), 36–61.

—— 'The Quaker Lobby and its Influence on Irish Legislation, 1692–1705', *Eighteenth-Century Ireland/Iris an dá chultúr*, 19 (2004), 9–36.

Clark, J.C.D. 'Whig Tactics and Parliamentary Precedent: The English Management of Irish Politics, 1754–1756', *Historical Journal*, 21.2 (1978), 275–301.

Erwin, Timothy. 'Parody and Prostitution', *Huntington Library Quarterly*, 68.4 (2005), 677–84.

Falkiner, Caesar Litton. 'The Irish Guards, 1661–1798', *Proceedings of the Royal Irish Academy*, 24 (1902–4), 7–30.

Foster, Sarah. 'Buying Irish: Consumer Nationalism in Eighteenth Century Dublin', *History Today*, 47.6 (1997).

Hayton, D.W. 'The Stanhope/Sunderland Ministry and the Repudiation of Irish Parliamentary Independence' *English Historical Review*, 113.452 (1998), 610–36.

Hill, Berekeley. 'Illustrations of the Working of the Contagious Diseases Act', *British Medical Journal*, 1.386 (1868), 505–6.

Hill, Jacqueline. 'Allegories, Fictions, and Feigned Representations: Decoding the Money Bill Dispute, 1752–6' *Eighteenth-Century Ireland*, 21 (2006), 66–88.

Kelly, James. 'Harvests and Hardship: Famine and Scarcity in Ireland in the Late 1720s', *Studia Hibernica*, 26 (1992), 65–105.

Kent, D.A. 'Ubiquitous but Invisible: Female Domestic Servants in Mid-Eighteenth Century London', *History Workshop*, 28 (1989), 111–28

Kirkland, Richard. 'Reading the Rookery: The Social Meaning of an Irish Slum in Nineteenth Century London', *New Hibernia Review*, 16.1, (2012), 16–30.

Livesey, James. 'The Dublin Society in Eighteenth Century Political Thought', *Historical Journal*, 47.3, (2004), 615–40.

Mulvey-Roberts, Marie. 'Hogarth on the Square: Framing the Freemasons', *Journal for Eighteenth Century Studies*, 26.2, (2003), 251–70.

Murphy, Séan. 'Irish Jacobitism and Freemasonry', *Eighteenth-Century Ireland/Iris an dá chultúr*, 9 (1994), 75–82.

Nettels, Curtis. 'The Menace of Colonial Manufacturing 1690–1720', *New England Quarterly*, 4.2 (1931), 230–69.

Pink, Andrew. 'A music club for freemasons: *Philo-musicae et -architecturae societas Apollini*, London, 1725–1727', *Early Music*, 38.4, (2010), 523–36.

Rogers, Nicholas. 'Money, Land and Lineage: The Big Bourgeoisie of Hanoverian London', *Social History*, 4.3 (1979), 437–54.

Stevenson, David. 'James Anderson: Man & Mason', *Heredom*, 10 (2002), 93–138.

Swift, Roger. 'Heroes or Villains?: The Irish, Crime, and Disorder in Victorian England' *Albion*, 29.3 (1997), 399–421.

Selected Secondary Sources

Barnard, Toby. *Improving Ireland?* (Dublin, 2008).

Beames, *The Rookeries of London* (London, 1852).

Benjamin, Lewis. *South Sea Bubble* (Manchester (NH), 1967).

Berry, Henry. *A History of the Royal Dublin Society* (London, 1915).

Burke, Sir Bernard. *The Landed Gentry of Ireland* (London, 1912).

Burke, John. *A Genealogical and Heraldic history of The Commoners of Great Britain and Ireland* (London, 1838).

Callaghan, John Cornelius. *History of the Irish Brigades in the service of France* (Glasgow, 1885).

Crawley, Chetwode. *Caementaria Hibernica* (London, 1895).

Crossle, Philip. *Transactions* (Dublin, 1923), pp. 109–112.

Cullen, Louis M. *Anglo-Irish Trade, 1660–1800* (Manchester, 1968).

Curl, James Stevens. *The Honourable The Irish Society and the Plantation of Ulster, 1608–2000* (Chichester, 2000).

Deane, Phyllis and Cole W.A., *British Economic Growth, 1688–1959* (Cambridge, 1969) 2nd ed.

Dickinson, David. *Arctic Ireland: the Extraordinary Story of the Great Frost and Forgotten Famine of 1740–41* (Belfast, 1997).

Dickinson, David et al., *Irish and Scottish Mercantile Networks in Europe and Overseas in the Seventeenth and Eighteenth Centuries* (Gent, 2006).

Dyer, Colin, *The Grand Stewards and their Lodge* (London, 1985).

Eccleshall, George. *A History of the Old King's Arms Lodge, 1725–2000* (London, 2001).

Engels, Frederick. *The Condition of the Working-Class in England in 1844* (London, 1887.

Glover, Richard. *Memoirs by a Celebrated Literary and Political Character* (London, 1814), 2nd edn.

Gould, R.F. *Atholl Lodges* (London, 1879).

—— *The History of Freemasonry: Its Antiquities, Symbols, Constitutions, Customs, Etc* (London, 1885).

—— *The History of Freemasonry* (Philadelphia, 1902).

—— *The Concise History of Freemasonry* (London, 1951).

—— *Military Lodges: the Apron and the Sword* (London, 1899).

—— *Gould's History of Freemasonry throughout the World, vols I, II and III* (New York, 1936).

Hervey, John. *Memoirs of the Reign of George II* (Philadelphia, 1884).

Hewitt, Regina and Rogers, Pat (eds.), *Orthodoxy and Heresy in Eighteenth Century London* (Cranbury, N.J., 2002).

Kelly, James. *Poynings' Law and the Making of Laws in Ireland, 1660–1800* (Dublin, 2007).

Lepper, J.H. & Crossle, P. *History of the Grand Lodge of Ireland* (Dublin, 1925).

Livesey, James. *Civil Society and Empire: Ireland and Scotland in the Eighteenth-Century Atlantic World* (New Haven, 2009).

Lodge, John (rev. Mervyn Archdall). *The Peerage of Ireland* (Dublin, 1789).

Malcolmson, A.P.W. *Nathaniel Clements: Government & the Governing Elite in Ireland* (Dublin, 2005).

The Pursuit of the Heiress: Aristocratic Marriage in Ireland, 1740–1840 (Belfast, 2006).

McLynn, Frank. *Crime and Punishment in Eighteenth Century England* (Abingdon, 1989).

Meaney, Lisa. *Freemasonry in Munster, 1726–1829* (Mary Immaculate College, Ireland, 2005).

Melville, Lewis. *South Sea Bubble* (London, 1921).

Mirala, Petri. *Freemasonry in Ulster, 1733–1813: A Social and Political History of the Masonic Brotherhood in the North of Ireland* (Dublin, 2007).

—— 'Masonic sociability and its limitations: the case of Ireland' in James Kelly & Martin J. Powell (eds.), *Clubs and Societies in Eighteenth-Century Ireland* (Dublin, 2010).

Money, John. *Experience and Identity: Birmingham and the West Midlands, 1760–1800* (Manchester, 1977).

Munter, Robert. *The History of the Irish Newspaper 1685–1760* (Cambridge, 1967).

Paley, Ruth (ed.), *Justice in eighteenth century Hackney: The Justicing notebook of Henry Norris* (London, 1991).

Power, Bill. *White Knights, Dark Earls: The Rise and fall of an Anglo-Irish Dynasty* (Cork, 2000).

Redding, Moses W. *Illustrated History of Freemasonry* (New York, 1910.)

Relton, F.B. *An Account of the Fire Insurance Companies, Associations, Institutions, Projects and Schemes Established and Projected in Great Britain and Ireland during the Seventeenth and Eighteenth Centuries* (London, 1893).

Stewart, A.T.Q. *A Deeper Silence: Hidden Origins of the United Irishmen* (London, 1993).

Stone, Richard. *Some British Empiricists in the Social Sciences, 1650–1900* (Cambridge, 1997).

Thornbury, Walter. *Old and New London* (London, 1878).

Trumbach, Randolph. *Sex and the Gender Revolution: Heterosexuality and the Third Gender in Enlightenment London* (Chicago, 1998).

Truxes, Thomas M. *Irish American Trade, 1660–1783* (Cambridge, 2004).

Williams, Basil. *The Whig Supremacy, 1714–1761* (Oxford, 1997), 2nd edn.

Windele, John. *Historical and Descriptive Notices of the City of Cork* (Cork, 1839).

Selected Online Resources

British Periodicals Online	britishperiodicals.chadwyck.co.uk
Burney Collection	gale.cengage.co.uk
Early English Books Online	gale.cengage.co.uk
Eighteenth Century Collections Online	gale.cengage.co.uk
History of Parliament	histparl.ac.uk
House of Commons Parliamentary Papers	parlipapers.chadwyck.co.uk
Institute of Historical Research	history.ac.uk
Irish Dictionary of Biography	dib.cambridge.org
London Lives, 1690–1800	londonlives.org.
Old Bailey Online	oldbaileyonline.org
Oxford Dictionary of National Biography	oxforddnb.com
Royal Dublin Society	rds.ie.
Royal Society of London	royalsociety.org

Index

Page numbers in italics refer to tables or illustrations.